Change and Continuity in the 1984 Elections

Change and Continuity in the 1984 Elections

Paul R. Abramson
Michigan State University

John H. Aldrich
University of Minnesota

David W. Rohde
Michigan State University

PRESS

A Division of Congressional Quarterly Inc.
1414 22nd Street N.W., Washington, D.C. 20037

Copyright © 1986, Congressional Quarterly Inc.

All rights reserved. No part of this publication may be reproduced or transmitted in any form or by any means, electronic or mechanical, including a photocopy, recording, or any information storage and retrieval system, without permission in writing from the publisher.

Printed in the United States of America

Library of Congress Cataloging in Publication Data

Abramson, Paul R.
    Change and continuity in the 1984 elections.

    Bibliography: p.
    Includes index.
    1. Presidents—United States—Election—1984.
2. United States. Congress—Elections, 1984.
3. Elections—United States. I. Aldrich, John Herbert,
1947- . II. Rohde, David W. III. Title.
JK526 1984e   324.973′0927   86-2630
ISBN 0-87187-384-2

To
David
Heather and Lee
Jennifer and Margaret

Contents

Tables and Figures

Tables

Figures

Preface

Ronald Reagan's 1984 reelection victory was a landslide of historic proportions, but the long-term significance of his win remains controversial. Although the president carried 49 states, the Republican party made only a modest gain of 14 seats in the U.S. House of Representatives and lost 2 seats in the Senate. This mixed pattern led many analysts to view the 1984 contest as merely a personal triumph for the president. Following this initial reaction, commentators more often emphasized the overall pattern of Republican success in postwar presidential elections and argued that the 1984 elections marked the beginning, or perhaps even the continuation, of a pro-Republican realignment.

The Republicans, some argue, are going to be the new majority party, a view shared by Reagan. Speaking to former campaign aides celebrating the first anniversary of his reelection, he declared, "We stand poised to become the party of a new governing coalition—the party of the future."

Have the Republicans become, or are they about to become, the dominant party in presidential elections? Can they translate their presidential victories into control of both houses of the U.S. Congress? To answer these questions, one cannot view the 1984 elections as isolated events, but must place them in a broad historical context. To do this, we have examined a broad range of evidence, from past election results to public opinion surveys of the electorate conducted over the past four decades.

Our goal in writing this book was to provide a solid social-scientific analysis of the 1984 elections using the best data available to study voting behavior. We employ many sources, but rely primarily on the 1984 survey of the American electorate conducted by the Survey Research Center-Center for Political Studies of the University of Michigan as part of an ongoing project funded by the National Science Foundation. In the course of our analysis, we use every one of the 17 election studies conducted by the Michigan SRC-CPS, a series often referred to as the National Election Studies.

These surveys can be analyzed by scholars throughout the United States because they are disseminated by the Inter-University Consortium for Political and Social Research. The ICPSR provided a preliminary version of the data for the 1984 election survey to scholars in late April 1985; another version, which included a study to determine whether respondents actually voted, was provided in late July 1985. Unless otherwise indicated, all the tables and figures in Chapters 1 and 2, 4 through 8, and 10 are based upon data from the ICPSR. The standard disclaimer holds: the consortium is not responsible for our analyses or interpretations.

We are grateful to Harriet Dhanak of the Politometrics Laboratory at Michigan State University for helping us analyze these surveys. Michael J. Keefe of Michigan State University and Tom Trump and John Williams of the University of Minnesota assisted with the data analysis. Several of our colleagues gave us helpful suggestions and we are grateful to Ada W. Finifter, Jack H. Knott, and Joseph A. Schlesinger for their comments. Walter Dean Burnham of the Massachusetts Institute of Technology provided us with unpublished estimates of turnout as well as comments on Chapter 4. Richard G. Niemi of the University of Rochester provided extensive and helpful comments on the entire manuscript. We also thank Joanne Daniels, Carolyn Goldinger, and Carolyn McGovern of CQ Press for their help and encouragement.

This book was a collective enterprise, but we divided the labor. Paul Abramson had primary responsibility for Chapters 3, 4, 5, and 11, John Aldrich for Chapters 1, 6, 7, and 8, and David Rohde for Chapters 2, 9, and 10. None of us is responsible for the presidential election result, although one of us contributed to the 3,761-vote Mondale margin in Minnesota that denied Reagan a 50-state sweep. While we disagreed about the most appropriate electoral choice, we share our interpretation of the elections. The 1984 elections, in our view, raised fundamental questions about the future of American politics that cannot yet be answered. But a thorough analysis of the data at hand can help us understand the changes these elections may produce and gain a broader appreciation of current American politics.

Paul R. Abramson
John H. Aldrich
David W. Rohde

PART I

The 1984 Presidential Election Contest

Presidential elections in the United States are partly ritual, reaffirming our democratic values. But they are far more than that. The office confers great powers upon the occupant, and those powers have been expanded during the course of American history. It is precisely because of these immense powers that at least some presidential elections have played a major role in determining the course of American history.

For example, the election of 1860, which brought Abraham Lincoln and the Republicans to power and ousted a divided Democratic party, focused on whether slavery should be extended into the western territories. Following Lincoln's victory, 11 southern states attempted to secede from the Union, the Civil War erupted, and, ultimately, slavery itself was abolished. An antislavery plurality that did not necessarily favor the abolition of slavery (Lincoln received only 40 percent of the popular vote) set in motion a chain of events that freed some four million blacks.

And the election of 1896, in which the Republican William McKinley defeated the Populist and Democrat William Jennings Bryan, beat back the challenge of western and southern agrarian interests against the prevailing financial and industrial power of the East. Although Bryan mounted a strong campaign, winning 47 percent of the popular vote to 51 percent for McKinley, the election set a clear course for a policy of high tariffs and the continuation of the gold standard for American money.

The twentieth century also has witnessed presidential elections that determined the fate of public policy. The 1936 contest, in which incumbent Franklin D. Roosevelt won 61 percent of the vote and his Republican opponent, Alfred E. Landon, only 37 percent, allowed the Democrats to continue and consolidate the economic policies of the New Deal.

Lyndon B. Johnson's 1964 landslide victory over Republican Barry M. Goldwater probably provided the clearest set of policy alternatives of any election in this century. Johnson, who received 61 percent of the popular vote to 38 percent for Goldwater, saw his triumph as a mandate for his Great Society reforms, the most far-reaching social legislation enacted since World War II.

Goldwater offered "a choice, not an echo," advocating far more conservative social and economic policies than Johnson, but the electorate rejected him. Ironically, the election also appeared to offer a choice between escalating American involvement in Vietnam and restraint. Given Johnson's subsequent actions, most of Goldwater's policies about the war ultimately were implemented by Johnson himself.

What Did the 1984 Election Mean?

Only the future can determine the ultimate importance of the 1984 election. In some respects, it was an uninteresting contest with a predictable outcome. Two leading journalists, Jack W. Germond and Jules Witcover, entitled their book on the 1984 presidential contest *Wake Us When It's Over*.[1] Although the general election campaign was relatively dull, the election itself may prove important.

Ronald Reagan had been remarkably successful, especially during the first year and a half of his presidency, in translating many of his 1980 campaign promises into policy changes. There had been a cutback in social programs, a slowing of government growth, and an acceleration of government deregulation that had begun under Jimmy Carter. Reagan's promise of a 30 percent cut in federal income taxes had been largely implemented, and, as of 1985, these taxes were indexed to prevent inflation from pushing Americans into higher tax brackets. While many of Reagan's policies, especially the tax cuts, benefited the well-to-do, most Americans were profiting from the relatively low inflation during Reagan's presidency.[2] In 1980, when Reagan was elected, the annual inflation rate was 12.4 percent; in 1984 it was only 4.0 percent.

Under Reagan there were substantial increases in defense spending, with calls for further investment in new defense technologies. Reagan had maintained a belligerent posture toward the Soviet Union. He used military force with drastically unsuccessful results in Lebanon and with dramatically successful results in Grenada. While promising not to send American troops into combat, Reagan increased U.S. military involvement in Central America.

The Democratic candidate, Walter F. Mondale, sensing a conservative mood among the electorate, planned his campaign strategy accordingly. He avoided commitments to major new social programs, concentrating on the growing federal deficits and the need to increase taxes. But there seemed little doubt that, as a long-time liberal Democrat, he was far more supportive of aiding disadvantaged Americans than Reagan was and that he would foster a more active government involvement in the economy. His long-established ties to organized labor had secured the endorsement of the AFL-CIO even before the election year began.

Mondale's support for the civil rights movement over the course of two decades had earned him black support, including Jesse Jackson's begrudging endorsement. By selecting Rep. Geraldine Ferraro of New York as his running mate, Mondale hoped to appeal to Roman Catholics, to Italian-Americans, and especially to women.

While the electorate was offered a clear choice in 1984, the range of choices was not as wide as it had been four years earlier, for there were no reasonably viable third-party candidates. The percentage of Americans voting for third-party candidates was the lowest it had been in two decades. Moreover, about 80 million Americans chose not to vote.

But among those who did, nearly three out of five chose Reagan. Reagan's win, as we will show, was a landslide of historic proportions. The Republicans, however, lost two seats in the Senate and gained only 14 seats in the House of Representatives. Reagan's failure to carry more Republicans to victory has led some analysts to view his election landslide as merely a personal triumph.

The mixed pattern of results in 1984 raises some fundamental questions. To what extent did Republican successes, and especially Reagan's landslide, result from conservative policy preferences among the electorate? To what extent was the election a favorable endorsement of Reagan's performance as president? And did the 1984 election, as well as the Reagan victory of 1980, provide the basis for a shift in partisan fortunes that will establish the Republicans as the dominant party?

As we will show, the Reagan win in 1984 did not result from a conservative shift in the policy preferences of the electorate, but resulted mainly from favorable views of his performance as president. Did the 1980 and 1984 elections demonstrate that there has been a partisan realignment? If not, do they provide a signal that a realignment is imminent? These are more difficult questions to answer.

Political scientists define realignment in different ways, but all are influenced by the seminal writings of V. O. Key, Jr., who began by developing a theory of "critical elections" that specified the conditions under which "new and durable electoral groupings are formed." [3] He later argued that realignments can take place over a series of elections—a pattern he called "secular realignment." During these periods "shifts in the partisan balance of power" occur. [4]

James L. Sundquist has pointed out that all scholars agree that durability is an essential element of realignment. [5] Most scholars also agree that realignments seldom if ever involve across-the-board shifts to the same party among all segments of the electorate. Shifts occur instead in the regional bases of partisan support and in the voting patterns of social groups. Realignments may also be accompanied by the mobilization of new groups into the electorate. Sundquist also stresses the importance of new issues in bringing about a realignment. Moreover, many political scientists argue that partisan realignments result not just from shifts in the way people vote, but from shifts in feelings of party loyalty among the electorate.

Most political scientists would agree that the old alignment, formed in the 1930s, that made the Democrats the majority party, no longer exists. But most do not believe there has been a new partisan realignment, even though there may be the potential for one. Rather, they believe that the American party system is in a state of "dealignment"—a condition under which old voting patterns break down without being replaced by new ones.[6] As Russell J. Dalton and his colleagues point out, dealignment was originally viewed as a preliminary stage leading to a new partisan realignment. But, they argue, dealignment itself "may be a regular feature of electoral politics."[7]

Despite Reagan's massive victory, neither politicians nor political scientists agree about the implications of the 1984 elections for long-term partisan change. The most optimistic interpretation for the Democrats is that Reagan won because he mastered the art of communicating on television and Mondale did not. Mondale subscribes to this interpretation, admitting that he never felt comfortable with television. But this explanation seems superficial, especially in the light of past Republican victories. Richard Nixon, for example, was considered ineffective on television, but he defeated his Democratic opponent in 1972 by an even larger popular vote margin than Reagan did.

Another interpretation is that the presidential contest has been divorced from partisan politics, and that Reagan's massive win has few implications for nonpresidential politics. According to Theodore J. Lowi, "First and foremost, the results of the election demonstrate the existence of two separate constituencies, one for the presidency and one for Congress and state and local offices."[8] "Despite its landslide proportions," Lowi continued, "the election of 1984 does not qualify as ... a critical realignment, because the Republican victory failed to penetrate local and state electoral patterns."[9] Lowi believes we are in a stage of "dealignment," although he objects to negative terminology to define this condition.

Gerald M. Pomper rejects the thesis that the presidency has become completely nonpartisan. "In the long run," he wrote, "the presidency cannot be totally isolated from the rest of American politics."[10] With effective leadership, Pomper believes, the Republicans could become the majority party. "With a skilled political leader and efficient organization," he argued, "the party will have the opportunity to extend its gains beyond the White House, toward control of the state governments, and, after 1990, the redistricting and capture of Congress."[11]

In a speech in August 1985 to a Republican fund-raiser in California, Reagan suggested that a realignment may already have been achieved.

"The other side would like to believe that our victory last November was due to something other than our philosophy," he asserted. "I just hope they keep believing that. There's a change happening in America. Realignment is real." [12]

While we find little support for Reagan's claim, it should be apparent that whether a realignment has been attained depends largely upon how the term is defined. Our knowledge of historical patterns provides a guide to understanding the present distribution of partisan forces, but it should not become a blinder that limits our understanding of current conditions. And debates about the best definition of realignment may not be very useful for understanding contemporary American politics.

In our evaluation of the 1984 elections we are interested in the broader implications of the elections for the future of American politics. We ask two basic questions. First, is the current Republican dominance of the presidency likely to continue for the remainder of the century? Second, can the Republican dominance of the presidency be translated into control of both houses of the U.S. Congress?

Survey Research Sampling

Our book relies heavily upon surveys of the American electorate. It draws upon telephone polls conducted during the election year, exit polls by the television networks outside of voting stations, and interviews conducted in respondents' households by the Gallup organization, the National Opinion Research Center of the University of Chicago, and the U.S. Bureau of the Census. But we rely mainly upon interviews conducted in the respondents' households during the two months before and the two months after the 1984 election by the Survey Research Center-Center for Political Studies (SRC-CPS) of the University of Michigan.[13] Because the SRC has been studying American voting behavior since 1948, we are able to examine it for the entire postwar period. Since 1952 the SRC also has measured party identification and feelings of political efficacy. The CPS, founded in 1970, has developed valuable questions for measuring issue preferences. The SRC-CPS data provide the best and most comprehensive source of information about the political attitudes and partisan loyalties of the American electorate.

Readers may question our reliance on the 1984 SRC-CPS survey of 2,257 Americans, when some 165,000,000 are of voting age.[14] Would we have obtained similar results if all adults were surveyed? The Michigan SRC-CPS uses a procedure called multistage probability sampling to select the specific individuals to be interviewed. These procedures assure that the final sample is very likely to represent the entire U.S. adult citizen population (except for Americans living in institutions, on military installations, or abroad).[15]

Given the probability procedures the SRC-CPS uses, we are able to assess the likelihood that the results of these surveys represent the total U.S. resident citizen population. The 1984 survey sampled only about one American in 73,000, but the representativeness of a sample depends far more upon the size of the sample than on the size of the population being studied. For most purposes, samples of about 1,500 respondents are adequate to study the American electorate. With a sample of this size, we can be fairly confident (confident to a level of .95) that the results we obtain fall within plus or minus 3 percentage points of the result we would get if the entire adult population were surveyed.[16] For example, when we find that 49 percent of the electorate named an economic issue as the most important problem facing the nation, we can be fairly confident that between 46 percent and 52 percent of the entire nation considered an economic problem as the most important. The actual results for the entire electorate *could* be less than 46 percent or more than 52 percent. But a confidence level of .95 means that the odds are 19 to 1 that the entire electorate falls within this range.

The range of confidence becomes wider when we look at subgroups of the electorate. When we examine groups of 500 respondents, the range of confidence grows to plus or minus 6 percentage points. For only 100 respondents, the range of confidence expands to plus or minus 14 points. Because the likelihood of error grows as our subsamples become smaller, we often supplement our analysis with the reports of other surveys.

Somewhat more complicated procedures are necessary to determine whether the difference between groups is likely to reflect the relationship that would obtain if the entire population were surveyed. The probability that such differences reflect real differences in the total population is largely a function of the size of the samples of the groups being compared.[17] Generally speaking, when we compare the results of the total 1984 survey with the results of an earlier SRC survey, a difference of 4 percentage points is sufficient to be reasonably confident that the differences are real.

When we compare subgroups of the electorate sampled in 1984 (or subgroups sampled in 1984 with the same subgroup sampled in earlier surveys), a larger percentage difference would be necessary to be reasonably confident that differences did not result from chance. For example, when we compare men with women a difference of about 6 points would be necessary. When we compare blacks with whites, a difference of about 9 points would be necessary, since one of the two groups will be relatively small (generally only about 200 blacks are sampled in any given survey).

These numbers provide only a quick "ballpark" estimate of the chance that the reported results are likely to represent the entire population. Better estimates can be obtained by using formulas presented in statistics textbooks. To make such calculations or even a ballpark estimate of the chance of error, the reader must know the size of the groups being compared. For this reason we always report in our tables and figures either the number of cases upon which our percentages are based or the information necessary to approximate the number of cases.

The 1984 Contest

Part I of our book follows the chronology of the campaign itself. We begin with the struggle to gain the Democratic presidential nomination. In 1984 Reagan faced no opposition for the Republican nomination. But there were eight major candidates for the Democratic presidential nomination, and that contest developed into a fascinating two-man race between Mondale and Sen. Gary Hart of Colorado, complicated by the presence of Jesse Jackson.

Chapter 1 focuses on the Democratic nomination struggle. It explains why some potential candidates chose to run and why others did not. It demonstrates that an understanding of the opportunities available to politicians, as well as their past office-seeking choices, can help us understand who runs for president. We then examine the rules changes for the Democratic nomination and show how these changes, although relatively modest compared with past reforms, helped to assure Mondale's victory. Candidates always begin the nomination contest with a strategy for victory, and we analyze these strategies.

Turning to the primaries and caucuses—the actual stage at which delegates to the convention are chosen—we first explain the winnowing process that quickly forced five contenders to withdraw. We then study the long struggle between Mondale and Hart and show how Mondale's organizational advantages eventually led to his victory. We also examine Jackson's candidacy because, although he had no chance of winning the nomination, his presence throughout the campaign helped to prolong the Mondale-Hart contest. We also examine Mondale's important first step once his nomination had been assured—the choice of Ferraro as his running mate. Finally, we assess the lessons of the 1984 nomination contest and see how that struggle revealed major divisions within the Democratic party.

Having won the nomination, Mondale faced an even more formidable task: to defeat Ronald Reagan in the general election. As a popular incumbent, Reagan had the luxury of choosing among a variety of strategies in his reelection campaign, and in Chapter 2 we analyze those choices. Mondale's choices were more limited, but we examine his major decisions. Although Reagan made mistakes throughout the campaign and performed poorly in the first of his two televised debates, he still proved unbeatable. In our view, victory was beyond Mondale's grasp at the outset, and our analyses suggest that the campaign had little effect on the presidential election results.

Chapter 3 presents and interprets the election results. Because states are the building blocks upon which electoral vote majorities are won, the results are discussed on a state-by-state basis. The 1980 and 1984 elections should bury the myth that the Democrats are the majority party. As we shall see, the Republicans have built an electoral vote base that may aid them in future presidential elections. The pattern of Republican electoral vote successes during the postwar years presents a bleak outlook for the Democratic party. At the same time, however, the way people vote has become more similar throughout the nation, and regional differences are becoming less important. While the Democrats have virtually no electoral vote base, the Republican base may not be as secure as it initially appears. Despite their electoral vote dominance, the Republicans may not be a majority party either.

Notes

1. Jack W. Germond and Jules Witcover, *Wake Us When It's Over: Presidential Politics of 1984* (New York: Macmillan, 1985). Another excellent journalistic account was prepared by a team of *Newsweek* reporters. See Peter Goldman and Tony Fuller, with others, *The Quest for the Presidency—1984* (New York: Bantam Books, 1985).
2. For two excellent summaries of the domestic policy consequences of Reagan's first term, see John L. Palmer and Isabel V. Sawhill, eds., *The Reagan Record: An Assessment of America's Changing Domestic Priorities* (Cambridge, Mass.: Ballinger, 1984); and John E. Chubb and Paul E. Peterson, eds., *The New Direction in American Politics* (Washington, D.C.: The Brookings Institution, 1985).
3. V. O. Key, Jr., "A Theory of Critical Elections," *Journal of Politics* 17 (February 1955): 4.
4. V. O. Key, Jr., "Secular Realignment and the Party System," *Journal of Politics* 21 (May 1959): 198.
5. James L. Sundquist, *Dynamics of the Party System: Alignment and Realignment of Political Parties in the United States,* rev. ed. (Washington, D.C.: The Brookings Institution, 1983), 4.
6. For discussions of "dealignment," see Ronald Inglehart and Avram Hochstein, "Alignment and Dealignment of the Electorate in France and the United States," *Comparative Political Studies* 5 (October 1972): 343-372; Paul Allen Beck, "The Dealignment Era in America," in *Electoral Change in Advanced Industrial Democracies: Realignment or Dealignment,* ed. Russell J. Dalton, Scott C. Flanagan, and Paul Allen Beck (Princeton, N.J.: Princeton University Press, 1974), 240-266; and Bo Särlvik and Ivor Crewe, *Decade*

of Dealignment: The Conservative Victory of 1979 and Electoral Trends in the 1970s (Cambridge: Cambridge University Press, 1983).

7. Dalton, Beck, and Flanagan, "Electoral Change in Advanced Industrial Democracies," in *Electoral Change*, 14.

8. Theodore J. Lowi, "An Aligning Election: A Presidential Plebiscite," in *The Elections of 1984*, ed. Michael Nelson (Washington, D.C.: CQ Press, 1985), 293. For a more extensive discussion of this thesis, see Theodore J. Lowi, *The Personal President: Power Invested, Promise Unfulfilled* (Ithaca, N.Y.: Cornell University Press, 1985).

9. Lowi, "An Aligning Election," 295.

10. Gerald M. Pomper, "The Presidential Election," in *The Election of 1984: Reports and Interpretations*, Gerald M. Pomper, with colleagues (Chatham, N.J.: Chatham House, 1985), 86.

11. Ibid.

12. Phil Gailey, "Republicans Start to Worry About Signs of Slippage," *New York Times*, Aug. 25, 1985, E5.

13. To be more precise, all of the interviews before the election were conducted in the respondents' households. Following the standard SRC-CPS procedures for presidential election surveys, the same individuals were reinterviewed after the election. However, in 1984 half of these postelection interviews were conducted by telephone. In some instances the same questions were asked before and after the election. In those cases, we rely upon the preelection interview response.

14. Because we are usually analyzing responses to key questions measured only in the postelection interview (e.g., how the respondent said he or she voted for president or for Congress), we often confine our analysis to the 1,989 respondents who were included in the 1984 SRC-CPS postelection interview.

15. For an excellent introduction to sampling procedures used by the University of Michigan Survey Research Center, see Herbert F. Weisberg and Bruce D. Bowen, *An Introduction to Survey Research and Data Analysis* (San Francisco: W. H. Freeman, 1977), 27-35. For a more detailed description of SRC survey methods, see Survey Research Center, *Interviewer's Manual*, rev. ed. (Ann Arbor, Mich.: Institute for Social Research, 1976).

16. The probability of sampling error is partly a function of the result for any given question. The probability of error is greater for proportions near 50 percent and diminishes somewhat for proportions above 70 percent or below 30 percent. The probability of error diminishes markedly for proportions above 90 percent or below 10 percent. For the sake of simplicity, we report the confidence levels for percentages near 50 percent.

17. For an excellent table that allows us to evaluate differences between groups, see Leslie Kish, *Survey Sampling* (New York: John Wiley & Sons, 1965), 580. Kish defines the difference between two groups to be significant if the results are two standard errors apart.

Chapter 1

The Nomination Struggle

The story of the 1984 nomination campaign is a Democratic story. It is the story of Walter F. Mondale's victory, of Gary Hart's surprisingly strong and John Glenn's surprisingly weak performances, of the Reverend Jesse Jackson, and of Geraldine Ferraro.

As in all recent contested nomination campaigns, the Democrats produced a great deal of activity. From early 1981 to January 1984, eight candidates decided to run, organized, raised money, and jockeyed for position. They presented their cases to the voters and tried to gain support in primaries and caucuses. All this effort culminated in the July convention with Mondale winning the nomination and selecting Ferraro as the first female vice-presidential nominee of a major party in American history.

Before we examine the Democratic campaign, however, we must look at the Republican side and the context that set the stage for the Democratic struggle. While the "action" belonged to the Democrats, Ronald Reagan's foreboding presence was always in the background. We begin our account of nomination politics in 1984 with that presence.

The Republicans

Reagan played the incumbent's cat-and-mouse game of delaying the announcement of his reelection bid as long as possible, thereby generating as much attention, commentary, and spectacle as he could. In fact, he ran for and won renomination, as have all incumbents beginning with the 1972 election. Yet Reagan's renomination differed in several important respects.

Reagan was unchallenged. His immediate predecessors, Jimmy Carter in 1980 and Gerald Ford in 1976, had faced difficult nomination challenges. The reason Reagan faced no challengers was simple. He was truly in charge of his party, and, as events would prove to the Democrats' chagrin, in political control of the nation.

A simple index of Reagan's command is his approval rating. In December 1983 the Gallup poll reported that a nationwide majority, 54 percent, approved of his handling of the presidency, while a whopping 83 percent of Republicans approved. In contrast, Carter's approval rating stood at only 39 percent nationwide and 42 percent among Democrats in August 1979; Ford's was 39 percent nationwide and 59 percent among Republicans in December 1974. Even Richard Nixon, on the verge of an easy renomination and historically sweeping reelection, was no more popular. Nixon stood at 49 percent nationwide and 85 percent approval among Republicans in December 1971.[1]

And, of course, it was not just that people liked Reagan, though surely many did. After a deep recession, the nation's economy was growing rapidly, and unemployment was receding. Inflation had been low throughout his term. In foreign affairs, Lebanon and Central America were troubling, and people were concerned about the prospect of nuclear war with the Soviet Union. Still, the nation was not at war, and no foreign problem was nearly as acute as the Iranian hostage crisis had been to Carter four years earlier. All in all, the nation appeared to most Americans to be in better shape than it had been for years. According to the Gallup poll, only 17 percent claimed to be "satisfied with way things [were] going" when Reagan took office in 1981. By early 1984, a full 50 percent were.[2]

This context meant two things. First, Reagan would be able to set the agenda for the campaign. He could run virtually as he wanted. Without a nomination challenge, his reelection campaign could begin whenever he chose, while Democrats competed among themselves. He had the freedom, as we will see in the next chapter, to set the tone of the reelection campaign.

Second, the Democrats were almost naturally on the defensive. Their intense intraparty competition only detracted from establishing the central theme of the fall campaign—why a Democrat should be elected instead of Reagan. Many commentators reasonably asked whether any Democrat could beat Reagan. Still, as usual, many Democrats felt the urge to run.

The Democrats

Eight Democrats sought their party's presidential nomination, a number about typical for the "out party" (the party that does not control the White House) during the 1972-1984 period. In some ways, eight is a large field, offering a wide menu of choice. In other ways, it is small. There are several reasons "only" eight would try: a presidential nomination campaign is long, difficult, and extremely costly in terms of time, energy, political credit, and money. Most important, however, the field is very competitive and only one can win, so the odds are long. The reason that as many as eight ran is that the presidency is an extremely valuable, prestigious, rewarding, and powerful office, the absolute pinnacle of a political career. Moreover, as the nomination successes of candidates such as Sen. George S. McGovern of South Dakota in 1972 and Jimmy Carter in 1976 indicate, even little-known and little-regarded challengers can hope to do well under the new nomination system.

In any case, the decision to run is not undertaken lightly. A campaign consumes most of a candidate's time and energy for at least one year, if not four long years. Thus, it should come as no surprise that potential candidates painstakingly calculate their decision to run. Let us look at the eight contenders and see how they illustrate this careful planning that we call the "calculus of candidacy." [3]

The eight Democrats were led by "front-runner" Mondale of Minnesota, former vice president and senator and a leading spokesman for Democratic and liberal causes. Candidate Gary Hart of Colorado was an incumbent senator who had learned how to run under the current nomination process while serving as campaign manager for McGovern in 1972.

Three other incumbent senators also ran. One was John Glenn of Ohio, the first American astronaut to circle the globe. Many expected that this two-term senator would be able to establish a successful candidacy as a moderate. Another was Alan Cranston of California, who had been targeted for defeat by the National Conservative Political Action Committee (NCPAC) in his reelection bid for the Senate in 1980. He was one of the few so targeted who won—and won handily. He had also sought to become a leading spokesman for the nuclear freeze movement. Ernest F. Hollings of South Carolina was a southerner hoping to provide a more moderate alternative, much as Jimmy Carter had eight years earlier, and like Carter he hoped his southern support would prove crucial in the election.

Former senator and 1972 nominee McGovern made a belated campaign. Given the magnitude of his defeat in 1972 (as well as his NCPAC-targeted defeat for reelection to the Senate in 1980), his showing was rather surprising, if short lived. Former Florida governor Reubin Askew, often mentioned as a potential national contender, was a moderate and well-respected, if little-known, southerner.

The eighth candidate presented the most unusual set of credentials. Jesse Jackson had never held elected office, but he proved to be the first black to make a strong showing in presidential politics. Jackson had been one of Rev. Martin Luther King, Jr.'s, chief lieutenants in the civil rights movement. Although from South Carolina, he had moved to Chicago to carry on his civil rights activism. He had established his political credentials in support of the 1983 election of Harold Washington, the first black mayor of Chicago. Jackson had demonstrated special acumen in registering blacks and turning them out to defeat white opposition and the remnants of Chicago's political machine.

This capsule description of the contenders illustrates several points. First, all except Jackson had long and distinguished careers in elective offices. Three offices serve as the gateway to presidential politics: the vice presidency, the Senate, and state governorships, because they provide a strong "electoral base." [4] That is, those who have won major state or national offices are in the strongest position to build a national constituency.

Second, Mondale, Askew, McGovern, and Jackson were not in office in 1984. This gave them the freedom their office-holding peers did not have to pursue a long, enervating campaign. Carter, Reagan, George Bush, and others before them had demonstrated the advantages of running as a "gainfully unemployed" politician. The failures of potentially strong contenders, such as Republican senator Howard H. Baker, Jr., of Tennessee, in 1980, were attributed in part to the demands of their offices. Baker retired from his majority leadership position and Senate seat in 1984 in part to prepare the way for a full-time campaign for 1988.

The four who held office in 1984, all senators, had some advantages over many of the 41 Democratic senators who did not run. None of these four was in his first term in the Senate; thus they had the experience of office and at least one reelection to cement their electoral credentials.[5] None of the four had to stand for reelection to the Senate in 1984. A senator who is up for reelection may have to forfeit defending his Senate seat if he gains his party's nomination. If he does not get nominated, this losing bid may hurt his efforts to defend his seat. None of these four candidates had any of the other observable electoral liabilities that reduced the chances of some of their senatorial peers. In other words, these four were in a particularly strong and convenient position to run.

We can go one step further. While these candidates might have been in a good position to run, there were others (13 other senators, by our count) also well situated. But these 4 shared one other characteristic. When they first ran for Senate, they demonstrated a willingness to enter risky situations.[6] Of course, many who seek a Senate seat are taking a risk. Indeed, 23 of the 45 incumbent Democrats faced long odds during their first campaigns. But only 10 of the 45 senators were both well situated and proven risk-takers, and all 4 of those who ran were drawn from this group.

The Rules

Two major sets of rules govern nomination campaigns, and both underwent important changes between 1968 and 1972. These rules concern the way delegates are selected to attend the national convention and how money is raised and allocated in presidential contests. After 1972 these rules were modified further, and these changes also had a substantial impact on who won, as we will see for the 1984 contest.

Delegate Selection Rules

Since 1832 all major party presidential nominees have been chosen by the votes of delegates at the national nominating conventions. In principle, delegates can nominate anyone they want. In reality, they have rarely been that free. Most delegates these days are chosen by competition among presidential contenders in the primaries and caucuses. The candidates, in other words, campaign to get the public to select delegates who back them.

National convention delegates are chosen by the various states in one of two ways. One method is the primary election. A primary is an official election held by the state, in which voters choose which presidential candidate's delegates attend the national convention.

Other states use the caucus method for choosing delegates. While these procedures are often very complex, the key action usually happens in the very first step, often at the precinct level. A precinct caucus is a meeting of those partisans who live in the precinct and are interested enough to attend. At the caucus, partisans declare their preference among presidential candidates. While the process from then onward is long and complicated, in the Democratic party at least, a caucus is like a primary, in that all Democrats in the state can go to the caucus and declare a preference for the presidential candidate of their choice, and delegates, when finally selected, must reflect the results of that "vote." [7] However, very few people attend caucuses. Turnout of 5 percent to 10 percent is unusually high. Therefore, while candidates might run an election-like campaign in a caucus state, the important campaign is to find the candidate's supporters and get them to attend the caucus meetings. Success in caucuses, therefore, turns less on general popularity, media coverage, and advertising, and much more on a strong, well-financed campaign organization.

There is one more crucial fact about delegate selection. It is a months-long process; in 1984 it began in late February and ended in the middle of June. As a result, candidates can use success in one primary or caucus to generate enthusiasm, media coverage, and, the candidate hopes, greater popular support in a later state's primary or caucus. The result is a long, rapidly changing, and some would say chaotic campaign. Whatever the case, it is a campaign run by candidates through the media to obtain grass-root support. The party and its leadership play a small role in the selection of its national standard bearer. How did we get to a position in which the party plays such a small role in choosing its own leader?

The basic shape of Democratic delegate selection reforms was set in reaction to the tumultuous nomination process in 1968. In that year, Sen. Eugene J. McCarthy of Minnesota and Sen. Robert F. Kennedy of New York ran public, primary-oriented campaigns. Before the second primary, Wisconsin's, President Lyndon B. Johnson surprisingly announced he would not seek renomination. Vice President Hubert H. Humphrey took his place as a candidate. Humphrey, however, made no *public* campaign, winning nomination without entering a primary. The controversial nomination split the Democratic party and led it to initiate reforms, including those designed to open the nomination to more diverse candidacies and to more public participation.

The most obvious consequence of these reforms was the rapid increase in the use of primaries to select delegates. In 1968, 17 states held Democratic presidential primaries. That figure jumped to 23 in 1972, 30 in 1976, and 31 in 1980. The proportion of delegates to the Democratic convention chosen by primary elections increased even more dramatically. In 1968, 38 percent were chosen via primaries, 61 percent in 1972, and 73 percent and 72 percent, respectively, in the next two elections. Most of the rest were chosen by caucus. However, reforms succeeded in making caucuses more open to public participation—more timely, better publicized, more primary-like. By 1976, for example, the Iowa caucuses, the first delegate-selection proceedings in the nation, had become as widely covered in the media and as hotly contested and important to the candidates as any primary.

The important point in these changes was the greater role played by the public. No candidate could avoid a public campaign. Indeed, the eventual nominees in all campaigns in this period won because they won in the primaries and caucuses. Moreover, candidates discovered not only that they needed to win in the "primary season," but also that they could use early primary and caucus events as launching pads toward prominence and victory, gathering, in the favored catchword, "momentum." [8]

There were several significant changes for 1984. In 1980 the Democratic party had established the Hunt Commission to recommend changes in delegate selection procedures.[9] The party was concerned that, in an attempt at rejuvenation, it instead had weakened itself and had lost control of its destiny. The party's nomination was decided by individual candidates, by the media, by the public, by just about anyone but the party.[10]

To correct some of the excesses of reform, the Hunt Commission recommended, and the party accepted, the creation of so-called "superdelegates." About 14 percent (568 delegate seats) were reserved for party and elected leaders. Moreover, these superdelegates were free to vote for whomever they chose, unbound by popular sentiment expressed in primaries, caucuses, or public opinion polls.

For 1984 the Democratic party also shortened its primary season. The Iowa caucuses were moved five weeks closer to the convention and were held on February 20 instead of the middle of January. The New Hampshire primary was held on February 28, and all other primaries and caucuses were held in March or later. In addition, six fewer states (25 altogether) held Democratic primaries in 1984 than in 1980. The net effect of these changes was that fewer delegates were chosen in primaries in 1984. Only 53 percent of Democratic delegates were chosen in primaries, a drop of 19 percent; 32 percent were chosen by caucuses, up 4 percent from 1980; and 14 percent were superdelegates.

The Democratic party also modified its rules relating votes cast in primaries and caucuses to delegate selection. For some time, reformers had objected to so-called "winner-take-all" rules. Under such a rule, the candidate who got more votes than any other candidate would win every delegate selected, thus denying even one delegate to a candidate who lost by, say, a 51-to-49 plurality. Reformers favored a rule of proportionality where, as in the last example, the leading candidate would receive about 51 percent and the other about 49 percent of the delegates. A compromise called the "loophole primary" had been reached in 1976. In such a case, delegates could be awarded on a winner-take-all basis, but only at the level of a congressional district, not statewide. In 1980 the Democrats prohibited the "loophole," and states had to allocate delegates on the basis of proportional representation. In 1984 the Democrats not only allowed states to reintroduce the loophole, but also added new modifications to proportionality. Under "winner-take-more" procedures, most delegates would be awarded proportionately, but states could add a bonus to the overall statewide winner. In addition, most states raised the "threshold" needed to gain any delegates to 20 percent.

One other change was the so-called "front loading" of primaries. In earlier years, voting was spread out over several months, culminating in what journalists took to calling "Super Tuesday," which, in June 1980, featured eight Democratic primaries. Most of the action, however, had occurred earlier in the primary season. By Super Tuesday most nominations were already decided. Moreover, the greatest media attention and campaign money were showered on the earliest races. It made sense to many states to advance their primary dates. As a result, Super Tuesday 1984 fell on March 13, only two weeks after New Hampshire's primary. Five states held primaries, and four others began their caucuses on the 13th. More delegates were selected on that day than any other.

Some candidates could expect to be helped more than others by these changes. In general, the shortening of the season, front loading, and increased use of caucuses were more likely to help the already well-known, well-organized, and best-financed candidate. Moreover, the superdelegates, coming from the ranks of party and government leadership, would be more likely to support a well-established party figure than a little-known outsider.

In 1984 Mondale was the best-known, best-organized, best-financed, and most experienced candidate. In the long run, Mondale's victory rested in large part on the advantages the rules brought him.

Financial Rules

The 1970s also brought major changes in campaign financing procedures. The Federal Election Campaign Act of 1971 opened these reforms. The act was substantially amended in 1974 and 1976 and has been revised in less important ways since then. In general, the major features of the reforms fell into three areas of immediate concern.[11]

First, individuals and groups (the political action committees or PACs of current notoriety) were severely limited in the contributions they could make to any campaign. The old-style "fat cats" who gave hundreds of thousands, even millions, of dollars to a candidate were thereby eliminated. That meant that funds would have to be raised in a massive, public campaign, paralleling the candidates' public campaign for votes.

Second, presidential nomination candidates could receive a dollar-for-dollar match of small, individual contributions (up to the first $250 of an individual's contribution), thus providing as much as 50 percent federal funding. Candidates could refuse federal funding, but in 1984 none did.

Third, presidential candidates who accepted federal funding were subject to limits on what they could spend. Candidates for nomination in 1984 could spend no more than $20.2 million on the primary season (plus $4 million more on fund raising). Moreover, there were limits to spending in each state. Because state limits add up to nearly three times the overall limit, candidates who could raise the full amount of money had to plan carefully where to spend it.

Given the importance of the early events in states such as Iowa and New Hampshire, there is a natural desire to spend to the limit early to be as competitive as possible in these crucial states. It is fortunate for the lesser-known candidates that these states are small and thus have relatively low expenditure ceilings. Even so, spending in 1984 was very heavily "front loaded," too. Gary R. Orren calculated that by the end of April 1980, the four leading candidates (Reagan, Bush, Carter, and Edward M. Kennedy) had spent three-quarters of the legal maximum, but only half of the delegates had been selected.[12] Orren's calculations indicate that in 1984 Mondale and Hart each had expended two-thirds or more of their total spending by the end of March, about one-third of the way through the primary season.[13]

Surviving

To win nomination, a candidate needs to win a majority of the votes at the party convention. The best way to do this in the new nomination system is to ensure that delegates who back the candidate are selected to attend the convention. In turn, that means winning public support in a primary or caucus.

These steps require resources. The candidate must become known to the participating public, and some candidates, such as Mondale, start off with a sharp advantage in name recognition *(Table 1-1)*. Those who need to achieve name recognition can do so most effectively through media coverage and advertising campaigns. But little-known candidates usually do not have much money. Hart, for example, was able to spend just over half of the legal limits because he never was able to raise more, while Mondale raised and spent more than 90 percent of the overall limits.[14] These candidates lack other organizational resources such as contacts with and likely support from key party leaders throughout the nation, the ability to attract skilled strategists, and the means to hire the best polling, media, and advertising people. Because of their lack of recognition and resources, these candidates have less credibility and therefore receive less news coverage. The first problem for a candidate in this predicament is to break the vicious cycle of little public recognition and support, little media attention, and little money.

The new nomination system provides a way out. If, by dint of long, hard campaigning in the early and small states such as Iowa and New Hampshire, the little-known candidate can do "surprisingly" well (a solid second place, for example, if not an outright win), then that candidate receives a good deal of news coverage. People take notice and begin to support the candidate financially and, ultimately, at the polls. Of course, only one or two candidates can do well in Iowa or New Hampshire. Those who do not are, in the words of 1976 Democratic candidate Fred Harris of Oklahoma, "winnowed out" of contention.[15]

A front-runner, such as Mondale, invariably attempts to follow the "knock-out blow" strategy of so dominating the early primaries and caucuses that no other candidate can break the cycle. Virtually no candidate, however, is so popular that absolute domination is very likely. Besides, someone has to come in second, and, if the media turn their attention to that second-place finisher, the cycle is broken. In fact, Hart finished a distant second to Mondale in Iowa and still received extensive media coverage.[16]

Candidates who break the cycle do not merely survive, they achieve momentum. They become media phenomena and display consistent growth in popularity, attention, and resource support. At this point, the race becomes truly competitive, a head-to-head race between the survivors. The media and public begin to scrutinize these survivors more carefully. Their issue positions, personalities, and leadership abilities grow increasingly relevant. In short, the race becomes more like a "real" election.

The first step toward surviving is to achieve name recognition, but not all candidates start from the same position. To see this, we examined data collected by the Survey Research Center-Center for Political Studies (SRC-CPS) continuous monitoring study of 1984. The center interviewed a small, representative sample of the national public each week from January 1984 through early December in a "continuous monitoring," or "rolling cross-sectional" telephone survey.[17] This ingenious research design permits us to isolate key periods in the campaign and examine changes over time. In this chapter, we use these data to look at the nation as a whole, excluding the Republicans in the electorate.

In Table 1-1, we look at those Democrats who were interviewed between January 1 and the Iowa caucuses. Respondents were asked whether they had "heard anything about" the various candidates. By early 1984 nearly all Democrats recognized the names of Mondale, Glenn, Jackson, and McGovern. About 7 in 10 recognized Cranston, but less than half recognized Hart, Hollings, and Askew. Clearly, the latter three had a long way to go.

Name recognition is but the first step, for people also must have enough information to evaluate a candidate. In Table 1-1 we report how Democrats felt about each candidate on a 100-point "thermometer." A score of 0° indicates the respondent feels very "cold" toward the candidate, 50° is a neutral position, and 100° indicates very "warm" feelings. These thermometers have proven to be very accurate indicators of individual preference.[18] Only Mondale was evaluated much above the neutral point, having a clear lead over Glenn, whose average score was second highest. Note that far fewer people felt they could even rate Hart, Hollings, or Askew.

Finally, the data in Table 1-1 demonstrate that most Democrats felt Mondale had a very good chance at the nomination. These data are based on another 100-point scale, where 0 indicates the belief that the candidate had no chance at victory and 100 that his nomination was certain. Glenn was seen as having about an even chance, while the others were seen as prospective "also rans."

Table 1-1 Recognition and Evaluation of 1984 Democratic Candidates by Democrats, January, February 1984

Candidate	Recognition: Percentage Who Had Heard of Candidate	Evaluations: Average Score on 100° Thermometers	(N)	Perceived Chances at Nomination: 100-point Scale	(N)
Askew	43.6	40.4	(78)	—	(NA)
Cranston	69.1	46.0	(120)	27.5	(122)
Glenn	97.3	52.1	(177)	48.8	(178)
Hart	48.9	44.4	(87)	—	(NA)[1]
Hollings	38.8	42.6	(69)	—	(NA)
Jackson	96.3	48.5	(176)	38.3	(178)
McGovern	96.8	46.2	(175)	—	(NA)
Mondale	96.3	60.8	(176)	67.7	(178)

Source: SRC-CPS 1984 continuous monitoring study.

[1] Only 23 people ranked Hart on this scale, too few to give a reliable estimate. The question was not asked about the others listed as NA.

Note: "Democrat" is defined as a self-proclaimed Democrat or an independent who leans toward the Democratic party. Based on interviews completed by February 21, 1984. The average used is the mean. The percentages are based upon 183 cases. The numbers in parentheses are the totals upon which the mean scores are based.

Understood in these terms, the importance of the Iowa and New Hampshire races becomes clear. *All* candidates need to do well in at least one of them. Unknowns *must* become known quickly. Those who need to establish their position and credibility *must* do it in these states. Front-runners *must* hold their lead or lose credibility. In fact, only Mondale and Hart, by splitting first and second place in these two events, remained as credible candidates by early March.

By Super Tuesday, Cranston, Askew, Hollings, and McGovern had withdrawn—and for good reasons. The "unknowns" had remained that way, and the losers had gained no popularity, as reflected in their average thermometer evaluations. Of those candidates asked about, the public rated the losers' chances even lower (Cranston by about 7 points, Jackson by nearly 10 points). Thermometer ratings of Glenn fell nearly 3 points, and his perceived nomination chances fell to just over one in three. His candidacy teetered on the edge and, following a poor outcome on Super Tuesday, he withdrew.

On the other side of the coin, Hart's recognition jumped to 70 percent and then to nearly 100 percent among Democrats in this crucial two-week period. Second, his thermometer-popularity jumped from 44 percent to 59 percent. Third, the few people who rated him believed Hart had a very good chance to win (an average rating of 73). The race had become a two-man race, as both Hart and Mondale were far more popular than the opponents, and people believed these two—and only these two—had very strong prospects.

Public knowledge, feelings, and expectations are only part of the overall picture candidates form about their chances. The steady flow of campaign money and "free advertising" via news coverage in the media are also signs of success.

Mondale had raised more than enough money for this first round of primaries. He had spent nearly a third of the permissible $20.2 million by the end of January, reflecting his strong and early organizational efforts nationwide. Hart was far worse off financially. He had spent barely 10 percent of the overall limit by the end of January, mostly because money was not on hand. He had enough money, however, to spend two-thirds of the limit in Iowa and 90 percent in New Hampshire. With successes there, money began to flow in more rapidly, although he ended up spending less than two-thirds of the amount permitted overall.[19]

Media coverage followed a similar pattern. According to figures collected by Thomas E. Patterson and Richard Davis, nearly 60 percent of the *New York Times* coverage in January and February concerned Mondale; only 30 percent went to Hart and about 10 percent to Cranston. However, with Hart's nine-point victory over Mondale in New Hampshire, the *Times* spent 60 percent of its coverage on him, with only 40 percent going to the other seven combined.[20]

Thus only Mondale and Hart remained viable contenders. Lack of recognition, support, money, and media coverage forced the others out. Only Jackson's special candidacy permitted him to remain active. Let us look first at the two-man, Mondale-Hart race and then at Jackson's campaign.

The Mondale-Hart Race

Mondale had the advantages of recognition, attention, resources, and organizational strength at the outset. He had received many endorsements, the most important of which was the early backing of the AFL-CIO. So strong did he appear that it was often said that he would lose the nomination only if he made serious mistakes. And yet Hart turned the publicity of his Iowa "success"—as well as hard campaigning—into a narrow (37 percent to 28 percent) victory over Mondale in New Hampshire, followed by wins in the Vermont primary and the Maine caucuses. Suddenly Hart was a major competitor, Mondale was reeling, and some polls showed Hart ahead. Indeed, Mondale's three victories on Super Tuesday (with Hart winning the other six contests) were seen as necessary for rekindling his drive. By some accounts,

Mondale was prepared to quit the campaign if he lost all the primaries on Super Tuesday. The media mattered because their coverage focused on Mondale's resurrection rather than Hart's victories. By defeating Hart in the next few key primaries, especially Illinois, New York, and Pennsylvania, Mondale was able to reestablish front-runner status and carry on to victory. How did he do so?

Let's begin with the bottom line—delegates won. By July 5 Mondale had more than 2,000 delegate commitments; he needed only 1,967 to win.[21] He ultimately won 2,191 delegate votes or 56 percent to Hart's 1,200.5 votes, about 30 percent, and Jackson's 465.5 or 12 percent. (The remaining votes were scattered or abstaining.)

Where did Mondale's delegate support come from? There were only three sources: primaries, caucuses, and superdelegates. Mondale won 49 percent of the delegates selected in primaries to Hart's 36 percent, noticeably better than the 39 percent to 36 percent edge he won among voters *(Table 1-2)*. Mondale won more than his proportionate share of the delegates selected in primaries because his strongest showings were in those states that used "bonus" or "loophole" rules.

Reflecting his greater organizational strength and resources, Mondale soundly defeated Hart in caucus states. There he won 52 percent of the delegates to Hart's 33 percent, again bettering the 43 percent to 31 percent lead over Hart in estimated support among those attending.[22] In this case, Mondale picked up delegates from the 14 percent who attended caucuses as uncommitted. Once again, coming in first was more than proportionately rewarded.

Mondale's biggest edge came from the superdelegates. Of the 568 such delegates, about 450 or 80 percent probably voted for Mondale, by our best estimates.[23] Only 62 superdelegates were reported as favoring Hart.[24] Indeed, without any superdelegate support, Mondale would have fallen short of the nomination (1,740 delegate votes or about 44 percent). However, had Mondale received the same proportion of superdelegate votes as he did from those chosen by primary and caucus, he probably would have won—but just barely. It is impossible to know with certainty how many votes Mondale would have received had there been no superdelegates. After the last primaries, he made a major effort, including personally telephoning individual delegates, to line up the support he needed to put him over the top. Without the strong support he held already among superdelegates, Mondale might have looked less invincible and might have found it far harder to line up this extra support.

In sum, Mondale's winning edge must be attributed to three factors. The first was his organizational and resource lead that permitted him to seek delegates everywhere, while Hart was unable to do so. The second was the fortuitous fact—and the good planning—that enabled Mondale to win more than his proportionate share of delegates in primaries and

Table 1-2   Democratic Nomination Results under Different Rules (CQ estimates)

	Mondale	Hart	Jackson	Other/Un-committed
Statewide proportional represen-tation (No superdelegates)[1]	1,591	1,307	645	390
Statewide winner-take-all (No superdelegates)[1]	2,157	1,502	88	186
CQ projection as of June 23, 1984 (Includes superdelegates)	2,045	1,249	384	253
ABC estimate of superdelegate preferences[2]	363	62	26	77
Final roll call (Including superdelegates)	2,191	1,200.5	465.5	66*[4]

* 26 for other candidates; 40 uncommitted.

Percentage of Primary Vote Received and Delegate Share

	Mondale	Hart	Jackson	Others
Percentage of primary vote received	39	36	18	7
Percentage of delegates as of June 23 CQ estimate[3]	52	32	10	6
Percentage of delegates on final roll call[3]	56	31	12	2[4]

[1] Assumes that the same total number of delegates would be selected, but that all would be selected through primaries and caucuses.
[2] Excluding those who were not polled.
[3] Includes superdelegates.
[4] Includes abstentions.

caucuses. The third was his great following among the elected and party leadership that gave him a huge lead in superdelegates. In short, Mondale capitalized on his assets and the new rules of nomination for 1984.

Hart, as we saw, relied on the "momentum" strategy employed by McGovern, Carter, and others. Mondale used his front-runner status and resource and organizational strength to run the "marathon" strategy of competing everywhere delegates were to be selected. But these strategies are only one side of the dynamic nature of nomination campaigns. The public also reacted to—and was an intimate part of—the 1984 campaign. We have seen already how their votes were distributed overall, but that tells only part of the story. The views of the electorate were influenced by (and in turn affected) the flow of events and by strategic considerations.

Roughly, the Hart-Mondale primary season can be divided into six parts. The first was the Iowa to New Hampshire period in which Hart emerged as the major competitor to Mondale. The two-week period between New Hampshire and Super Tuesday was the only time when Hart was in command of the race. Even though Hart did well on Super Tuesday, Mondale's victories in two primaries and one caucus revived his campaign. The next week, highlighted by Mondale's Illinois primary victory, reestablished the view that Mondale was the front-runner. The next month (through about April 24) saw a split in victories but with Mondale carrying the largest states—the New York and Pennsylvania primaries and the Virginia, Wisconsin, and Missouri caucuses. The following month (to about May 22) saw Hart win many important primaries (Indiana, Ohio, Nebraska, Oregon, and Idaho). But Mondale won a few primaries (Tennessee, Maryland, and North Carolina), thereby maintaining credibility, and he easily won the key caucus state of Texas. Thus, while Hart attracted attention with his sometimes narrow victories, Mondale piled up delegates. The final round of primaries was about evenly split. Hart won three on June 5, including California; Mondale two, including shutting Hart out of delegates completely in New Jersey. We next turn to the public's perceptions of the campaign and how those views changed during the six parts of the campaign.

Public Beliefs and Perceptions

How did the public react to the ebb and flow of the candidates' fortunes? First, we will examine the "strategic" variables relevant to the public's decisions. Then we will turn to the traditional variables of electoral choice: parties, candidates' images, and issues.

By "strategic" variables we mean three things. The first is candidate preference. The second is the public's perception of who would win the nomination. The third is the most obviously strategic: How likely was it that Mondale or Hart, respectively, would be able to defeat Reagan in the fall? This question became a crucial campaign debating point as each contender claimed, with increasing urgency, that he would be more likely to win in the fall.

We will divide the dates of completion of the SRC-CPS continuous monitoring surveys into the time periods described above. (There are, of course, relatively few interviews in the shorter periods, so sampling error will be greater.) Three measures of candidate preference are available. The first is the candidate "thermometer" already described. The second is the response to the questions of who is the respondent's first and who is the second choice for the nomination. The third is the Gallup poll measure of "head-to-head" choices among Mondale, Hart, and Jackson.

The perceived likelihood of nomination is measured by the 100-point scale, while the SRC-CPS provided a comparable measure of likelihood of winning in November.

The preferences for candidates are reported in Figure 1-1. Mondale began and ended as the first choice of about half of the Democrats in the nation, including independents who lean toward the Democratic party. In between, however, his fortunes changed. March was a difficult month for

Figure 1-1   Choice of Democrats for 1984 Democratic Nomination, by Time Periods

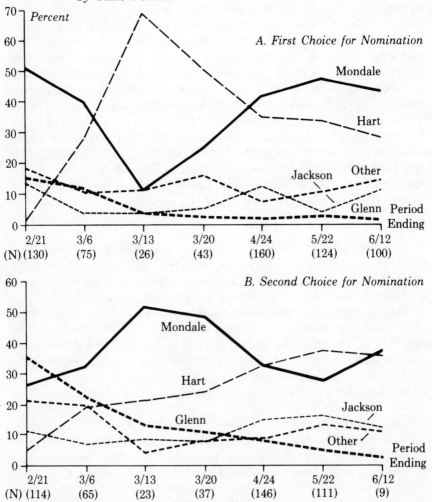

Source: SRC-CPS 1984 continuous monitoring study.

Note: Democrats include those who are strong and weak partisans and independents who lean to the party.

him, as he dipped very far behind Hart in the weeks following New Hampshire. By the end of March he was reestablishing his hold among Democrats, and from April on he was once again the leading candidate. Even at low ebb, however, he was always a strong candidate. If he was not the first choice of most Democrats, he was their second.

Figure 1-1 shows Hart's rise. Even by the New Hampshire primary, he had become the second leading candidate and, as can be seen in Figure 1-1B, he had broadened his base considerably. From then on it was a two-man race. Then Hart's lead disappeared, and Mondale held about a 15-point lead thereafter. However, as we will see, Hart drew much greater support from independents, while Mondale did so among self-proclaimed Democrats.

As the average thermometer evaluations of candidates in Figure 1-2 indicate, both Mondale and Hart were well regarded by Democrats. Indeed, the average evaluations of the two were virtually indistinguishable from the middle of March on. That means that people liked Hart as much as Mondale but were choosing Mondale for the nomination. Why?

Figure 1-2 Average Evaluation of Candidates for 1984 Democratic Nomination by Democrats, by Time Periods

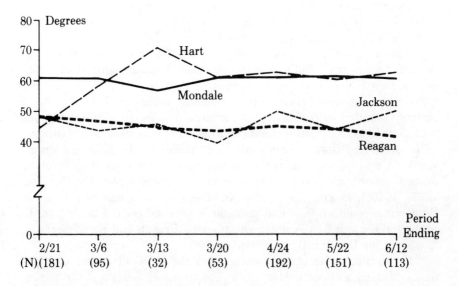

Source: SRC-CPS 1984 continuous monitoring study.

Note: Entries are average (mean) scores on the SRC-CPS 100° "thermometer" evaluations among Democrats and independents who lean toward the Democratic party. Ns will vary somewhat among the four candidates.

One strategic advantage Mondale had was that Democrats thought he was more likely than Hart to win the nomination *(Figure 1-3)*. He fell behind Hart significantly only for the single week preceding Super Tuesday. By April, just when Mondale became again the leading choice of Democrats, he had clearly established the perception that he would win. Interestingly, there was very little difference in the perceptions of whether Mondale and Hart, if nominated, would defeat Reagan. In fact, the typical Democrat thought their chances were equally good—or, more accurately, equally bad. Even Democrats recognized that neither candidate had much of a chance to defeat Reagan.

Campaign Themes and the Public's Bases of Choice

The Mondale-Hart race was, of course, far more than merely a simple game of who's ahead and who's behind. Underlying this "horse race" was a contest of the candidates' campaign themes—their answers to the public's question, "Why should I vote for you?"—and the goals and perceptions, the needs and preferences of the public. A candidate's themes and the public's goals must mesh if the candidate has any hope of attracting support in a competitive campaign. In analyzing voter behavior in an election, political scientists focus on four factors: the social and demographic composition of electoral coalitions and the public's attitudes toward the parties, the candidates, and the issues. We will see that the candidates' themes were built around—and designed to accentuate—these factors. First a bit about the themes of the two-man campaign and their reflection in demographics.

The campaign strategies of Mondale and Hart were based, of course, on their backgrounds, beliefs, and experiences. Mondale, long at the heart of traditional New Deal liberal causes, was the favorite of unions and other long-time members of the Democratic coalition. Thus, his basic strategy was that of traditional Democratic politics. In 1984 that meant attacking Reagan's cuts of domestic programs—the so-called "fairness" issue—declaring that Reagan's cuts were unfair to the poor, the disadvantaged, and the average worker. It also meant an emphasis on reducing unemployment and supporting programs to reinvigorate the "smokestack" industries and their cities. In short, it was a call to revive the Democratic coalition that had dominated national politics from 1932 to about 1968, and it was as much an attack on Reagan and Republicans as it was on his Democratic opponents.

If the blue-collar union member was the symbolic center of Mondale's campaign appeals, Hart's was the so-called "yuppie," the young, upwardly mobile professional. Hart's central claim was that the old Democratic coalition needed to be changed to be more in tune with the present and the future. His economic program, for example, called for developing new, high-technology industries. He proposed that govern-

Figure 1-3 Percentage That Ranked Various Candidates as Most Likely to Win Nomination (Democratic) and Election, by Time Periods

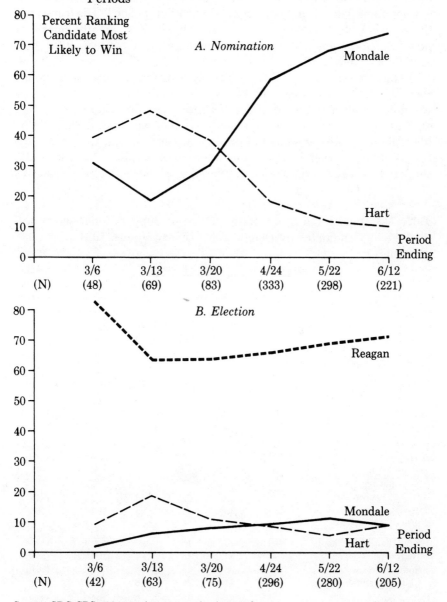

Source: SRC-CPS 1984 continuous monitoring study.

Notes: 1. Based on 100-point probability "thermometers," point plotted is percentage ranking candidate higher than all other candidates.
2. Jackson was ranked first in both cases by too few (never exceeding 2.5 percent) to include.
3. Questions not asked about Hart before 2/21.

ment, business, and labor coordinate their efforts in research and development via a "national industrialization policy." His campaign themes were "new ideas" and "new leadership." Therefore, the campaign pitted the old Democratic coalition against a call for a new order, new agenda, and new Democratic alignment.

The electoral impact of these competing claims among social groups was clear. Table 1-3 uses "exit" polls to estimate the way social groups voted in the Democratic primaries. It shows that Hart did relatively well among young voters, while Mondale fared very well among the elderly. Mondale drew greater support from union members and those with less money and education. Hart appealed more to the yuppies. Note how little support Hart drew from blacks, compared to Mondale. Despite Jackson's

Table 1-3 Social and Demographic Bases of Support for Democratic Candidates by Democratic Primary Voters, 1984

Voter Category	Voters for:					Percentage of Primary Electorate
	Mondale	Hart	Jackson	Other	Total Percent	
Gender:						
Men	38%	36	17	9	100%	(46)
Women	39%	35	20	6	100%	(54)
Race:						
White	42%	43	5	10	100%	(78)
Black	19%	3	77	1	100%	(18)
Age:						
18-29	26%	39	26	9	100%	(17)
30-44	30%	38	23	9	100%	(30)
45-59	41%	34	18	7	100%	(24)
60 and over	52%	31	10	7	100%	(28)
Family income:						
Under $25,000	40%	32	22	6	100%	(54)
$25,000 and over	36%	40	15	9	100%	(46)
Education:						
Less than high school	51%	26	18	5	100%	(14)
High school graduate	43%	34	16	7	100%	(33)
Some college	33%	38	21	8	100%	(27)
College graduate	31%	41	20	8	100%	(26)
Union household	45%	31	19	5	100%	(33)
Non-union household	36%	37	18	9	100%	(67)

Source: Adapted from Adam Clymer, "The 1984 National Primary," *Public Opinion*, Vol. 7, (August/September 1984): 53. These results are based on a computer model of the combined primary elections using exit polls, mainly from the *New York Times*/CBS News. A total of 35,118 voters were polled. Non-union household results calculated by authors.

candidacy, 1 black voter out of 5 voted for Mondale, whereas only about 1 black in 33 voted for Hart.

Party. It may sound odd that party identification was important in a contest between two Democrats. But Mondale stood at the core of the established Democratic party, and Hart stood at the periphery.

As Figure 1-4 illustrates, Hart was more popular among independents than Mondale, even when he had fallen behind Mondale nationwide. Democrats, however, favored Mondale, even at his campaign's lowest ebb, and by May he held a two-to-one advantage over Hart. Rarely

Figure 1-4 Democratic Nomination Choices in 1984 Gallup Polls

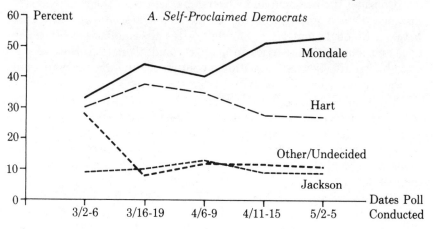

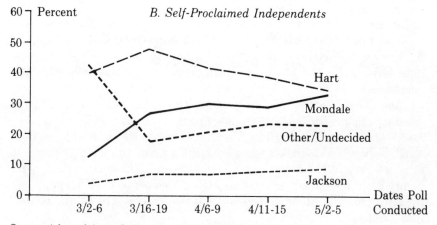

Source: Adopted from *Gallup Report* No. 224, May 1984, 18-19.

Note: These percentages are based upon about 400 Democrats and 300 independents for each time period.

have such partisan differences been as clear in a nomination campaign as in 1984. Only Rep. John B. Anderson of Illinois in the 1980 Republican primaries drew as much support from independents. Significantly, his appeal was based on "the Anderson difference," just as Hart's was based on "new ideas." Indeed, Hart, like Anderson, drew from the discontent with the two parties that has led increasing numbers of people to think of themselves as independents first and partisans second.[25]

Candidate Evaluations. Recent studies of voting behavior in primary campaigns have concluded that choice is based more on perceptions of candidate "image" than on the issues or ideology.[26] But 1984 provides something of an exception.

Consider the personal and leadership qualities of the candidates, for instance. One might expect the public to have seen vast differences between Mondale and Hart. Mondale, after all, emphasized his experience and long faithful service to his party and his nation. Hart emphasized his relative newness to national politics, that he was unencumbered by the old ways or tied to special interest groups.

Both claims sounded attractive, and both found a ready audience. In fact, the continuous monitoring study demonstrates that there were surprisingly few differences overall on several key dimensions of competence, personality, and leadership *(Table 1-4)*. In general, both candidates were highly regarded among Democrats and less highly so among independents.

There were a few differences, to be sure, and these generally favored Hart slightly, such as the "inspiring," "commands respect," and, perhaps, "provides strong leadership" questions. But even these small differences are more apparent than real. For example, the perception that Hart was "inspiring" began to decline among Democrats (from nearly 50 percent) as his fortunes fell in late March *(data not shown)*. From April on, about 20 percent so described him, putting evaluations of him at just about the same level as those of Mondale. Much the same is true for the other two questions.

We cannot tell, of course, whether these declines reflected Hart's waning primary successes, weakening prospects for nomination, increased media attention on "negatives," such as his name change or questions about his age, or Mondale's more frequent attacks. In truth, probably all were relevant. What does matter is that, overall, these evaluations gave no net advantage to either. At least among Democrats and independents, the criticisms that Mondale was dull and that Hart lacked substance were not taken very seriously.

There were two differences between Democrats and independents. First, Hart was better received among independents than Mondale. The tag that Mondale was dull or uninspiring hit home much more among

Table 1-4 Impressions of Personal Qualities of Mondale and Hart by Democrats and by Independents, January-June 1984

Quality	Percentage Saying Quality Fits Candidate a Great Deal			
Candidate	Democrats		All Independents	
		(N)		(N)
Decent				
Mondale	52.2	(594)	40.5	(580)
Hart	53.9	(399)	43.3	(402)
Compassionate				
Mondale	41.1	(582)	27.1	(569)
Hart	38.2	(400)	30.2	(400)
Commands respect				
Mondale	39.2	(589)	27.0	(577)
Hart	44.0	(402)	36.0	(400)
Inspiring				
Mondale	26.2	(591)	13.0	(581)
Hart	35.8	(400)	28.8	(399)
Knowledgeable				
Mondale	50.6	(591)	34.8	(584)
Hart	49.4	(403)	36.7	(401)
Really cares about you				
Mondale	33.8	(585)	21.9	(572)
Hart	33.7	(400)	25.6	(399)
Provides strong leadership				
Mondale	32.9	(590)	16.0	(574)
Hart	34.1	(402)	23.4	(397)

Source: SRC-CPS 1984 continuous monitoring study.
Note: The numbers in parentheses are the totals upon which percentages are based.

independents, with Hart holding a two-to-one edge over Mondale as inspiring. Hart held the advantage, though often a small one, over Mondale on all other dimensions among independents, too. Neither candidate held a clear advantage among Democrats.

Second, and the more important difference, is that Democrats thought both contenders were much stronger on these personal and leadership dimensions than did independents. In short, judgments about personal qualities reflected the respondent's partisan feelings very strongly. It appears, therefore, that "candidate image" did not provide either candidate with any clear advantage. Given the importance of candidate image found in other contests, this conclusion is rather surprising. Party appears to have been a far more important force than were evaluations of the candidate in 1984.

Issues. The role of issues in elections is always controversial. Many political scientists consider voting on the basis of the issue positions advanced by the candidates as the closest to the democratic ideal. Except on such divisive issues as the Vietnam War in the McGovern-Nixon race of 1972, citizens seem to fall well short of this ideal.[27] People have, it is usually argued, relatively poorly defined preferences on issues; they see candidate positions dimly and with distortion. [28] Therefore, issues play a smaller role in elections than, say, candidate image. Most studies of primary voters reach an even stronger and more dismal conclusion. One study of the 1980 primary electorate was entitled *Uninformed Choice,* and the authors, Scott Keeter and Cliff Zukin, say they even "toyed for awhile with the title 'Random Selection.' " [29]

And yet, candidates spend a great deal of effort developing complex issue positions and put their general stances at the heart of their campaign themes. Mondale, for instance, was attacked for making too *many* commitments to too many groups. One political scientist examined seven of Mondale's most important nomination campaign speeches, tabulating the number of references in five categories: promises, the future, experience, Reagan, and Hart.[30] There were more than twice as many references to promises as to any other category. While Mondale accused Hart of a lack of substance, "new ideas" were as central to Hart's campaign as any other theme, and they were backed up with specifics such as the new industrial policy program.

Two major reasons have been advanced to explain the lack of issue voting. Some find the fault lying, at least in part, with the news media coverage of the campaign. The media, especially in nomination contests, pay great attention to the election "game" or "horse race"—who is winning and who is losing.[31] As Patterson and Davis reported about the 1984 contest "the media's concern with the election game makes it difficult for candidates to communicate their ideas, despite the great efforts they make to do so." [32] They found that even in the *New York Times,* the candidates' themes received little coverage, and specific issues received even less. Only Hart's "new leadership" theme—that portion of his theme that dealt with personal image rather than policy—was mentioned in as many as 15 percent of the stories covering him. Observers find even less detailed coverage in local and regional papers, and the television news is regularly castigated for lack of substance. In response, it is often said that the media report what the public wants to read or see. And the second major argument, carefully documented by Keeter and Zukin, is that the public knows very little about policy matters, especially in nomination campaigns.[33]

There is a third reason why issues may play a less important role in nomination campaigns than in the general election. Candidates of the same party usually hold much more similar positions on issues than do candidates from opposing parties, and the same is true for Democrats and Republicans in the electorate. In short, there is relatively little basis of choice on issues in a nomination campaign compared to what comes later.

The 1984 race illustrates that point extremely well. The continuous monitoring study asked respondents where they stood and where they thought Mondale, Hart, and Reagan stood on four key political controversies: spending for defense, spending for domestic programs, the responsibility of the government to enhance the social and economic position of women, and relations with the Soviet Union. The key point is that the public saw *very* little difference, on average, between Mondale and Hart on any of these issues. The largest average difference between perceptions of Mondale and Hart on all four issues was only 0.1 out of a possible 4-point difference. Such differences were dwarfed by the much clearer distinction between either Democrat and Reagan (at least one and as much as two full points on these issues). It is also worth noting that the average Democrat and the average independent were less liberal than they saw either Mondale or Hart, but were still closer to both Democratic candidates than to Reagan. The only exception was on the government spending on social services question, where the Democrats were slightly *more* liberal on average than their perceptions of either candidate.

There is an obvious explanation for these results. The issues are those that divide Democrats from Republicans and do not divide Democrat from Democrat very much. This does not mean, however, that there were not issues that divided Democrats in 1984, nor, more important, that Democratic voters were unable to base their choices in part on policy concerns.

On many issues, policy-based evaluations may not rest on what *goals* to seek, for Democrats share the same goals, broadly speaking. Clearer differences exist over the *means* of achieving those goals. Here we find the real differences between Hart and Mondale. Hart called for new approaches, while Mondale relied on the traditional Democratic approach and his long experience and successes with it. Neither disagreed, for example, that unemployment was a major problem and must be reduced. They differed over how to do it.

In Table 1-5 we report results of a Gallup poll conducted in late April and early May that asked Democrats and independents whether Mondale or Hart would be better able to handle a series of problems. The problems chosen were based on Gallup's measurement of what most concerned Americans. In the first half of 1984, foreign affairs, defense, and unemployment were the three biggest concerns, followed by inflation and budget deficits.[34] Democrats generally agreed, except more than one-

Table 1-5   Democrats' and Independents' Beliefs about Competence of Mondale and Hart (in percentages)

Problem	Mondale	Hart	No Difference	No Opinion	Total Percentage
Democrats: Candidate Better					
Foreign affairs	69	17	3	11	100
Relations with Russia	55	19	6	20	100
Central America	53	22	6	19	100
Avoiding war	49	27	6	18	100
Reducing unemployment	51	29	4	16	100
Controlling inflation	47	32	5	16	100
Improving the economy	49	30	6	15	100
Improving conditions for minorities	49	25	7	19	100
Women's rights	42	32	10	16	100
Environmental problems	45	34	5	16	100
Independents: Candidate Better					
Foreign affairs	46	31	9	14	100
Relations with Russia	40	31	12	17	100
Central America	36	34	9	21	100
Avoiding war	35	37	13	15	100
Reducing unemployment	36	34	12	18	100
Controlling inflation	31	40	11	18	100
Improving the economy	32	38	14	16	100
Improving conditions for minorities	34	35	10	21	100
Women's rights	28	41	10	21	100
Environmental problems	27	47	8	18	100

Note: Based on responses from 384 Democrats and 309 independents.

Source: Adapted from Gallup poll conducted April 23-May 6, 1984, reported in *Gallup Report*, No. 225, June 1984, 20-29.

third picked unemployment as most important, outdistancing foreign affairs and defense.[35]

The data in Table 1-5 lead us to two conclusions. The first is that Democrats and independents had very different views of Mondale and Hart on policy. At this point in the campaign, Mondale was seen among Democrats as substantially better than Hart on every issue. On some matters, especially foreign affairs and unemployment, the differences were overwhelming. Significantly, these were the two major concerns of

Democrats—and the entire public. Among independents, the picture was more mixed. On some issues Mondale was seen as better, on others Hart was, and on many issues the views were quite balanced. Second, there were differences by issue, regardless of party. Mondale held the advantage among both groups on foreign affairs and relations with Russia. Hart did much better on the inflation issue, women's rights, the environment, and, to a lesser extent, improving the economy.

Mondale's Edge. The surprising finding is the substantial importance of partisan identification in the Democratic campaign. Mondale was the clear choice of Democrats, while Hart held the advantage among independents. Both were generally seen as effective, promising candidates. Democrats evaluated both candidates more positively than independents, but there was no advantage for either candidate in these terms. Issues appeared to matter more than usually thought. However, what mattered was not where the candidates stood, for they were often seen to stand for quite similar policies. What mattered was how effective people expected Mondale and Hart to be on issues. On relations with Russia, for example, Democrats and independents saw few differences in what the candidates wanted to achieve, but both groups thought Mondale was the better choice. Once again, on many issues there were clear partisan differences, with Mondale holding the advantage among Democrats, but independents giving neither candidate a clear edge.

In sum, Mondale won his small edge in the Democratic primaries and caucuses because he was the choice of his party on party principles and loyalty and on expected performance on issues. And, while many independents participated in the nomination campaign—to Hart's great advantage—analysis of exit polls suggests that about three-quarters of the voters in the Democratic primaries were Democrats, and only one in five was an independent.

It may strike one as odd that Mondale held such a clear advantage in many ways among Democrats, that Democrats made up the overwhelming proportion of the primary and caucus electorate, and yet that he received only a small edge in votes cast. The reason he did not win more handily was Jackson's candidacy.

Jesse Jackson's Candidacy

Jesse Jackson played an unprecedented role in the 1984 nomination campaign. As already noted, he was the first black presidential contender to have a significant impact on the nomination process, and he brought no elective political experience to his campaign.

What made him run? The answer was, as usual, a mixture of motives. Blacks began debating the merits of a black candidacy shortly after Washington won the Chicago mayoralty election in April 1983 and when W. Wilson Goode won the Democratic nomination for mayor of Philadelphia the following month. There was no illusion that a black would win the nomination, but there was hope that the black vote, united under a prominent black politician, would give them some leverage over the nomination and, perhaps more important, on issues of concern to them within the Democratic party and in the government.

Blacks were divided over the question. Some argued they would be more influential united behind a white candidate who understood black concerns—and who could win. Also, some feared that supporting a black candidacy would in effect promote the personal ambitions of Jesse Jackson. Despite disagreement among black leaders, in November 1983 Jackson announced his decision to run.

Jackson aimed for a "rainbow coalition," an alliance of blacks, whites, and Hispanics who shared concerns for the poor, minorities, and the problems of the cities. In fact, his electoral base was concentrated among blacks. Still, blacks make up as much as a quarter of the typical Democratic electorate, and they are concentrated in areas crucial for any Democratic nominee.

Jackson received about three-quarters of the black vote but only about 1 white vote in 20 in Democratic primaries *(Table 1-3)*. Jackson won the Washington, D.C., and Louisiana primaries outright, gained about 20 percent or more of the vote in nine others, and earned 18 percent of the vote overall. His strongest support was in the South and the large, industrial states where blacks are concentrated. In many states where Jackson did well, the rules, such as loophole and bonus provisions, worked against him. In those states where Jackson fared poorly, he was often hurt by "threshold" rules requiring 20 percent support to gain any delegates.

Upon achieving the status of solid third-place candidate—the candidate who could not win but could pull significant support—Jackson's campaign focused on black issues. Within the party, for example, his main concerns were registration drives, black voter turnout, and reforms, such as the abolition of "runoff" (or "second") primaries that he claimed hurt black candidates.[36] National concerns remained focused on those relevant to the poor, blacks, and other minorities, and on urban revitalization. Money to address these problems would be found by cutting defense spending, which was also a key issue for Jackson. He also challenged the direction of U.S. foreign policy, attempting to link the demands of blacks to the concerns of Third World countries. He urged a more "balanced" approach to Middle East policies, whereas Mondale and Hart urged even greater support for Israel.

What resulted from Jackson's candidacy? In the short run, he was unable to achieve many of his specific objectives. His special concerns

Table 1-6 Impressions of Personal Qualities of Jackson among All Democrats and of All the Candidates among Black Democrats, January-June 1984

| | Percentage Saying Quality Fits Candidate a Great Deal | | | | | | | |
| Quality | White Democrats | | Black Democrats | | | | | |
	Jackson	(N)	Jackson	(N)	Mondale	(N)	Hart	(N)
Decent	38.2	(683)	70.2	(121)	56.8	(118)	43.6	(78)
Compassionate	40.1	(684)	76.9	(121)	50.4	(117)	33.3	(78)
Commands respect	32.1	(683)	71.9	(121)	50.0	(116)	46.8	(77)
Inspiring	34.5	(685)	76.9	(121)	43.1	(117)	37.2	(78)
Knowledgeable	25.2	(685)	66.9	(121)	59.0	(117)	51.3	(78)
Really cares about you	25.2	(675)	79.2	(120)	39.7	(116)	29.9	(77)
Provides strong leadership	22.4	(683)	62.5	(120)	47.0	(117)	35.9	(78)

Source: SRC-CPS 1984 continuous monitoring study.

Note: Democrat includes self-professed Democrats and independents who claim to lean toward the Democratic party. Numbers in parentheses are the totals upon which percentages are based.

were generally rejected at the Democratic National Convention. On the other hand, he did place these items before the public and the party, and his success as a candidate might serve well as a role model for other black candidates. Finally, he was successful in spurring black voter registration. But the most immediate impact of his candidacy was on the Mondale-Hart race. By our best guess, the majority of his support would have gone to Mondale and not to Hart.

Blacks not only voted for Jackson, but also liked him very much. In Table 1-6, we report the assessments of Jackson by white Democrats and the assessments of all three candidates by black Democrats. Jackson received significantly lower marks from the average white Democrat than either of his opponents *(Table 1-4)*. Blacks, however, gave him high marks on all dimensions. He truly had generated a great deal of enthusiasm among his core followers.

Table 1-6 also tells us that blacks liked Mondale more than Hart. Among blacks, Mondale scored better than Hart on all dimensions, sometimes substantially so, even on issues where Mondale was considered weakest. Clearly, blacks much preferred Jackson to either opponent, but they preferred Mondale to Hart.

To some extent, blacks followed up on these preferences by giving 19 percent of their votes to Mondale but only 3 percent to Hart. However, if Jackson had not been a candidate, many more blacks probably would have supported Mondale. Among blacks, 72 percent ranked Mondale higher than Hart or ranked only Mondale; only 28 percent ranked Hart higher or ranked only Hart.[37] If Jackson had not been a candidate, we estimate both Mondale and Hart would have received about 45 percent of the white vote. If Jackson had not been a candidate, Mondale, we assume, would have received 72 percent of the black vote, but fewer blacks would have voted. As Table 1-3 shows, 18 percent of the voters in the Democratic primaries were black. Assuming that black primary turnout would have dropped and that blacks would have made up only 15 percent of the Democratic electorate, Mondale would have defeated Hart by about 49 percent to 42 percent overall. Although the specific details of our assumptions could be altered, it seems clear that Mondale would have defeated Hart more substantially without Jackson's candidacy.

Choosing the Running Mate

After the primary season, Mondale retreated to his Minnesota home to woo the last delegates and to make plans for the convention and fall campaign. Chief among these was the selection of his vice-presidential running mate. He attempted to follow the lead of Carter in 1976 to consider carefully who his running mate should be, to interview the finalists in the sweepstakes, and to announce his choice. Mondale, however, began to come under increasing pressure from Democratic constituency groups, such as women, blacks, and Hispanics, to pick one of their own. What had been intended as a careful weighing of this most important decision turned increasingly into a media and political brouhaha.

His historic decision to select Ferraro led to a positive and immediate swell of approval. Unfortunately for him and the Democrats, neither he nor Ferraro was able to maintain the euphoria. Some observers questioned whether Mondale, by picking a liberal female from New York, had hurt his chances of winning votes in other regions, especially the South. As we note in Chapter 2, Lee Atwater, the deputy director of the Reagan campaign, analyzed the electoral strength of the candidates and concluded that Reagan would win, once Mondale chose Ferraro. Mondale hoped to balance the selection of Ferraro by picking Georgian Bert Lance, a key adviser to Jimmy Carter, to chair the Democratic National Committee. The incumbent, Charles T. Manatt, however, fought his removal, and Lance's suitability was questioned. In the end Mondale backed down, and, amidst the controversy, lost much of what positive press coverage his selection of Ferraro had generated. Moreover, he appeared unable to bend the party to his will and was unable to pick up points in the South.

Ferraro suffered the fate of all nationally prominent politicians, as the media began to study her record closely. Both her husband's and her own financial affairs became controversial. It appeared that she had not fully reported to Congress her financial involvement with her husband's businesses, and questions were raised about campaign contributions. Ultimately, the House investigated, found her in technical noncompliance, but concluded that the transgressions were not worth major reprimand or action. The controversy, however, took much of the positive glow off her nomination.

At the convention, Mondale and Ferraro were nominated with enthusiasm. The party endorsed a platform that was consistent with most of Mondale's campaign stances. On some matters, Mondale's forces compromised with those backing Hart, but there were few compromises made with Jackson. In effect, then, the platform reflected the nomination, with Mondale winning the majority of contested issues, Hart receiving some victories, and Jackson gaining very little.

The Lessons of the 1984 Nomination Campaign

What basic conclusions about electoral politics can be drawn from the 1984 nomination campaign? The first is that there is likely to be much more competition for the nomination for the party out of office than for the nomination of the incumbent's party. Under the new, post-1968 nomination system, the out party has consistently fielded a large set of challengers. In no case has such a candidate been able to win nomination easily. The contest among those who survived the early "winnowing" has been intense. Nonetheless Mondale in 1984, like his predecessors, was able to secure nomination before the convention. In many ways, Mondale's fate paralleled that of Reagan in 1980. Both began as odds-on favorites to win. Both suffered an early set-back (Reagan's was in Iowa) that permitted a lesser-known challenger to grab an early advantage. Both, however, were able to reestablish the lead and emerge victorious.

The incumbent has, in all post-1968 nomination campaigns, won renomination, sometimes with challenges and sometimes, as in 1984, without. The 1988 campaign will present a most interesting situation. For the first time under the new nomination system, there will be no incumbent, assuming Reagan completes his second term. It remains an open question, however, whether the Republican campaign of 1988 will look just like an out-party campaign or be dominated by George Bush, running on the successes of the current administration.

The second lesson of 1984 is that the public responds quickly to changing electoral conditions. The early part of the campaign was the period of most rapid learning and change in attitudes among the public.

The public, for example, quickly learned who Hart was and developed opinions about him. There was also substantial change in the strategic variables, such as the public's perception of who would win nomination. Shortly after Super Tuesday, however, the campaign settled down, and the overall distribution of attitudes changed relatively little. The two-man race had become a campaign increasingly similar to a two-candidate presidential campaign in the fall.

In this instance, candidate support was based on the different coalitions the two men put together: Mondale's base among traditional Democratic support groups—older citizens, union members, and the like—and Hart's base among the younger and the better educated. Most important, party identification played a crucial role. Democratic identifiers, that is, those voters who consider themselves strong Democrats, backed Mondale, while more independent-leaning partisans supported Hart. Those differences were reflected in evaluations of the candidates as leaders and as policy makers.

The third lesson of 1984 is that successful candidates adapt to changing party rules. Mondale and Hart succeeded in large part because they were able to use the nomination system to their advantage, although they followed very different routes. Hart used the classic route of unknowns, the momentum strategy. Like Bush in 1980, he faced a strong opponent who was able to stop his momentum. Mondale capitalized on his initial front-runner status to raise huge sums of money before the campaign began and to develop a strong, nationwide organization. And as a result of changes in the rules and of his superior organization, Mondale won more than his proportionate share of delegates in both caucus and primary states. But Mondale's biggest advantage was among the superdelegates. He won a great number of commitments from them because he was a long-time Democratic leader and because he was the leading contender for nomination.

A final lesson of 1984 is that there are important divisions within the Democratic party. There well may be such divisions among Republicans, too, but they were not revealed by the 1984 nominating process. But 1984 highlighted the plight of the Democratic party. The basic split is along the lines revealed by the Mondale-Hart campaign. Is the party a continuation of coalitions, goals, and policies struck in the New Deal-Great Society Democratic party, the party to which Mondale appealed? Or must the party redefine its goals, its policies, and hence its coalitions?

Once again, 1988 looms as a crucial campaign year. Perhaps, in the absence of a popular leader like Reagan, a traditional Democrat such as Gov. Mario Cuomo of New York can revitalize the old alignment, appeal strongly enough to the more independent portions of the public, and build a viable election coalition. Perhaps the party must redefine itself. If so, just what new ideas it uses will depend on what new leaders emerge in

1988 and what vision they offer to reshape a Democratic coalition. For now, however, it is time that we turn to the general election campaign to see just how and why Reagan won reelection so handily.

Notes

1. These figures come from Gallup poll data, as reported in the *Gallup Opinion Index*, various issues; since 1981, the *Gallup Report.*
2. Ibid.
3. For more on this "calculus of candidacy," see Paul R. Abramson, John H. Aldrich, and David W. Rohde, *Change and Continuity in the 1980 Elections,* rev. ed. (Washington, D.C.: CQ Press, 1983) and sources cited therein.
4. The terminology comes from Robert L. Peabody, Norman J. Ornstein, and David W. Rohde, "The United States Senate as a Presidential Incubator: Many Are Called but Few Are Chosen," *Political Science Quarterly* 91, (Summer 1976): 237-58.
5. See Abramson, Aldrich, and Rohde, *Change and Continuity in the 1980 Elections,* rev. ed., 274-79, for a detailed analysis of the 46 Democratic senators at the beginning of the 98th Congress. Note that we are using a base of 45 Democratic senators, since one of them, Henry M. Jackson of Washington, died before the 1984 election year began.
6. "Risk-taking" is measured by the situation faced by Senate candidates the first time they ran for the Senate. A situation is said to be "risky" if they faced an incumbent in the primary or the general election campaign or if the opposition party had averaged at least 57 percent of the vote over the four preceding Senate races in that state. Others may, of course, have been risk takers, but were not in a position to reveal that fact.
7. Our description of caucuses describes the most commonly used form (e.g., that used in the highly publicized Iowa caucuses). There are, however, many different ways state parties can and do conduct caucuses. In some states (e.g., Michigan) the caucus consists only of a vote for president. In that state, there were very few places for "voting," and, in 1984, many of these were at union halls, presumably aiding the union-backed candidacy of Mondale. In all cases, caucuses differ from primaries since voting often is not secret and since it is more difficult for most voters to learn where and how to participate.
8. See John H. Aldrich, *Before the Convention: Strategies and Choices in Presidential Nomination Campaigns* (Chicago: University of Chicago Press, 1980) and sources cited therein.
9. The commission was named after its chairman, James B. Hunt, then governor of North Carolina. For more information about the commission, see David E. Price, *Bringing Back the Parties* (Washington, D.C.: CQ Press, 1984), 159-83.
10. Many have argued that these reforms weakened the political parties. See Nelson W. Polsby, *Consequences of Party Reform* (Oxford: Oxford University Press, 1983); David S. Broder, *The Party's Over: The Failure of Politics in America* (New York: Harper & Row, 1972); and William Crotty and John

S. Jackson III, *Presidential Primaries and Nominations* (Washington, D.C.: CQ Press, 1985).

11. Crotty and Jackson, *Presidential Primaries.*
12. Gary R. Orren, "The Nomination Process: Vicissitudes of Candidate Selection," in Michael Nelson, ed., *The Elections of 1984* (Washington, D.C.: CQ Press, 1985), 44.
13. Ibid., 45-50.
14. Ibid., 49.
15. Quoted in Jules Witcover, *Marathon: The Pursuit of the Presidency, 1972-1976* (New York: Viking, 1977), 205.
16. Mondale won 48.9 percent in the Iowa caucuses, Hart was the second-place candidate with only 16.5 percent, but "uncommitted" came in second overall with 23.7 percent.
17. The survey was conducted by telephone by the Survey Research Center-Center for Political Studies, University of Michigan. A small, random sample was interviewed in each of 46 weeks of the campaign, to provide a "continuous monitoring" of the public throughout the campaign. An average of 76 respondents were interviewed each week. Note that interviewees seem to be of higher status and presumably hold greater political information and interest than the nation as a whole. For instance, about a quarter of the respondents report holding college degrees, which is about 8 percent higher than in the SRC-CPS face-to-face survey conducted in the general election campaign.
18. See Abramson, Aldrich, and Rohde, *Change and Continuity in the 1980 Elections,* rev. ed., 174-75.
19. These figures are from Orren, "The Nomination Process."
20. Thomas E. Patterson and Richard Davis, "The Media Campaign: Struggle for the Agenda," in *The Elections of 1984,* 114.
21. Most accounts, such as the UPI's count reported in the *Congressional Quarterly Weekly Report,* July 7, 1984, 1629, had Mondale with 2,000 or more votes by about July 5. Congressional Quarterly, based on the June 5 primaries, reported a "hard" (i.e., certain) count of Mondale delegates of 1,497.05, but a "grand total" that included estimated results of unfinished caucuses and superdelegates of 1,974, or 7 more delegates than minimally necessary. See their count on June 9, 1984, 1345. It was this sort of "grand total" projection that Mondale used as a basis for declaring himself "over the top" in that week, and thus the victor.
22. Caucus figures are based on estimates reported in the *Congressional Quarterly Weekly Report,* since records of actual attendance and voting are not always kept statewide.
23. These estimates of superdelegate support are based on a poll conducted in early July by ABC News and kindly made available to us by Rhodes Cook of Congressional Quarterly. In our estimates, we assume that those who said they were uncommitted in the poll or who were not contacted by ABC News divided their vote in the same proportion as those who stated a candidate preference.
24. In addition, there were 26 supporting Jackson and 76 uncommitted.
25. For a recent analysis of the rise of independents, see Martin P. Wattenberg,

The Decline of American Political Parties 1952-1980 (Cambridge, Mass: Harvard University Press, 1984).

26. See Scott Keeter and Cliff Zukin, *Uninformed Choice: The Failure of the New Nominating System* (New York: Praeger, 1983).
27. Abramson, Aldrich, and Rohde, *Change and Continuity in the 1980 Elections*, rev. ed., 122-31.
28. Richard A. Brody and Benjamin I. Page, "Comment: The Assessment of Policy Voting," *American Political Science Review* 66 (June 1972): 450-58; and Benjamin I. Page and Richard A. Brody, "Policy Voting and the Electoral Process: The Vietnam War Issue," *American Political Science Review* 66 (September 1972): 979-95.
29. Keeter and Zukin, *Uninformed Choice*, vii.
30. Paul Light, "As Good as Their Word: Mondale's Message," *Public Opinion* (June/July 1984): 13-17.
31. See, for example, Donald R. Matthews, "Winnowing," in James D. Barber, ed., *Race for the Presidency* (Englewood Cliffs, N.J.: Prentice-Hall, 1978), 55-78.
32. Patterson and Davis, "The Media Campaign," 116.
33. Keeter and Zukin, *Uninformed Choice*.
34. The first two were picked by about one quarter as the most important problem.
35. About a quarter picked a foreign or defense concern as the most important problem. Fewer Democrats than others were concerned about budget deficits and, especially, "excessive government spending."
36. Some form of runoff primary is currently used in nonpresidential contests in every one of the former Confederate states except Tennessee. As a general rule, candidates must receive an absolute majority of the vote to win without a runoff. If no candidate wins a majority, the runoff primary is held between the two leading vote-gatherers in the first round of voting. For more specific information, see Congressional Quarterly, *Guide to U.S. Elections*, 2d ed. (Washington, D.C.: Congressional Quarterly, 1985), 1067-71.
37. Based upon the "thermometer" scale used in the continuous monitoring study.

Chapter 2

The General Election Campaign

Once nominated, candidates choose their general election campaign strategies based on their perceptions of what the electorate wants, of the relative strengths and weaknesses of their opponents and themselves, and their chances of winning. A candidate who has a substantial lead in the polls will choose strategies that are very different from those used by a candidate who is far behind. A candidate who believes that his or her opponent has significant weaknesses is more likely to run an aggressive, attacking campaign than one who does not perceive such weaknesses.

As the preceding chapter indicated, there was a substantial difference in Ronald Reagan's and Walter F. Mondale's situations, and these differences carried over into the general election campaign. The contrast is best expressed by the candidates' standings in the polls. For example, in the Harris poll taken after the Republican convention, the Republican ticket received the support of 55 percent of the respondents, and the Democrats received 40 percent, a 15-point Reagan advantage.[1] For Mondale to win, he would have to find a way to overcome this enormous lead. Reagan, on the other hand, merely had to hold his own and could even lose some ground. Mondale had to get the voters to change their minds about Reagan, and he had only a few months to do it.

Part II of this book will consider in detail the impact of particular factors (like issues or evaluations of Reagan's job performance) on the voters' decisions. This chapter will provide an overview of the campaign—an account of its course and a description of the context within which strategic decisions were made.

Candidates' Perceptions and Strategy Choices

As we said, candidates base their strategies on their perceptions of the political climate. Both candidates and their campaign staffs understood the reality described by the Harris poll and its implications.

Mondale started the general election campaign not only behind in the national polls, but also with a sizable disadvantage in potential electoral votes. To win, Mondale would have to carry enough states (plus D.C.) to earn 270 electoral votes, an absolute majority of the 538 votes to be cast. The Democrats had won only three of the eight presidential elections between 1952 and 1980, and two of those wins (1960 and 1976) were by the narrowest of margins. The Republicans had won substantial victories in four of the five others, most recently in 1980. The pattern of state voting in these elections established the boundaries within which the campaign strategists had to work.

As Figure 2-1 reveals, there were 17 states that had voted Republican

Figure 2-1   States That Voted Republican at least Six out of
Eight Times, 1952-1980

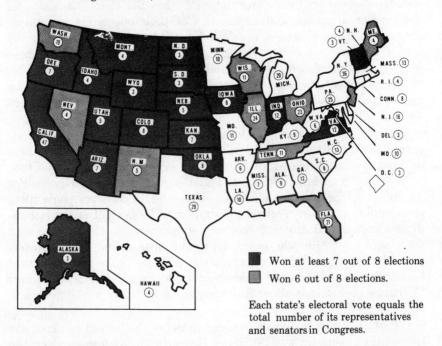

■ Won at least 7 out of 8 elections
▨ Won 6 out of 8 elections.

Each state's electoral vote equals the total number of its representatives and senators in Congress.

Note: The Republicans won Arizona in all 8 elections. The Republicans won Alaska in 5 of the 6 elections in which it voted.

Source: *Presidential Elections Since 1789,* 3d ed. (Washington, D.C.: Congressional Quarterly, 1983).

in seven out of eight elections and 1 (Arizona) that had voted Republican in all eight.[2] The Republicans also had carried Alaska in five of the six elections that had taken place since it attained statehood. These 19 states could provide 153 electoral votes in 1984, more than half of the votes needed to win. There were 10 additional states, with 129 electoral votes, that had voted Republican six of the eight times. If these states kept to their historical patterns, they would yield Ronald Reagan 282 votes and victory. Not all of them, to be sure, were certain to end up in the Republican column. Because of anger among farmers about their economic situations, Iowa and Wisconsin were vulnerable.[3] The Democrats had carried Illinois in 1960 and Ohio in 1976, and some observers (mainly Democratic activists) argued that California could be taken from the Republicans. On the other hand, these 29 potentially Republican states included only 3 southern states. In 1980 Reagan had carried all of the South except Jimmy Carter's home state of Georgia. Reagan could afford to lose all 5 of the questionable states from the list and still win if he carried all 11 southern states and the Border State of Kentucky.

This was a bleak set of figures for the Democrats and a rosy picture for the Republicans. Each campaign organization reacted to the situation in its own way. The Reagan campaign, facing no competition for the nomination, had begun to plan for the general election early, when the only major unanswered question was who the Democratic nominee would be. In November 1983 Lee Atwater, the deputy director of the Reagan campaign, produced a memorandum describing a strategy based on targeting the South and West.[4] Using calculations similar to ours above, but with somewhat different definitions of the regions, he claimed at least 107 of the West's 111 electoral votes and all 155 southern votes for Reagan, yielding a total of 262—only 8 short of victory without winning a single eastern or midwestern state.

All the Reagan campaign had to do, most of its managers believed, was to emphasize the president's leadership and the improved economic situation in the country (they chose the slogan "Leadership That's Working") and to avoid any catastrophic mistakes. There was some disagreement about this approach. Some members of the campaign team believed that Reagan should not rest on the first-term record, but instead should spell out a vision of what he would do in his second term.

This debate continued until the Democratic convention, after which there was general agreement, based on the composition of the Democratic ticket, that looking ahead was not necessary.[5] The "feel good" strategy emphasizing past accomplishments would be enough. Immediately after the Democratic convention, Atwater produced another memo claiming outright victory for the president. He said that the choice of Geraldine Ferraro, giving the Democrats a "North-North" ticket (a combination that had not won for them since 1944) had written off the South. This had, he argued, solidified all 266 western and southern votes and guaranteed a Reagan win. The analysis ended with the statement: "It's over, folks." [6] To nail down the last few electoral votes for certain victory, they chose two of Mondale's must-win states—Ohio and Michigan—and decided to "*carpet*-bomb them—saturate them with mail, media, surrogates, and presidential visits as if Reagan were campaigning for governor instead of president." [7]

The Mondale campaign had little time to plan. Jim Johnson, Mondale's chief strategist, had based his long-range planning on Mondale's wrapping up the nomination early. When this did not happen, general election planning became a spur-of-the-moment affair, starting at the end of the convention and immediately after it. The campaign did not seem to grapple directly with the political situation in geographic terms, and apparently it did not have a specific plan to reach 270 electoral votes. Instead the campaign was conceived in demographic terms, targeting weak Democrats and independent voters.

Mondale's people believed that the old Democratic coalition of minorities, ethnics, union members, and Jews could be brought together once again. Polls done for the campaign showed "that people liked Reagan but preferred Mondale's side of the big issues—the deficit, the arms race, the environment." [8] Thus the candidate would emphasize the issues, and eventually wayward Democrats and independents would come over to the Mondale-Ferraro ticket. As a geographic manifestation of this strategy, the Democratic campaign chose to emphasize Reagan's strongest area, the South and West, in the early going. [9]

From the Conventions to the First Debate

The Democratic Muddle

Mondale began his issue-based attack in his acceptance speech at the Democratic convention. He claimed that under the Reagan administration, only the rich were better off, working people were worse off, and "the middle class is standing on a trap door." [10] The wealthy were the beneficiaries of the Reagan tax cuts, and the deficits that were their consequence damaged the economy and undermined the future. Mondale promised to cut the deficit by two-thirds in his first term.

He then took the major gamble of his campaign. To deal with the budget squeeze caused by the deficit, he said taxes would have to be raised. "Mr. Reagan will raise taxes, and so will I. He won't tell you, I just did." [11] He also said that his tax increases would be fair and Reagan's would not, and that he would couple the tax raise with holding the line on spending. Mondale challenged Reagan to put his plan for dealing with the deficit on the table and debate both plans. He also promised to deal with the trade deficit, work for human rights, and negotiate a nuclear freeze with the Soviet Union.

The Democrats were happy with their convention. The choice of Ferraro as the vice-presidential nominee had, the Mondale managers felt, given them a boost. Although Mondale's staff had no coherent plan for winning the general election, they decided to launch the campaign right away rather than wait for the traditional Labor Day beginning. The week after the convention Mondale and Ferraro appeared in Mississippi and Texas. But even before this, things had already started to go wrong.

It is customary for a nominee to pick a new national party chairman, and the Mondale organization wanted their new person in place at the convention to help plan campaign strategy. They chose Bert Lance, Georgia party chairman and Carter's former budget director, who had been forced to resign in 1977 because of charges of banking irregularities. Lance had been indicted on these charges in 1979, but was acquitted in 1980.

Lance was chosen partly because the campaign felt the need to appeal to the South after the choice of Ferraro and partly because they felt grateful to him for his support that helped Mondale win the Georgia primary on Super Tuesday. What the Mondale people failed to recognize was that the choice would further remind voters of Mondale's past links to Carter, and that picking a "tarnished" chairman would lead others to question Mondale's judgment. Furthermore, other party leaders had not been consulted and reacted negatively when word leaked out. The day the convention opened, the decision was already made to pass over Lance and leave the current chairman in place. Jack W. Germond and Jules Witcover wrote that Mondale's "selection of Geraldine Ferraro to be his running mate had electrified the party and the country, but almost at once he had short-circuited the charge with the Lance ... debacle." [12]

Once the campaign was launched, things got even worse. Ferraro had promised to reveal all the details of her family finances, including the tax returns of her husband, John A. Zaccaro. In mid-August, however, she responded to a question from a reporter by revealing (without first informing Mondale) that her husband had refused to make his returns public. Mondale's staff was angry, and there was a great deal of press speculation about what might be hidden. After four days of pressure, Zaccaro relented, and Ferraro scheduled a press conference for four days after that. She faced 250 reporters for 90 minutes, answering all questions. Virtually every observer agreed that she did an excellent job, but the campaign had paid a heavy price. Beyond the negative publicity, Mondale-Ferraro lost the opportunity to gain ground on Reagan— something candidates so far behind could ill afford. As the data in Figure 2-2 (derived from Richard B. Wirthlin's daily polling for the Reagan

Figure 2-2 Reagan's Margin in Tracking Polls, June–November 1984

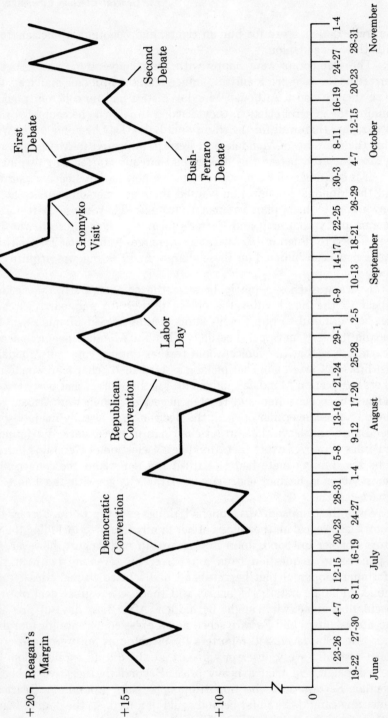

Source: Based upon daily telephone polls conducted by Richard B. Wirthlin. For further details, see note 13.

campaign) show, Reagan's lead stayed stable at about 12 points in early August and then expanded later in the month.[13]

The uncertainty of direction of the Democratic campaign is well illustrated by Mondale's Labor Day speech in Merrill, Wis. The speech had been planned to spell out the issue differences between Mondale and Reagan—the deficit, the proper place of religion in politics, and arms control. Just before the speech was to be delivered, Mondale was given a memorandum written by Patrick H. Caddell, Gary Hart's former pollster. The memo urged that "the election should be made a referendum on national character and values and about the future, as a way to deal with the leadership problem, and had in it the phrase 'What kind of people are we?' " [14] Mondale was impressed by the memo, but many on the staff resisted the change of focus. The result was a rewritten speech that did not go clearly in one direction or the other; it retained Caddell's "what kind of people" line, but little else was new. To make matters worse, Mondale's appearance at the New York City Labor Day parade had been poorly attended because it had occurred very early that morning, and that was the image that went on television in the evening.

In mid-September Caddell asked why the Mondale campaign had not implemented his plan; he was incredulous when he was told that campaign polls showed that Mondale was "only" 11 points behind. Caddell knew that a *New York Times* poll would be released the next day showing a 21-point gap, and he told this to the Mondale team. "You are the first campaign ever to come into September trailing and lose more ground," he said. "The first in *history*. You people are going down the tubes and the party's going with you." [15] A quick poll confirmed Caddell's numbers, and the campaign began to adopt his ideas.

Caddell's influence was reflected in a major speech Mondale gave at George Washington University on September 25. The message was still mixed, but there was a change of emphasis. The beginning was another attack on Reagan, this time for shifting his positions to the center to gain votes. The second half, however, (drafted in part by Caddell) talked less about Reagan and more about the values the Democratic campaign stood for. Mondale said he had been advised to cut loose from past positions, but "my answer is no. I would rather lose a race about decency than win one about self-interest." [16] Mondale and his staff were encouraged by the positive reaction to his speech. Buoyed, they looked forward to the first presidential debate.

Reagan: Taxes and Teflon

As we have just seen, the tale of a campaign in difficulty can be lengthy. By the same token, the tale of a campaign going well can be comparatively brief. When Mondale came out in favor of tax increases in his acceptance speech, what little debate there was in the Republican campaign over strategy came to an end. They would hammer at Mondale on the tax issue and emphasize the successes of the first administration. The attack began right after the Democratic convention. In Austin, Texas, on July 25 Reagan charged that the Democrats were "going so far left they've left America," and that they "never stop pining for their days of tax and tax, spend and spend." [17]

The attack continued in earnest at the Republican convention. In his acceptance speech Reagan characterized the campaign as offering the "clearest political choice of half a century." The choices were: "between two different visions of the future, two fundamentally different ways of governing—their government of pessimism, fear and limits—or ours of hope, confidence and growth." [18] The speech was a long one, and the president hammered repeatedly at the tax issue: "Our friends in the other party have never met a tax they didn't like—they didn't like, or hike." [19]

The tax issue, Reagan's managers believed, was their vehicle for guaranteeing victory. There was, however, one trap they felt needed to be neutralized: How would the deficit be handled if Reagan absolutely refused to raise taxes? Reagan argued that economic growth would lead to increased federal revenue, although few economists believed that his projections were realistic. But if economic growth proved inadequate, it was hard to see how the deficit could be trimmed without raising taxes. Because Reagan also would not cut defense spending, the Democrats plausibly could claim that the cuts would come from Social Security and Medicare. To defuse this, Reagan's team proposed that the president keep open the option of raising taxes as a *last* resort, and he agreed.

In contrast to the Democrats, the Republicans kicked off their campaign superbly on Labor Day, and that too came across on television. It opened in a park in Orange County, Calif., before an estimated crowd of 69,000 people.[20] Reagan spoke of his vision of America and his objectives for the second term. In closing he said that America's message to the world was: "You ain't seen nothin' yet." [21] The crowd responded warmly.

It was not that the Reagan campaign did not make any mistakes, but rather that they did not seem to matter. For example, in mid-August, while the president was testing his microphone before a radio broadcast, he jokingly announced: "My fellow Americans. I am pleased to tell you I just signed legislation outlawing Russia forever. The bombing begins in five minutes." [22] The mike was open and the joke became public. There was a brief flurry of reaction in the press, but virtually no impact on voter preferences. Like so often before, a negative event did not stick to the "Teflon president."

Thus as September came to a close, the Mondale campaign had generated some much needed enthusiasm, while the Reagan machine proceeded forward virtually without a hitch. Both sides looked forward to the first presidential debate, on domestic policy. To the Democrats it was a final hope; to the Republicans a chance for a *coup de grâce*. Two days before the debate, however, the magnitude of the gulf between the candidates was clear. A *Washington Post* poll of 12,000 respondents in the 48 contiguous states showed an 18-point gap and revealed that Mondale did not lead in even a single state.[23]

The Presidential Debates: The Rise and Demise of Walter Mondale

Televised presidential debates seem to have become a political institution. Until 1960 there had never been a debate between two major party presidential candidates. But in the contest between John F. Kennedy and Richard Nixon, there were four televised presidential debates. Lyndon B. Johnson refused to debate Barry M. Goldwater in 1964, Nixon refused to debate George S. McGovern in 1972, but Gerald R. Ford, who was far behind in the polls, challenged Jimmy Carter to a series of debates in 1976. Eventually there were three presidential debates, as well as a vice-presidential debate between Mondale and Robert Dole. In 1980 there were two debates, one between Reagan and independent candidate John B. Anderson and a head-to-head debate between Carter and Reagan one week before the election. Carter, like Ford, was trailing in the polls when he agreed to debate Reagan.

Mondale challenged Reagan to six debates. Reagan recognized that even agreeing to debate Mondale would give a boost to the challenger. Incumbent presidents who were ahead in the polls had never agreed to debate their opponents. But by 1984 it seemed potentially costly to refuse to debate, and, in any event, Reagan had done well in debates four years earlier. Eventually three debates were scheduled, two between the presidential candidates and one between the vice-presidential candidates, Ferraro and George Bush.

Recognizing the possibilities and risks inherent in the event, both campaign organizations put in a great deal of preparation for the first debate. Both candidates had briefing books to study (although Reagan's was considerably briefer than Mondale's), and both engaged in a number of practice debates. David A. Stockman played Mondale's part for Reagan's practices, as he had played Jimmy Carter in the debate preparations four years earlier. The president's managers assumed that Mondale would take an attacking posture and come after Reagan on the issues, so that is what Stockman did—with a vengeance. Reagan did poorly in the first rehearsal, four days before the debate, and the subsequent practice attempted to better prepare him to respond.

Mondale's preparation was more extensive, because he knew the whole ball game was at stake. Caddell prepared a memo that argued that

Mondale had not merely to defeat the president, but to "rout" him. To do this he had to surprise Reagan, adopting a strategy the president was unprepared to meet. Instead of directly attacking him, Mondale should adopt a " 'gold-watch approach' suitable to a family business retiring one of its elders—'sort of embracing a grandfather,' Caddell wrote, 'and gently pushing him aside.' " [24] To conceal this strategy from the Reagan camp, the Democrats deliberately leaked information that indicated Mondale would make a slashing attack.

When the candidates met in Louisville, Ky., on October 7, it was clear that—whether because of nervousness or Mondale's strategy or other reasons—the first debate would not go to the president. From the beginning, Reagan got bogged down in specifics and statistics and was unable to articulate the broad themes and witty lines to which voters had always responded. It was not that Mondale's performance was so good (he too often seemed nervous), but that Reagan's clearly was not. Even so, Reagan's managers thought the two were about even, up to the summations. Then the president, talking about whether Americans were better off than four years ago, got tangled up in an itemized defense of his record. Watching the event, Mondale's people were jubilant and Reagan's were decidedly not. "The summing up had been disjointed, Wirthlin worried aloud; the president had sounded old." [25]

Data on responses to the debate illustrate how public perceptions are shaped by press coverage. A poll taken by CBS immediately after the debate showed that respondents perceived that Mondale had outper-formed Reagan by only a 9 percentage point margin (43 to 34).[26] The press reaction to Reagan's performance, however, was almost uniformly negative, and there was much discussion of the "age issue"—whether Reagan was mentally and physically fit enough to hold office. Two days later, another *New York Times*/CBS News poll showed respondents perceiving Mondale to have won by a margin of almost four to one (66 percent to 17 percent).

Certainly both campaign organizations thought Mondale had won. The president's people were depressed and some, including his wife, were angry. Nancy Reagan and Sen. Paul Laxalt of Nevada, the official campaign chairman, thought that he had been overprepared—stuffed full of facts and figures.

Mondale and his people were, on the other hand, reinvigorated. The Democratic candidate declared the campaign "a brand new race" be-fore a responsive crowd in New York City the day after the debate.[27] During the next weeks, both the candidate and the crowds he encoun-tered showed renewed enthusiasm. Campaign workers all over the country reported more positive reactions; local press coverage in-creased and became more positive. Mondale's campaign polls showed that the gap had been narrowing, and this was borne out by most public polls (and by the Reagan campaign—*see the Wirthlin results in Figure 2-2)*.

The Reagan campaign concentrated on regaining its stride and restoring its candidate's confidence. These tasks were begun on a one-day whistlestop tour in Ohio using the same railroad car that Harry S Truman had used. Crowds were large and enthusiastic, and Reagan was heartened by them. He also received personal encouragement from many quarters. For example, Nixon called a member of the campaign staff and told him: "Don't panic. [Reagan's lead in] the polls will go down to 12 or 13; then they'll stabilize, and by Saturday, they'll go back up again. You'll be fine." [28] Nixon's prophecy about the polls proved precisely correct.

While the first debate produced improved morale in the Mondale camp and some apparent gain for him in voter support, a daunting task remained. Virtually all the polls showed the Reagan lead in double digits, and time was running out. If the Democrats were to have a chance of winning the election, Mondale would have to trounce Reagan in the second presidential debate, in Kansas City, Mo., on October 21. And although the nominal subject of the debate would be foreign policy, it was clear that for electoral purposes, the real issue would be Reagan's age and competence.

Both campaigns again prepared carefully. The Mondale camp again disagreed over strategy, with some advocating a calm discussion of the issues and Caddell advising a slashing attack on Reagan, to "break" him. Reagan, not wanting to repeat the fiasco of his closing statement the first time around, practiced many times with a stop watch. Against the possibility that Reagan would lose the second debate, his staff readied a plan, described in a memo as the "Great American Fog Machine," to limit damage. It advocated using top foreign policy (and even Pentagon) officials to defend the president. It also recommended direct attacks on Mondale on television by Ford, Dole, and Reagan himself. Excuses would be offered, downplaying the role of debates and saying "national security" precluded discussing certain things. The memo even suggested a possible trip by Reagan to Grenada on October 25, the first anniversary of the invasion.

As it turned out, the fog machine was not necessary. On television Mondale looked tired and drawn, and Reagan appeared rested and fit. The president had some trouble on the first question, which dealt with a CIA pamphlet for Nicaraguan rebels that seemed to advocate assassination, and his planned closing statement—despite all his practice—ran too long and was never completed. In between, however, he seemed to do quite well. He handled easily a question about his belief in the biblical prophecy of Armageddon, and, probably more important, he did not appear to let Mondale's attacking strategy throw him off stride.

Although Mondale's aggressive strategy may have been his only real option, there is some evidence that it was counterproductive. Wirthlin devised a technique for instantly measuring responses to debates. He selected a "focus group" of 40 persons, representing a cross-section of the electorate. Group members were given hand-held electronic devices on which they could register the degree to which they liked or disliked what they saw and heard in the debate. The responses were totaled by a computer every six seconds and could be superimposed visually on a video tape of the debate for later playback and analysis. The responses indicated that whenever Mondale attacked Reagan and his leadership, the reactions were strongly negative.[29]

Much of Mondale's attack was directed at Reagan's knowledge of issues, indicating that the president was not really in control of his administration. This was designed to keep raising the age issue, but indirectly. One of the reporters asking the debate questions was more blunt. He noted the tremendous pressures John Kennedy had faced during the Cuban missile crisis and asked Reagan whether he could function in circumstances like those. Reagan responded that he certainly felt up to doing the job. Then he said, "I will not make age an issue in this campaign. I am not going to exploit, for political purposes, my opponent's youth and inexperience."

The audience in Kansas City laughed, and so did viewers all across the country. Even Mondale laughed, and the reactions of Wirthlin's electronic focus group were enormously positive. Reagan had deftly defused the age issue, and at that moment, for all intents and purposes, the presidential campaign of 1984 was over.

The End Game: How Big a Victory?

The public reaction to the debate, measured by polls, was that it was close, although the Reagan margin grew somewhat over the next few days. Close or not, it certainly was not the big win Mondale needed. As a consequence, both sides began to adjust to the view that the outcome on election day had been determined and now the only question was the magnitude of Reagan's victory. Wirthlin employed an elaborate computer model of the electorate a few days after the second debate. He "punched in every nightmare assumption he could think of" and "the number at the bottom line still showed 430 electoral votes for Reagan."[30]

The Mondale campaign continued on, and some observers find it ironic that he finally was able to articulate why he was running. He spoke little about Reagan's competence in office and instead challenged the president on his administration's values. Mondale said that Reagan's television commercials depicted an America in which everything was all right: "It's all picket fences and puppy dogs. No one's hurting. No one's alone. No one's hungry. No one's unemployed. No one gets old. Everybody's happy." [31] There was, Mondale said, another America, but the president did not seem to know or care about it. At the end of his campaign, Mondale had returned to his original political motivations. The crowds he faced were large and they responded positively, but none of this would change the result.

Having concluded that they had won, the Reagan campaign concentrated on winning every state. Shortly after the debate, Wirthlin's polls showed Reagan's lead surging from 11 to 19 points, and a clean sweep seemed within their grasp. To this end, Reagan was scheduled to spend the final days of the campaign in the Northeast and the industrial Midwest, before going home to California. Indeed, he even made a stop in Mondale's home state of Minnesota. Republican strategists also tried to use the president in the last week to help the party's congressional candidates. Reagan made appearances in Iowa and Illinois on behalf of embattled Republican Senate incumbents Roger W. Jepson and Charles H. Percy, Jr., respectively, and in Arkansas for Senate challenger Ed Bethune. All lost.

Reagan closed the campaign with a half-hour television broadcast on election eve from his home state. The Mondale campaign could not afford any more television; they closed quietly in St. Paul. The voters would now register their preferences for real, not just in public opinion polls.

Did the Campaign Matter?

It is appropriate to ask whether the general election campaign made any difference. The answer depends on the yardstick used to measure the campaign's effects. Did it determine the winner? Did it affect the choices of voters? Did it put issues and candidates' positions clearly before the voters? Did it produce events that will have a lasting impact on American politics?

Regarding the outcome and voter choices, the answers appear to be no and yes. That is, voter choices seem to have been affected, but not enough of them ever to put the outcome in doubt. Table 2-1 presents data on voter choices for president based on responses in the Survey Research Center-Center for Political Studies 1984 postelection survey. The table shows the percentage voting for Reagan, by the time voters said they decided how to vote, presenting the results separately for each party identification category.[32] The data show that among Republicans Reagan was the overwhelming choice regardless of the time of decision, although there was a little slippage near the end. Among Democrats the rate of defection to Reagan was higher for those who decided during the general election campaign. Most important for our purposes, more than 70 percent of the respondents reported having made up their minds by the time the conventions ended. Of this group, 61 percent chose Reagan. This means that more than 43 percent of the voters had chosen Reagan by the time the conventions ended and had found nothing in the campaign to change their minds. The president did not need many votes in addition to this to guarantee victory.

About 30 percent of the voters decided after the conventions. Mondale needed 75 percent of these voters to pull even with Reagan. In fact, he won only 48 percent of the voters who made their choice during the general election campaign. Mondale possibly could have won if the campaign had led to a *much* larger turnout and if the additional voters were *very heavily* Democratic. But projected landslides do not stimulate a large turnout. In 1984 turnout increased only about 1 percentage point over the low levels of 1980. Moreover, as we show in Chapter 4, Democratic hopes to win by increasing turnout were unrealistic.

Looking back, it is difficult to see how any campaign strategy could have made a difference in the outcome. The Carter-Mondale ticket had won a fairly narrow electoral vote victory in 1976 (297 to 240), while carrying 10 of the 11 southern states with 118 electoral votes. In 1980 the ticket had lost all of those states but Georgia. Did anyone seriously believe that Mondale was going to win any of them back? And if not, which states that Gerald Ford had won was Mondale likely to take to make up the deficit? There were few plausible possibilities.

Table 2-1 Major Party Voters Who Voted for Reagan, by Time of Vote Decision and Party Identification, 1984

	Knew All the Time		Through the Conventions		After Conventions Through 1st Debate		After 1st Debate	
Strong Democrat	4%	(92)	11%	(106)	30%	(20)	20%	(41)
Weak Democrat	33%	(25)	29%	(93)	37%	(30)	35%	(75)
Independent, leans Democrat	16%	(31)	15%	(41)	23%	(13)	31%	(39)
Independent, no partisan leanings	87%	(23)	77%	(39)	[4]	(7)	67%	(33)
Independent, leans Republican	98%	(55)	95%	(75)	95%	(19)	82%	(33)
Weak Republican	100%	(61)	96%	(90)	95%	(21)	77%	(31)
Strong Republican	99%	(104)	98%	(80)	93%	(14)	77%	(13)

Note: Numbers in parentheses are totals on which percentages are based. Numbers in brackets are the number voting for Reagan in cases where the total N is less than 10.

The Democrats have won only one presidential election after 1948 with a northern Democrat at the top of the ticket (1960), and *none* without a southerner on the ticket at all. The reason is that, without any southern electoral votes, it is difficult to put together any conceivable winning coalition. It is not that it was *logically* impossible for Mondale to win in 1984, but that the combination of events for a win were so unlikely as to make it *practically* impossible. To be fair, one would have probably had to make the same judgment regarding any other Democratic ticket. Some observers might argue that a southerner as the vice-presidential nominee could have won a couple of southern states back into the fold, or that perhaps Gary Hart could have broken through to some degree in the West. Yet in the end, in our judgment, the result would have been largely the same.

One must conclude that issues and the candidates' policy positions also did not matter very much. This, however, is not unique to this campaign. The same could be said of virtually any campaign with a popular incumbent. Such candidates, and Reagan was no exception, are drawn almost inexorably to issue-free strategies that extol their achievements because such strategies have low risks. The challenger tries to raise issues, but if voters are basically satisfied, it is hard to make much headway.

Finally, in terms of events of lasting impact, at least two could be so considered. The first is the selection of Ferraro as the Democratic vice-presidential nominee. To be sure, there is little evidence of a substantial positive impact on the campaign. Poll results indicate that Bush may have had a more positive effect both in general and in the vice-presidential debate.[33] There is, on the other hand, also little evidence that she had any significant negative impact. (Indeed, there is little evidence that a vice-presidential candidate ever has had much impact on the outcome, beyond helping to carry his home state.) Most observers agree that she conducted her side of the campaign fairly well, and her selection may open up the top of national tickets to other women.

The second is the outcome itself in light of Mondale's selection. Since 1972 Democratic insiders have blamed Democratic defeats on the fact that the nomination process was open to seizure by outsiders. In 1972 an outsider, McGovern, led the party to a massive defeat. In 1976 an outsider, Carter, won a lucky victory, but he was soundly defeated in 1980. In 1984 the Democratic insiders stacked the nomination rules and won the nomination for their candidate. This led to another electoral disaster. If recent history convinces leaders of the Democratic party that the American people have been reacting negatively to the message of the party—whether the messenger has been insider or outsider—and, as a consequence, the party devises a new approach to the electorate, then the

1984 presidential campaign may turn out to have been very important indeed.

Notes

1. "See How They Ran," *Public Opinion* 7 (October/November 1984): 39.
2. For a discussion of the way these states changed their voting patterns over the past half-century, see Chap. 3.
3. Indeed, Iowa and Wisconsin were to be Mondale's sixth and eighth best states respectively, in terms of his share of the popular vote.
4. The memo is reprinted in Peter Goldman and Tony Fuller, with others, *The Quest for the Presidency—1984* (New York: Bantam Books, 1985), 383-86.
5. See Jack W. Germond and Jules Witcover, *Wake Us When It's Over: Presidential Politics of 1984* (New York: Macmillan, 1985), 469.
6. Goldman and Fuller, with others, *The Quest for the Presidency*, 414.
7. *Newsweek*, "Election Extra," November/December 1984, 89.
8. Ibid., 100.
9. See Germond and Witcover, *Wake Us When It's Over*, 465.
10. *Congressional Quarterly Weekly Report*, July 21, 1984, 1792.
11. Ibid., 1793.
12. Germond and Witcover, *Wake Us When It's Over*, 397.
13. The data in the figures are averages of the margins shown in Wirthlin's daily polls. The samples employed varied as follows: from June 19 through October 4, nightly tracking samples of 250 interviews per night aggregated over four days for a sample size of 1,000; from October 5 through October 30, nightly tracking samples of 500 aggregated over two days for a sample size of 1,000; from October 31 through November 4, nightly tracking samples of 1,000 aggregated over two days for a sample size of 2,000. The data and descriptions of the same are taken from Goldman and Fuller, with others, *Quest for the Presidency*, 454. Other polls show similar patterns (see "See How They Ran"). We focus here on the Wirthlin poll because it was based upon a much larger number of cases than any other poll and because it tracked Reagan's and Mondale's standing on a daily basis.
14. Elizabeth Drew, "A Political Journal," *New Yorker*, Dec. 3, 1984, 117. The memorandum can be found in Goldman and Fuller, with others, *Quest for the Presidency*, 420-26.
15. *Newsweek*, "Election Extra," 102.
16. Ibid.
17. Quoted in David Hoffman, "Reagan Rips into Mondale," *Washington Post*, July 26, 1984, A1.
18. *Congressional Quarterly Weekly Report*, Aug. 25, 1984, 2123.
19. Ibid.
20. Germond and Witcover, *Wake Us When It's Over*, 459.
21. Ibid., 463.
22. Ibid., 468-69.

23. David S. Broder and Barry Sussman, "Poll Shows Landslide for Reagan," *Washington Post,* Oct. 5, 1984, A1.
24. Goldman and Fuller, with others, *The Quest for the Presidency,* 314.
25. *Newsweek,* "Election Extra," 106.
26. These poll results and results cited in this paragraph are from CBS/*New York Times* polls cited in Kathleen A. Frankovic, "The 1984 Election: The Irrelevance of the Campaign," *P.S.* 18 (Winter 1984): 43.
27. Milton Coleman and Rick Atkinson, "Challenger Declares Campaign Is 'Brand New Race,'" *Washington Post,* Oct. 9, 1984, A1.
28. *Newsweek,* "Election Extra," 107.
29. Drew, "A Political Journal," 126-27.
30. *Newsweek,* "Election Extra," 110.
31. Ibid., 111.
32. For a discussion of the concept of party identification, see Chap. 8. For the questions used to measure party identification, see Chap. 4, note 40. The question used to measure the time the respondent decided how to vote was asked in the postelection interview and read as follows: "How long before the election did you decide that you were going to vote the way you did?"
33. On the latter point, see Frankovic, "The 1984 Election: The Irrelevance of the Campaign," 43.

Chapter 3

The Election Results

By election day, November 6, 1984, there was no suspense over who would win the presidency. During the last week of the campaign Walter F. Mondale and Geraldine Ferraro pointed to their large enthusiastic crowds as evidence that the public opinion polls were wrong. But Mondale's staff, if not the candidate himself, knew his chances were all but nonexistent once he failed to gain ground after the second televised presidential debate.[1] By making a last-minute campaign stop in Mondale's home state of Minnesota, Ronald Reagan underscored the only remaining question: Could he win all 50 states?

By 7:30 p.m. (eastern standard time) Dan Rather, the CBS anchor, reported early election returns and asked, "Can Ronald Reagan make it a 50-state sweep?"[2] A minute after 8 p.m., just after the polls had closed in 15 states, CBS News announced that Reagan had won the election. ABC News followed 12 minutes later, and at 8:30 NBC News declared Reagan the winner. When the last of the three networks "called" the election for Reagan, the polls were still open in 24 states.[3]

Reagan did not win all 50 states, but he fell short of this goal by only 3,761 votes of the 2,084,449 votes cast in Minnesota. Mondale held on to his home state by less than one-fifth of a percentage point, and, as expected, won the District of Columbia by a wide margin. Reagan had won nearly 54.5 million votes to 37.6 million for Mondale, a margin of 16.9 million votes, far greater than Reagan's 8.4 million vote margin over Jimmy Carter four years earlier. In 1984 Reagan won 58.8 percent of the vote to Mondale's 40.6 percent, an 18.2-point margin. Reagan's 1980 margin over Carter was only 9.7 points.

All third party candidates fared poorly. In 1980 independent candi-

Table 3-1 Official Presidential Election Results by State, 1984

State	Total Vote	Republican	Democratic	Other*	Percentage of Total Votes Rep.	Dem.	Other
Alabama	1,441,713	872,849	551,899	16,965	60.5%	38.3%	1.2%
Alaska	207,605	138,377	62,007	7,221	66.7%	29.9%	3.5%
Arizona	1,025,897	681,416	333,854	10,627	66.4%	32.5%	1.0%
Arkansas	884,406	534,774	338,646	10,986	60.5%	38.3%	1.2%
California	9,505,423	5,467,009	3,922,519	115,895	57.5%	41.3%	1.2%
Colorado	1,295,380	821,817	454,975	18,588	63.4%	35.1%	1.4%
Connecticut	1,466,900	890,877	569,597	6,426	60.7%	38.8%	.4%
Delaware	254,572	152,190	101,656	726	59.8%	39.9%	.3%
Florida	4,180,051	2,730,350	1,448,816	885	65.3%	34.7%	.0%
Georgia	1,776,120	1,068,722	706,628	770	60.2%	39.8%	.0%
Hawaii	335,846	185,050	147,154	3,642	55.1%	43.8%	1.1%
Idaho	411,144	297,523	108,510	5,111	72.4%	26.4%	1.2%
Illinois	4,819,088	2,707,103	2,086,499	25,486	56.2%	43.3%	.5%
Indiana	2,233,069	1,377,230	841,481	14,358	61.7%	37.7%	.6%
Iowa	1,319,805	703,088	605,620	11,097	53.3%	45.9%	.8%
Kansas	1,021,991	677,296	333,149	11,546	66.3%	32.6%	1.1%
Kentucky	1,369,345	821,702	539,539	8,104	60.0%	39.4%	.6%
Louisiana	1,706,822	1,037,299	651,586	17,937	60.8%	38.2%	1.1%
Maine	553,144	336,500	214,515	2,129	60.8%	38.8%	.4%
Maryland	1,675,873	879,918	787,935	8,020	52.5%	47.0%	.5%
Massachusetts	2,559,453	1,310,936	1,239,606	8,911	51.2%	48.4%	.3%
Michigan	3,801,658	2,251,571	1,529,638	20,449	59.2%	40.2%	.5%
Minnesota	2,084,449	1,032,603	1,036,364	15,482	49.5%	49.7%	.7%
Mississippi	941,104	582,377	352,192	6,535	61.9%	37.4%	.7%
Missouri	2,122,783	1,274,188	848,583	12	60.0%	40.0%	.0%

State	Total						
Montana	384,377	232,450	146,742	5,185	60.5%	38.2%	1.3%
Nebraska	652,090	460,054	187,866	4,170	70.6%	28.8%	.6%
Nevada	286,667	188,770	91,655	6,242	65.8%	32.0%	2.2%
New Hampshire	389,066	267,051	120,395	1,620	68.6%	30.9%	.4%
New Jersey	3,217,862	1,933,630	1,261,323	22,909	60.1%	39.2%	.7%
New Mexico	514,370	307,101	201,769	5,500	59.7%	39.2%	1.1%
New York	6,806,810	3,664,763	3,119,609	22,438	53.8%	45.8%	.3%
North Carolina	2,175,361	1,346,481	824,287	4,593	61.9%	37.9%	.2%
North Dakota	308,971	200,336	104,429	4,206	64.8%	33.8%	1.4%
Ohio	4,547,619	2,678,560	1,825,440	43,619	58.9%	40.1%	1.0%
Oklahoma	1,255,676	861,530	385,080	9,066	68.6%	30.7%	.7%
Oregon	1,226,527	685,700	536,479	4,348	55.9%	43.7%	.4%
Pennsylvania	4,844,903	2,584,323	2,228,131	32,449	53.3%	46.0%	.7%
Rhode Island	410,492	212,080	197,106	1,306	51.7%	48.0%	.3%
South Carolina	968,529	615,539	344,459	8,531	63.6%	35.6%	.9%
South Dakota	317,867	200,267	116,113	1,487	63.0%	36.5%	.5%
Tennessee	1,711,994	990,212	711,714	10,068	57.8%	41.6%	.6%
Texas	5,397,571	3,433,428	1,949,276	14,867	63.6%	36.1%	.3%
Utah	629,656	469,105	155,369	5,182	74.5%	24.7%	.8%
Vermont	234,561	135,865	95,730	2,966	57.9%	40.8%	1.3%
Virginia	2,146,635	1,337,078	796,250	13,307	62.3%	37.1%	.6%
Washington	1,883,910	1,051,670	807,352	24,888	55.8%	42.9%	1.3%
West Virginia	735,742	405,483	328,125	2,134	55.1%	44.6%	.3%
Wisconsin	2,211,689	1,198,584	995,740	17,365	54.2%	45.0%	.8%
Wyoming	188,968	133,241	53,370	2,357	70.5%	28.2%	1.2%
District of Columbia	211,288	29,009	180,408	1,871	13.7%	85.4%	.9%
United States	92,652,842	54,455,075	37,577,185	620,582	58.8%	40.6%	.7%

* Other includes David Bergland (Libertarian party), who received 228,314 votes; Lyndon H. LaRouche, Jr. (independent), who received 78,807; Sonia Johnson (Citizens Party), who received 72,200; and a variety of other candidates.

Source: *American Votes 16: A Handbook of Contemporary American Election Statistics*, compiled and edited by Richard M. Scammon and Alice V. McGillivray (Washington, D.C.: Congressional Quarterly, 1985), 41.

date John B. Anderson won 5.7 million votes, 6.6 percent of the votes cast; Ed Clark, the Libertarian party candidate, won more than 900,000 votes, 1 percent of the votes cast; and Barry Commoner, the Citizens party candidate, received 230,000 votes, a fourth of a percentage point. In 1984 the most successful third party candidate was David Bergland, the Libertarian candidate, who was on the ballot in 38 states and D.C. He won only 228,000 votes, a fifth of 1 percent of the votes cast. Lyndon H. LaRouche, Jr., running as an independent, won 79,000 votes, while Sonia Johnson, the Citizens party candidate, won 72,000 votes. None of these minor party candidates did as well as Commoner, the fifth-place candidate in 1980.[4] Table 3-1 presents the official presidential election results by states in the 1984 election.[5]

Reagan's electoral college margin was even more impressive than his popular vote tally. Figure 3-1 presents the electoral college results by states in 1980 and 1984. Admittedly, Reagan's margin was impressive in both elections. But in 1980 Carter held on to 6 states (Georgia, Hawaii, Maryland, Minnesota, Rhode Island, and West Virginia) as well as D.C. In 1984 Reagan carried 49 states.

The Pattern of Results

The 1984 election may be placed in perspective by comparing it with all previous presidential elections and by studying the overall pattern of presidential election results. Three conclusions emerge. First, Reagan's win was a truly historic landslide. Second, his win continues a pattern of Republican dominance in postwar presidential elections. Third, Reagan's victory must still be seen as part of a pattern of electoral volatility that began after the 1948 election.

Although the term "landslide" has been used very loosely by American political commentators, Reagan's 1984 win qualified by even the most stringent standards. Stanley Kelley, Jr., uses three criteria for calling an election a landslide.[6] A presidential election is a landslide if the winning candidate wins 53 percent of the popular vote, *or* wins 80 percent of the electoral vote, *or* wins 80 percent of the states. Kelley finds that 20 presidential elections of the 39 held between 1828 and 1980 met at least one of these criteria. In our view this definition is too loose, as Kelley himself realizes. For example, we do not view Reagan's 1980 win as a landslide because he won only 51 percent of the popular vote. But any presidential election that meets *all three* conditions certainly is a landslide.

Reagan's 1984 triumph is among nine elections that meet all three conditions. (The others are Abraham Lincoln's in 1864, Herbert Hoover's in 1928, Franklin D. Roosevelt's in 1932 and 1936, Dwight D. Eisenhower's in 1952 and 1956, Lyndon B. Johnson's in 1964, and Richard Nixon's

Figure 3-1 Electoral Votes by States, 1980 and 1984

Map 3-1A Electoral Votes by States, 1980

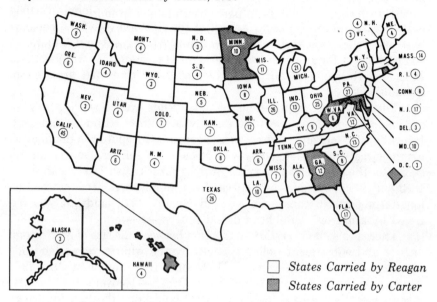

Note: Reagan won 489 electoral votes; Carter won 49 electoral votes.

Source: *Congressional Quarterly Weekly Report,* Nov. 8, 1980, 3297.

Map 3-1B Electoral Votes by States, 1984

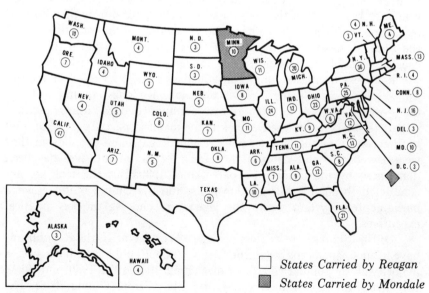

Note: Reagan won 525 electoral votes; Mondale won 13 electoral votes.

Source: *Congressional Quarterly Weekly Report,* Nov. 10, 1984, 2893.

in 1972.) Reagan received the fifth largest share of the popular vote in American history,[7] falling just 2 percentage points below Johnson's 1964 record of 61.1 percent. Reagan's share of the electoral vote (97.6 percent) falls just below Roosevelt's 1936 record of 98.5 percent and thus ranks second highest for any contested presidential election.[8] By winning 49 of 50 states, Reagan tied Nixon's 1972 record for contested presidential elections.

The long-term implications of a landslide win, however, may be minimal. Landslides do not necessarily lead to partisan realignment. Hoover's 1928 landslide did not create continued Republican dominance, for the Great Depression, along with Roosevelt's policies, led to minority status for the Republican party. Most political scientists see Eisenhower's 1952 and 1956 landslides as victories for a popular war hero that had no long-term partisan consequences. And Nixon's 1972 landslide was followed by a narrow Republican defeat four years later.

There is also no necessary connection between the size of an electoral victory and subsequent policy changes by the winner. Some landslide victories, such as Roosevelt's in 1932 and 1936 and Johnson's 1964 triumph, led to major policy initiatives. Others—Hoover's 1928 victory, Eisenhower's two wins, and Nixon's 1972 landslide—did not. Moreover, some elections that were not landslides were followed by major policy changes. In 1860, for example, Lincoln won only 39.8 percent of the popular vote, only 54.5 percent of the states, and only 59.4 percent of the electoral vote, but his election led to the end of slavery. Woodrow Wilson won only 41 percent of the popular vote in 1912, but during the first year of his presidency there was a major tariff reform and the establishment of the Federal Reserve System. While it is too early to judge the policy consequences of the 1984 election, it appears that Reagan's 1984 landslide will have less dramatic policy consequences than his victory in 1980.

While the size of Reagan's win may not have long-term implications, the postwar pattern of Republican dominance does. Many political scientists still consider the Democrats the majority party because, at least until recently, public opinion polls revealed that more people said they were Democrats and because the House of Representatives has been dominated by the Democratic party since 1930. But elections are not conducted through public opinion polls, and the United States is not a parliamentary system where the legislature chooses the key political executives.

Of the 10 presidential elections since World War II, the Republicans have won 6, including 4 of the last 5. The Republicans have won a majority of the popular vote five times (1952, 1956, 1972, 1980, and 1984); the Democrats have gained a majority only twice (1964 and 1976). The average (mean) level of Republican support in the 10 postwar elections is 50.7 percent; the average level of Democratic support is only 45.9 percent.

Moreover, during these elections, Republican presidential candidates have won 40 million votes more than the Democratic candidates—a total of 369,232,000 cast for Republican candidates and 329,132,000 cast for the Democrats.

Although the Republicans hold a clear edge over the Democrats, the overall pattern of postwar results also demonstrates considerable electoral volatility. Since the war, no party has been able to win more than two presidential elections in a row. The failure of either party to win a string of victories sets the postwar era in sharp contrast with most of American electoral history. Table 3-2 shows the presidential election results since 1832, the first year the candidate of the modern Democratic party, Andrew Jackson, ran for reelection. Since 1832, we find four periods in which a single party won a series of three or more elections. The Republicans won six consecutive elections between 1860 and 1880, although in 1876 Rutherford B. Hayes beat Samuel J. Tilden by a single electoral vote, and Tilden had a majority of the popular vote cast. The Republicans also won four elections between 1896 and 1908, as well as three between 1920 and 1928. The Democrats won five straight elections between 1932 and 1948.

Although no party has managed three straight wins during the postwar era, until 1980 the winning party was able to pull off a second presidential victory. The Republicans won in 1952 and 1956, the Democrats in 1960 and 1964, and the Republicans in 1968 and 1972. In all these elections, the second win was by a bigger margin than the first. The 1980 and 1984 elections fit this pattern, with a win followed by a bigger win. But the 1976 and 1980 elections do not fit the pattern, for the Democrats ousted a Republican incumbent in 1976 but lost four years later. The 1976 and 1980 elections are the only contests in the twentieth century in which the incumbent party lost two elections in a row.

The incumbent party lost four elections in a row between 1840 and 1852, a period of alternation between the Democrats and the Whigs, and again between 1884 and 1896, a period of alternation between the Republicans and the Democrats. Both of these intervals preceded major party realignments. After the Whig loss of 1852, the Republicans replaced them as the second major party. Although many Whigs, including Lincoln, became Republicans, the Republican party was not just the Whig party renamed. The Republicans had transformed the American political agenda by capitalizing upon opposition to extending slavery into the territories.[9] They had a different regional base from the Whigs, for, unlike the Whigs, they had no southern support. But they created a regional base in the Midwest, which the Whigs had never established.

The 1896 election, the last in a series of four incumbent party losses, is also seen as "critical" because it solidified Republican dominance. In 1896 the Republicans emerged as the clearly dominant party, gaining a

Table 3-2 Presidential Election Results, 1832-1984

Election	Winning Candidate	Party of Winning Candidate	Success of Incumbent Political Party
1832	Andrew Jackson	Democrat	Won
1836	Martin Van Buren	Democrat	Won
1840	William H. Harrison	Whig	Lost
1844	James K. Polk	Democrat	Lost
1848	Zachary Taylor	Whig	Lost
1852	Franklin Pierce	Democrat	Lost
1856	James Buchanan	Democrat	Won
1860	Abraham Lincoln	Republican	Lost
1864	Abraham Lincoln	Republican	Won
1868	Ulysses S. Grant	Republican	Won
1872	Ulysses S. Grant	Republican	Won
1876	Rutherford B. Hayes	Republican	Won
1880	James A. Garfield	Republican	Won
1884	Grover Cleveland	Democrat	Lost
1888	Benjamin Harrison	Republican	Lost
1892	Grover Cleveland	Democrat	Lost
1896	William McKinley	Republican	Lost
1900	William McKinley	Republican	Won
1904	Theodore Roosevelt	Republican	Won
1908	William H. Taft	Republican	Won
1912	Woodrow Wilson	Democrat	Lost
1916	Woodrow Wilson	Democrat	Won
1920	Warren G. Harding	Republican	Lost
1924	Calvin Coolidge	Republican	Won
1928	Herbert C. Hoover	Republican	Won
1932	Franklin D. Roosevelt	Democrat	Lost
1936	Franklin D. Roosevelt	Democrat	Won
1940	Franklin D. Roosevelt	Democrat	Won
1944	Franklin D. Roosevelt	Democrat	Won
1948	Harry S Truman	Democrat	Won
1952	Dwight D. Eisenhower	Republican	Lost
1956	Dwight D. Eisenhower	Republican	Won
1960	John F. Kennedy	Democrat	Lost
1964	Lyndon B. Johnson	Democrat	Won
1968	Richard M. Nixon	Republican	Lost
1972	Richard M. Nixon	Republican	Won
1976	Jimmy Carter	Democrat	Lost
1980	Ronald Reagan	Republican	Lost
1984	Ronald Reagan	Republican	Won

Source: *Congressional Quarterly's Guide to U.S. Elections,* 2d ed. (Washington, D.C.: Congressional Quarterly, 1985).

solid hold in New York, Connecticut, New Jersey, and Indiana, states they frequently had lost between 1876 and 1892. After William McKinley's defeat of William Jennings Bryan in 1896, the Republicans established firmer bases in the Midwest, New England, and the mid-Atlantic states. They lost the presidency only in 1912, when the GOP was split, and in 1916, when Wilson ran for reelection.

The Great Depression ended Republican dominance. The emergence of the Democrats as the majority party was not preceded by a series of incumbent losses. The Democratic coalition, forged between 1932 and 1936, relied heavily upon the emerging industrial working class and the mobilization of new groups into the electorate.[10] Clearly, a series of incumbent party losses is not a prerequisite for a partisan realignment.

If the Republicans win in 1988, it will be the first time in four decades that the incumbent party will have won the White House for two consecutive elections. Moreover, if Reagan is still president in 1988, the Republicans would need to win with a nonincumbent, something the party holding the White House has not done since 1928. If this happens, many political scientists will argue that Republican presidential dominance must be viewed as a realignment. The two consecutive incumbent party losses of 1976 and 1980 may then be seen as a signal that a realignment was underway.

The 1988 election may prove the crucial test for Republican hopes to emerge as a majority party. If they win, they will break the postwar pattern of electoral volatility. Because Reagan cannot be the candidate, a 1988 Republican victory is unlikely to be viewed as the personal triumph of a politician who has mastered the electronic media. Thus, the 1988 election will be a major test for the Republican party.

State-by-State Results

Politicians, journalists, and political scientists are fascinated by how presidential candidates fare in each state because the states deliver the electoral votes needed to win the presidency. The presidential contest can be viewed as 51 separate elections, one for each state and one for the District of Columbia.

Although there are some minor exceptions, the candidate with the most votes in each state wins all of its electoral votes. The number of electoral votes for each state is the sum of the number of its senators (two), plus the number of representatives in the House. In 1984 the number of votes per state ranged from a low of 3 in Alaska, Delaware, North Dakota, South Dakota, Vermont, Wyoming, and the District of Columbia, to a high of 47 in California. Naturally, the quest for the 270 electoral votes needed to win is focused on the more populous states. Candidates usually focus more attention on large states that often switch their allegiance from election to election. In 1984 Mondale spent a great deal of time and money in California, even though it had voted Republican in seven elections of the past eight. But the vote in California often has been fairly close; thus, a Democrat could imagine carrying its 47 electoral votes— more than a sixth of the votes needed to win.

States are the building blocks of winning electoral coalitions, but state-by-state results can be overemphasized and may even be misleading. First, in all 24 presidential elections between 1892 and 1984, the candidate with the largest number of popular votes also gained an absolute majority of the electoral votes. Thus, candidates can win by gaining broad-based support throughout the nation, even though they must also think in terms of states. Moreover, given the importance of national television coverage, candidates must run national campaigns. They can make special appeals to specific states or regions, but these appeals will be broadcast to the entire country by the national media.

Second, comparing state-by-state results can be misleading because it may conceal change. To illustrate this point we compare such results for two of the closest postwar presidential elections—John F. Kennedy's win over Nixon in 1960 and Carter's win over Gerald R. Ford in 1976.

There are many striking parallels between these two Democratic victories. In 1960 and 1976 the Republicans did well in the West, and both Kennedy and Carter needed southern support to win.[11] Kennedy carried 6 of the 11 states of the old Confederacy (Arkansas, Georgia, Louisiana, North Carolina, South Carolina, and Texas), as well as 5 of Alabama's 11 electoral votes, for a total of 81 electoral votes. Carter carried 10 of these states (all but Virginia) for a total of 118 electoral votes.

The demographic basis of Carter's support was completely different, however. In 1960 only 29 percent of the black adults in the South were registered to vote, compared with 61 percent of the whites. According to our analysis of survey data from the University of Michigan's Survey Research Center, only 1 voter out of 15 supporting Kennedy in the South was black *(Chapter 5).* After the Voting Rights Act of 1965, however, black registration and voting increased dramatically. In 1976, 63 percent of black adults were registered to vote, compared to 68 percent of the whites.[12] We estimate that about 1 voter out of 3 for Carter in the South was black. A comparison of state-by-state victories conceals this massive change in the social composition of the Democratic presidential coalition.

Third, state-by-state comparisons do not tell us why a presidential candidate received support. Of course, such analyses lead to interesting speculation, especially when dominant political issues are clearly related to regional differences. In Part II we will turn to surveys that question individual voters to understand the dynamics of electoral change.

With these qualifications in mind, we now turn to the state results. Figure 3-2 shows Reagan's margin of victory over his Democratic opponents in 1980 and 1984. Unlike the win-loss map in Figure 3-1, the margin of victory maps reveal clear regional differences, and comparing the 1980 and 1984 maps reveals sharp differences between the two elections.

In 1980 Carter did best in his native South. Although he won only 1 of the 11 states of the old Confederacy, his margin of defeat was 5 points or less in 6 of the remaining. Carter did less poorly in these states because they have a relatively large black population: blacks were the only major group that gave Carter their solid support. Carter's margin of defeat was also relatively small in the 6 New England states where he won 1 state and lost by 5 points or less in 2 others.

In 1980 Reagan did far better in the West than in other regions. We consider 18 states as western from the standpoint of presidential elections, and Reagan won 13 of them by a margin of 20 points or more, while winning 2 others by 15 to 20 points.[13]

Once we turn to the state-by-state results for 1984, the West no longer appears distinctive. Reagan won by a larger overall margin in 1984, and his wins in many more states were more impressive than in 1980. Reagan's margin of victory increased in 37 states, and he won 5 states that he had lost four years earlier. He also lost Minnesota by a narrower margin. His margin of victory fell only in California, Iowa, Montana, Nevada, North Dakota, South Dakota, and Utah, and he lost the District of Columbia by a larger margin.[14] In 1980 Reagan won 14 states by 20 percentage points or more, but he carried 31 states by this margin in 1984.

While Reagan still had a massive victory margin in the West, he now carried 17 states outside the West by a margin of 20 points or more. His biggest gains were in the South. In 1980 he had carried none of the 11 southern states by a 20-point margin. In 1984 he carried 10 of them by a margin of at least 20 points, and he carried Tennessee by 16 points. In 1980 Carter, aided by a strong black vote, fared less poorly in the South than elsewhere. Although blacks voted overwhelmingly for Mondale, his losses in the South were massive. Only about one white southern voter in four supported Mondale.

For the nation as a whole Reagan's margin of victory increased by 8.5 percentage points. It increased by at least 12 points in every southern state, and in Alabama, Arkansas, Mississippi, North Carolina, and South Carolina, it increased by more than 20 points. In Georgia, Reagan had lost to Carter by 15 points, but defeated Mondale by 20 points. Combining the votes of all southern states in 1980, Reagan's margin of victory was only 6.9 percentage points; in 1984 it was 25.2. Outside the South, Reagan's margin of victory increased far less, rising from 10.6

Figure 3-2 Reagan's Margin of Victory, 1980 and 1984

Map 3-2A Reagan's Margin of Victory Over Carter

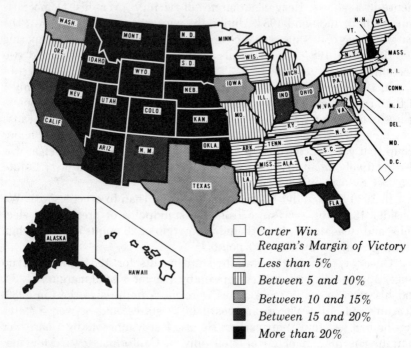

Carter Win
Reagan's Margin of Victory
Less than 5%
Between 5 and 10%
Between 10 and 15%
Between 15 and 20%
More than 20%

Map 3-2B Reagan's Margin of Victory Over Mondale

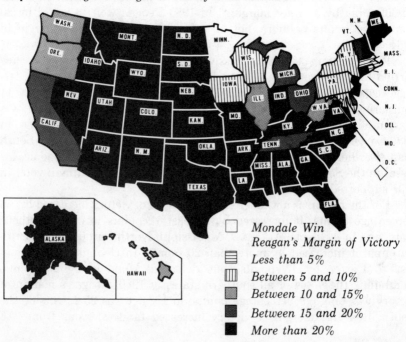

Mondale Win
Reagan's Margin of Victory
Less than 5%
Between 5 and 10%
Between 10 and 15%
Between 15 and 20%
More than 20%

points in 1980 to 15.9 points in 1984.

There were no regions where Mondale did well in 1984, but there were some where he lost less badly. Although he won no New England states and lost three of these states by a margin of 20 points or more, he lost two of them (Massachusetts and Rhode Island) by less than 5 percentage points. Mondale also did less poorly in the mid-Atlantic states, where he lost by 5 to 10 points in New York and Pennsylvania. He did less badly in the North Central states, where he lost by 5 to 10 points in Iowa and Wisconsin and actually won Minnesota. And while Mondale lost by at least 10 points in all three of the Pacific Coast states, he lost them less badly than the national average.

Perhaps the most striking feature of the 1984 election is the relative absence of regional differences, which can be shown by statistical analysis. Joseph A. Schlesinger has analyzed state-by-state variation in all the presidential elections from 1824 through 1984. His measure is the "standard deviation" among the states in the percentage of the Democratic vote.[15] In 1984 the state-by-state variation was only 5.84 points, the second lowest of all 10 postwar presidential elections.[16] State-by-state variation in 1980 was higher, at 7.95 points, placing it in the middle range (fifth highest) of the postwar elections. But what is most striking in Schlesinger's analysis is the relatively low level of state-by-state variation in all 10 of the elections after World War II. According to Schlesinger's analysis, all 15 of the presidential elections between 1888 and 1944 displayed more state-by-state variation than any of the 10 postwar elections.

As Schlesinger's analysis suggests, the 1980 and 1984 elections can be seen as part of a trend toward a more nationalized electorate, at least in presidential elections. And, in recent years, this has been an increasingly Republican electorate.

Viewed from a regional perspective, the Reagan victories continue two basic trends in postwar American politics: Republican dominance in the West and a continued breakdown of Democratic dominance in the South. These shifts began well before these elections and can be illustrated by maps that capture the watershed elections in which they took place.

Figure 3-3 presents six maps that portray this shifting regional strength. Maps 3-3A and 3-3B show election results by state in the five elections between 1932 and 1948; that is, the four Roosevelt victories and Harry S Truman's defeat of Thomas E. Dewey. Maps 3-3C and 3-3D show the results for the three elections between 1952 and 1960; that is, Eisenhower's two wins and Kennedy's win over Nixon. Maps 3-3E and 3-3F present the results of the six most recent elections, of which the Republicans have won four.

Maps 3-3A and 3-3C show the states that supported the Democratic

Figure 3-3 How States Voted for President between 1932 and 1948, 1952 and 1960, 1964 and 1984

Map 3-3A States That Voted Democratic at least Three out of Five Times, 1932-1948

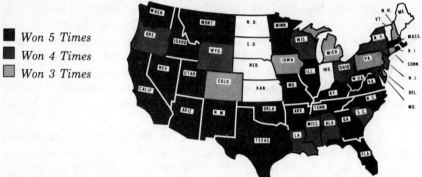

- ■ *Won 5 Times*
- ■ *Won 4 Times*
- □ *Won 3 Times*

Map 3-3B States That Voted Republican at least Three out of Five Times, 1932-1948

- ■ *Won 5 Times*
- ■ *Won 3 Times*

Map 3-3C States That Voted Democratic at least Two out of Three Times, 1952-1960

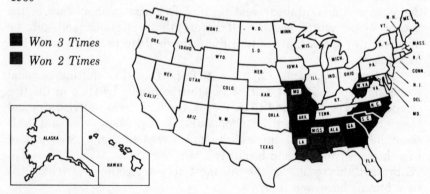

- ■ *Won 3 Times*
- ■ *Won 2 Times*

* Hawaii attained statehood in 1959 and voted Democratic in 1960.

Map 3-3D States That Voted Republican at least Two out of Three Times, 1952-1960

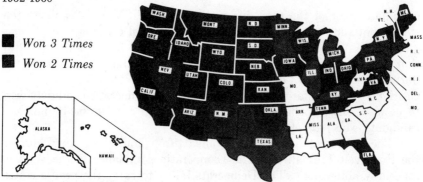

■ *Won 3 Times*
■ *Won 2 Times*

* Alaska attained statehood in 1959 and voted Republican in 1960.

Map 3-3E States That Voted Democratic at least Three out of Six Times, 1964-1984

■ *Won 5 Times*
■ *Won 4 Times*
▨ *Won 3 Times*

(6 times)

Map 3-3F States That Voted Republican at least Four out of Six Times, 1964-1984

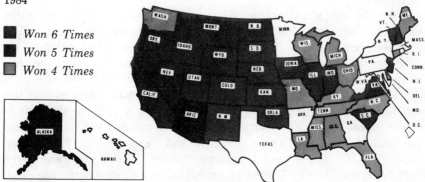

■ *Won 6 Times*
■ *Won 5 Times*
▨ *Won 4 Times*

Note: States that voted for third party candidates are as follows: Alabama, Louisiana, Mississippi, and South Carolina voted for J. Strom Thurmond in 1948; all of the electors from Mississippi and the majority of the electors from Alabama voted for Harry F. Byrd in 1960; and Alabama, Arkansas, Georgia, Louisiana, and Mississippi voted for George C. Wallace in 1968.

candidate most of the time during these periods. Map 3-3E shows the states that supported the Democratic presidential candidate in *at least half* of these six elections. Maps 3-3B, 3-3D, and 3-3F show the states that supported the Republican presidential candidate most of the time during these periods. Readers should remember that for the last six elections we show states as Democratic if the Democratic candidate won *three* elections; we show a state as Republican only if the Republican candidate won *four* elections.[17]

The Democrats generally prevailed throughout the country during the Roosevelt-Truman era. The Democratic dominance in the West is especially noteworthy. The Democrats failed to carry the prairie states from North Dakota south through Kansas, but they won six of the mountain states in all five elections and most of the elections in the remaining two. In addition, the Democrats won Oklahoma, Washington, and California in all five elections, and Oregon in four out of five. Map 3-3A also shows the beginning of a crack in the "Solid South." Alabama, Louisiana, Mississippi, and South Carolina voted for J. Strom Thurmond, the States' Rights Democrat in 1948, but no southern state went Republican during this era.

The 1932-1948 period was a lean time for the Republicans, as Map 3-3B illustrates. The GOP carried only seven states in three or more of these elections.

The years between 1952 and 1960 show a marked move to the Republicans among the western states. It is not surprising that these states voted Republican during Eisenhower's landslide victories. What is more important is that only two western states (Nevada and New Mexico) returned to the Democratic fold in 1960. The two new western states split, with Alaska voting for Nixon, and Hawaii for Kennedy.

All the western states but Arizona voted Democratic in Johnson's landslide over Barry M. Goldwater, but most western states voted consistently Republican after 1964, as Map 3-3F makes apparent. If we total the results in Maps 3-3D and 3-3F, we find that Hawaii is the only western state the Republicans have failed to dominate.[18]

As Map 3-3C shows, the Democrats won only nine states most of the time between 1952 and 1960, and seven of them were in the South. However, the Republicans made some inroads, carrying Virginia, Tennessee, and Florida in all three elections, and Texas in both Eisenhower contests. They also gained Louisiana in 1956. The Republicans never succeeded in capturing Mississippi or Alabama, although both bolted the Democratic column in 1960. Schlesinger's analysis shows state-by-state variation to be low in all three of these elections, and this decline results mainly from the declining percentage of southerners supporting Democratic presidential candidates.

As Maps 3-3E and 3-3F show, neither party has dominated the South during the last six elections, although the Republicans have been far more successful than the Democrats. The major breakthrough came in 1964, when Goldwater carried Alabama, Georgia, Louisiana, Mississippi, and South Carolina. In 1968 Hubert H. Humphrey carried only 1 former Confederate state (Texas), while George C. Wallace, the American Independent party candidate, carried 5 (Alabama, Arkansas, Georgia, Louisiana, and Mississippi). In 1972 Nixon carried all 11 of the former Confederate states, but in 1976 Carter carried every one but Virginia. Four years later, he held only his home state, Georgia. In 1984, as in 1972, the Republicans carried all 11 states of the old Confederacy. Texas is the only southern state carried by the Democrats in even half of the last six elections. Although Republican success in the South does not match their dominance in the West, the South is clearly no longer part of the Democratic presidential coalition.

What explains the Republican strength in the West? No simple answer accounts for this regional shift. Historically, the Democratic party enjoyed Western support after Bryan's Democratic and Populist candidacy in 1896. In the 1920, 1924, and 1928 Republican victories, however, the West voted solidly Republican. Roosevelt's agricultural policies may have earned him western support, and Truman's appeals to farmers may have helped him carry the region. Perhaps Kennedy failed to regain the West partly because he was a Roman Catholic, and most western states are less Catholic than the nation as a whole. Another reason may be that Kennedy was an easterner who did not emphasize agricultural issues.

During the Bryan contests of 1896 and 1900 and perhaps during the Roosevelt years, many westerners looked to the federal government to protect them from powerful banking and railroad interests in the East. Today, when most social and economic policies emerge from Washington, westerners may resent the federal government and vote for the party that favors less federal regulation. The Democratic reliance on black votes hurts them in this region, because many western states have a smaller proportion of blacks than the nation as a whole. Finally, the Democrats tend to emphasize conservation, while the Republicans tend to favor the economic development of federal lands, which are concentrated in the West.

The reason for the Democratic loss of the South is readily apparent. As V. O. Key, Jr., brilliantly demonstrated in *Southern Politics in State and Nation* (1949), the crucial factor in southern politics is race: "In its grand outlines the politics of the South revolves around the position of the Negro . . . Whatever phase of the southern political process one seeks to understand, sooner or later the trail of inquiry leads to the Negro." [19] And it is the changed role of the national Democratic party toward black Americans that smashed the Democratic dominance in the South. [20]

During the 12 presidential elections from 1880 (after Reconstruction ended) through 1924, the Democrats won all 11 former Confederate states, with one exception—Tennessee in 1920. Even in 1928, when the Democrats ran Alfred E. Smith, a Roman Catholic, 6 of the most "solid" of these states voted Democratic (Alabama, Arkansas, Georgia, Louisiana, Mississippi, and South Carolina), even though all but Louisiana are overwhelmingly Protestant. After the southern blacks lost the vote during the late nineteenth and early twentieth centuries, the Republicans ceded these states to the Democrats. While the Republicans, as the party of Lincoln, had black support in the North, they did not attempt to enforce the Fifteenth Amendment that bans restrictions on voting on grounds of "race, color, or previous condition of servitude."

In 1932 a majority of black voters remained loyal to Hoover, although by 1936 Roosevelt won the support of northern blacks. Roosevelt made no effort to win the votes of southern blacks, most of whom remained effectively disfranchised. Even as late as 1940 about 70 percent of the nation's blacks lived in the 11 states of the old Confederacy. Roosevelt carried all 11 of these states in all four of his elections. His 1944 victory, however, was the last election in which the Democratic presidential candidate carried all 11 southern states.

World War II led to massive black migration to the North, and by 1948 Truman, through his support of the Fair Employment Practices Commission, made explicit appeals to blacks. These policies led to defections by the "Dixiecrats" and cost Truman four southern states. Adlai E. Stevenson deemphasized appeals to blacks and held most of the deep southern states, although Eisenhower made some inroads. Kennedy also played down appeals to blacks, and southern support was essential for his narrow win over Nixon.[21] By choosing Texan Lyndon Johnson as his running mate, Kennedy may have helped himself in the South. Clearly, Johnson's presence on the ticket helped Kennedy narrowly win Texas.

But if Johnson as running mate aided the Democrats in the South, Johnson as president played a different role. His support for the Civil Rights Act of 1964 and his explicit appeals to blacks helped end the Democratic dominance in the South. Goldwater, the Republican candidate in 1964, had voted against the Civil Rights Act, creating a sharp contrast between the presidential candidates. By 1968, Humphrey, who had long been a champion of black demands, carried only one southern state, Texas, which he won with only 41 percent of the vote. (He was probably aided by Wallace's candidacy, since Wallace gained 19 percent of the vote, and national surveys suggest that he took more votes from Nixon than from Humphrey.) Even in 1976, Carter carried a minority of the vote among white southerners.

Today the South belongs to neither political party, although, on balance, it is more Republican than Democratic in presidential voting. With massive support from black voters, Carter won the South in 1976 perhaps because southern pride led a substantial minority of whites to support him. Carter failed to carry the South four years later, despite continued support from southern blacks. And in 1984, with no southerner on the ticket, the Democrats did worse in the South than in the nation as a whole. The 1980 and 1984 results underscore the problems the Democrats face in this region. As long as the Democratic party is seen as the supporter of blacks, it will have substantial difficulty gaining enough white votes to carry the South. And yet without the black vote the Democrats are unlikely to carry the South itself or the northern industrial states they also need to gain the presidency.

Conclusion

The 1980 and 1984 election results, when placed in the historical context of postwar presidential American politics, present a bleak outlook for Democrats. The party lacks an electoral base. Only the District of Columbia has voted consistently Democratic in the last six elections, and only one state, Minnesota, has voted Democratic in five of the last six contests. Five other states have voted Democratic in four of the last six elections. Together, these states and D.C. have only 50 electoral votes. Three states, New York, Pennsylvania, and Texas, have voted Democratic in three of the last six elections. They have a total of 90 electoral votes.

The Republican base is impressive, especially in the West. Among the 18 states we have classified as western, the Republicans have won 16 in the last five elections. These states alone provide 123 electoral votes, nearly half the 270 needed to win the presidency.

But the solid West does not constitute an insurmountable Republican advantage. Kennedy was elected in 1960 even though he won only three western states (Hawaii, Nevada, and New Mexico) with a total of 10 electoral votes, and Carter won in 1976 even though he carried only one western state (Hawaii) with 4 electoral votes. Despite the three reapportionments since the 1960 election and the one reapportionment since 1976, a Democrat could have won in 1984, or could win in 1988, with the same set of states won by either Kennedy or Carter.[22]

The Republican base may not be as solid as it appears. California, with its 47 electoral votes, is far larger than any other western state. While California has voted Republican in eight of the last nine presidential elections, it is not as firmly Republican as this record makes it appear. Although California has a Republican governor and one Republican senator, it also has one Democratic senator, and its congressional delegation has 27 Democrats and 18 Republicans. Both houses of its state legislature are controlled by the Democratic party.

In presidential elections California has not voted very differently from the nation as a whole. During the 10 postwar presidential elections, its average level of Republican support has been 51.2 percent, only half a percentage point more Republican than the national average. In 1968 it voted four points more Republican than the nation as a whole, but in 3 elections, 1956, 1972, and 1984, it voted less Republican. In every close presidential election, California also has been close. In retrospect, Mondale's efforts in California seem futile, since he lost the state by a million and a half votes. But while Mondale may have been the wrong Democrat in the wrong year to win California, another Democrat in another year could win it.

No state can be considered safe for the Democrats. But as American presidential elections are increasingly nationalized, no state may be safe for the Republicans either. Given the high level of volatility in postwar presidential elections, the District of Columbia may be the only electoral unit that cannot be won by both political parties.

The 1980 and 1984 presidential elections should bury the myth that the Democrats are the majority party. In postwar elections, the Republicans have the edge, whether one focuses on elections won, popular votes cast, or states that usually support the same party. We should not judge Republican prospects, however, without a close examination of the attitudes and behaviors of individual voters, the subject of Part II of our study.

Notes

1. Peter Goldman and Tony Fuller, with others, *The Quest for the Presidency—1984* (New York: Bantam Books, 1985), 344-50.
2. John Corry, "TV: The Differing Network Moods on Election Night," *New York Times*, Nov. 8, 1984, C28.
3. We rely on the poll-closing times for states reported in *U.S.A. Today*, Nov. 2, 1984, 7A. Eleven states closed their polls before 8 p.m. EST, and 15 states set their closing times at either 8 p.m. EST or 7 p.m. CST. Arkansas closed its polls at 7:30 p.m. CST.
4. For a perceptive analysis of the conditions that contribute to third party voting, see Steven J. Rosenstone, Roy L. Behr, and Edward H. Lazarus, *Third Parties in America: Citizen Response to Major Party Failure* (Princeton, N.J.: Princeton University Press, 1984).
5. We report the 1980 results in Paul R. Abramson, John H. Aldrich, and David W. Rohde, *Change and Continuity in the 1980 Elections*, rev. ed. (Washing-

ton, D.C.: CQ Press, 1983), 52-53. These results are widely available in other sources as well. See, for example, *Presidential Elections Since 1789,* 3d ed. (Washington, D.C.: Congressional Quarterly, 1983), 119.

6. See Stanley Kelley, Jr., *Interpreting Elections* (Princeton, N.J.: Princeton University Press, 1983), 26. Kelley was modifying three criteria advanced earlier by Max Frankel. See "Nixon Is Re-elected in a Landslide Vote," *New York Times,* Nov. 8, 1972, 34.

7. For the popular vote for president by state from 1824 through 1980, see *Presidential Elections Since 1789,* 3d ed., 82-119.

8. James Monroe won 231 of the 232 electoral votes cast in 1820. All of the electors who voted in 1789 and 1792 named George Washington. In those elections, however, each elector had two votes and named two choices, so Washington got half the total electoral votes cast. Because Washington received the maximum number of votes possible, he was, in effect, elected unanimously.

9. For an analysis of agenda setting during this era, see William H. Riker, *Liberalism Against Populism: A Confrontation Between the Theory of Democracy and the Theory of Social Choice* (San Francisco: W. H. Freeman, 1982), 213-32).

10. There has been an interesting controversy in recent years over the extent to which the New Deal realignment was based upon the mobilization of new voters and the extent to which it relied upon converting Republicans. For the most sustained support of the mobilization thesis, see Kristi Andersen, *The Creation of a Democratic Majority, 1928-1936* (Chicago: University of Chicago Press, 1979). For the evidence supporting the conversion thesis, see Robert S. Erikson and Kent L. Tedin, "The 1928-1936 Partisan Realignment: The Case for the Conversion Hypothesis," *American Political Science Review* 75 (December 1981): 951-62.

11. Although the U.S. Bureau of the Census classifies several Border States and the District of Columbia as part of the South, we use an explicitly political definition—the 11 states of the old Confederacy, which are Alabama, Arkansas, Florida, Georgia, Louisiana, Mississippi, North Carolina, South Carolina, Tennessee, Texas, and Virginia.

12. U.S. Department of Commerce, Bureau of the Census, *Statistical Abstract of the United States,* 101st ed. (Washington, D.C.: U.S. Government Printing Office, 1980), 514.

13. According to the U.S. Bureau of the Census, only Alaska, Arizona, California, Colorado, Hawaii, Idaho, Montana, Nevada, New Mexico, Oregon, Utah, Washington, and Wyoming are the West. But as Walter Dean Burnham points out, for presidential elections the 96th meridian of longitude provides a dividing line. See Walter Dean Burnham, "The 1980 Earthquake: Realignment, Reaction, or What?" in *The Hidden Election: Politics and Economics in the 1980 Presidential Campaign,* ed. Thomas Ferguson and Joel Rogers (New York: Pantheon Books, 1981), 111. For our discussion in this chapter we therefore also consider Kansas, Nebraska, North Dakota, South Dakota, and Oklahoma as western. Even though Texas lies mainly west of this meridian, we have classified it as southern since it was a former Confederate state.

14. Iowa is the only state on our maps that actually shows a pro-Democratic shift between 1980 and 1984. In the other six states where Reagan's margin was reduced, he won by the same general range as in 1980.

15. Joseph A. Schlesinger, "The American Party System on the Scales" (Unpublished manuscript, Michigan State University, March 1985). Schlesinger treats each state as an equal unit. His key value for each state is the percentage of voters who voted Democratic, and his overall measure for each election is the standard deviation in the percentage of the Democratic vote among the states.

    The standard deviation measures the extent to which all states differ from the average (mean) level of Democratic voting in a given election year. The standard deviation is considered the best measure of the extent to which values are dispersed. The actual formula for computing the standard deviation is available in social statistics textbooks and the computations can be performed easily with many desk calculators.

    Including the District of Columbia, which has voted only since the 1964 election, increases the standard deviation somewhat, since it is always more Democratic than the most Democratic state. We report here only Schlesinger's results for states, not his alternative results that include D.C.

16. According to Schlesinger, the postwar election with the lowest variation by state was 1960, with a state-by-state standard deviation in the Democratic vote of only 5.42 percentage points.

17. Since the 1964-1984 period includes an even number of elections, we have a problem in classifying New York, Pennsylvania, and Texas because they voted three times for each party. Rather than leave these states unshaded on both maps, we shaded them as Democratic. While they have not voted Democratic most of the time during this period, they were clearly more Democratic than most states.

18. See Figure 2-1, which shows states that the Republicans won six or more times in the eight elections between 1952 and 1980. Because Reagan won all of these states in 1984, Figure 2-1, in effect, combines the result of Maps 3-3D and 3-3F.

19. V. O. Key, Jr., *Southern Politics in State and Nation* (New York: Alfred A. Knopf, 1949), 5.

20. There have been many studies of partisan change in the South. For a recent book that presents state-by-state results, see Alexander P. Lamis, *The Two-Party South* (New York: Oxford University Press, 1984).

21. Kennedy made a major symbolic gesture that helped him win black votes. Three weeks before the election, Martin Luther King, Jr., was arrested in Atlanta for taking part in a sit-in demonstration. Although all of the other demonstrators were released, King was held on a technicality and sent to the Georgia State Penitentiary. Kennedy telephoned King's wife to express his concern, and his brother, Robert F. Kennedy, made a direct plea with a Georgia judge that led to King's release on bail. This incident received little notice in the press, but had a major impact among the black community. For an account, see Theodore H. White, *The Making of the President, 1960* (New York: Atheneum, 1961), 350-53.

22. Kennedy won 303 of the 537 electoral votes in 1960. A Democrat who carried the same states that Kennedy won (and who, like Kennedy, won 45 percent of Alabama's electoral vote), would have won 281 electoral votes in 1984. Assuming that Democrat also carried D.C., he would have won 284 electoral votes. Carter won 297 of the 538 electoral votes in 1976. A Democrat who won the same states that Carter won would have gained 294 electoral votes.

Voting Behavior in the 1984 Presidential Election

PART II

Voting Behavior in the
1984 Presidential Election

The collective decision reached by the electorate on November 6, 1984, was the product of 165 million individual decisions.[1] Two choices faced American citizens 18 years and older: whether to vote and, if they decided to vote, how to cast their ballots. The way voters make up their minds is one of the most thoroughly studied subjects in political science—and one of the most controversial.[2]

Voting decisions can be studied from at least three theoretical perspectives. First, individuals can be viewed primarily as members of social groups. Voters belong to primary groups of family members and peers; secondary groups, such as private clubs, trade unions, or voluntary associations; and broader reference groups, such as social classes and ethnic groups. Understanding the political behavior of these groups is the key approach to understanding voting itself, according to the pioneers of this approach, Paul F. Lazarsfeld, Bernard R. Berelson, and their colleagues. Using a simple "index of political predisposition," they classified voters according to their religion (Catholic or Protestant), socioeconomic level, and residence (rural or urban) to predict how they would vote in the 1940 presidential election. Lazarsfeld and his colleagues maintain that "a person thinks, politically, as he is, socially. Social characteristics determine political preference."[3] This perspective is still very popular, although more so among sociologists than political scientists. The writings of Robert R. Alford, Richard F. Hamilton, and Seymour Martin Lipset provide excellent examples of this sociological approach.[4]

A second approach emphasizes psychological variables. To explain voting choices in the 1952 and 1956 presidential elections, Angus Campbell and others at the University of Michigan's Survey Research Center (SRC) developed a model of political behavior based on social-psychological variables.[5] They focused on attitudes likely to have the greatest effect just before the moment of decision, particularly attitudes toward the parties, candidates, and issues. Party identification emerged as the major social-psychological variable that influences voting decisions. The Michigan approach is the most prevalent among political scientists, although many deemphasize its psychological underpinnings. The SRC has collected data on presidential elections since 1948, and students of voting behavior throughout the country often use the questions originally developed by the Michigan researchers. Indeed, in the following chapters we shall rely mainly upon the Michigan data because they clearly provide the best surveys of the American electorate. The writings of Philip E. Converse provide an outstanding example of this research tradition.[6]

A third approach to voting decisions draws heavily upon the work of economics. According to this perspective, voters weigh the costs of voting against the expected benefits of voting when deciding whether to go to the polls. And when deciding whom to choose on election day, voters calculate which candidate favors policies closest to their policy preferences. Voters are thus viewed as rational actors who attempt to maximize their expected utility. Anthony Downs and William H. Riker are the major theoretical founders of this rational choice approach.[7] The writings of Riker, Peter C. Ordeshook, John A. Ferejohn, and Morris P. Fiorina provide excellent examples of this tradition.[8]

How, then, do voters decide? In our view none of these perspectives provides a complete answer. Although individuals are members of groups, they are not always influenced by these memberships. Moreover, classifying voters by social groups often does not explain why they are influenced by social forces. On the other hand, too great an emphasis on psychologically based variables can lead us away from the important political forces that shape voting behavior. And while the assumptions of economic rationality may result in clearly testable propositions, the data necessary to test them are often weak, and the propositions that actually can be tested are sometimes trivial.

Although individually none of these perspectives adequately explains voting behavior, taken together they are largely complementary. Therefore, we have chosen an eclectic approach that draws upon the most useful insights from each research perspective. Where appropriate, we focus on sociological variables, but we also employ social-psychological variables such as party identification and sense of political efficacy. The rational choice approach guides our study of how issues influence voting decisions.

Part II begins with an examination of the most important decision of all: whether to vote. One of the most profound changes in postwar American politics has been the decline of electoral participation. Although turnout grew fairly consistently between 1920 and 1960, it decreased in 1964 and in each of the four subsequent elections. From a record high of 63 percent of the adult population voting for president in 1960, turnout fell to below 53 percent in 1980. Despite massive efforts to increase electoral participation in 1984, turnout rose only slightly, less than a single percentage point. Turnout was still nearly 10 points lower than it was a quarter of a century earlier. But although turnout was low in 1984, it was not equally low for all social groups, and we will examine group differences in detail. From a social-psychological perspective,

Chapter 4 studies the attitudes that contribute to electoral participation and attempts to account for the decline in turnout during the past quarter century. Last, we try to determine whether low turnout has political consequences.

In Chapter 5 we examine how social forces influence the vote. Data from the Survey Research Center and the Center for Political Studies enable us to analyze the vote for Ronald Reagan and Walter F. Mondale by race, gender, region, age, occupation, union membership, educational level, and religion. As we shall see, the impact of these social forces has changed considerably during the last four decades. Support for the Democratic party among the traditional "New Deal" coalition of southerners, union members, the working class, and Catholics has eroded, and it is very unlikely that this coalition will ever be restored in its previous form.

Did Reagan's massive victory result from conservative policy preferences among the electorate? Chapter 6 attempts to answer this important question by looking at how issues influence the way Americans vote. We will compare issue preferences among the electorate in the last four presidential elections and conclude that a major shift toward conservative policy preferences did not occur in 1984. Issue preferences contributed to voting choices, but as we will show, Reagan's gains between 1980 and 1984 did not result from a pro-Republican shift in such preferences.

This leads to a consideration of the way presidential performance influences voting choices. Recent research suggests that many voters decide how to vote on the basis of "retrospective" evaluations of incumbents. In other words, what the incumbent has done while in office—not what he promises to do if reelected—affects how the voter decides. In Chapter 7 we assess the role of retrospective evaluations in 1972, 1976, 1980, and 1984—four presidential elections in which an incumbent ran. As we shall see, voters' evaluations of Gerald R. Ford's and Jimmy Carter's performances played a major role in electing Carter in 1976 and defeating him four years later. And in 1984, positive evaluations of Reagan as president, as well as positive evaluations of the government's performance and of the Republican party, played a central role in assuring Reagan's reelection.

How closely do voters identify with a political party? And how does this identification shape issue preferences and retrospective evaluations of the incumbent and the incumbent party? Chapter 8 explores the impact of party loyalties on voting choices in the postwar era. We will find that the 1984 election was marked by two major changes: a sizable shift toward the Republicans in the party loyalties of the electorate and an increase in the impact of partisan loyalties upon voter choice. This shift toward Republican party loyalties played a major role in increasing

Reagan's margin of victory and could create additional burdens for the Democratic party in future elections.

Notes

1. The U.S. Bureau of the Census estimated the voting age population to be 173,936,000. However, it also estimated that this number included about 6 million legal aliens and about 2 million illegal aliens. Another half million persons were ineligible to vote because they were in prisons, mental hospitals, or other institutions. See U.S. Department of Commerce, Bureau of the Census, *Projections of the Population of Voting Age for States: November 1984*, Series P-25, No. 948, April 1984, 3.
2. For an excellent collection of articles dealing with some of the major controversies, see Richard G. Niemi and Herbert F. Weisberg, eds., *Controversies in Voting Behavior*, 2d ed. (Washington, D.C.: CQ Press, 1984).
3. Paul F. Lazarsfeld, Bernard Berelson, and Hazel Gaudet, *The People's Choice: How the Voter Makes Up His Mind in a Presidential Campaign* (New York: Columbia University Press, 1944), 27. See also Bernard R. Berelson, Paul F. Lazarsfeld, and William N. McPhee, *Voting: A Study of Opinion Formation in a Presidential Campaign* (Chicago: University of Chicago Press, 1954).
4. See Robert R. Alford, *Party and Society: The Anglo-American Democracies* (Chicago: Rand McNally & Co., 1963); Richard F. Hamilton, *Class and Politics in the United States* (New York: John Wiley & Sons, 1972); and Seymour Martin Lipset, *Political Man: The Social Basis of Politics*, expanded edition (Baltimore: Johns Hopkins University Press, 1981).
5. Angus Campbell, Gerald Gurin, and Warren E. Miller, *The Voter Decides* (Evanston, Ill.: Row, Peterson, 1954); and Angus Campbell, Philip E. Converse, Warren E. Miller, and Donald E. Stokes, *The American Voter* (New York: John Wiley & Sons, 1960).
6. For the single best essay summarizing Converse's view on voting behavior, see Philip E. Converse, "Public Opinion and Voting Behavior," in *Handbook of Political Science, Volume 4: Nongovernmental Politics*, ed. Fred I. Greenstein and Nelson W. Polsby (Reading, Mass.: Addison-Wesley Publishing Co., 1975), 75-169. For an excellent summary of recent research from a social-psychological point of view, see Donald R. Kinder and David O. Sears, "Public Opinion and Political Action," in *Handbook of Social Psychology, Volume II: Special Fields and Applications*, 3d ed., ed. Gardner Lindzey and Elliot Aronson (New York: Random House, 1985), 659-741.
7. Anthony Downs, *An Economic Theory of Democracy* (New York: Harper & Row, 1957); and William H. Riker, *The Theory of Political Coalitions* (New Haven, Conn.: Yale University Press, 1962).
8. See, for example, William H. Riker and Peter C. Ordeshook, "A Theory of the Calculus of Voting," *American Political Science Review* 62 (March 1968): 25-42; John A. Ferejohn and Morris P. Fiorina, "The Paradox of Not Voting: A

Decision Theoretic Analysis," *American Political Science Review* 68 (June 1974); 525-36; and Morris P. Fiorina, *Retrospective Voting in American National Elections* (New Haven, Conn.: Yale University Press, 1981). For a recent introduction to much of this research, see James M. Enelow and Melvin J. Hinich, *The Spatial Theory of Voting: An Introduction* (New York: Cambridge University Press, 1984).

Who Voted

Before attempting to discover how people voted in the 1984 presidential election, we should answer an even more basic question: Who voted? Only 53 percent of the adults voted for president. If the nonvoters had participated, who would have been elected? Even though Ronald Reagan won by 18 percentage points, the 47 percent who did not vote could have made Walter F. Mondale the winner. In principle, nonvoters could have selected any alternative candidate, since many more Americans chose not to vote than voted for Reagan. Yet, as we will see, it is highly unlikely that increased turnout would have affected the outcome of the presidential election. Before we study turnout in the 1984 election, however, it is useful to place the low turnout for this contest in a broader historical context.

Turnout between 1824 and 1916

Historical records can be used to determine how many people voted in presidential elections, and we can derive meaningful estimates of turnout as early as 1824. Turnout is calculated by dividing the total number of votes cast for president by the voting-age population. Should the turnout denominator (i.e., the voting-age population) include all persons old enough to vote or should it include only those *eligible* to vote? The answer to this question will greatly affect our estimate of turnout in all presidential elections through 1916, for, until 1920, few women were legally eligible to vote.

Although women gained the right to vote in the Wyoming Territory as early as 1869, even by the 1916 presidential election only 11 of the 48 states had enfranchised women, and these were mainly western states with small populations.[1] The Nineteenth Amendment, which granted women the right to vote in all the states, was ratified only a few months before the 1920 election. Because women were already voting in some states, it is difficult to calculate turnout before 1920. Clearly, women were part of the turnout denominator in those states where they could vote. Including them as part of the denominator where they could not vote leads to very low estimates of turnout.

There are at least two legitimate ways to calculate national turnout during the years before 1920, and Table 4-1 presents two sets of estimates for the years between 1824 and 1916. Both sets of results have been published by the U.S. Bureau of the Census, although in presenting the second set of results, we have relied upon more recent estimates provided by Walter Dean Burnham. The first column, compiled by Charles E. Johnson, Jr., calculates turnout by dividing the total number of votes cast for president by the total voting-age population. The second column, based upon results compiled by Burnham, calculates turnout by dividing the total presidential vote by the total number of Americans eligible to vote. Burnham excludes southern blacks before the Civil War and attempts to exclude noncitizens after 1860. But the major difference between Burnham's calculations and those by Johnson is that Burnham excludes women from his turnout denominator in those states where they were not able to vote.

Most political scientists would consider Burnham's estimate to be more meaningful than Johnson's. For example, most political scientists argue that turnout was higher in the nineteenth century than it is today. But even if we reject this interpretation, both sets of estimates reveal the same pattern of change. There was clearly a large jump in turnout after 1836, for the Whigs turned to popular appeals to mobilize the electorate against the Democrats. Turnout jumped markedly in the 1840 election, the famous "Log Cabin and Hard Cider" campaign in which William Henry Harrison, the hero of Tippecanoe, ran against the incumbent Democrat, Martin Van Buren. Turnout waned after 1840, but rose rapidly after the Republican party, founded in 1854, polarized the nation by taking a clear position against the extension of slavery into the territories. In Abraham Lincoln's election in 1860, four white males out of five went to the polls.

Turnout waxed and waned in the post-Civil War period, peaking in the 1876 contest between Rutherford B. Hayes, the Republican winner, and Samuel J. Tilden, the Democrat. As a price of Hayes's contested victory, the Republicans agreed to end Reconstruction in the South. When federal troops were withdrawn, many blacks were prevented from voting. Although some southern blacks could still vote in 1880, overall turnout among blacks dropped sharply, decreasing southern turnout.

Table 4-1 Turnout in Presidential Elections, 1824-1916

Election Year	Winning Candidate	Party of Winning Candidate	Percentage of Voting-Age Population Who Voted	Percentage Eligible to Vote Who Voted
1824[1]	John Quincy Adams	National Republican	—	28.6
1828	Andrew Jackson	Democrat	22.2	57.3
1832	Andrew Jackson	Democrat	20.6	57.0
1836	Martin Van Buren	Democrat	22.4	57.7
1840	William H. Harrison	Whig	31.9	80.3
1844	James K. Polk	Democrat	30.6	79.0
1848	Zachary Taylor	Whig	28.6	72.8
1852	Franklin Pierce	Democrat	27.3	69.5
1856	James Buchanan	Democrat	30.6	79.4
1860	Abraham Lincoln	Republican	31.5	81.8
1864[2]	Abraham Lincoln	Republican	24.4	76.3
1868	Ulysses S. Grant	Republican	31.7	80.9
1872	Ulysses S. Grant	Republican	32.0	72.1
1876	Rutherford B. Hayes	Republican	37.1	82.6
1880	James A. Garfield	Republican	36.2	80.6
1884	Grover Cleveland	Democrat	35.6	78.3
1888	Benjamin Harrison	Republican	36.3	80.5
1892	Grover Cleveland	Democrat	34.9	75.9
1896	William McKinley	Republican	36.8	79.7
1900	William McKinley	Republican	34.0	73.7
1904	Theodore Roosevelt	Republican	29.7	65.5
1908	William H. Taft	Republican	29.8	65.7
1912	Woodrow Wilson	Democrat	27.9	59.0
1916	Woodrow Wilson	Democrat	32.1	61.8

[1] No estimate of turnout for the voting-age population.
[2] The estimate for the voting-age population is based upon the entire U.S. adult population. The estimate for the eligible population excludes the 11 Confederate states that did not take part in the election.

Source: The estimates of turnout among the voting age population are based upon Charles E. Johnson, Jr., *Nonvoting Americans* (U.S. Department of Commerce, Bureau of the Census, Washington, D.C.: U.S. Government Printing Office, Current Population Reports, Series P-23, No. 102, May 1980), 2. The estimates of turnout among the population eligible to vote are based upon calculations by Walter Dean Burnham. Burnham's earlier estimates were published in U.S. Department of Commerce, Bureau of the Census, *Historical Statistics of the United States: Colonial Times to 1970* (Washington, D.C.: U.S. Government Printing Office, 1975), Series Y-27-78, 1071-1072. The results in this table, however, are based upon Burnham's most recent estimates, which he kindly provided to us in a personal communication, Sept. 9, 1985.

Turnout began to fall nationwide by 1892, but it shot up dramatically in the 1896 contest between William Jennings Bryan (Democrat and Populist) and William McKinley. Turnout dropped in the 1900 rerun between the same two contenders.

By the late nineteenth century blacks were being effectively disfranchised throughout the South, and, along with blacks, poor whites often were effectively denied the right to vote.[2] Moreover, registration requirements, at least partly designed to discourage voter fraud, became more widespread.[3] Because individuals were responsible for getting their names on the registration rolls and usually had to register months before the election, the procedure created a barrier that reduced electoral participation.

Introduction of the secret ballot also reduced turnout. Before this innovation, most voting in U.S. elections was public. Ballots were printed by the political parties, with each party producing its own. Ballots differed in size and color, and, because voters usually cast their ballots in public, their choices were obvious. In 1856 Australia adopted a law calling for a secret ballot to be printed and administered by the state. The "Australian ballot" was first used in statewide elections in the United States by Massachusetts, which introduced it in 1888. By the time of the 1896 election, 9 states out of 10 had followed Massachusetts's lead.[4] Although the secret ballot was introduced to cut fraud, its use also cut turnout. When voting was public, men could sell their votes, but candidates were less willing to pay for a vote if they could not see it delivered. Ballot-stuffing was also more difficult when the state printed and distributed the ballots.

As Table 4-1 shows, turnout trailed off rapidly in the early twentieth century. By the time of the three-way contest among Woodrow Wilson (Democrat), William Howard Taft (Republican), and Theodore Roosevelt (Progressive) of 1912, fewer than three eligible Americans out of five went to the polls. In 1916 turnout rose slightly, but just over three eligible Americans out of five voted, only about a third of the total adult population.

Turnout between 1920 and 1984

It is easier to calculate turnout in elections since 1920, and we have provided estimates based upon Census Bureau statistics. Although there are still alternative ways to compute the turnout denominator, they lead to relatively small differences in the overall estimate of turnout.[5]

In Table 4-2 we show the percentage of the voting-age population that voted for the Democratic, Republican, and minor party candidates in the 17 elections between 1920 and 1984. It also shows the percentage that did not vote and the overall size of the voting-age population. In

Table 4-2 Percentage of Adults Who Voted for Each Major Presidential Candidate, 1920-1984

Election Year	Democratic Candidate		Republican Candidate		Other Candidates	Did Not Vote	Total Percent	Voting-Age Population
1920	14.8	James M. Cox	26.2	*Warren G. Harding*	2.4	56.6	100%	61,639,000
1924	12.7	John W. Davis	23.7	*Calvin Coolidge*	7.5	56.1	100%	66,229,000
1928	21.1	Alfred E. Smith	30.1	*Herbert C. Hoover*	.6	48.2	100%	71,100,000
1932	30.1	*Franklin D. Roosevelt*	20.8	Herbert C. Hoover	1.5	47.6	100%	75,768,000
1936	34.6	*Franklin D. Roosevelt*	20.8	Alfred M. Landon	1.5	43.1	100%	80,174,000
1940	32.2	*Franklin D. Roosevelt*	26.4	Wendell Willkie	.3	41.1	100%	84,728,000
1944	29.9	*Franklin D. Roosevelt*	25.7	Thomas E. Dewey	.4	44.0	100%	85,654,000
1948	25.3	*Harry S Truman*	23.0	Thomas E. Dewey	2.7	48.9	100%	95,573,000
1952	27.3	Adlai E. Stevenson	34.0	*Dwight D. Eisenhower*	.3	38.4	100%	99,929,000
1956	24.9	Adlai E. Stevenson	34.1	*Dwight D. Eisenhower*	.4	40.7	100%	104,515,000
1960	31.2	*John F. Kennedy*	31.1	Richard M. Nixon	.5	37.2	100%	109,672,000
1964	37.8	*Lyndon B. Johnson*	23.8	Barry M. Goldwater	.3	38.1	100%	114,090,000
1968	26.0	Hubert H. Humphrey	26.4	*Richard M. Nixon*	8.4	39.1	100%	120,285,000
1972	20.7	George S. McGovern	33.5	*Richard M. Nixon*	1.0	44.8	100%	140,777,000
1976	26.8	*Jimmy Carter*	25.7	Gerald R. Ford	1.0	46.5	100%	152,308,000
1980	21.6	Jimmy Carter	26.7	*Ronald Reagan*	4.3	47.4	100%	164,473,000
1984	21.6	Walter F. Mondale	31.3	*Ronald Reagan*	.4	46.7	100%	173,936,000

Note: The names of winning candidates are italicized.

Source: Results for 1920 through 1928 are based upon U.S. Department of Commerce, Bureau of the Census, *Statistical Abstract of the United States, 1972* (Washington, D.C.: U.S. Government Printing Office, 1972), 358, 373; results for 1932 through 1980 are based upon *Statistical Abstract of the United States, 1985* (Washington, D.C.: U.S. Government Printing Office, 1985), 238, 251. For 1984 the voting-age population is based upon U.S. Department of Commerce, Bureau of the Census, *Projection of the Population of Voting Age for States: November 1984*, Series P-25, No. 948 (Washington, D.C.: U.S. Government Printing Office, 1984), 1; the number of votes cast for each candidate and the total number of votes cast are based upon *America Votes 16: A Handbook of Contemporary Election Statistics*, compiled and edited by Richard M. Scammon and Alice V. McGillivray (Washington, D.C.: Congressional Quarterly, 1985), 41.

Figure 4-1 Percentage of Voting-Age Population That Voted for President, 1920-1984

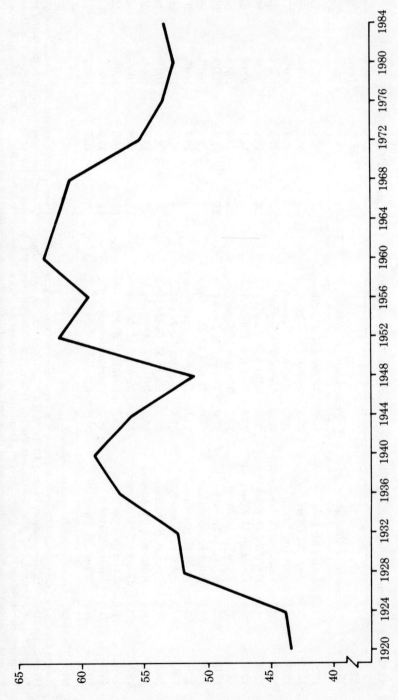

Source: See Table 4-2.

Figure 4-1 we show the percentage of the voting-age population that voted in all 17 elections.

As Table 4-2 shows, Reagan received the votes of only 31 percent of the voting-age population. In the 16 elections between 1920 and 1980, this percentage has been exceeded six times (Franklin D. Roosevelt in 1936 and 1940, Dwight D. Eisenhower in 1952 and 1956, Lyndon B. Johnson in 1964, and Richard Nixon in 1972). Reagan's overall share was still higher than most presidential winners; although overall turnout was low, he received nearly three votes out of every five cast.

Mondale's overall total was identical to Jimmy Carter's share four years earlier. Both received the support of only 21.6 percent of the voting-age population. This is a remarkably poor showing for candidates of a "majority party." In the 12 elections between Roosevelt's first victory in 1932 through Carter's victory in 1976, the Democrats fared this poorly only once—in George S. McGovern's crushing defeat by Nixon in 1972. During these years, the Democrats' average (mean) share was 28.9 percent of the voting-age population—fully 7 points better than their share in the last two contests. The very low share attained by Carter in 1980 and Mondale in 1984 results from a combination of two factors. Both received just over two votes out of five cast, and in both elections just over half of the voting-age population went to the polls.

The low turnout in 1984 appears to be part of a trend that has been under way for the past quarter century. As Figure 4-1 shows, however, turnout increased in 7 elections of the 10 held between 1920 and 1960. Two of the three exceptions—1944 and 1948—resulted largely from the social dislocations during and shortly after World War II. Specific political events explain why more people voted in certain elections. The jump in turnout between 1924 and 1928 resulted from the candidacy of Alfred E. Smith, the first Roman Catholic to receive a major party nomination, and the increase between 1932 and 1936 resulted from Roosevelt's efforts to mobilize voters from the lower social strata— particularly the industrial working class. The extremely close race between Nixon and another Catholic candidate, John F. Kennedy, partly accounts for the high turnout in 1960. Turnout rose to 62.8 percent. This was far below the level of eligible voters that voted between 1840 and 1900, although it was the highest percentage of the total voting-age population that ever had voted in a presidential election *(Table 4-1)*.

Changing social characteristics of the electorate contributed to the long-term trend toward increasing turnout. For example, women who came of voting age before the Nineteenth Amendment often failed to exercise their right to vote, but women who came of voting age after 1920 had higher levels of turnout. Because it was necessary to be a citizen to vote (a requirement imposed by state law, not by the Constitution) many immigrants failed to enter the electorate. But after 1921, as a result of restrictive immigration laws, the percentage of the population that was foreign-born declined. Moreover, levels of formal education have been growing throughout the twentieth century—a change that boosted turnout because Americans with higher educational levels are much more likely to vote than those with lower levels.

By 1960 the first two population trends had run their course and no longer played an important role in increasing turnout. However, educational levels continued to increase, a factor that might have been expected to push turnout upward. Political changes might also have been expected to increase turnout. After passage of the Voting Rights Act of 1965, turnout rose among southern blacks, which often led to increased electoral participation among southern whites. Less restrictive registration laws enacted during the last 20 years have made it easier to vote. Despite these changes, turnout declined after 1960 and continued to decline through 1980.

Given the low turnout in 1980, many political leaders saw the potential for increased electoral participation as a way to increase their chances of winning. As was widely recognized, nonvoters tended to have social characteristics that would make them likely Democratic voters. They were, for example, more likely to be black, Hispanic, and poor. By 1984 many Democratic leaders, along with many groups sympathetic to the Democrats, launched massive voter registration drives.[6] Registration forms were circulated at shopping centers, welfare agencies, and unemployment offices. Jesse Jackson's presidential candidacy helped spur black voter registration and turnout in the presidential primaries. By the spring of 1984, according to the Gallup poll, blacks were as likely to say they were registered to vote as whites were.[7] While the Gallup result was not confirmed by later Census Bureau surveys, there is little doubt that black registration increased substantially between 1980 and 1984.[8]

Fearing Democratic efforts, the Republicans also attempted to register prospective GOP voters. Because potential Republican voters are more likely to be registered already, adding new Republicans to the voting rolls is more difficult and more expensive. Some help was provided by evangelical groups, especially in registering southern whites. But the Republicans also used expensive computer technology to locate potential supporters and to screen out likely Democratic voters.[9] By most estimates the Republicans more than matched Democratic registration efforts.[10]

Despite the massive get-out-the-vote efforts in 1984, turnout rose only slightly, by less than a single percentage point. Turnout was still nearly 10 percentage points lower in 1984 than it was in 1960. As we saw in Chapter 3, 92.7 million Americans voted for president in 1984. But if turnout in 1984 had been as high as it was in 1960, more than 109 million Americans would have voted. The decline in turnout, then, resulted in a shortfall of 16.5 million voters. Coincidentally, this turnout deficit closely matched the margin by which Reagan defeated Mondale.

Turnout among Social Groups

Turnout in 1984 was not equally low among all social groups, as Table 4-3 shows. Because respondents sometimes claim to vote when they have not, reports of electoral participation derived from postelection surveys can lead to substantial overestimates of turnout. Fortunately, the 1984 survey by the Survey Research Center-Center for Political Studies (SRC-CPS) at the University of Michigan conducted a check of local registration and voting records to determine whether respondents voted. In this chapter we will rely upon this actual check of voting records in most of our analysis.[11] Even this check of the registration records revealed an overall turnout of 67 percent, about 12 points more than the overall turnout among the voting-age citizen population.[12] But this is less than the 73 percent level of reported turnout registered by the SRC-CPS survey.[13] Despite this inflation in overall levels of turnout, the SRC-CPS surveys provide the best source of data for studying the way attitudes contribute to turnout and are the best source of data for studying why turnout declined.[14]

Although we rely on the SRC-CPS surveys, wherever possible we will supplement our analysis with Census Bureau surveys of turnout. Beginning in 1964, and in every subsequent midterm and presidential election, the Census Bureau has conducted a survey to determine who voted. As a government agency, however, the bureau cannot ask some of the more interesting questions posed by political scientists. The bureau asks no questions about political attitudes or religion, for example. These surveys cannot be used to determine *how* people voted, for such a question would be inappropriate for a government agency.

Despite these limitations, these studies have two major advantages. First, the Census Bureau is able to survey the lower social strata more effectively than the SRC-CPS. This partly explains why the overall level of turnout in the census surveys is always much lower than the SRC-CPS surveys.[15] In 1984, for example, reported turnout in the bureau survey was 59.9 percent, only 7 points higher than the actual turnout among the voting-age population.[16] Second, the Census Bureau surveys are much larger than those conducted by the SRC-CPS. In the 1984 survey, for example, interviews were conducted in 58,000 households, and registration and voting information was gathered on about 120,000 Americans.[17] Because the sample is larger, the subgroups of the survey will also be larger. This allows comparisons that are impossible with the SRC-CPS surveys. For example, in the vote validation study it would be difficult to compare the relative turnout of black men and black women because we

Table 4-3 Percentage That Voted for President According to Vote Validation Study, by Social Group, 1984

Social Group	Voted (%)	Did Not Vote (%)	(N)
Electorate, by race			
White	70	30	(1588)
Black	52	48	(198)
Whites, by Hispanic identification			
Identify as Hispanic	54	46	(98)
Do not identify	71	29	(1487)
Whites, by gender			
Male	70	30	(695)
Female	70	30	(893)
Whites, by region			
New England and mid-Atlantic	75	25	(310)
North Central	74	26	(492)
South	59	41	(291)
Border	62	38	(151)
Mountain and Pacific	73	27	(344)
Whites, by birth cohort			
Before 1924	74	26	(372)
1924-1939	80	20	(328)
1940-1954	72	28	(523)
1955-1966	53	47	(356)
Whites, by social class			
Working class	61	39	(707)
Middle class	80	20	(726)
Farmers	67	33	(67)
Whites, by occupation of head of household			
Unskilled manual	53	47	(187)
Skilled, semiskilled manual	64	36	(520)
Clerical, sales, other white collar	75	25	(268)
Managerial	83	17	(239)
Professional and semiprofessional	84	16	(219)
Whites, by annual family income			
Less than $10,000	52	48	(296)
$10,000 to $14,999	62	38	(195)
$15,000 to $19,999	65	35	(153)
$20,000 to $24,999	73	27	(179)
$25,000 to $34,999	75	25	(158)
$30,000 to $34,999	77	23	(145)
$35,000 to $39,999	83	17	(90)
$40,000 to $49,999	80	20	(133)
$50,000 to $59,999	85	15	(84)
$60,000 and more	92	18	(95)

Table 4-3 (continued)

Social Group	Voted (%)	Did Not Vote (%)	(N)
Whites, by level of education			
Eight grades or less	53	47	(144)
Some high school	51	49	(168)
High school graduate	65	35	(570)
Some college	77	23	(398)
College graduate	87	13	(211)
Advanced degree	92	8	(90)
Whites, by union membership†			
Member	75	25	(338)
Nonmember	69	31	(1247)
Whites, by religion			
Protestant	68	32	(952)
Catholic	75	25	(430)
Jewish	81	19	(43)
No preference	60	40	(119)
Whites, by social class and religion			
Middle-class Protestants	81	19	(409)
Working-class Protestants	56	44	(435)
Middle-class Catholics	81	19	(196)
Working-class Catholics	73	27	(196)

† Whether respondent or family member in union.

Note: Based upon respondents who were included in the postelection interview. The 152 respondents who were not classified in the vote validation study have been excluded from these calculations, as well as from calculations for Tables 4-4 and 4-5. Seven validated voters who said they did not vote for president have been classified as nonvoters.

can compare only 74 black men with 124 black women. The Census Bureau survey includes information for approximately 6,000 black men and 7,000 black women.

Race, Gender, Region, and Age

Our own analysis begins with a comparison of blacks and whites. In spite of the massive effort to turn out the black vote and the stimulus provided by Jackson's candidacy in registering blacks, the vote validation study found black turnout to be 18 points lower than white. Part of the low participation among blacks results from their relatively lower level of formal education, but even when we take educational differences into account, blacks were still much less likely to vote than whites. The SRC-

CPS surveys actually suggest that racial differences in turnout increased between 1980 and 1984, but we must remember that the survey is based upon a relatively small sample of blacks. The census survey shows blacks to be less likely to vote than whites, but the gap between the races was only about 6 points. According to their survey, reported turnout among whites was 61.4 percent and 55.8 percent among blacks. But this is the smallest differential registered by the bureau in the six presidential elections it has studied. Four years earlier, reported turnout was 60.9 percent among whites and only 50.5 percent among blacks, a 10-point gap. According to the bureau survey, turnout rose 5 percentage points among blacks, while rising only half a point among whites.[18]

Because relatively few blacks were sampled in the SRC-CPS study, we will rely upon the census survey to make comparisons among blacks. According to the census survey, 59.2 percent of black women voted, but only 51.7 percent of black men. Reported turnout was 53.2 percent among southern blacks, but was 58.9 percent among blacks outside the South.[19] And young blacks were far less likely to vote than were middle-aged blacks, or even than blacks above the age of 75. Among blacks between the ages of 18 and 24, reported turnout was only 40.6 percent; among black males of this age, it was only 36.0 percent.

As Table 4-3 shows, among whites, those who identified themselves as Hispanic had much lower levels of turnout, mainly because few Chicanos voted.[20] While the Census Bureau results are not comparable to ours, their survey shows that reported turnout among Hispanics was only 32.6 percent, although it was 48 percent among Hispanics who said they were citizens. Although total Hispanic turnout had risen 2.7 percent since 1980, this increase fell far short of the gains hoped for by Hispanic leaders.

Our table also shows that in 1984 there was no difference in turnout between white men and white women. Surveys show that men consistently outvoted women in all postwar elections through 1976. By 1980 these differences had become negligible. The 1980 vote validation survey revealed that white men were more likely to vote than white women, although the census survey showed reported turnout to be the same for both groups. In 1984 the census survey found that white women were marginally more likely to vote than white men. Among white women reported turnout was 62.0 percent; among white men it was 60.8 percent. For all races, reported turnout was 60.8 percent among women, 59.0 percent among men. Overall turnout had risen 1.4 percent among women, while dropping a negligible .1 percent among men. While Geraldine Ferraro's candidacy may have stimulated interest among women, it clearly did not lead to a substantial increase in turnout. However, the 1980 and 1984 elections marked a turning point, for the historical participation advantage among men was eliminated.

Of course, we do not need surveys to study turnout in the various regions of the country. Because the Census Bureau estimates the total voting-age population for each state, we can measure turnout merely by dividing the total number of votes cast for president within each state by its voting-age population. We do need surveys, however, to study the relative levels of turnout among whites and blacks within the regions. As Table 4-3 shows, white turnout was lower in the South than it was outside the South.[21] Fifty-nine percent of the southern whites voted for president; outside of the region, 73 percent did. The census surveys also show reported turnout lower among white southerners. According to their survey, 58.1 percent of the southern whites voted, while outside the South, 63 percent did. The relatively low turnout in the South results partly from the lower levels of education in that region.[22] But regional differences have declined dramatically during the past two decades. According to the 1964 census survey, southern whites were 15 percentage points less likely to vote than whites outside the South, and nonwhite southerners were 28 points less likely to vote than nonwhites outside the South.[23]

The 1984 vote validation survey reveals the same general pattern by age that previous surveys show. Turnout was very low among the young (born between 1955 and 1966), highest among the middle-aged (born between 1924 and 1939), and somewhat lower among the elderly (born before 1924). However, as Raymond E. Wolfinger and Steven J. Rosenstone's analysis of census surveys shows, low turnout among the elderly results from their relatively low level of formal education.[24] The 1984 census survey presents reported turnout by age among whites. Among whites between 18 and 24 years old, reported turnout was only 41.6 percent. But turnout rose to 56.1 percent among whites between 25 and 34, and to 66.5 percent among those between 35 and 54. Among whites between 55 and 64 turnout was 73.2 percent, and even among those between 65 and 74 it was 72.9 percent. Turnout falls only when we examine the very elderly, those 75 years and over. But even among this group reported turnout, at 62.1 percent, was much higher than turnout among the young.

While the somewhat lower turnout among the elderly is consistent with the overall relationship between level of education and turnout, the low turnout by the young is not. Young Americans have relatively high levels of formal education. However, low turnout by the young is clearly a function of their youth—as young people age, marry, have children, and develop community ties, their turnout tends to increase.

Social Class, Income, and Union Membership

As Table 4-3 shows, social class differences in turnout were pronounced in 1984, a finding consistent with the relationship of formal education to turnout. Middle-class whites (here defined as nonmanually employed workers and their dependents) were substantially more likely to vote than working-class whites (manually employed workers and their dependents).[25] Farmers registered average levels of turnout, but the number of farmers sampled was too small to lead to reliable conclusions. Although the distinction between the middle class and the working class is crude, it appears to capture a politically meaningful division, for when we further divide respondents according to the occupation of the head of household, we find that turnout among clerical, sales, and other white-collar workers (the lowest level of the middle class) is markedly higher than that among skilled and semiskilled manual workers.

Annual family income also was related to turnout, with substantially lower turnout among whites with family incomes below $10,000.[26] Turnout was very high among whites with annual family incomes of $60,000 and above. While persons with a high family income tend to have higher levels of formal education, and while both income and education contribute to turnout, level of education appears to have a more direct impact on turnout than does family income.[27]

Surveys over the years have found only a weak and inconsistent relationship between union membership and turnout. While being in a household with a union member leads to organizational ties that should stimulate turnout, members of union households tend to have somewhat lower levels of formal education. In 1984 members of union households were somewhat more likely to vote than persons in households with no union members.

As a final note, we may add that turnout was very low among the unemployed. Among whites where the head of household was unemployed ($N = 67$), only 52 percent voted, while among whites where the head of household was currently employed ($N = 1,104$), 70 percent voted. The census survey also shows low turnout among the unemployed, although the census report does not differentiate between whites and blacks. According to the census survey, reported turnout was only 44.0 percent among the unemployed, but it was 61.6 percent among the employed. Unemployed Americans tend to have lower levels of formal education than those who are employed, but unemployment also weakens feelings of personal and political effectiveness and the social ties that contribute to electoral participation.[28]

Religion

In most postwar elections, white Catholics have voted more than white Protestants, but these differences have eroded. In 1980 there was virtually no difference in turnout between these groups. In 1984, however, Catholics once again were more likely to vote than white Protestants. Turnout was particularly high among Catholic women, who may have been more motivated to vote than Protestant women by Ferraro's presence on the Democratic ticket. Jews have much higher levels of formal education than gentiles and have always had high levels of turnout. They registered very high turnout, although the number of Jews sampled is too small to reach any reliable conclusions. Whites with no religious preference had lower than average turnout.

Given attempts by fundamentalist leaders to register potential Reagan supporters, we examined turnout among white Protestants in considerable detail. Unlike the 1980 election, in which there was little evidence of successful mobilization by fundamentalist leaders, there is at least some evidence of success in 1984. Among the major Protestant denominations, the highest levels of turnout were registered by Episcopalians, Lutherans, and Presbyterians. But turnout was as high among Southern Baptists as among white Protestants as a whole. Among white Southern Baptists ($N = 111$), 69 percent voted, a relatively high turnout for a group with lower than average levels of formal education.

We also explored turnout among white Protestants with differing religious values. Those who said religion was important in their lives were more likely to vote than those who said it was not. On the other hand, there were negligible differences in turnout among those who said religion provided "quite a bit" of guidance in their lives, those who said it provided "a great deal" of guidance, and those who said it provided only "some" guidance.[29] There were only negligible differences in turnout between white Protestants who felt close to evangelical groups and those who did not.[30] And white Protestants who said they had been "born again" were somewhat less likely to vote than those who said they had not had this religious experience.[31]

In Table 4-3 we also present the combined effect of social class and religion upon electoral participation. Among middle-class whites, religion is unrelated to turnout. Middle-class Protestants are as likely to vote as middle-class Catholics. Among the working class, however, religion is strongly related to turnout, for white working-class Catholics were 17 percentage points more likely to vote than were white working-class Protestants.

Education

We found a strong relationship between formal education and turnout. As Wolfinger and Rosenstone document, education is the major variable in explaining differences in turnout in the United States.[32] Better-educated Americans are more likely to develop attitudes that contribute to participation in politics, especially feelings that citizens have a duty to vote and can be politically effective.

Among whites who had not graduated from high school, only 52 percent voted. Among whites with advanced degrees, 92 percent voted.

The census survey also shows a strong relationship between level of formal education and turnout, although the published results do not differentiate among whites and blacks. According to the census survey, among Americans who did not graduate from high school, only 43.7 percent reported voting, while among those with four years of high school, 58.7 percent did. For Americans with one to three years of college, reported turnout was 67.5 percent, and with four or more years of college, it was 79.1 percent.

The strong relationship between level of education and turnout underscores the paradox of declining levels of electoral participation. After all, levels of education have been rising since 1960. Why have these increases in education not pushed turnout upward, continuing the 1920 through 1960 trend of increased participation?

Why Has Turnout Declined?

Clearly, turnout within educational groups must have been declining so fast that it canceled out the impact of rising educational levels. We therefore examined the relationship between education and *reported* turnout in all presidential elections from 1952 through 1984, dividing the electorate into five educational levels: college graduate, some college, high school graduate, some high school, and eight grades or less.[33] Blacks have substantially lower levels of formal education than whites, and southern blacks have been effectively enfranchised only since 1965. Therefore, including blacks in any analysis of trends in participation would partly obscure the relationships we are studying.

College graduates have maintained their high levels of turnout throughout the postwar period and were as likely to vote in 1984 as they were in 1960, when overall turnout was highest. But turnout declined among all four of the remaining educational categories, and it dropped markedly among the three groups that had not attended college. Therefore, consistent with patterns found in examining Census Bureau data, the greatest declines in turnout have occurred among Americans who are relatively disadvantaged.[34]

While increased education among the electorate did not prevent turnout from declining, it played a major role in slowing down the decline. Between 1960 and 1984, the level of education of the white electorate rose substantially, an increase that resulted almost entirely from generational replacement.[35] According to the SRC-CPS surveys, the percentage of the white electorate that had not graduated from high school decreased from 47 percent in 1960 to 21 percent in 1984. During the same period, the percentage that were college graduates rose from 11 percent to 18 percent. Nevertheless, reported turnout among the white electorate dropped 7 percentage points. If there had been no increase in educational levels, the decline would have been 14 percentage points. In other words, if levels of formal education among the electorate had not increased during the last quarter century, the decline in turnout would have been twice as great as the decline that actually occurred.

Demographic changes and changing attitudes toward the political system appear to have contributed to the decline of turnout over the past quarter century. As we saw in Table 4-3, as well as through our examination of the census surveys, young adults are less likely than their elders to vote. Because young adults are less likely to vote, the enfranchisement of 18-, 19-, and 20-year-olds in 1971 reduced turnout. While the total number of voting age adults increased by definition (increasing the turnout denominator), the total number of actual voters increased by a smaller rate. Wolfinger and Rosenstone estimate that about one-fifth of the decline in turnout between 1968 and 1972 results from enfranchising young Americans.[36] Moreover, as the "baby boom" generation entered the electorate, young adults made up a larger share of the voting-age population. Richard W. Boyd estimates that about one-fourth of the decline in turnout between 1960 and 1976 resulted from the changing age distribution of the electorate.[37] However, the average age of the electorate has increased slightly since 1976 and will continue to increase through the 1980s.[38] This change could produce a long-term force that may gradually increase turnout.

Changing attitudes toward the political system also eroded electoral participation. Our analyses focus on the erosion of party loyalties and declining beliefs that the government is responsive, or what George I. Balch and others have called feelings of "external" political efficacy.[39] The measure of party identification is based upon questions designed to gauge psychological attachment to a partisan reference group.[40] It is widely recognized that partisan loyalties have declined, although a closer examination reveals that this decline has been most marked among whites. The percentage of whites who strongly identified with either the Republican or Democratic party dropped from 36 percent in 1960 and 1964 to 23 percent in 1980. In 1984, however, the percentage of strong partisans rose back to 29 percent, still 7 points less than it was two decades earlier. In all the SRC surveys between 1952 and 1964, the percentage of independents with no party leanings never rose above 9 percent. This figure rose to 14 percent by 1980, although it fell back to 11 percent in 1984. For a more detailed discussion of party loyalties and tables showing the distribution of party identification between 1952 and 1984, see Chapter 8.

Strong feelings of partisan identification contribute to psychological involvement in politics, Angus Campbell and his colleagues argue.[41] We would also expect partisanship to contribute to electoral participation, because partisan loyalties reduce the time and effort needed to learn how to vote and thus reduce the costs of voting.[42] Indeed, in every presidential election since 1952, strong partisans have been more likely to report voting than any other partisan strength category. In every election since 1960, independents with no party leanings have been the least likely to say that they voted.

During the two decades between 1960 and 1980, feelings of political effectiveness declined markedly, although they rebounded somewhat in 1982 and 1984.[43] Scores on our measure are based upon responses to these two statements: "I don't think public officials care much what people like me think" and "People like me don't have any say about what the government does." [44] In 1956 and 1968, 64 percent of the white electorate were scored as highly efficacious. The decline in "external" political efficacy began in 1964. By 1980 only 39 percent scored high. After 1980, however, the percentage of whites scoring high rose, and in 1984, 52 percent scored high. Despite this rebound, however, the percentage scoring high was still 12 points below the 1956 and 1960 levels. The percentage scoring low on our measure was only 15 percent in 1956 and 1960, but it rose fairly steadily through 1976. In 1980, 30 percent scored low. The percentage of whites with feelings of low political efficacy declined in 1984, and only 23 percent scored low on this measure. Despite this drop in the proportion of Americans who felt politically powerless, the percentage scoring low on this measure was 8 points higher than it was a quarter century earlier.

Feelings of political effectiveness also contribute to electoral participation. Persons who feel politically capable may feel psychologically motivated to participate. Those who feel overwhelmed by the political process may withdraw from political activity. In addition, citizens are more likely to see benefits from voting if they believe that government is responsive to citizen demands. In every presidential election since 1952, persons scoring "high" on our measure have been the most likely to report voting, and those scoring "low," the least likely.

Although feelings of partisan loyalty and feelings of political efficacy are both related to turnout, they are only weakly related to each other. In other words, there is little tendency for persons who have strong party loyalties to have high levels of "external" political efficacy. Table 4-4 examines the combined effect of these attitudes upon the entire electorate in 1984. Since there were virtually no differences in turnout between weak partisans and independents who leaned toward a party, we have combined both groups into a single category.

By reading across each row of Table 4-4 we see that strength of party identification is consistently related to turnout, regardless of scores on our measure of political efficacy. By reading down the columns, we see that feelings of political efficacy are related to turnout, regardless of partisan strength. These attitudinal variables together have a strong

Table 4-4 Percentage That Voted for President According to Vote Validation Study, by Strength of Party Identification and Sense of "External" Political Efficacy, 1984

Scores on External Political Efficacy Index	Strong Partisan		Weak Partisan or Independent Who Leans toward a Party		Independent, With No Partisan Leaning	
		(N)		(N)		(N)
High	84	(308)	71	(530)	67	(88)
Medium	83	(139)	66	(272)	47	(38)
Low	68	(104)	50	(252)	34	(62)

Note: Numbers in parentheses are the totals upon which percentages are based.

cumulative effect. Eighty-four percent of the strong partisans who have high feelings of "external" political efficacy voted; only 34 percent of the pure independents with low feelings of political efficacy voted.

The decline in partisan loyalties and the erosion of feelings of political effectiveness play a major role in contributing to the decline of turnout. According to our calculations, based upon a simple algebraic technique, the weakening of partisan loyalties accounts for 18 percent of the decline of reported turnout among whites between 1960 and 1984, while the erosion in feelings of "external" political efficacy accounts for 30 percent of the decline.[45] When we examined the combined effects of these attitude changes, we found that 44 percent of the decline in reported turnout resulted from weakening partisanship and eroding feelings of political effectiveness.

Political parties—a major mechanism for mobilizing the electorate— appear to have lost much of their appeal—especially to Americans who entered the electorate since World War II. While older Americans usually retained their strong party loyalties, young adults, who entered the electorate with weak partisan loyalties, usually did not become stronger partisans as they grew older. To a large extent the overall erosion of partisan loyalties resulted from the replacement of older cohorts with cohorts that entered the electorate in a less partisan era.[46]

Low levels of political effectiveness appear to spring from a generalized disaffection that may be a response to political events. Dissatisfaction with government policies in Vietnam, the Watergate scandals, and a more generalized sense that the government has failed to solve economic and social problems may have contributed to the feeling that the government does not respond to the people.[47] However, positive feelings toward the government have increased during the Reagan years, resulting in an increase in feelings that the government is responsive, as well as to increased feelings of political trust.[48]

Although we see the low level of turnout in 1984 as part of a long-term trend caused by long-term attitude change, our model does not work as well as it did in accounting for low turnout in the 1980 election. Our analyses through 1980 suggested that between two-thirds and seven-tenths of the decline in reported turnout resulted from the erosion of partisanship and declining feelings of political effectiveness.[49] Given our model we would have expected that the increased strength of partisanship and in feelings of political efficacy would have done more to increase turnout between 1980 and 1984. From this attitude change we would have predicted a 3.9 point increase in reported turnout among the white electorate; the actual SRC-CPS surveys revealed only a 2.3 percent increase.[50]

We suspect that short-term forces kept turnout from rising more, despite attitude change. However, the SRC-CPS survey provides no immediate clue about what these short-term forces were. As we will show in Chapter 6, the electorate saw clear policy differences between Reagan and Mondale. Moreover, concern about the electoral outcome was much higher in 1984 than it was four years earlier. In 1980 only 54 percent of the whites "cared a good deal" which party won the election. Concern was measured by responses to the question: "Generally speaking, would you say that you personally care a good deal which party wins the presidential election this fall, or that you don't care very much which party wins?"—a question asked in every SRC presidential election survey since 1952. But in 1984, 66 percent of the whites questioned said they "cared a good deal," only slightly below the 69 percent level recorded in 1960 when turnout was highest. In 1984, as in every previous election, Americans who cared which party would win were more likely to vote than those who did not care. Among whites who cared ($N = 1,039$), 76 percent voted; among those who did not ($N = 502$), only 59 percent voted. But this relationship only adds to the puzzle, because the greater concern about the election's outcome did very little to increase turnout.

The most obvious short-term factor keeping turnout from rising was the widespread expectation that Reagan would win by a landslide. The SRC-CPS surveys were conducted during the two months before the election, when 49 percent of the whites and 65 percent of the blacks said they expected the election to be close.[51] Considering how strongly the polls were running in Reagan's favor, this percentage seems high, but it is far lower than the proportion who thought the 1980 election would be close. In the 1980 SRC-CPS survey, 85 percent of the whites and 76 percent of the blacks expected the election to be close.

In most elections, voters who think the election will be close are more likely to vote than those who think that the winner will win by quite a bit.[52] Even though these relationships are usually not strong, the percentage viewing the election as close has varied greatly from contest to contest. Orley Ashenfelter and Stanley Kelley, Jr., report that the single most important factor accounting for the decline in turnout between 1960 and 1972 was "the dramatic shift in voter expectations about the closeness of the race in these two elections."[53] But in 1984 whites who thought the election would be close were actually somewhat less likely to vote than those who thought the winner would win by quite a bit. Given this relationship the SRC-CPS survey provides no direct evidence that Reagan's expected landslide reduced turnout.

It is possible that these results, based upon surveys conducted on average a month before the election, do not reflect last-minute changes in perceptions about the election. Our analysis of the SRC-CPS continuous monitoring survey shows that after the second presidential debate, the public's perception that Reagan was likely to win increased markedly. In addition, early network projections of Reagan's victory may have depressed turnout.[54]

The failure of turnout to rise by more than a negligible amount in 1984 reinforces our earlier conclusions that the decline in turnout results mainly from long-term forces. This does not mean that turnout will not rise in the future. At the very least, the 1984 election stopped and even slightly reversed a trend toward declining turnout that was consistent for five straight presidential elections. But given the massive get-out-the-vote efforts in 1984, as well as attitudinal change that should have increased turnout more, it appears that restoring even moderately high levels of turnout may be a more difficult task than we earlier had imagined.

Does Low Turnout Matter?

While, in principle, nonvoters in 1984 could have elected Mondale, their turnout would have changed the outcome only if they voted very heavily Democratic. As we will see in Chapter 5, blacks were the only large social group that provided high levels of support for Mondale. According to the Census Bureau, there were about 19 million blacks of voting age in 1984, and 55.8 percent reported voting. Let us assume that roughly half of the black adults actually voted. This would leave 9.5 million black nonvoters. Even if every one of them had voted for Mondale, Reagan still would have won by more than seven million votes. But it is unrealistic to imagine a massive increase in turnout among blacks that would not also be accompanied by a sizable increase in turnout among whites.

A more reasonable way to estimate the effects of higher turnout among Mondale supporters is to ask how much better he would have done if groups that supported him had voted at the same level as the electorate as a whole. Rather than assuming that all the new voters from these groups would have supported Mondale, we may ask how much better he would have done if the new voters brought to the polls had voted Democratic at the same rate as members of the groups that did vote. But very few groups of whites gave a majority of their vote to Mondale, and, even among these groups, he usually won only a slight majority. As we will see in Chapter 5, Mondale received a majority of the vote from Hispanics, whites with annual family incomes of less than $10,000 a year, whites with an eighth grade education or less, unemployed whites, whites with no religious preference, and Jews. Among these six groups, all but Jews had lower than average turnout. But among the five low turnout groups, Mondale received just over half the vote. Bringing extra voters from these groups to the polls would have had virtually no effect on Mondale's total share of the vote, unless they were far more heavily in favor of Mondale than group members who actually voted. Assuming that black turnout was as high as white turnout and that Mondale would have received 9 out of 10 of the new black voters brought to the polls, Mondale's overall share of the vote would have increased only one and one-half percentage points.

Some scholars have argued that low turnout matters little unless it can be shown that the partisan or policy preferences of voters and nonvoters differ markedly. Wolfinger and Rosenstone's analysis of the 1972 SRC-CPS survey suggests that there were negligible differences in the policy preferences of voters and nonvoters.[55] Similarly, analyses of the SRC surveys by Paul Kleppner and by Steven D. Shaffer suggest that the policy preferences of voters and nonvoters differed only slightly during the postwar years.[56] And our own analysis of the 1980 election survey demonstrated that the voters and nonvoters differed little in their policy preferences.[57]

Our analysis of the 1984 SRC-CPS survey, however, shows that there were differences in both the partisan loyalties and the policy preferences of voters and nonvoters. Table 4-5 summarizes our results. First, we examined turnout according to party identification. Strong Republicans were somewhat more likely to vote than strong Democrats, weak Republicans were somewhat more likely to vote than weak Democrats, while independents who felt closer to the Republican party were clearly more likely to vote than those who felt closer to the Democrats. But even if each Democratic group had voted at the same level as its Republican counterpart, and assuming these extra voters had voted Democratic at the same rate as members of each Democratic group that did vote, this increased turnout would have added about 2 percentage points to Mondale's share of the vote.

Table 4-5 Percentage That Voted for President According to Vote Validation Study, by Party Identification, Issue Preferences, and Retrospective Evaluations, 1984

Attitude	Voted (%)	Did Not Vote (%)	(N)
Electorate, by party identification			
Strong Democrat	78	22	(312)
Weak Democrat	63	37	(350)
Independent, leans Democratic	55	45	(204)
Independent, no partisan leaning	52	48	(190)
Independent, leans Republican	69	31	(228)
Weak Republican	71	29	(275)
Strong Republican	85	15	(240)
Electorate, by balance of issues measure			
Strongly Democratic	75	25	(113)
Moderately Democratic	65	35	(229)
Slightly Democratic	63	37	(374)
Neutral	64	36	(707)
Slightly Republican	74	26	(258)
Moderately Republican	79	21	(119)
Strongly Republican	84	16	(37)
Electorate, by summary measure of retrospective evaluations			
Strongly Democratic	76	24	(198)
Moderately Democratic	63	37	(233)
Leans Democratic	64	36	(192)
Neutral	57	43	(240)
Leans Republican	73	27	(364)
Moderately Republican	76	24	(282)
Strongly Republican	78	22	(169)

Unlike in the 1980 election, there were differences in the policy preferences of voters and nonvoters. In Chapter 6 we analyze policy preferences on seven major issues—domestic spending, government aid for minorities, U.S. involvement in Central America, defense spending, government aid for women, cooperation with Russia, and government support for guaranteed jobs. On all four of the domestic issues, respondents who opposed government involvement were more likely to vote than those who favored it. These turnout differences are reported in Table 4-5, where we use our balance of issues measure that summarizes the overall direction of policy preferences for each respondent.[58] Respondents who were strongly, moderately, and slightly Republican were more likely to vote than those who were strongly, moderately, and slightly Democratic. Despite these turnout differences, the net impact on the way people voted was small. Assuming that respondents in each pro-Democratic group were as likely to vote as members of the comparable pro-Republican group and that the extra voters brought to the polls were as likely to vote for Mondale as voters with similar policy preferences who actually voted, Mondale's overall share of the vote would have increased only 2 percentage points.

Last, we found that respondents with a positive evaluation of Reagan's performance in office were more likely to vote than those who disapproved of Reagan; respondents who thought the Republicans would do a good job solving the most important problem facing the country were more likely to vote than those who thought the Democrats would do a good job. On the other hand, those who thought the government was doing a good job solving the nation's most important problem were no more likely to vote than those who thought it was doing a poor job. In Table 4-5 we present the percentage that voted according to scores on our summary measure of "retrospective" evaluations, which combines the responses to all three questions.[59]

There were negligible differences in turnout between respondents who strongly favored the Republicans and those who strongly favored the Democrats. But respondents who were moderately supportive of the Republican party were more likely to vote than those who moderately supported the Democrats, and whose who leaned toward the Republicans were more likely to vote than those who leaned toward the Democrats. However, even if respondents with favorable views of the Democrats were as likely to vote as those who favored the Republicans, and assuming they voted for Mondale at the same rate as members of these pro-Democratic groups who did vote, Mondale's overall share would have increased by only 2 percentage points.

On balance, there is no reasonable scenario under which increased turnout would have altered the outcome of the presidential election. Despite early Democratic hopes that increased turnout could throw Reagan out of office, these hopes proved to be unrealistic for three basic reasons.

First, mobilizing disadvantaged Americans proved to be more difficult than expected. Even when the disadvantaged are placed on the registration rolls, they may not vote on election day. Some studies suggest that although the percentage of citizens registered to vote increased, the percentage of those who actually voted declined. According to the Committee for the Study of the American Electorate, the percentage of people registered who did go to the polls dropped nearly 3 points.[60] It is difficult to know, however, just how many Americans are registered to vote. The Census Bureau survey shows that the percentage of Americans who said they were registered, but reported that they did not vote, increased only 1 point. The survey found no increase percentage of registered nonvoters among blacks. In any event, turnout was still substantially lower among blacks than among whites.

Second, the Democratic efforts failed because the Republicans engineered get-out-the-vote drives of their own. Several studies suggest that the Republicans were at least as successful in signing up new voters as the Democrats were.

Third, and most important, the major problem for the Democrats is not low turnout, but low levels of support. Simple arithmetic dictates that relying upon increased turnout to win has a fundamental disadvantage. It takes two new voters to match every one voter who switches to the opposition.[61] During the postwar years, millions of traditionally Democratic voters have been voting Republican, at least in presidential elections. Recouping these losses through increased turnout among Americans who are difficult to get to the polls is not a practical strategy.

Given that increased turnout would not have altered the election's outcome, some argue that low turnout does not matter. Some scholars point out that in most elections (although not in 1984) the policy preferences of voters have been similar to those who did not go to the polls. Turnout has been low in most postwar elections, but, in most of these, the voters reflected the sentiments of the electorate as a whole. Despite these arguments, we do not accept the conclusion that low turnout is unimportant. We are concerned that turnout is especially low among disadvantaged Americans. From the Johnson-Goldwater contest of 1964 through 1980, turnout declined most among the relatively disadvantaged members of our society. Turnout remained low among disadvantaged Americans in 1984. While black turnout is up from the early 1960s, as a result of the enfranchisement of southern blacks, turnout among disadvantaged whites is much lower than it was two decades ago. During the past two decades turnout also declined among blacks outside the South. Some believe this is because political leaders are structuring policy alternatives in a way that provides the disadvantaged little choice. The similarity of issue preferences among voters and nonvoters, they argue, results from the way policy choices are structured.[62]

We cannot endorse this argument, mainly because the empirical evidence to support such conclusions is weak. The difficulty in supporting this point of view may result from the nature of survey research, because questions about policy preferences are usually framed along the lines of controversy as defined by mainstream political leaders. Occasionally, however, surveys pose radical policy alternatives, and they often ask open-ended questions that allow respondents to state their preferences. We find little concrete evidence that current political leaders are ignoring the preferences of the electorate.

Nevertheless, the very low turnout of Americans can scarcely be healthy for a democracy. Even if current low levels of turnout seldom alter electoral outcomes, they may undermine the legitimacy of elected political leaders. Moreover, the large bloc of nonparticipants in the electorate may be potentially dangerous because this means that many people may have weak ties to established political leaders. The prospects for electoral instability, and perhaps political instability, are thus increased.[63]

Does the low turnout in 1984 have implications for partisan realignment? Four years ago the low level of turnout led some scholars to question whether Reagan's first victory presaged Republican party dominance. As Gerald M. Pomper then argued, "Elections that involve upheavals in the party coalitions have certain hallmarks, such as popular enthusiasm." [64] Indeed, the historical data show that in the past realignments have been characterized by marked increases in turnout. As Table 4-1 shows, turnout rose markedly between 1852 and 1860, a period during which the Republican party was formed, replaced the Whigs, and gained control of the presidency. Turnout also rose in the Bryan-McKinley contest of 1896, generally considered a realigning election. As both Table 4-2 and Figure 4-1 show, turnout also rose markedly after 1924, increasing in 1928 and again in 1936, a period when the Democrats emerged as the majority party.

But the historical evidence may not provide a guide for the future. Although past realignments were characterized by increased turnout, future realignments may not be. At the same time, however, it is difficult to view any alignment as stable when such a large percentage of the electorate does not vote. Burnham has called the nonparticipants the "party of nonvoters." [65] Nonvoters could alter the balance of political power, either by voting Democratic or, as Burnham hopes, supporting a genuine party of the left. We view these prospects as highly unlikely, however. In 1984, more than in 1980, it appears that the Republican party could attain long-term dominance despite the ever-present threat of future participation by some 80 million nonvoting Americans.

Notes

1. During the 1916 presidential election, women could vote only in Arizona, California, Colorado, Idaho, Kansas, Montana, Nevada, Oregon, Utah, Washington, and Wyoming. Only 10 percent of the U.S. population lived in these states. For a provocative discussion of the struggle for women's right to vote, see Alan P. Grimes, *The Puritan Ethic and Woman Suffrage* (New York: Oxford University Press, 1967).

2. For a penetrating discussion of the way voting restrictions reduced southern turnout, see V. O. Key, Jr., *Southern Politics in State and Nation* (New York: Alfred A. Knopf, 1949), 531-663. For a more general discussion of the decline of turnout in the late nineteenth and early twentieth century, see Paul Kleppner, *Who Voted? The Dynamics of Electoral Turnout, 1870-1980* (New York: Praeger, 1982), 55-82.

3. There has been considerable controversy over the reasons for and the consequences of these registration requirements. For some of the more interesting arguments, see Walter Dean Burnham, "The Changing Shape of the American Political Universe," *American Political Science Review* 59 (March 1965): 7-28; Philip E. Converse, "Change in the American Electorate," in *The Human Meaning of Social Change*, ed. Angus Campbell and Philip E. Converse (New York: Russell Sage, 1972), 266-301; Burnham, "Theory and Voting Research: Some Reflections on Converse's 'Change in the American Electorate,'" *American Political Science Review* 68 (September 1974): 1002-23, as well as a comment by Converse and a rejoinder by Burnham in the same issue.

4. For a rich source of information about the introduction of the Australian ballot and its effects, see Jerrold G. Rusk, "The Effect of the Australian Ballot Reform on Split Ticket Voting: 1876-1908," *American Political Science Review* 64 (December 1970): 1220-38. Rusk's analysis has also led to an interesting exchange with Burnham. See a comment by Burnham and a rejoinder by Rusk in the *American Political Science Review* 65 (December 1971): 1149-57, as well as further discussion by both authors in the September 1974 issue, 1028-49, 1052-57.

5. For example, see Burnham's most recent published estimates for the years between 1920 and 1980, which appear in "The 1980 Earthquake: Realignment, Reaction, or What?" in *The Hidden Election: Politics and Economics in the 1980 Campaign*, ed. Thomas Ferguson and Joel Rogers (New York: Pantheon Books, 1981), 101. His preliminary estimate for 1984 appears in "The 1984 Election and the Future of American Politics," in *Election 1984: Landslide Without a Mandate?*, ed. Ellis Sandoz and Cecil V. Crabb (New York: New American Library, 1985), 216. Based upon his personal communication to us of Sept. 9, 1985, Burnham estimates turnout among the U.S. adult citizen population in 1980 to be 54.3 percent and turnout in 1984 to be 55.2 percent. We are grateful to Burnham for providing us with his most recent turnout estimates.

Because Burnham's turnout denominator is smaller than ours, his estimates of turnout are always somewhat higher. Although there are advantages to Burnham's calculations, we use the total voting age as our base for two reasons. First, it is very difficult to estimate the size of the noncitizen population, and official estimates of turnout published by the U.S. Bureau of the Census use the voting-age population as the turnout denominator. Second, citizenship is not a constitutional requirement for voting. The time it takes to become a citizen is a matter of national legislation, and imposing citizenship as a condition of voting is a matter of state law.

6. For an excellent assessment of attempts to register members of minority groups, see Sam Roberts, "Blacks Form United Front in Vote Drive," *New*

York Times, July 8, 1983, B1, 4. See also John Herbers, "Legal Moves Ease Signup of Voters," *New York Times,* Aug. 18, 1984, 1, 8; and Robert Reinhold, "Hispanic Leaders Open Voter Drive," *New York Times,* Aug. 9, 1983, A15.

7. *The Gallup Report,* No. 224 (May 1984), 9. These results are based upon Gallup polls conducted between November 1983 and April 1984. Given that blacks appear to be more likely to falsely report voting than whites, this result should be interpreted with caution. But it is probably safe to say that racial differences in registration levels had been reduced substantially.

8. According to surveys conducted by the U.S. Bureau of the Census, the percentage of blacks who reported that they were registered to vote rose from 60 percent in November 1980 to 66.3 percent in November 1984. Among whites, the percentage who said they were registered rose from 68.4 percent to 69.6 percent. See U.S. Department of Commerce, Bureau of the Census, *Voting and Registration in the Election of November 1984 (Advance Report),* Series P-20, No. 397, January 1985, 3.

9. See Thomas B. Edsall and Haynes Johnson, "High Tech, Impersonal Computer Net Is Snaring Prospective Republicans," *Washington Post,* April 22, 1984: A1, A8.

10. See Charles Green and Paul Magnusson, "Republican Voter Drive May Cancel Dem Hopes," *Detroit Free Press,* Sept. 16, 1984, A1, A11; and John Herbers, "Drives to Sign Up New Voters Bring Surge in the Polls," *New York Times,* Oct. 29, 1984: A1, A20.

11. We use the vote validation results made available by the Inter-University Consortium for Political and Social Research in July 1985. We are grateful to Santa Traugott of the Center for Political Studies for providing us with information about the conduct of this study.

12. The main reason for being classified as a nonvoter in the vote validation study is that the SRC field staff fails to find a record that the respondent is registered. There will always be some cases in which the staff fails to find a registration record, leading an actual voter to be wrongly classified as a nonvoter. In 1984 the SRC improved its vote validation procedures, mainly by relying upon field supervisors to check the registration record. This led to a lower level of "overreporting" than in any of the four previous vote validation efforts. Since more records were found, overall levels of turnout were higher compared with actual turnout than in any of the four previous vote validation efforts.

  Because the SRC-CPS validation procedures were changed, the results we report in Tables 4-3, 4-4, and 4-5 cannot be compared directly with similar tables (Tables 4-2, 4-3, and 4-4) in Paul R. Abramson, John H. Aldrich, and David W. Rohde, *Change and Continuity in the 1980 Elections,* rev. ed., (Washington, D.C.: CQ Press, 1983). While relative levels of turnout among social and attitudinal groups can be compared, any comparisons of the absolute levels of turnout between 1980 and 1984 will be misleading. Since these changed procedures make comparisons over time very difficult, we have relied upon measures of reported turnout to study postwar trends.

13. There are biases in the extent of voting overreports. In addition to the 1984 vote validation study, similar studies were conducted by the SRC-CPS in

1964, 1976, 1978, and 1980. Most analyses that compare results of reported turnout and turnout as measured by these vote validation studies suggest that relative levels of turnout can be measured using reported turnout. However, research suggests that blacks are more likely to falsely claim to vote than whites, and turnout differences between the races are greater when the vote validation studies are used to measure electoral participation. See Paul R. Abramson and William Claggett, "Race-Related Differences in Self-Reported and Validated Turnout," *Journal of Politics,* 46 (November 1984): 719-38; and Abramson and Claggett, "Race-Related Differences in Self-Reported and Validated Turnout in 1984," *Journal of Politics,* 48 (May 1986). For an extensive analysis of the factors that contribute to false reports of voting, see Brian D. Silver, Barbara A. Anderson, and Paul R. Abramson, "Who Overreports Voting?" *American Political Science Review* 80 (June 1986).

14. For a discussion of reasons why these surveys provide the best data set for studying trends and turnout, see Paul R. Abramson and John H. Aldrich, "The Decline of Electoral Participation in America," *American Political Science Review* 76 (September 1982): 502-21.

15. Another factor that may contribute to relatively higher turnout in the SRC surveys is that in presidential years the Michigan survey interviews respondents before the election and measures turnout by interviewing the same respondents after the election. Being interviewed may itself stimulate respondents to vote. See Michael W. Traugott and John P. Katosh, "Response Validity in Surveys of Voting Behavior," *Public Opinion Quarterly* 43 (Fall 1979): 359-77.

16. We must compare the SRC-CPS and the Census Bureau surveys with different real-world populations. The census surveys are based upon the total noninstitutionalized voting-age population, and the SRC-CPS surveys are based upon the total noninstitutionalized politically eligible voting-age population.

17. We are grateful to Jerry T. Jennings of the U.S. Bureau of the Census for providing us with the information about the size of the 1984 sample. The census surveys use the respondent to report information about registration and turnout for all voting-age residents of the household. Studies by the bureau indicate that relying upon this information about how other adults voted leads to no significant biases.

18. U.S. Department of Commerce, Bureau of the Census, *Voting and Registration in the Election of November 1984 (Advance Report),* Series P-20, No. 397, January 1985, 1. All of our reports from the Census Bureau surveys are based upon this publication.

19. The U.S. Bureau of the Census survey definition of the South differs somewhat from ours. The bureau includes several Border States as southern. For the definition we use in our analysis of the SRC surveys, see note 21 below.

20. Respondents who identified as Hispanics were divided into three categories— Mexican-American or Chicano, Puerto Rican, and other Hispanic—but the total number of Hispanics surveyed was too small to permit careful analysis of their political behavior.

21. As we state in Chapter 3, we consider the South to include the 11 states of the old Confederacy. In our analysis of SRC-CPS surveys, however, we do not classify residents of Tennessee as southerners because the SRC-CPS samples respondents in Tennessee to represent the Border States. In the following analysis, as well as in analysis of regional differences using the SRC-CPS election studies later in our book, Alabama, Arkansas, Florida, Georgia, Louisiana, Mississippi, North Carolina, South Carolina, Texas, and Virginia are considered southern.

22. See Raymond E. Wolfinger and Steven J. Rosenstone, *Who Votes?* (New Haven, Conn.: Yale University Press, 1980), 93-94.

23. The 1964 census survey used the category "nonwhite," rather than black.

24. Wolfinger and Rosenstone, *Who Votes?*, 46-50.

25. We use this distinction mainly because it allows us to make comparisons across a long time period and thus is extremely valuable for studying change during the entire postwar period. See our analysis in Chapter 5.

    For a comprehensive analysis of the meaning of social class to the American public and the political implications of feelings of class identification, see Mary R. Jackman and Robert W. Jackman, *Class Awareness in the United States* (Berkeley: University of California Press, 1983).

26. Our measure of income is based upon the respondent's estimate of his or her family's 1983 annual family income before taxes. For respondents who refused to answer this question and for those the interviewer thought answered dishonestly, we relied upon the interviewer's assessment of family income.

27. See Wolfinger and Rosenstone, *Who Votes?*, 13-36.

28. See Steven J. Rosenstone, "Economic Adversity and Voter Turnout," *American Journal of Political Science* 26 (February 1982): 25-46.

29. The following two questions were asked: "Do you consider religion to be an important part of your life, or not?" Those who say religion is important are asked, "Would you say your religion provides *some* guidance in your day-to-day living, *quite a bit* of guidance, or *a great deal* of guidance in your day-to-day living?"

30. Respondents were given a list of groups and asked to identify "those groups you feel particularly close to—*people who are most like you in their ideas and interests and feelings about things.*" We have analyzed turnout among those who identified with "Evangelical Groups, Such as the Moral Majority."

31. The following question was used to measure whether the respondent was "born-again": "Some people have had deep religious experiences which have transformed their lives. I'm thinking of experiences sometimes described as 'being born again in one's faith,' or 'discovering Jesus Christ in one's life.' There are deeply religious people who have not had an experience of this sort. How about you; have you had such an experience?"

32. Wolfinger and Rosenstone, *Who Votes?*, 13-36.

33. Given problems of comparability between the 1984 vote validation study and previous validation studies, we rely upon reported turnout to study change over time.

34. Walter Dean Burnham, "The 1976 Election: Has the Crisis Been Adjourned?" in *American Politics and Public Policy,* ed. Walter Dean Burnham

and Martha Wagner Weinberg (Cambridge, Mass.: MIT Press, 1978), 24; and Thomas E. Cavanagh, "Change in American Voter Turnout: 1964-1976," *Political Science Quarterly* 96 (Spring 1981): 53-65.

35. See Paul R. Abramson, *Political Attitudes in America: Formation and Change* (San Francisco: W. H. Freeman, 1983), 56-61.
36. Wolfinger and Rosenstone, *Who Votes?*, 58.
37. Richard W. Boyd, "Decline of U.S. Voter Turnout: Structural Explanations," *American Politics Quarterly* 9 (April 1981): 133-59.
38. See U.S. Department of Commerce, U.S. Bureau of the Census, *Projections of the Population of Voting Age for States: November 1984*, Series P-25, No. 948, April 1984, 1.
39. George I. Balch, "Multiple Indicators in Survey Research: The Concept 'Sense of Political Efficacy,'" *Political Methodology* 1 (Spring 1974): 1-43. For an extensive discussion of feelings of political efficacy, see Abramson, *Political Attitudes*, 135-89.
40. Respondents are asked, "Generally speaking, do you usually think of yourself as a Republican, a Democrat, an independent, or what?" Persons who call themselves Republicans or Democrats are asked, "Would you call yourself a strong (Republican, Democrat) or not a very strong (Republican, Democrat)?" Respondents who call themselves independents, answer "no preference," or name another party are asked, "Do you think of yourself as closer to the Republican party or to the Democratic party?" Respondents who have no partisan preference are usually classified as independents by the SRC-CPS. They are classified as "apoliticals" only if they have very low levels of political interest and involvement.
41. Angus Campbell, Philip E. Converse, Warren E. Miller, and Donald E. Stokes, *The American Voter* (New York: John Wiley & Sons, 1960), 120-67.
42. This expectation follows from a rational-choice perspective. For the most extensive discussion of party identification from this point of view, see Morris P. Fiorina, *Retrospective Voting in American National Elections* (New Haven, Conn.: Yale University Press, 1981), 84-105.
43. For scores on this measure among blacks and whites from 1952 through 1980, see Abramson, *Political Attitudes*, 176.
44. Respondents who disagreed with both of these statements were scored as highly efficacious; those who disagreed with one, but agreed with the other, were scored as medium; those who agreed with both were scored as low. Respondents with ambiguous responses to one question were scored as either high or low according to their response to the remaining question, and those with ambiguous responses to both questions were excluded from our analysis.
45. This calculation is based upon the assumption that the percentage of respondents in each partisan strength and each sense of political efficacy category was the same as that observed in 1960, but that for each group reported turnout was the same as that observed in 1984. For a full explanation of this technique, see Abramson, *Political Attitudes*, 296.
46. Ibid., 105-19.
47. For a discussion of the decline in feelings of political efficacy among the American electorate, see Converse, "Change in the American Electorate," 322-37; James D. Wright, *The Dissent of the Governed: Alienation and*

Democracy in America (New York: Academic Press, 1976), 168-200; Seymour Martin Lipset and William Schneider, *The Confidence Gap: Business, Labor, and Government in the Public Mind* (New York: Free Press, 1983), 19-24; and Abramson, *Political Attitudes*, 172-89.

48. For example, the percentage of whites who trusted "the government in Washington to do what is right" just about always or most of the time rose from 25 percent in 1980 to 34 percent in 1982, and reached 46 percent in 1984—still far below the all-time high of 77 percent attained two decades earlier. Between 1980 and 1984 there was little change in trust among blacks. We do not focus on political trust in our analysis because feelings of political trust are not related to turnout. This finding, demonstrated by our previous analyses, was confirmed in 1984. We conducted an extensive analysis of the relationship of political trust to turnout in 1984 and found no evidence of a relationship between trust and voter participation among the white elector-ate.

49. See Abramson, Aldrich, and Rohde, *Change and Continuity in 1980 Elections*, rev. ed., 86-87. For a more detailed and technical analysis that uses a probability technique as well as the algebraic correction technique, see Abramson and Aldrich, "The Decline of Electoral Participation in America." In our analyses, we introduce no controls for level of education, for reasons we make clear in our article. However, a similar analysis by Kleppner estimates the effect of declining feelings of party identification and sense of political efficacy among nonsouthern whites and introduces simultaneous controls for education, income, age, and sex. Despite these controls, his estimates on the effects of attitude change upon the decline of turnout between 1960 and 1980 differ only negligibly from ours. See Kleppner, *Who Voted?*, 122-30.

50. This estimate is based upon assuming that each of the partisan strength and sense of political efficacy categories retained their 1980 levels of turnout, but that the distribution of these categories was the same as that observed in 1984.

51. The following questions were asked. Respondents were first asked who they thought would win the upcoming presidential election. Those who predicted a winner were asked, "Do you think the presidential race will be close, or will (name of predicted winner) win by quite a bit?" Those who did not predict a winner were asked, "Do you think the presidential race will be close or will one candidate win by quite a bit?"

52. See John H. Aldrich, "Some Problems in Testing Two Rational Models of Participation," *American Journal of Political Science* 20 (November 1976): 713-33.

53. Orley Ashenfelter and Stanley Kelley, Jr., "Determinants of Participation in Presidential Elections," *Journal of Law and Economics* 18 (December 1975): 721.

54. "Report Says Projections Reduced Voter Turnout," *New York Times*, Nov. 18, 1984: L27. For attempts to estimate the effects of early projections upon turnout in 1980, see John E. Jackson, "Election Night Reporting and Voter Turnout," *American Journal of Political Science* 27 (November 1983): 615-35; and Michael X. Delli Carpini, "Scooping the Voters? The Consequences of the Networks' Early Call of the 1980 Presidential Race," *Journal of*

Politics 46 (August 1984): 866-85.
55. Wolfinger and Rosenstone, *Who Votes?*, 109-14.
56. Kleppner, *Who Voted?*, 160-61; Stephen D. Shaffer, "Policy Differences Between Voters and Nonvoters in American Elections," *Western Political Quarterly* 35 (December 1982): 496-510.
57. Abramson, Aldrich, and Rohde, *Change and Continuity in the 1980 Elections*, rev. ed., 89-90.
58. For a discussion of this measure as well as a description of how it was constructed, see Chapter 6.
59. For a discussion of this measure as well as a description of how it was constructed, see Chapter 7.
60. Mike Feinsilber, "Non-voter May Also Be Making a Choice," *Lansing State Journal*, Nov. 19, 1984, 9A.
61. If you are a member of a three-person committee in which one voter opposes you, you will still win if you can count on the remaining vote. If your one supporter leaves the committee, you can still win if you add another member who will support you. But if your supporter joins your opponent, one new supporter added to the committee would only produce a tie. It would take two new supporters to regain a majority. The same logic applies to electoral coalitions with millions of members. See Robert Axelrod, "Where the Votes Come From: An Analysis of Electoral Coalitions, 1952-1968," *American Political Science Review* 66 (March 1972): 11-20.
62. Walter Dean Burnham, "Shifting Patterns of Congressional Voting Participation," in *The Current Crisis in American Politics*, ed. Walter Dean Burnham (New York: Oxford University Press, 1982), 166-203.
63. See Seymour Martin Lipset, *Political Map: The Social Bases of Politics*, expanded edition (Baltimore, Md.: Johns Hopkins University Press, 1981), 226-29. Lipset emphasizes the dangers of sudden increases in political participation.
64. Gerald M. Pomper, "The Presidential Election," in *The Election of 1980: Reports and Interpretations*, Gerald M. Pomper, with colleagues (Chatham, N.J.: Chatham House, 1981), 86.
65. Walter Dean Burnham, "The Eclipse of the Democratic Party," *Democracy* 2 (July 1982): 7-17. This essay was reprinted, along with comments by eight political scientists, and a rejoinder by Burnham, in *Society* 21 (July/August 1984): 5-42. For discussions of turnout, see, in particular, comments by Paul R. Abramson, "Nonvoters and the Future," 11-14; and D. Roderick Kiewiet, "American Voting and Nonvoting, 24-26.

Chapter 5

Social Forces and the Vote

The result of the 1984 presidential election was the product of more than 92 million individual votes. But most Americans also belong to primary groups comprised of families and friends and to secondary groups such as social classes, ethnic groups, and religions. Many belong to voluntary associations such as trade unions, churches, or professional associations, and are thus formal members of a group.

Although voting is an individual act, social group memberships influence voting choices. People who share social characteristics may share political interests. Group similarities in voting behavior may reflect political conditions that existed generations earlier. The partisan loyalties of blacks, for example, were shaped by the Civil War and the postwar Reconstruction, with black loyalties to the party of Lincoln lasting through the 1932 presidential election. The Democratic voting of southern whites, a product of those same historical conditions, lasted even longer, perhaps through 1960.

It is easy to see why group-based loyalties persist over time. Studies of pre-adult political learning suggest that partisan loyalties are often transmitted from generation to generation. And because religion, ethnicity, and, to a lesser extent, social class are also transmitted from generation to generation, social divisions among the electorate have considerable staying power. Moreover, the interaction of social group members with each other may reinforce similarities in political attitudes and behavior.

Politicians often think in group terms. They recognize that to win they must mobilize those social groups that have supported their party in the past and that it is helpful to cut into their opponent's established bases of support. The Democrats think in group terms more than Republicans do, for the Democrats are a coalition of minorities. To win they must earn high levels of support from the social groups that traditionally have supported their broad-based coalition.

In 1984 many traditionally Democratic groups cast a majority of their votes for Ronald Reagan, and others split their votes about evenly between Reagan and Walter F. Mondale. The decline of the Democratic party during the last five presidential elections may be attributed to its failure to hold the basic loyalties of the social groups that made up the winning coalition forged by Franklin D. Roosevelt during the 1930s.

This chapter examines the voting patterns of social groups in the 1984 presidential election. To put the 1984 results in perspective, the voting choices of key social groups for the entire postwar period will then be considered. By studying the social bases of partisan support since 1944, we will show how the 1984 election results are part of a long-term trend that has severely weakened the New Deal coalition upon which Democratic victories traditionally have depended.

How Social Groups Voted in 1984

Our basic results are presented in Table 5-1, which shows how various social groups voted for president in 1984.[1] Excluding respondents for whom the direction of vote was not ascertained, 57.7 percent said they voted for Reagan, 41.4 percent for Mondale, and .9 percent for other candidates—results that are close to the official voting statistics *(Table 3-1)*.[2] The Survey Research Center-Center for Political Studies study, based upon 1,389 voters, is the single best source of survey data and is especially valuable for studying change over time. However, once we begin to examine subgroups of the electorate, the number of persons sampled in some social groups becomes rather small. We therefore supplement our analysis by referring to the exit polls conducted by the three television networks and by the *Los Angeles Times*,[3] as well as with the final Gallup preelection survey.[4]

Race, Gender, Region, and Age

Political differences between blacks and whites are far sharper than any other social cleavage. According to the SRC-CPS survey, 89 percent of the black voters supported Mondale, compared to only 36 percent of the white voters. The *New York Times*/CBS News, NBC News, and *Los Angeles Times* exit polls all showed that 91 percent of the blacks voted for Mondale, compared with only 33 or 34 percent of the whites, and the ABC News poll result was almost identical to the SRC-CPS survey. According to the Gallup poll, 92 percent of the black voters supported Mondale, compared with only 34 percent of the whites. Even though blacks make up only one-ninth of the electorate and have relatively low turnout, a fifth of Mondale's total vote came from black voters.[5] Mondale received 37.6 million votes; about 7.5 million from blacks.

Because race is such a profound social division, our analysis in this chapter will examine divisions among blacks and whites separately. Among blacks, social divisions were relatively unimportant, and we do not present the results in Table 5-1. Among blacks, as among whites, women were more likely than men to vote Democratic. About 1 black man out of 8 voted for Reagan, whereas fewer than 1 black woman in 10 did.[6] On the other hand, blacks did not mirror the regional differences found among whites. Among whites, southerners were more likely to vote for Reagan than those outside the South.[7] Given the small number of black voters in the SRC-CPS survey, we cannot comment further on differences among blacks.[8] But one finding seems clear. Among every subset of blacks we examined, a large majority voted for Mondale.

Among whites, the small proportion who identified themselves as Hispanic were much more likely to vote for Mondale than those who were non-Hispanic, and a majority of Hispanics probably voted Democratic. Polls vary a great deal in reporting the Hispanic vote, ranging from a high of 68 percent Democratic in the NBC News poll to only 49 percent Democratic in the Gallup poll. These discrepancies probably result from the relatively small number of Hispanics sampled,[9] as well as to different ways of classifying voters as Hispanic.[10] It is clear, however, that at least a substantial minority of Hispanics voted for Reagan.

Gender differences in voting behavior have been pronounced in some European countries, but historically they have been negligible in the United States.[11] In 1980, however, polls showed that women were less likely than men to vote for Reagan, and throughout his administration women were consistently less likely to approve of Reagan's performance in office.[12] These differences between women and men, along with the tendency of women to vote more Democratic in the 1982 midterm election, led to a much-discussed "gender gap." Some feminists proclaimed that women would play a major role in defeating Reagan.[13] Women, some political analysts argued, were more likely to oppose Reagan because of his militaristic foreign policy, his opposition to the Equal Rights Amendment, and his cuts in domestic spending. However, most discussions of the gender gap ignored an obvious fact: a gap in the voting behavior of men and women would not necessarily aid the Democrats.[14]

As Table 5-1 reveals, there was a gender gap among whites, and, as we saw above, among blacks as well. But the bottom line was that an absolute majority of both men and women voted for Reagan. According to the SRC-CPS survey, 54 percent of all women and 62 percent of all men voted for Reagan—a gap of 8 points. All four exit polls, as well as the Gal-

Table 5-1 How Social Groups Voted for President in 1984*

Social Group	Reagan (%)	Mondale (%)	Other (%)	Total Percent	(N)
Electorate, by race					
White	63	36	1	100%	(1231)
Black	9	89	2	100%	(131)
Whites, by Hispanic identification					
Identify as Hispanic	47	53	0	100%	(66)
Do not identify	64	35	1	100%	(1163)
Whites, by gender					
Male	66	33	1	100%	(546)
Female	61	39	1	101%	(685)
Whites, by region					
New England and mid-Atlantic	64	35	1	100%	(245)
North Central	66	34	1	101%	(384)
South	70	29	†	99%	(222)
Border	56	44	0	100%	(101)
Mountain and Pacific	54	44	2	100%	(279)
Whites, by birth cohort					
Before 1924	60	38	2	100%	(289)
1924-1939	63	36	1	100%	(283)
1940-1954	65	35	†	100%	(435)
1955-1966	63	36	†	100%	(215)
Whites, by social class					
Working class	58	42	1	101%	(477)
Middle class	65	34	1	100%	(640)
Farmers	75	23	2	100%	(57)
Whites, by occupation of head of household					
Unskilled manual	55	44	1	100%	(105)
Skilled, semiskilled manual	58	41	1	100%	(372)
Clerical, sales, other white collar	64	35	1	100%	(229)
Managerial	73	26	1	100%	(215)
Professional and semiprofessional	59	41	1	101%	(196)
Whites, by annual family income					
Less than $10,000	43	54	2	99%	(175)
$10,000 to $14,999	63	35	2	100%	(130)
$15,000 to $19,999	61	39	0	100%	(114)
$20,000 to $24,999	59	40	1	100%	(145)
$25,000 to $29,999	62	37	1	100%	(132)
$30,000 to $34,999	73	27	0	100%	(122)

Table 5-1 (continued)

Social Group	Reagan (%)	Mondale (%)	Other (%)	Total Percent	(N)
$35,000 to $39,999	68	32	0	100%	(82)
$40,000 to $49,999	64	36	0	100%	(116)
$50,000 to $59,999	70	29	1	100%	(76)
$60,000 and more	81	19	0	100%	(91)
Whites, by level of education					
Eight grades or less	41	55	4	100%	(85)
Some high school	57	42	1	100%	(93)
High school graduate	66	34	†	100%	(418)
Some college	69	31	1	101%	(344)
College graduate	64	34	2	100%	(191)
Advanced degree	50	49	1	100%	(94)
Whites, by union membership††					
Member	47	51	1	99%	(282)
Nonmember	68	32	1	101%	(948)
Whites, by religion					
Protestant	71	28	1	100%	(717)
Catholic	55	44	1	100%	(362)
Jewish	31	69	0	100%	(36)
No preference	44	55	1	100%	(80)
Whites, by social class and religion					
Middle-class Protestants	75	23	1	99%	(363)
Working-class Protestants	62	37	1	100%	(271)
Middle-class Catholics	58	42	1	101%	(178)
Working-class Catholics	52	47	1	100%	(157)

* Percentages read across.
† Less than one percent.
†† Whether respondent or family member in union.
Note: The 60 voters for whom direction of vote was not ascertained have been excluded from these calculations.

lup poll, reported that a majority of women voted for Reagan. Estimates of the female vote for Reagan ranged from 54 percent by ABC News to 58 percent by the *New York Times*/CBS News. All these surveys revealed that men were more likely than women to vote for Reagan. The gender gap ranged from a low of 4 points in the *New York Times*/CBS News exit poll to a high of 9 points by the NBC News poll and by Gallup.

In Table 5-1 we report the SRC-CPS results for white men and for white women. Three out of five white women voted for Reagan, while nearly two out of three white men did. The *New York Times*/CBS News exit poll revealed similar results: 64 percent of the white women and 68 percent of the white men voted for Reagan.[15]

According to Everett Carll Ladd's analysis of the exit polls, the gender gap was greatest among the college-educated and in the Northeast. It was small or nonexistent among the elderly, those who had not gone to college, and southerners.[16] Our analysis of the SRC-CPS survey, which focuses on differences between white men and white women, shows no gender gap among whites who had not graduated from high school. But we found only an average gender gap among college graduates. Unlike Ladd, we found an 8-point gender gap in the South, mainly because of the very strong Reagan showing among white men. Seventy-four percent of the southern white males ($N=97$) supported Reagan. Like Ladd, we found a relatively low gender gap among the elderly. The largest gap among age groups, some 7 points, was found among whites born after 1954. We also found a gender gap among white Catholics. Among men ($N=150$), 61 percent voted for Reagan; among women ($N=212$), 51 percent did. But this 10-point gap should not obscure the more basic finding: the Mondale-Ferraro ticket failed to carry a majority among white Roman Catholic women.

Among both men and women, those who were married were a good deal more likely to vote for Reagan than were those who had never been married.[17] Among all women who had never been married ($N=103$), 59 percent voted for Mondale; among white women who had never been married ($N=79$), 49 percent did. White females who had never been married were 13 percentage points more likely to vote for Mondale than were white women who were currently married.[18] The *New York Times*/CBS News exit poll did not identify respondents who had never been married, but compared married and unmarried respondents, including those who were divorced. Thirty-seven percent of the married respondents and 47 percent of the singles voted for Mondale. Among all single women, 49 percent voted for Mondale. According to Maureen Dowd, single voters were more likely to support Mondale partly because they have lower annual family incomes than married voters, and partly because they are less supportive of the family values that Reagan stressed in his campaign.[19]

Our analysis in Chapter 3 shows that regional differences were relatively small. There were, however, more pronounced regional differences among whites. Among white voters in the states of the old Confederacy, 70 percent voted for Reagan and only 29 percent for Mondale. The *New York Times*/CBS News exit poll also showed that southern whites were more supportive of Reagan than were whites in any other region. According to their survey, 72 percent of the whites in the

South voted Republican and only 28 percent voted for Mondale.

Throughout the general election campaign, many pollsters expected Reagan to do especially well among young voters and for Mondale to do somewhat better among the elderly. Our analysis of the SRC-CPS survey shows that Mondale fared slightly better among whites born before 1924 (60 years old and older), but age differences were relatively small among our broadly defined cohorts. All four exit polls revealed small age-group differences. The Gallup poll, however, found that voters 65 and older were more likely to support Mondale than any other age group. Among the elderly, according to Gallup, 46 percent voted for Mondale. Our more detailed age-group analysis, which divides the electorate into four age cohorts, does not reveal a high level of Mondale support among voters 65 and older. On the other hand, Reagan did especially well among the handful of white voters too young to have voted in 1980. Among these young whites (N=44), he received 70 percent of the vote.[20] The *New York Times*/CBS News exit poll, however, reported results for all first-time voters and did not find them to be politically distinctive. Sixty percent voted for Reagan, about the same as the electorate as a whole.[21]

Social Class, Income, Education, and Union Membership

Traditionally, the Democratic party has appealed more to the relatively disadvantaged. It has done better among the working class, the poor, and voters with lower levels of formal education. Moreover, since the 1930s, most union leaders have supported the Democratic party, and union members have traditionally been a mainstay of the Democratic presidential coalition. These bases of support persisted in 1984, but most of these relationships were weak.

As we shall see, the weak relationship between social class and voting behavior is part of a long-term trend that has eroded class differences. Class-based voting might have been expected to rise in 1984. Mondale was a liberal Democrat with well-established ties to organized labor. He had received strong support from labor leaders during both the nomination and the general election campaigns. Moreover, Reagan had presided over the nation's worst postwar recession, in which unemployment had reached higher than 10 percent nationwide and 16 percent among blue-collar workers. On the other hand, Reagan's strong defense policies and his championing of traditional family values may have been especially attractive to the working class. On balance, however, the 1984 contest might have been expected to polarize the electorate along social class lines. In fact, it did not.

When we examine the relationship of social class, occupation, income, trade union membership, and level of education to voting behavior, we find very few groups that gave Mondale a majority of the vote. A clear majority of working-class whites (manually employed workers and their dependents) voted for Reagan, although he did somewhat better among the middle class. Among whites, unskilled workers and their dependents were more likely to vote for Mondale than any other occupational group, but even they gave half their vote to Reagan. Among the entire working class (including blacks), Reagan and Mondale split the vote evenly (50 percent for Reagan, 49 percent for Mondale). According to the *New York Times*/CBS News poll, 53 percent of the blue-collar vote went for Reagan.[22] As with our analysis, Gallup found that unskilled workers were the most likely to vote for Mondale, but even among these voters he received only a slight majority (51 percent) of the vote.

Mondale clearly fared better among the poor than among the more affluent. According to our analysis, Mondale actually gained a majority of the vote among whites with annual family incomes below $10,000; among whites with annual family incomes above $60,000, four out of five voted for Reagan. But among the eight middle-income categories in our analysis, there was a fairly weak relationship between income and voting choices. All four exit polls used different income categories, but all showed Mondale doing best among the poorest voters, with Reagan faring best among the most affluent. According to the ABC News poll, Mondale gained 69 percent of the vote among voters with incomes below $5,000. At this lower income range, however, a substantial proportion of the voters are black. We found, for example, that among all voters with annual family incomes below $5,000 ($N=69$), 65 percent voted for Mondale; among white voters with incomes this low ($N=49$), only 55 percent did.

Less educated voters were more likely to vote for Mondale than those with higher levels of education, and, among the small number of white voters with an eighth grade education or less, a slight majority voted for Mondale. Still, the overall relationship between formal education and the way people voted was relatively weak. Support for Reagan did not rise continuously as educational levels rose. White high school graduates were as likely to vote for Reagan as whites who had attended college or as whites who were college graduates. Among the relatively small number of whites with advanced degrees, support for Reagan dropped, and these highly educated whites appear to have split their votes about evenly for Reagan and Mondale. Gallup also found a weak relationship between level of education and voting choices. Among all voters who had not graduated from high school, Mondale and Reagan each received 50 percent of the vote. But Gallup found virtually no difference among high school graduates, voters with some college education, and college graduates. Reagan received three votes out of five in all three of these educational categories.

Mondale clearly did better among union households than among non-union households. As Table 5-1 shows, Mondale won a slender majority of the vote in white union households and only about a third of the vote among non-union households. All four exit polls, as well as the Gallup poll, showed that Mondale won a slight majority of the union vote, ranging from an estimated 52 percent in the *Los Angeles Times* poll and the Gallup poll to 55 percent in the ABC News poll. Put differently, however, despite organized labor's effort for Mondale, Reagan won nearly half the union vote.

As a final note we may add that Mondale did well among the minority of voters who were unemployed. Among all voters for whom the head of household was either unemployed or permanently disabled ($N=97$), he won 68 percent of the vote; among whites ($N=72$), he won 60 percent. According to the *New York Times*/CBS News exit poll, Mondale won 68 percent of the vote of the unemployed. As we saw in Chapter 4, however, the unemployed have relatively low turnout. Although unemployment was 7.2 percent in November of 1984, only 3 percent of the voters polled by the *New York Times*/CBS News survey were unemployed.

Religion

Religious differences, which partly reflect ethnic differences between Catholics and Protestants, also have played a major role in American electoral politics. Roman Catholics have tended to support the Democratic party, and white Protestants, especially outside the South, have tended to favor the Republicans. In all of Roosevelt's elections, and in every postwar election through 1976, Jews strongly supported the Democratic presidential candidate. In 1980 a substantial minority of Jews voted for John B. Anderson, depriving Jimmy Carter of an absolute majority of Jewish votes, but Carter still received a plurality of the Jewish vote.

As Table 5-1 shows, in 1984 Reagan won more than half of the vote among white Catholics, while winning 7 voters out of 10 among white Protestants. According to the *New York Times*/CBS News poll, 58 percent of the white Catholics and 73 percent of the white Protestants voted for Reagan.[23] Reagan was strongly supported by numerous fundamentalist leaders, the most prominent of whom was Jerry Falwell, the leader of the Moral Majority. In a speech to religious leaders during a prayer breakfast in Dallas the day after his nomination, Reagan endorsed their views so enthusiastically that critics argued he was coming close to ignoring the First Amendment prohibition against established religion. Reagan's appeals to fundamentalists appear to have been translated into votes. Our analysis of voting among white Protestants shows that Reagan won 86 percent of the vote among those who felt close to evangelical groups ($N=133$). On the other hand, Reagan fared only marginally better among white Protestants who said they had been born again than among white Protestants who had not had this religious experience. However, the *New York Times*/CBS News showed that 81 percent of the white born-again Protestants voted for Reagan, while he received 69 percent from white Protestants who had not had this religious experience.[24]

The Democratic nomination campaign had caused considerable concern among Jews. Several of Jesse Jackson's statements and his association with Nation of Islam minister Louis Farrakhan during the nomination campaign had created considerable tension between Jews and blacks, two crucial constituent groups within the Democratic party. But Reagan's strong endorsement of fundamentalist principles also caused considerable concern among Jews. Mondale did substantially better among Jewish voters than Carter did. Reagan received a lower percentage of the Jewish vote in 1984 than he had in 1980, when that vote was divided among three candidates. Because the SRC-CPS survey sampled only 36 Jewish voters, we must rely upon other sources to determine how Jews voted. In all four exit polls, Mondale received a substantial majority of the Jewish vote, ranging from 65 percent (NBC News) to 69 percent (ABC News). A survey of 1,500 Jewish voters sponsored by the American Jewish Congress found that 78 percent supported Mondale.[25]

Although Jews were politically distinctive, the differences between Catholics and Protestants were relatively small. However, when religion and social class are combined, our ability to explain how people vote is improved. Because working-class voters are more likely to vote Democratic than middle-class voters, and because Catholics are more likely to vote Democratic than Protestants, we find that the tendency to vote Democratic is higher among those who are both working class and Catholic and that the Republicans do well among middle-class Protestants. But, as Table 5-1 shows, Mondale failed to carry a majority even among white working-class Catholics. That Mondale could not carry a majority among voters for whom both class and religion usually contribute to a Democratic vote merely serves to underscore how badly he fared among groups that formed the traditional Democratic coalition. Reagan, by contrast, received three votes out of four among a traditionally Republican group, white middle-class Protestants.

How Social Groups Voted during the Postwar Years

Although there were sharp racial differences, most social differences in voting behavior were relatively small in 1984. How does this compare with other presidential elections? Were the weak relationships in 1984 atypical, or were they the result of a long-term trend that has eroded the impact of social forces? To answer these questions we will examine the social behavior of groups that have been an important part of the Democratic presidential coalition during the postwar years. Our analysis begins with the 1944 presidential contest between FDR and Thomas E. Dewey and uses a simple measure of social cleavages to assess the impact of social forces over time.

In his lucid discussion of the logic of party coalitions, Robert Axelrod analyzes the behavior of six basic groups that made up the Democratic presidential coalition: the poor, blacks (and other nonwhites), union members (and members of their families), Catholics (including other non-Protestants), southerners (including those in Border States), and residents of the 12 largest metropolitan areas.[26] John R. Petrocik's more comprehensive study identifies 15 party coalition groups and classifies 7 of them as predominantly Democratic: blacks, lower-status native southerners, middle- and upper-status southerners, Jews, Polish and Irish Catholics, union members, and lower-status Border State whites.[27] Our own analysis focuses on race, region, trade union membership, social class, and religion.[28]

The contribution that a social group can make to a party's total coalition depends upon three factors: the relative size of the group in the total electorate, its level of turnout compared with the electorate as a whole, and its relative loyalty to the party.[29] The larger a social group, the greater its contribution can be.

Blacks, for example, make up about 11 percent of the electorate, and the white working class makes up 38 percent. Thus, the contribution that blacks can make to a political party is limited compared to the potential contribution of working-class whites. The electoral power of blacks is diminished further by their relatively low turnout. However, because blacks vote overwhelmingly Democratic, their contribution to the party can be greater than their size would indicate. And their contribution will grow to the extent that whites desert the Democratic party.

Let us begin by examining racial differences, which we can trace back to 1944 by using the National Opinion Research Center study for that year.[30] Figure 5-1 shows the percentage of whites and blacks among major party voters who voted Democratic for president in each presidential election from 1944 through 1984. Although most blacks voted Democratic between 1944 and 1960, a substantial minority voted Republican. The political mobilization of blacks caused by the civil rights movement and the candidacy of Barry M. Goldwater ended this Republican voting, and the residual loyalties of older blacks were discarded between 1962 and 1964.[31]

While the Democrats made substantial gains among blacks, they lost ground among whites. Between 1944 and 1964, the Democrats gained a majority of the white vote in three of six elections, but from 1968 on they have never won a majority from white voters. However, the Democrats

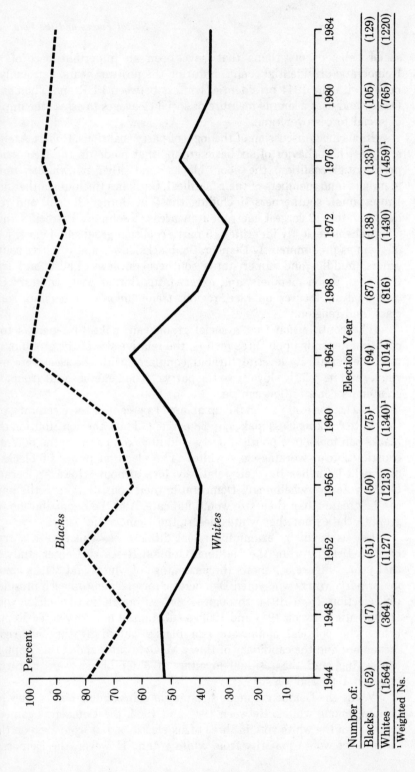

Figure 5-1 Major Party Voters Who Voted Democratic for President, by Race, 1944-1984 (in percentages)

	1944	1948	1952	1956	1960	1964	1968	1972	1976	1980	1984
Number of:											
Blacks	(52)	(17)	(51)	(50)	(75)[1]	(94)	(87)	(138)	(133)[1]	(105)	(129)
Whites	(1564)	(364)	(1127)	(1213)	(1340)[1]	(1014)	(816)	(1430)	(1459)[1]	(765)	(1220)

[1] Weighted Ns.

can win with just under half of the white vote, as the 1960 and 1976 elections demonstrate.

The gap between the two trend lines in Figure 5-1 illustrates the overall difference between white and black voting. Table 5-2 shows levels of "racial voting" during all 11 elections and also presents four other measures of social cleavage.[32] Between 1944 and 1960, differences in voting by blacks and whites ranged from a low of 12 percentage points to a high of 40. Although black support for the Democrats jumped in 1964, racial voting was held to 36 points because a substantial majority of whites voted Democratic. But racial differences jumped to 56 points in 1968, and never fell back to the levels of the 1944 to 1960 period.

Not only did black loyalty to the Democratic party increase sharply after 1960, but black turnout rose dramatically between 1960 and 1968 because southern blacks (about half the black population during this period) were enfranchised. Moreover, the relative size of the black population grew somewhat during the postwar years. Between 1960 and 1980 white turnout dropped about 10 percentage points, and it remained low in 1984. As a result of these changes, blacks have become a much larger component of the Democratic presidential coalition.

Between 1948 and 1960, blacks never made up more than 1 Democratic vote out of 12.[33] In 1964, however, Lyndon B. Johnson received about 1 in 7 of his votes from black voters, and blacks contributed a fifth of the Democratic totals in 1968 and 1972. In 1976, with Democratic gains among whites, the black total fell to just over 1 in 7. In 1980, according to our analysis of the SRC-CPS survey, Carter received about 1 in 4 of his total vote from blacks. As we saw, about 1 Mondale voter in 5 was black.[34]

Region

The desertion of the Democratic party by white southerners is among the most dramatic changes in postwar American politics. But the official voting returns are of limited utility in examining race-related differences in regional voting patterns because election results are not tabulated by race. Survey data allow us to document the dramatic shift in the voting behavior of southern whites.

As the data in Figure 5-2 reveal, white southerners were just a bit more Democratic than whites outside the South in the 1952 and 1956 Eisenhower contests and in the 1960 Kennedy-Nixon contest.[35] But in the next three presidential elections, regional differences were reversed, with white southerners voting Republican more often than whites outside the South. In 1976 and 1980, white southerners and whites outside the South voted very much alike. In 1984, as we saw, white southerners were less likely to vote for Mondale than whites in any other region. According to our analysis, Mondale received only 29 percent of the white southern vote; outside the South, he received 38 percent.

Table 5-2 Relationship of Social Characteristics to Presidential Voting, 1944-1984[1]

	Election Year										
	1944	1948	1952	1956	1960	1964	1968	1972	1976	1980	1984
Racial voting[2]	27	12	40	25	23	36	56	57	48	56	54
Regional voting[3]											
Among whites	—	—	12	17	6	−11	−4	−13	1	1	−9
Among entire electorate (SRC surveys)	—	—	9	15	4	−5	6	−3	7	3	3
Among entire electorate (official election results)	23	14	8	8	3	−13	−3	−11	5	2	−5
Union voting[4]											
Among whites	20	37	18	15	21	23	13	11	18	15	20
Among entire electorate	20	37	20	17	19	22	13	10	17	16	19
Class voting[5]											
Among whites	19	44	20	8	12	19	10	2	17	9	8
Among entire electorate	20	44	22	11	13	20	15	4	21	15	12
Religious voting[6]											
Among whites	25	21	18	10	48	21	30	13	15	10	16
Among entire electorate	24	19	15	10	46	16	21	8	11	3	9

[1] All calculations based upon major party voters.
[2] Percentage of blacks who voted Democratic minus the percentage of whites who voted Democratic.
[3] Percentage of southerners who voted Democratic minus the percentage of voters outside the South who voted Democratic.
[4] Percentage of members of union households who voted Democratic minus the percentage of members of households with no union members who voted Democratic.
[5] Percentage of working class that voted Democratic minus the percentage of middle class that voted Democratic.
[6] Percentage of Catholics who voted Democratic minus the percentage of Protestants who voted Democratic.

Figure 5-2 White Major Party Voters Who Voted Democratic for President, by Region, 1952-1984 (in percentages)

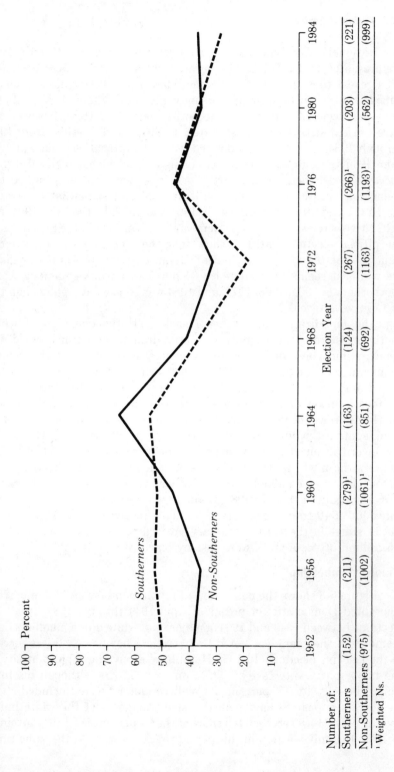

Number of:									
Southerners	(152)	(211)	(279)[1]	(163)	(124)	(267)	(266)[1]	(203)	(221)
Non-Southerners (975)	(1002)	(1061)[1]	(851)	(692)	(1163)	(1193)[1]	(562)	(999)

[1] Weighted Ns.

Regional differences in voting among whites from 1952 through 1984 are presented in Table 5-2. The negative signs for 1964, 1968, 1972, and 1984 reveal that the Democratic candidate fared better among whites outside the South than he did among white southerners. Table 5-2 also presents "regional voting" for the entire electorate. Here, however, we have presented two sets of estimates: 1) SRC survey results from 1952 through 1984, and 2) results derived using the official election statistics from 1944 through 1984. Both sets of figures show that regional differences have declined, but the SRC surveys somewhat overestimated the Democratic advantage in the South in 1956 and somewhat underestimated the Republican advantage in 1964 and 1972. In 1968 and 1984, the SRC surveys registered a slight Democratic advantage in the South, while the official election statistics show that the Democrats actually fared somewhat better outside the South.[36] Because most voters in both regions are white, it seems likely that the Republican advantage among white southerners in 1964, 1968, 1972, and 1984 was somewhat greater than the SRC surveys reveal.

The mobilization of southern blacks and the defection of white southerners from the Democratic party dramatically transformed the demographic composition of the Democratic coalition in the South. Democratic presidential candidates between 1952 and 1960 never received more than 1 vote out of 15 from black voters. In 1964 nearly 3 out of 10 of Johnson's southern votes came from blacks, and in 1968 Hubert H. Humphrey received nearly as many votes from southern blacks as from southern whites. In 1972, according to these data, George S. McGovern received more of his total votes from southern blacks than from southern whites. In 1976 blacks provided Carter with his margin of victory. He received about 1 of his southern votes out of 3 from blacks in 1976 and again in 1980. In 1984 Mondale received about 4 of his southern votes out of 10 from black voters. Mondale received 8.7 million votes in the 11 states of the old Confederacy. According to our estimates, about 3.5 million of these votes were cast by blacks.[37]

Union Membership

Figure 5-3 shows the percentage of union members and nonmembers who voted Democratic for president from 1944 through 1984. In all six elections between 1944 and 1964, a majority of white union members (and members of their families) voted Democratic. They have had less success in the last five elections. In 1968 Humphrey received a slight majority of the major party vote cast by white union members, although his total would be cut to 43 percent if Wallace voters were included. The Democrats appear to have gained a slight majority of the white union vote in 1984. However, they fell short of the 61 percent level they attained in 1976, the only election in this period that they won. At the same time,

Figure 5-3 White Major Party Voters Who Voted Democratic for President, 1944-1984 (in percentages)

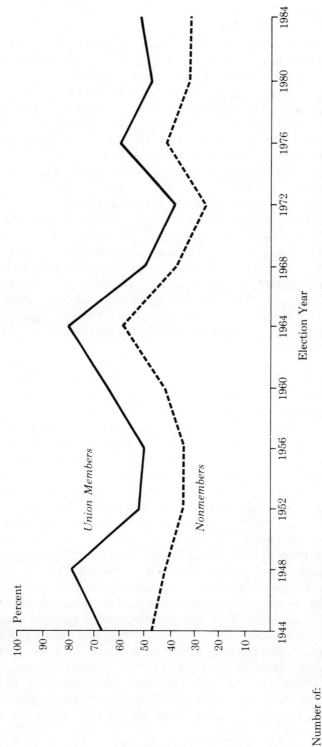

Election Year

Number of:

	1944	1948	1952	1956	1960	1964	1968	1972	1976	1980	1984
Union Members[1]	(322)	(94)	(305)	(334)	(342)[3]	(259)	(197)	(366)	(347)[3]	(193)	(278)
Nonmembers[2]	(1215)	(266)	(815)	(877)	(979)[3]	(755)	(617)	(1049)	(1099)[3]	(569)	(941)

[1] Union members or in household with union member.
[2] Not a union member and not in household with union member.
[3] Weighted Ns.

however, the Republicans gained an absolute majority of the union vote in only one of the last five elections, during Nixon's 1972 landslide.

Differences in the voting of union members and nonmembers rose in 1984 *(Table 5-2)*, reflecting Mondale's improved showing among union members, but it was still somewhat below the average (mean) level between 1944 and 1964. We have also reported "union voting" for the entire electorate, but, because blacks are about as likely to live in union households as whites are, including blacks has little effect on our results.

The percentage of the total electorate composed of white union members and their families has declined somewhat during the postwar years, and their turnout has declined at the same rate as that of non-union whites. These changes have not been as dramatic as the decline in union support for Democratic presidential candidates. All the above factors, as well as increased turnout among blacks, have reduced the total contribution of white trade unionists to the Democratic presidential coalition. Through 1960, a third of the total Democratic vote came from white trade union members. In the last six elections, only about one Democratic vote in four came from white trade unionists. Despite these changes, unions remain part of the Democratic presidential coalition.

Social Class

The broad cleavage between the political behavior of manually employed workers (and their dependents) and nonmanually employed workers (and their dependents) is especially valuable for comparative studies of voting behavior.[38] In every presidential election since 1936, the working class has voted more Democratic than the middle class. But, as Figure 5-4 shows, the percentage of working-class whites voting Democratic has varied considerably from election to election. It fell to its lowest level in 1972. Carter regained a majority of the white working-class vote in 1976, but he lost it four years later. In 1984, as in 1980, only about two working-class major party voters out of five supported the Democratic presidential candidate.

Although levels of "class voting" have varied since 1944, they appear to be following a downward trend, as Table 5-2 reveals. In 1984 working-class whites were only 8 points more Democratic than middle-class whites. Blacks are disproportionately working class, and, as we have seen, they vote overwhelmingly Democratic. In four of the last five elections, including blacks substantially raises class voting, and the overall trend toward declining class voting is dampened substantially if we study the entire electorate. However, black workers voted Democratic because they were black. Among blacks, class differences were negligible, because blacks in the middle class also voted Democratic. It seems reasonable, therefore, to focus on changing levels of class voting among the white electorate.

Figure 5-4 White Major Party Voters Who Voted Democratic for President, by Social Class, 1944-1984 (in percentages)

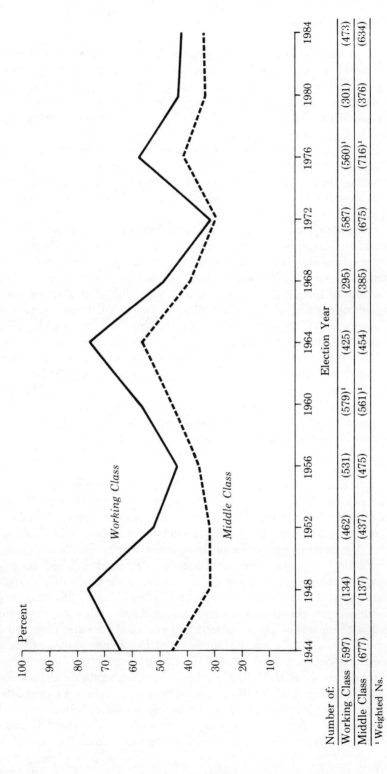

Number of:	1944	1948	1952	1956	1960	1964	1968	1972	1976	1980	1984
Working Class	(597)	(134)	(462)	(531)	(579)[1]	(425)	(295)	(587)	(560)[1]	(301)	(473)
Middle Class	(677)	(137)	(437)	(475)	(561)[1]	(454)	(385)	(675)	(716)[1]	(376)	(634)

[1] Weighted Ns.

During the postwar years, the proportion of the electorate made up of working-class whites has remained relatively constant, while the proportion of middle-class whites has grown. The percentage of whites in the agricultural sector has declined dramatically. After 1960 turnout fell among whites of both social classes, but it fell more among the working class. As we saw in Chapter 4, only 61 percent of working-class whites voted in 1984 compared with 80 percent of the middle-class whites. Declining turnout and defections from the Democrats among the white working class, along with increased turnout by blacks, have reduced the total contribution of working-class whites to the Democratic presidential coalition.

In 1948 and 1952, about half the total Democratic vote came from working-class whites, and between 1956 and 1964 more than 4 Democratic votes out of 10 came from this social group. In 1968 the white working-class contribution fell to 35 percent, and then to only 32 percent in 1972. In 1976, with the rise of class voting, the white working class provided 39 percent of Carter's total vote, but in 1980 just over a third of Carter's total support came from working-class whites. In 1984, 36 percent of the total Mondale vote came from working-class whites. The middle-class contribution to the Democratic presidential coalition was fewer than 3 votes in 10 in 1948 and 1952, just under one-third in 1956, stabilizing at just over one-third in the next five elections. In 1980, 33 percent of Carter's total vote came from middle-class whites. In 1984, 39 percent of the total Mondale vote came from middle-class whites, a somewhat larger share than from the white working class.

Religion

Voting differences among religious groups also have declined during the postwar years. As Figure 5-5 reveals, in every election since 1944, Jews have been more likely to vote Democratic than Catholics, and Catholics have been more likely to vote Democratic than Protestants.

A substantial majority of Jews voted Democratic in every election from 1944 through 1976, although in 1980 Carter failed to gain an absolute majority of the Jewish vote. Among the three religious groups, Jews were the only one to vote more Democratic in 1984 than in 1980. Even so, the proportion of Jews voting Democratic was substantially below the levels of Democratic voting recorded between 1944 and 1968.

A majority of white Catholics voted Democratic in six of the seven elections between 1944 and 1968. The percentage of Catholics voting Democratic peaked in 1960, when the Democrats fielded a Roman Catholic candidate, but it was also very high in Johnson's landslide four years later. Since then, Democratic voting among Catholics has declined precipitously. In 1968 a majority of white Catholics voted Democratic, although Humphrey's total would be reduced from 60 percent to 55

Figure 5-5 White Major Party Voters Who Voted Democratic for President, by Religion, 1944-1984 (in percentages)

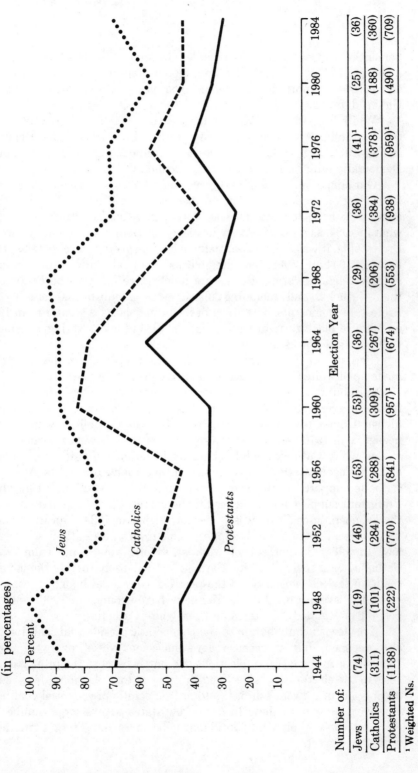

Number of:	1944	1948	1952	1956	1960	1964	1968	1972	1976	1980	1984
Jews	(74)	(19)	(46)	(53)	(53)[1]	(36)	(29)	(36)	(41)[1]	(25)	(36)
Catholics	(311)	(101)	(284)	(288)	(309)[1]	(267)	(206)	(384)	(378)[1]	(188)	(360)
Protestants	(1138)	(222)	(770)	(841)	(957)[1]	(674)	(553)	(938)	(959)[1]	(490)	(709)

[1] Weighted Ns.

percent if Wallace voters were included. In three of the last four elections, a majority of white Catholics have voted Republican. The erosion of Democratic support during the postwar years is also documented by Gallup data.

White Protestants have been far less volatile in their voting behavior than Catholics. An absolute majority of white Protestants voted Republican in 10 of the 11 elections we have studied, and a majority voted Democratic only in Johnson's 1964 landslide.

Our simple measure of "religious voting" shows considerable change from election to election, but, as the results in Table 5-2 show, there appears to be a downward trend. Although religious voting rose somewhat in 1984, as a result of very low levels of Democratic voting by white Protestants, it was still substantially below the average level for the years between 1944 and 1968. Including blacks in our calculations substantially reduces religious voting. Blacks are much more likely to be Protestant than Catholic, and including blacks adds a substantial number of Protestant Democrats. The effect of including blacks is greater from 1964 on because black turnout was higher. In 1984 religious voting is reduced to 9 points if blacks are included.

Throughout the postwar years, the total proportion of the electorate made up of white Catholics has remained constant, but between 1960 and 1980 turnout declined faster among Catholics than among white Protestants. In every election between 1948 and 1972, white Catholics had higher turnout than white Protestants, but the Catholic advantage was negligible in 1976 and was erased in 1980. In 1984, however, turnout rose among white Catholics, while changing little among white Protestants, and, once again, Catholics had higher turnout than Protestants. Although Catholic support for the Democrats remained constant in 1984, white Protestant support fell. As a result, the overall Catholic contribution to the Democratic coalition was somewhat higher in 1984 than in 1980. In 1980, only a fifth of Carter's support came from white Catholics, a record low. In 1984, 28 percent of Mondale's total vote came from white Catholics. The overall white Catholic contribution to the Democratic coalition in 1984 was close to the postwar average, although it was well below the level attained in the Kennedy-Nixon contest of 1960, when 37 percent of Kennedy's vote came from white Catholics.

The Jewish contribution to the Democratic presidential coalition has also declined, partly because Jews have not voted overwhelmingly Democratic in the last four elections and partly because the proportion of Jews in the electorate has declined. In the last four elections, Jews made up only about a twentieth of the total Democratic presidential coalition. However, since most Jews live in a few states with a large number of electoral votes, their contribution may be more important than these numbers suggest.

Figure 5-6 White Major Party Voters Who Voted Democratic for President, by Social Class and Religion, 1944-1984 (in percentages)

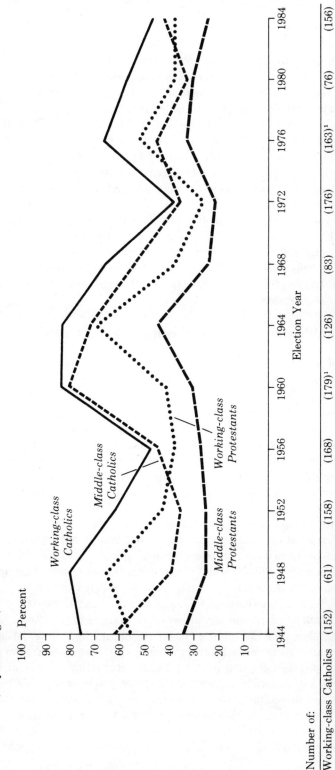

Number of:	1944	1948	1952	1956	1960	1964	1968	1972	1976	1980	1984
Working-class Catholics	(152)	(61)	(158)	(168)	(179)[1]	(126)	(83)	(176)	(163)[1]	(76)	(156)
Middle-class Catholics	(130)	(28)	(94)	(96)	(109)[1]	(121)	(96)	(176)	(179)[1]	(96)	(177)
Working-class Protestants	(405)	(59)	(279)	(329)	(374)[1]	(280)	(198)	(383)	(367)[1]	(197)	(268)
Middle-class Protestants	(479)	(91)	(302)	(336)	(405)[1]	(287)	(254)	(430)	(457)[1]	(226)	(359)

[1] Weighted Ns.

As the data in Figure 5-6 reveal, the effects of social class and religion are cumulative. In every election from 1944 through 1984, working-class Catholics have been more likely to vote Democratic than any other class-religious combination. In all 11 elections, white middle-class Protestants have been the least likely to vote Democratic. Of all the groups we studied, they show the most constancy in their vote. An absolute majority voted Republican in all 11 elections.

The relative importance of social class and religion can be assessed by comparing the voting behavior of middle-class Catholics with that of working-class Protestants. Religion was more important than class in predicting voting choices in 1944, 1956, 1960 (by a great margin), 1968, 1972, and 1984. Social class was more important than religion in 1948 (by a great margin), 1952, 1976, and 1980. And class and religion were equally important in 1964. However, during the last five elections all these trend lines have converged, suggesting that both class and religion have declined in importance.

Why the New Deal Coalition Broke Down

Except for race, all of the social factors we have examined—region, union membership, social class, and religion—have declined in importance as vote predictors during the postwar years. The decline in regional differences directly parallels the increase in racial differences. As the national Democratic party strengthened its appeals to blacks during the 1960s, party leaders endorsed policies opposed by southern whites. Several studies document the importance of issue preferences in contributing to a breakdown of Democratic support by white southerners.[39] The migration of northern whites to the South also reduced regional differences slightly.

To some extent, the Democratic party's appeal to blacks may have weakened its hold on white groups that traditionally supported it. But the erosion of Democratic support among trade union members, the working class, and Catholics results from other factors as well. During the postwar years, these groups have changed. Although trade union members do not hold high-paying professional and managerial jobs, they have gained substantial economic advantages. Differences in income between the working class and the middle class have diminished. And Catholics, who often came from more recent immigrant groups than Protestants, have grown increasingly middle class as the proportion of second- and third-generation Americans grew. During the 1950s and 1960s, white Catholics were more likely to be working class than white Protestants. This is no longer true. In 1976, 1980, and 1984 they were as likely to be middle class as white Protestants.

Not only have these groups changed economically and socially, but also the historical conditions that led union members, the working class, and Catholics to become Democrats have receded further into the past. While the transmission of partisan loyalties from one generation to another gives historically based coalitions some staying power, the success of family in transmitting partisan loyalties has declined as party identification has weakened.[40] Moreover, the total proportion of the electorate that directly experienced the politics of the Roosevelt years has progressively declined due to generational replacement. By 1984 only about one voter in four had entered the electorate before or during World War II. Among whites born before 1924, those who entered the electorate before or during the war, class voting was fairly high, some 19 points; it was only 2 points among whites born after 1954.[41] New policy issues, sometimes unrelated to the political conflicts of the New Deal era, have tended to erode Democratic support among traditional Democratic groups. Of all these policies, race-related issues have been the most important in weakening the New Deal coalition.[42]

Our study of changing social forces suggests that the Democrats are likely to have serious problems in future elections. While blacks vote solidly Democratic, they are a relatively small group with lower than average turnout. Blacks provide a weak base upon which to build a national coalition. A coalition of minorities needs the support of many minorities, and it needs high levels of support from them. During the 11 elections between 1944 and 1984, the Democrats have never won without *at least* three-fifths of the vote of white trade union members and *at least* two-thirds of the vote of white working-class Catholics. And they have never won without an absolute majority of both the white working class and of white Catholics. Moreover, the Democrats have never won an election in which blacks made up more than 15 percent of their coalition. Our calculations suggest that it would be difficult for the Democrats to win a two-candidate election in which more than a sixth of their total vote came from blacks.

Can the erosion of Democratic support among southerners, union members, the working class, and Catholics be reversed? Southern whites are no longer part of the Democratic presidential coalition. Even when the Democrats fielded a southerner against an unelected Republican incumbent in 1976, they failed to gain a majority among white southerners. On the other hand, the Democrats still do relatively better among trade unionists, the working class, and Catholics, demonstrating that the New Deal coalition is not totally defunct. After Carter's 1976 victory, political scientists saw signs of renewed vitality for the New Deal coalition, and some analysts saw signs of vitality after the 1982 midterm elections. But given the social changes that have occurred among the groups making up the New Deal coalition and the weak feelings of party identification that contribute to changes in voting preferences, it seems highly unlikely that the New Deal coalition will ever be restored in its previous form.

Notes

1. The basic social categories used in the chapter are the same we used in Chapter 4. The variables are described in the notes to that chapter.
2. We rely in this and all subsequent chapters (as well as in Table 2-1 above) on the way people said they voted. If we presented results only for validated voters, our analysis would not be comparable with the vast majority of previous analyses of the SRC data, and we would not be able to compare our results with most prior SRC surveys. In any event, the overall distribution of the presidential vote is virtually identical regardless of whether one analyzes all respondents who said they voted or the subset of respondents who were classified as voters by the vote validation study. The Mondale share of the votes is reduced by .3 percentage points when only validated voters are studied. Differences are slightly greater in the distribution of the congressional vote, but even here they are small. The total Democratic share of the House vote is reduced 1.6 percentage points when the analysis is restricted to validated voters.
3. The basic results of the four major exit polls are presented in "Opinion Roundup: The Exit Poll Results; Patterns in Group Voting," *Public Opinion* 7 (December/January 1985): 28-33. Unless otherwise indicated our reports about exit poll results are based upon this source.

   Exit polls have three main advantages. First, they are far less expensive to conduct than the surveys conducted by the University of Michigan Survey Research Center. Second, partly as a result of their lower cost, the networks can sample a large number of people. Third, because persons are questioned shortly after they have left the voting area, the vast majority will have actually voted for president. For our purposes here, the large size of the surveys is a major asset. The *New York Times*/CBS News poll sampled 8,671 voters; the NBC News survey sampled 11,671; ABC News sampled 11,023; and the *Los Angeles Times* national survey sampled 7,310 voters.

   Despite their large size, these surveys have some major disadvantages. First, the questionnaires used must be brief. Second, it is difficult to supervise the field work and to ensure that interviewers are using the proper procedures in selecting respondents. Last, a growing number of voters, especially in the West, are refusing to participate in exit polls. In California about two voters out of five refused to participate, and, in the state of Washington, legislation was passed making it difficult to interview voters close to the polling stations. The Washington State law was ruled unconstitutional by a federal district judge in December 1985. See "Polling at Voting Places Upheld by Federal Judge," *New York Times,* Dec. 19, 1985, A26.

4. For the Gallup results, see *The Gallup Report,* No. 230, November 1984, 7-9. All our reports about the Gallup poll are based upon this source.

   The Gallup polls are based upon in-person interviews conducted in the respondents' homes. Although Gallup surveys generally do not ask as many politically relevant questions as the Michigan SRC-CPS surveys, they provide a valuable source of information about change between 1952 and 1984. The final Gallup poll is based upon a survey of 3,456 respondents conducted on the weekend before the election. The actual analysis is based upon 1,985 respondents designated as "likely voters" on the basis of their responses to questions about their political interest, registration status, and previous voting behavior.

5. This analysis is based both upon our analysis of the SRC-CPS survey, and upon our recalculations of results presented from the *New York Times*/CBS News exit poll as presented in "Portrait of the Electorate," *New York Times,* Nov. 8, 1984, A19.

6. Ibid.

7. Ibid.

8. We have reported upon differences among blacks only where we could compare our results with those of one of the exit polls.

9. The *New York Times*/CBS News exit poll is based upon about 260 Hispanics.

10. The SRC-CPS surveys classify being Hispanic as a form of group identification, and it is a category that overlaps with race. The *New York Times*/CBS News survey apparently treats Hispanics as a separate category. According to the U.S. Bureau of the Census, persons of Spanish origin may be of any race.

11. This brief discussion cannot do justice to the growing research on women in politics. For two excellent discussions, see Sandra Baxter and Marjorie Lansing, *Women and Politics: The Visible Majority,* rev. ed. (Ann Arbor: University of Michigan Press, 1983); and Virginia Sapiro, *The Political Integration of Women: Roles, Socialization, and Politics* (Urbana: University of Illinois Press, 1983).

12. In the 1984 SRC-CPS preelection survey, 66 percent of the men interviewed approved of "the way Ronald Reagan is handling his job as president," and 61 percent of the women did. These differences, however, resulted mainly from the disproportionate number of black females in the sample. Among whites, sex differences were negligible. Sixty-nine percent of the men and 67 percent of the women approved of Reagan.

13. See Bella Abzug, with Mim Kelber, *Gender Gap* (Boston: Houghton-Mifflin, 1984); and Eleanor Smeal, *Why and How Women Will Elect the Next President* (New York: Harper & Row, 1984).

14. We make this point in Paul R. Abramson, John H. Aldrich, and David W. Rohde, *Change and Continuity in the 1980 Elections,* rev. ed. (Washington, D.C.: CQ Press, 1983), 290.

15. *New York Times,* "Portrait of the Electorate."

16. Everett Carll Ladd, "On Mandates, Realignments, and the 1984 Presidential Election," *Political Science Quarterly* 100 (Spring 1985): 1-25.

17. The SRC-CPS study reports six types of marital status: married and living with spouse, never married, divorced, separated, widowed, and partners who are not married. In this paragraph we compare the first two of these groups.

18. These differences are not just the result of women who have never been married being younger than those who are currently married. In the first place, as we report below, age was very weakly related to voting choices. Second, even when we compare married and never married women below the age of 30, those who were never married were more likely to vote for Mondale.
19. Maureen Dowd, "Singles Show Less Support for Reagan," *New York Times,* Dec. 16, 1984, 40.
20. Given the small number of cases, we must treat this finding with considerable caution. Moreover, the SRC surveys may not yield a representative sample of Americans below the age of 25. The SRC does not sample Americans living in college dormitories, prisons, and those serving in the military, all institutions populated disproportionately by young adults.
21. *New York Times,* "Portrait of the Electorate."
22. Ibid.
23. Adam Clymer, "Religion and Politics Mix Poorly for the Democrats," *New York Times,* Nov. 25, 1984, E2.
24. Ibid.
25. Dody Tsiantar, "Study Finds Jewish Vote Less Firm for Democrats," *Washington Post,* Nov. 14, 1984, A3.
26. Robert Axelrod, "Where the Votes Come From: An Analysis of Electoral Coalitions, 1952-1968," *American Political Science Review* 66 (March 1972): 11-20.
27. John R. Petrocik, *Party Coalitions: Realignment and the Decline of the New Deal Party System* (Chicago: University of Chicago Press, 1981).
28. For a discussion of the importance of working-class whites to the Democratic presidential coalition, see Paul R. Abramson, *Generational Change in American Politics* (Lexington, Mass.: D. C. Heath & Co., 1975).
29. For an insightful discussion of the factors that determine the total contribution a social group can make to a party's presidential coalition, see Robert Axelrod, "Where the Votes Come From." For Axelrod's analysis of the 1984 SRC-CPS survey, see Robert Axelrod, "Presidential Electoral Coalitions in 1984," *American Political Science Review* 80 (March 1986): 281-84.
30. The NORC survey, based upon 2,564 civilians, used a quota sample that does not follow the probability procedures employed by the University of Michigan Survey Research Center. Following quota sampling procedures common at the time, southern blacks were not sampled. Because the NORC survey overrepresented upper income and occupational groups, it cannot be used to estimate the contribution of social groups to the Democratic and Republican presidential coalitions.
31. Abramson, *Generational Change,* 65-68.
32. The results in Table 5-2 are based upon major party voters. In 1968 about 1 voter out of 7 supported George C. Wallace, the American Independent party candidate, and in 1980 about 1 voter in 15 supported the independent candidacy of John B. Anderson. Including Wallace voters in 1968 and Anderson voters in 1980 affects these measures somewhat. For a report on the way including these voters affects the scores, see Abramson, Aldrich, and Rohde, *Change and Continuity in the 1980 Elections,* rev. ed., 102-115.

33. As hote 30 explains, we cannot use the 1944 NORC survey to estimate the contribution of social groups to a party's electoral coalition.
34. Because blacks are somewhat more likely to overreport voting than whites, we examined the racial composition of the Democratic presidential coalition using the 1964, 1976, 1980, and 1984 vote validation studies. If we calculate the composition of the Democratic coalition based only upon respondents who actually voted, we find that the black contribution drops from 13 to 11 percent in 1964, from 15 to 13 percent in 1976, from 26 to 24 percent in 1980, and from 20 to 17 percent in 1984.
35. As we explained in Chapter 4, we consider the South to include the 11 states of the old Confederacy. Because we could not use our definition of the South with either the 1944 NORC survey or the 1948 University of Michigan Survey Research Center survey, we have not included these years in our analysis of regional differences among the white electorate.
36. The main source of error arises from the relatively small number of southern voters upon which these estimates are based. In 1984, for example, there were only 302 southern voters sampled, among whom 44.0 percent said they voted for Mondale. In fact, the official election returns show that only 37.2 percent of the southern vote went for Mondale. The survey was far closer in estimating the vote outside the South. Among the 1,087 nonsouthern voters, 40.7 percent said they voted for Mondale. Mondale's actual share outside the South was 41.7 percent.
37. We base this estimate upon both the 1984 SRC-CPS survey and the *New York Times*/CBS News exit poll, which used a slightly broader definition of the South. The SRC-CPS survey reports only 133 Mondale voters in the South, among whom 46 percent were black. But our recalculation of the exit poll result suggests that about 34 percent of Mondale's southern vote was black. The latter calculation, however, includes some Border States.
38. See Robert R. Alford, *Party and Society: The Anglo-American Democracies* (Chicago: Rand McNally & Co., 1963); Ronald Inglehart, *The Silent Revolution: Changing Values and Political Styles Among Western Publics* (Princeton, N.J.: Princeton University Press, 1977); Seymour Martin Lipset, *Political Man: The Social Bases of Politics,* expanded edition (Baltimore: Johns Hopkins University Press, 1981); and Ronald Inglehart, "Changing Paradigms in Comparative Political Behavior," in *Political Science: The State of the Discipline,* ed. Ada W. Finifter (Washington, D.C.: American Political Science Association, 1983): 429-69.
39. Paul Allen Beck, "Partisan Dealignment in the Postwar South," *American Political Science Review* 71 (June 1977): 477-96; and Bruce A. Campbell, "Realignment, Party Decomposition, and Issue Voting," in *Realignment in American Politics: Toward a Theory,* ed. Bruce A. Campbell and Richard J. Trilling (Austin: University of Texas Press, 1980), 82-109. For an alternative view, see Raymond E. Wolfinger, "Dealignment, Realignment, and Mandates in the 1984 Election," in *The American Elections of 1984,* ed. Austin Ranney (Durham, N.C.: Duke University Press, 1985), 287-90.
40. For evidence on this point, see Paul R. Abramson, *Political Attitudes in America: Formation and Change* (San Francisco: W. H. Freeman, 1983), 94-96.

41. For evidence that higher levels of class voting among the prewar electorate probably result from differences between the formative socialization experiences of younger and older Americans, see Abramson *Generational Change,* 29-49.
42. See Petrocik, *Party Coalitions,* 111-53; see also Edward G. Carmines and James A. Stimson, "The Racial Reorientation of American Politics," in *The Electorate Reconsidered,* ed. John C. Pierce and John L. Sullivan (Beverly Hills, Calif.: Sage Publications, 1980), 199-218.

Chapter 6

Issues, Candidates, and Voter Choice

In Chapter 5, we pointed out that social forces were weakly related to voter choice in 1984. Except for the sharp division between blacks and whites, the social and demographic groups that made up the Democratic presidential coalition largely deserted Walter F. Mondale. Only a handful of social groups among whites gave him a majority of their vote, and, except for Jews, those groups gave him only a slight majority.

The erosion of the Democratic presidential coalition may be part of a long-term breakup of the New Deal coalition. But this decline in the social divisions that defined the Democratic New Deal coalition does not in itself demonstrate that the Republicans will become the majority party. It certainly does not show that the Republicans can translate their hold of the presidency into control of Congress or the nation's state houses. It is generally agreed that new political alignments are forged when a party captures the majority position on newly emerging issues. In our analysis of the 1980 election, we found little evidence that the election was an endorsement of Ronald Reagan's policy proposals. By 1984, however, the electorate was in a far better position to judge those policies. Voters no longer needed to rely on what Reagan said he would do; they could see what changes he had implemented and could judge their results.

The 1984 election provided voters a chance to reject Reagan and his policies. The voters did not avail themselves of this opportunity, but this does not mean that they endorsed his specific programs. Nor does it indicate that the electorate supported the very conservative policy proposals embraced by the Republican party at the convention in Dallas.

The 1984 election also provided an opportunity to endorse Democratic party principles. Mondale represented much of the liberal agenda of the Democratic party, forged in the New Deal, extending through the Great Society programs of Lyndon B. Johnson in the mid-1960s, and culminating in the policies the Democrats endorsed at their convention in San Francisco. While the outcome in 1984 could indicate that voters rejected the Democratic platform in favor of the Republicans' platform, it could simply demonstrate support for a popular incumbent who had been seen as a successful president.

We viewed the 1980 election largely as a referendum on Jimmy Carter's performance as president, a referendum that Carter lost decisively. To what extent was the 1984 election a referendum that endorsed Reagan's performance, and to what extent did it result from conservative issue preferences among the electorate? We will address these questions in this chapter and the next.

Retrospective and Prospective Evaluations

Public policy concerns enter into the voting decision in two very different ways. One is in answer to two questions: "How has the incumbent president done on policy?" and "How likely is it that his opponent would be any better?" Voting based on this form of policy appraisal is called "retrospective" voting and will be analyzed in Chapter 7. The second form of policy-based reasoning and behavior is close to the standard view of "good citizenship" found in civics courses. It involves an examination of the policy platforms advanced by the two candidates and an assessment of which of these policy promises is more similar to what the individual believes the government ought to be doing. Policy voting, therefore, involves comparing the two sets of promises and voting for that set most like the voter's own beliefs. Voting based on these kinds of decisions may be referred to as "prospective voting," for it involves an examination of the promises of the two candidates about future actions. In this chapter, we will examine prospective evaluations of the two candidates and how these evaluations relate to voter choice.

The 1980 and 1984 elections show some remarkable similarities in terms of prospective policy evaluations and voting. Perhaps the most important similarity is the perception of where the Democratic and Republican candidates stood on issues. In both elections, the public saw clear differences between the major party candidates. In both elections, the public saw Reagan as a conservative, and most citizens saw Reagan as more conservative than they saw themselves. And in both elections, the public saw the Democratic candidate as a liberal, and most citizens saw the Democrat as more liberal than they saw themselves. As a result, people perceived a clear choice based on their understanding of the candidates' policy positions. The candidates presented, in the 1964 campaign slogan of Republican nominee Barry M. Goldwater, "a choice and not an echo." The *average* citizen, therefore, faced a difficult choice. For many, Mondale and Carter were seen to be as far to the left as Reagan was to the right. On balance, the net effect of prospective issues was to give neither party a clear advantage.

There were also important differences between the two elections. First, the mixture of just what issues concerned the public was quite different. Second, and equally important, the contexts for the two elections were very different and, as a result, candidate strategies on issues were quite different. In 1980 Reagan ran on a very clearly defined program, centered on economic issues and the size and scope of governmental activity.[1] The central planks of his campaign platform were substantial cuts in income taxes, massive reductions in government spending for domestic programs, and increased spending for defense. In 1984 Mondale also held a clear set of programs. He called for expansion of many of the domestic programs that Reagan had successfully reduced, for tax increases to help balance the looming budget deficits, and for slower growth in defense expenditures.

The more important difference, however, was in the reaction of the incumbent president. In 1980 Carter was perceived as a weak and ineffective incumbent. A crucial part of his campaign was to challenge the Reagan platform, saying in effect, "Whatever you might think of me, listen to what Reagan is saying he'll do. He'll only make things worse." In 1984 Reagan faced a much more receptive audience that, in general, thought he had been a successful president. As we saw in Chapter 2, he enjoyed the luxury of a choice of how to focus his campaign. Should he advance a new set of programs, earning a new mandate from the public to pressure Congress to pass these programs, or should he simply run on the argument that he had done a good job already and deserved to be returned to office?

Reagan chose the latter, and the 1984 campaign focused less on prospective issues than the 1980 campaign. Of course, this does not mean that the voters responded, in either election, to the campaign as conducted by the candidates. In 1980, for example, the vote was more clearly based on retrospective issues, on the negative views of Carter's incumbency. In short, Carter's campaign strategy did not work. In 1984, as we will see, voters responded to both retrospective and prospective issue assessments.

The Concerns of the Electorate

The first question in the study of prospective voting is what kinds of concerns moved the public. The Survey Research Center-Center for

Political Studies (SRC-CPS) survey asks, "What do you personally feel are the most important problems the government in Washington should try to take care of?" In Table 6-1, we have listed the percentage of responses to what respondents claimed was the single most important problem in broad categories of concerns over the four most recent elections.[2]

In 1984 concerns were more broadly distributed than in 1976 and 1980. In 1976 economic woes, especially unemployment and inflation, dominated the public's concerns. In 1980 inflation was mentioned by a third of the public, about twice as many as cited the Iranian hostage crisis, the second most cited problem. Together, they accounted for nearly half of the public's primary political concerns.

Table 6-1 Most Important Problem as Seen by the Electorate, 1972-1984 (in percentages)

Problem	1972		1976		1980		1984	
Economics	27		76		56		49	
Unemployment/recession		9		33		10		16
Inflation/prices		14		27		33		5
Deficit/govt. spending		1		9		3		19
Social issues	34		14		7		13	
Social welfare		7		4		3		9
Public order		20		8		1		4
Foreign/defense	31		4		32		34	
Foreign		4		3		9		17
Defense		1		1		8		17
Functioning of government								
(competence, corruption, trust, power, etc.)	4		4		2		2	
All others	4		3		3		3	
Total percent	100		101		100		101	
(N)	(842)		(2337)		(1352)		(1780)	
"Missing"	(63)		(203)		(56)		(163)	
Percent missing	7		7		4		7	

Notes: Foreign in 1972 includes 25 percent who cited Vietnam. Foreign in 1980 includes 15 percent who cited Iran. Questions asked of randomly selected half sample in 1972. Weighted N in 1976. All of the subcategories are not included. The total percentages for the subcategories, therefore, will not equal the percentages for the main categories. In 1984 total N is 1,943 because 46 respondents were not asked this question, being given a shortened postelection questionnaire.

In 1984 nearly half of the public cited economic problems as most important to them. But instead of inflation and unemployment, the public focused attention on the deficit and government spending. Nineteen percent of the respondents cited that as the most important concern, slightly more than those who mentioned unemployment or recession.

We cannot tell whether people were citing looming budget deficits or government spending as most important. This raises an important distinction. People who are concerned about unemployment have a clear preference: they want to see it reduced. This type of problem is political, but it involves asking which party or candidate is more likely to reduce unemployment. There is no question about the goal, merely over how—or who—to best achieve it. Deficits and spending are quite different.

First, citing "deficits" or "government spending" does not, by itself, tell us what the respondents wanted to achieve. Did respondents want to see government spending reduced, presumably as a way to reduce the deficit, or did they want to see government spending increased? Even if (as is likely the case) a respondent who mentioned government spending as the most important problem meant that the deficit should be reduced, that still does not tell us whom the respondent was likely to favor.[3] Mondale supporters might well have said "reduce the deficit," thinking that Mondale, with his proposed tax increase and lesser defense spending, was the better candidate to do so. Reagan supporters might have said "reduce the deficit" and meant "go with Reagan and reduce domestic spending, but do not raise taxes." In this case, prospective evaluations are called for. Moreover, it is not clear that the voter is thinking of this as an *economic* issue, although surely it is in part. But it is just as plausible that people were thinking of this as a more general domestic issue, further distinguishing it from economic issues like unemployment and inflation.

Foreign and defense issues were the next most commonly cited type of problem. They had been about equally commonly cited in 1972 and 1980. There is, once again, a big difference between 1984 and the earlier elections. In 1972, when people cited a foreign and defense issue, they almost always meant the war in Vietnam. In 1980 nearly half of the respondents meant Iran and the hostage crisis, and others cited the Soviet Union's invasion of Afghanistan. In 1984, when people's responses were coded into the foreign and defense category, they did not mean a particular hot spot in the world. Slightly more than half of the defense responses were coded into the specific category "nuclear war; the threat of nuclear war." More than two-fifths of the foreign responses were coded into the category "prevention of war, establishment of peace." Another fifth mentioned relations with Russia. If we combine these categories, 47 percent of all foreign and defense mentions, or 16 percent of all responses, concerned war, peace, or nuclear weapons. Clearly, the concern about war, nuclear weapons, or another aspect of arms control and arms negotiations with Russia weighed heavily on the minds of a far larger proportion of the electorate in 1984 than in other recent elections. Once again, just as with the budget deficit and government spending problem, there is no immediate translation of this concern into candidate choice. Again, the possibility for prospective choice, one based on a comparison of the candidates' promises for future policies, seems relatively high.

Finally in 1984 there was increased concern expressed over a variety of issues in the social welfare category. After a rapid decline in these and public order concerns over the last three elections, there was a resurgent interest in and concern about issues of social welfare programs, largely and unsurprisingly concentrated among those who felt that the Reagan administration had led the fight to cut them too far.

These findings indicate only what problems concerned the electorate. It does not follow necessarily, as we have pointed out, that concern about the budget deficit necessarily translated into support for Mondale's deficit reduction program, let alone a vote for him. A vote, after all, is an expression of a comparison between alternatives. To investigate these questions, we must look at the voters' issue preferences and their perceptions of where the candidates stood on these issues.

Issue Positions and Perceptions

In the four most recent presidential election surveys, the SRC-CPS questionnaires have included numerous issue scales designed to measure the preferences of the electorate and their perceptions of the positions the candidates took on these issues.[4] These questions, therefore, are especially appropriate for examining prospective issue evaluations and their relationship to voter choice. We hasten to add, however, that the perceptions of where the incumbent stands may well be based on what he has done in office, as well as what he promises to do if reelected. Perceptions of where Mondale stood on issues may have been based in part on the respondent's memory of what Mondale had done as senator or vice president. Both incumbent and challenger had been prominent politicians for nearly two decades, and during the campaign both reminded the public of their past achievements and of their opponent's alleged failures. These scales measure perceptions of where the candidates stand, and those perceptions will be affected by the current campaign, too. As we will see in the next chapter, these more prospective issue evaluations are quite different from the retrospective judgments of the public, and thus they tap different aspects of policy-based evaluations.

These issue scales will be used here for examining several questions. First, just what alternatives did the voters perceive the candidates to be offering? Second, to what extent did voters have issue preferences and perceptions of candidate positions? Finally, how strongly were voters' preferences and perceptions related to their choice of candidates?

The assumption that underlies this analysis is that voters make choices after comparing their own issue preferences with the alternatives presented to them. For example, if a voter preferred to see spending for defense increased, and perceived Reagan as the candidate proposing such an increase, then that voter would be disposed to vote for Reagan, at least on the basis of this one issue. In this view of issue voting, the candidates' promises about the policies they will pursue, if elected, shape voting behavior.

The 1984 Data

Figure 6-1 presents the text of one of the seven-point issue scale questions, along with an example shown to respondents as they considered their response. Figure 6-2 indicates the set of issue scales asked in the 1984 SRC-CPS survey. It also presents the average (median) position of respondents (labeled "self") and the average (median) perception of

Figure 6-1   An Example of a 7-Point Issue Scale: Jobs and Standard of Living Guarantees

Question asked by interviewers:
"Some people feel the government in Washington should see to it that every person has a job and a good standard of living. [For the first issue scale only, the following is added: "Suppose these people are at one end of the scale at point number 1."] Others think the government should just let each person get ahead on his own." [For the first scale, the interviewer says, "Suppose these people are at the other end, at point 7. And of course, some people have opinions somewhere in between, at points 2, 3, 4, 5, or 6."]

Interviewer then refers respondent to the appropriate page in the respondent booklet and asks, "Where would you place yourself on this scale, or haven't you thought much about this?"

If respondent places self on scale, the interviewer asks, "Where would you place _____ on this scale?" [Reagan, Mondale, etc.]

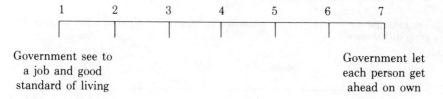

| 1 | 2 | 3 | 4 | 5 | 6 | 7 |

Government see to
 a job and good
standard of living

Government let
each person get
ahead on own

Source: 1984 National Election Studies Pre-Election Survey, Survey Research Center, Institute for Social Research, University of Michigan, Fall 1984, respondent booklet, 17.

Figure 6-2 Median Self-Placement of the Electorate and the Electorate's Placement of Candidates on Issue Scales, 1984

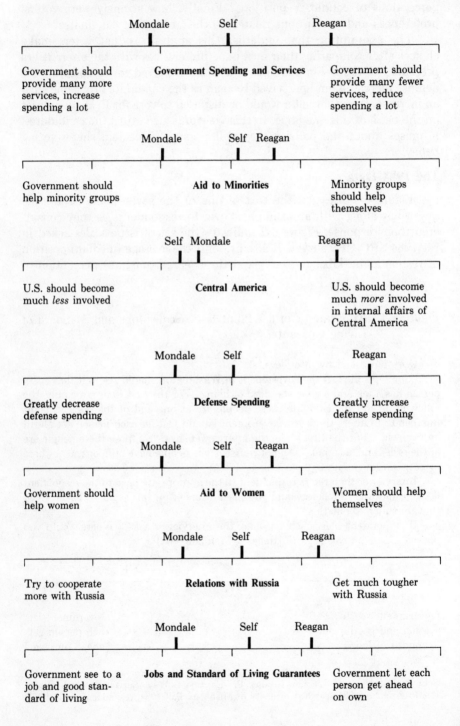

the positions of Reagan and Mondale.[5] The seven issue scales asked in 1984 probe a large variety of important concerns. Three dealt with international and defense issues: U.S. relations with the Soviet Union, U.S. involvement in Central America, and the level of defense spending the respondent believes appropriate. Four questions concerned domestic policy: should government spending for social services be increased or decreased, should the government provide for jobs and a good standard of living, should the government help women, and should the government help minority groups. While these issue scales are not a perfect mirror of the problems the public saw as most important to them (for example, there is no direct measure of arms control policies or the appropriate way to reduce the federal deficit, if at all), they do reveal most of the public's concerns and the issues most frequently discussed by the candidates in the campaign.

What then of the average respondent? These issues were selected precisely because they were controversial and generally tapped long-standing partisan divisions and differences between the two candidates of 1984. As a result, the average citizen comes out looking moderate on all issues. On six issues the average respondent is located close to the center of the issue scale, at point 4. Only on the Central America scale is the average respondent closer to some other point, in this case a score of 3, indicating at least a slight rejection of greater involvement in Central America. The moderate position of the average respondent reflects a nearly equal balancing of "liberals" and "conservatives," but also reflects the large number of respondents expressing a preference for moderate policies. On all scales, the mid-point (or 4) response is the most commonly chosen alternative, often followed by the two adjacent points, 3 and 5 *(see the Ns reported in Table 6-3)*.

In 1980 the average citizen was in favor of a more conservative policy on many issues.[6] For example, the average respondent favored decreased spending on social programs but increased spending on defense. Such was no longer the case in 1984, when the average citizen wanted to see neither an increase nor a decrease in spending in either area. A major reason for the apparent shift in preferences is simple: government policy had changed in the intervening years. The Reagan administration had achieved many of its domestic program cuts and had increased spending for defense. In both cases, the average respondent was saying that the shift in policy was just about right. There was no longer any overall sentiment for further domestic program reductions nor for increased spending for defense.

Perceptions of the two candidates' positions, however, were very similar to those in 1980. In both cases, the public saw clear and unmistakable differences between the positions taken by Reagan and his

Democratic opponents. The average distance separating perceptions of the two candidates was a bit over two points on the scale, out of a maximum possible difference of six points, in both years. In 1984, on two questions—aid to minorities and aid to women—the difference was only a point and a half, while on the government spending and services, it was two and a half points. The others were almost exactly two-point differences. Citizens did not perceive either candidate as an extremist overall or on any individual issue, but they did see them as offering quite different policy alternatives.

With the exception of the Central America issue, the average citizen placed himself half way between where Mondale and Reagan were seen to stand. On average, across all seven issues the typical respondent was about three-quarters of a point to the right of Mondale and a point and a quarter to the left of Reagan. However, if we exclude the Central America question, the average citizen is just about a point from both Mondale and Reagan. To be sure, there are a few differences among these six issues. For example, the average respondent is noticeably closer to where Reagan was seen to stand on aid to minorities, but closer to Mondale on defense spending. Still, the overriding point is that, excepting Central America, the average citizen was very close to the middle of the scale and equally close to both candidates.

Mondale supporters and advisers often stated that they felt the public's issue preferences were more in line with Mondale's than Reagan's positions. If only, they felt, other forces were not at work, Mondale would win on the issues. If these issues were typical of all of the issues in the campaign, then people were no closer to Mondale than to Reagan. No matter how closely these issue preferences and perceptions were related to the vote, it appears that neither candidate had a clear advantage. The number of citizens casting a prospective, issue-based vote for Mondale should have been just about the same as for Reagan. Of course, we must look beyond the preferences and perceptions of the average respondent before we can assess the role of these issues in electoral choice.

Issue Voting Criteria

The Problem

To this point we have looked at the public as a whole. Voting is, of course, an individual action, and we must look at the preferences of individuals to see if prospective issues influenced their vote. In fact, the question of prospective issue voting is quite controversial. The authors of the classic study of the American electorate, *The American Voter*, point out that the public often is ill informed about public policy and may not be able to vote on the basis of issues.[7] They asked what information a voter would need before an issue could influence the decision of how to vote, and they specified three conditions. First, the voter must hold an opinion on the issue; second, the voter must see what the government is doing on the issue; and, third, he or she must see a difference between the policies of the two major parties. According to their analysis, only about one-quarter to one-third of the electorate in 1956 could meet these three criteria on a given issue.

While it is impossible to replicate their analysis, we can adapt their procedures to the 1984 electorate. In some ways, currently available data focus more directly on the actual choice citizens must make, a choice between the two candidates. The first and most basic criterion is whether the respondent claims to have a opinion on the issue. This is measured by whether respondents placed themselves on the scale. (If they could not, they were asked no more questions about that issue.) Second, the respondents should have some perception of the positions taken by both candidates on that issue. This is measured by whether they could place both candidates on an issue scale.[8] It is possible that a respondent might perceive the position of only one candidate and so thoroughly agree or disagree with it that learning where the other candidate stands is irrelevant to the voter's decision. Still, prospective voting is, at base, a comparison of the promises of both candidates, so the expressed ability to perceive the stances of both contenders seems a minimal requirement. Third, the voter must see a difference between the positions of the two candidates. Failing to see a difference means that the voter perceived no choice on this issue.

A voter may be able to satisfy these criteria, but misperceive the offerings of the two candidates. This leads to a fourth condition that we are able to measure more systematically than was possible in 1956. Does the respondent accurately perceive the *relative* positions of the two candidates; that is, see Mondale as more "liberal" than Reagan? This criterion does not demand that the voter have an accurate perception of just what the candidate proposes, but it does expect the voter to see that Mondale, for instance, favored more spending than Reagan on social services.[9]

The Data

In Table 6-2 we report the percentages of the sample that met the four criteria on each issue scale in 1984. We also show the average proportion meeting these criteria for all seven scales and compare those averages to comparable averages in the three preceding elections.[10] As can be seen in Column I, most people felt capable of placing themselves on any issue scale, and this capability was common to all four election years.[11]

Fewer people could place both candidates on an issue scale than could place just themselves, as can be seen in Column II. Nonetheless,

Table 6-2 Four Criteria for Issue Voting, 1984, and Comparisons with 1980, 1976, and 1972 (in percentages)

Issue Scale	Percentage of Sample Who Placed:			
	I *Self on* *Scale*	*II* *Both* *Candidates* *on Scale**	*III* *Saw* *Differences* *between Mondale* *and Reagan*	*IV* *Saw Mondale* *More "Liberal"* *than Reagan*
Government spending/services	85	76	69	60
Aid to minorities	87	76	62	49
Central America	77	64	55	45
Defense spending	87	77	71	65
Aid to women	84	73	59	49
Relations with Russia	84	73	61	52
Jobs and standard of living	86	75	60	53
Average:				
1984 (7)**	84	73	62	53
1980 (9)	82	61	51	43
1976 (9)	84	58	36	26
1972 (8)	90	65	49	41

* If respondent could not place self on scale, respondent was not questioned further on that issue.

** Number in parentheses is the number of issue scales included in the average for each election year survey.

Note: Columns II, III, and IV compare Carter and Reagan in 1980, Carter and Ford in 1976, and McGovern and Nixon in 1972.

almost three out of four met these two criteria in 1984, and that is a noticeably higher percentage than in any of the other three election years. In other years, moreover, there was substantially greater variation across issues than was true in 1984. Indeed, with the exception of the Central America scale, there was a remarkably consistent three out of four who met these first two criteria. In 1980, by comparison, nine issue scales were used. In no case did the percentage placing themselves, Carter, and Reagan go beyond 72 percent, and on three scales fewer than half placed themselves and both major party candidates.

As can be seen in Column III, more than half of the sample met the first two criteria and also saw a difference between the positions of

Reagan and Mondale, and on two issues (government spending on social services and on defense) 7 out of 10 did. Overall, 3 respondents out of 5 met all three of these criteria, a proportion clearly higher than in 1972 and 1980, and much higher than in the 1976 Ford-Carter contest.

Many people were unable to satisfy these criteria, even in 1984. On average, nearly two in five did not satisfy them. Still, that leaves a bit more than three of five who could, compared to the one-third to one-half in earlier elections. What are we to conclude from these differences in the ability of the electorate to satisfy these criteria and thus be able to vote on the basis of issues? It seems highly unlikely that the ability of the public to comprehend the electoral process varies so greatly from election to election. Rather these differences from election to election result from changing political conditions and, in particular, from the strategies followed by the candidates. In 1984 the candidates adopted quite distinct positions on issues, and this relative clarity was picked up by the electorate.

In sum, we support Morris P. Fiorina's argument that failure to satisfy the criteria for issue voting does not mean that the electorate has ill-informed preferences and perceptions.[12] Rather, the "quality" of the response to these issue questions is based in part on how clearly the candidates articulate their positions. It is, in this light, not a coincidence that perceptions of the candidates' positions vary most sharply from election to election, and that 1976 stands out as having the lowest proportion satisfying the last two criteria.

The contest between Gerald R. Ford and Jimmy Carter featured candidates generally described as moderates, albeit moderately conservative and moderately liberal. In contrast, the 1972 election featured a clearly liberal alternative against a moderately conservative one, and the last two featured fairly liberal candidates opposing the more conservative Reagan.

The data in Column IV reflect the ability of the electorate to pick up these distinctions. Averaging the issues together, we see that in 1984 more than half of those sampled saw Mondale as more liberal than Reagan. The 1976 election, by this point, stands out in even starker contrast to the three other recent elections. In 1976 barely one in four could assess the relative positions of the two candidates. By contrast, the 1984 contest is the only election in which more than half the electorate met all four conditions.

The data in Table 6-2 suggest that the potential for prospective issue voting was unusually high in 1984. We might expect, therefore, that these issues were closely related to voter choice. We will examine voter choice on these issues in two ways. First, how often did people vote for the closer candidate on each issue? Second, how strongly related to the vote is the set of all issues taken together?

Apparent Issue Voting in 1984

Issue Criteria and Voting on Each Issue

The first question is to what extent did people who were closer to a candidate on a given issue actually vote for that candidate. That is, how strong was apparent issue voting? [13] In Table 6-3 we report the proportion of major party voters who voted for Reagan by where they placed themselves and the candidates.

We divided the seven points into the set of positions that were closer to where the average citizen placed Mondale and Reagan, along with, in four cases, those who were about equidistant between these two average perceptions (*Figure 6-2*). Of course, the individual might have thought Mondale or Reagan held a different position than did the public as a whole, but use of the samplewide perceptions reduces the possibility that people were "projecting" their own issue preferences onto their favored candidate, thereby "rationalizing" their issue perceptions to be consistent with their vote, rather than voting for the candidate whose views were closer to the citizen's own preferences.[14]

As can be seen in Table 6-3, for virtually all issues there is a strong relationship between the citizens' issue preferences and the candidate they supported. As we saw in Chapter 5, 58 percent of the voters in the SRC-CPS survey voted for Reagan. Voters who were closer to where Reagan was seen to stand on any issue never failed to give Reagan less than 66 percent of the vote, and he often received about 80 percent. For the most part, those closer to where Mondale was seen to stand were much less likely to vote for Reagan than the electorate as a whole. Indeed, in most cases, the relationship between issues and the vote is quite strong.

The richness of the information in Table 6-3 can be summarized in a way that, while losing some of the information, presents the relationship between issue preferences and candidate choice more clearly. In the first column of Table 6-4, we report the percentage of those who placed themselves closer to the average perception of Mondale and Reagan and who voted for the closer candidate. To be more specific, the denominator in our measure is the total number of major party voters who were closer to the electorate's perception of either Reagan or Mondale. The numerator is the total number of major party voters who were closer to Reagan and who voted for him plus the total number of major party voters who were closer to Mondale and voted for him.[15]

If voting were unrelated to issue positions, we would expect that across all seven issues 50 percent would vote for the closer candidate on average. In 1984, 65 percent voted for the closer candidate. Again, this is a higher percentage, on average, than in 1976, but about the same as in the

Table 6-3 Major Party Voters Who Voted for Reagan, by Seven-Point Issue Scales, 1984 (in percentages)

Issue Scale	Closer to Median Perceptions of Mondale			Equi-distant	Closer to Median Perceptions of Reagan			(N)
	1	2	3	4	5	6	7	
Government spending/services[1]	27.8	32.9	39.9	56.0	80.1	88.4	82.9	(1216)
(N)[2]	(79)	(85)	(228)	(391)	(196)	(155)	(82)	
Aid to minorities	17.8	33.3	50.8	58.4	69.2	79.0	76.9	(1247)
(N)	(90)	(96)	(193)	(409)	(227)	(124)	(108)	
Central America[1]	30.4	45.6	57.9	71.9	73.0	84.2	68.8	(1106)
(N)	(168)	(217)	(202)	(242)	(137)	(76)	(64)	
Defense spending	21.4	32.8	42.7	66.7	75.4	81.6	77.8	(1245)
(N)	(103)	(137)	(157)	(405)	(248)	(114)	(81)	
Aid to women	25.4	39.7	46.4	64.3	75.8	74.1	76.6	(1205)
(N)	(114)	(131)	(194)	(378)	(182)	(112)	(94)	
Relations with Russia	27.0	38.0	45.7	67.5	73.8	79.1	68.1	(1221)
(N)	(148)	(121)	(175)	(271)	(229)	(139)	(138)	
Jobs and standard of living	29.1	33.0	41.0	51.8	65.9	83.8	85.4	(1226)
(N)	(110)	(88)	(144)	(299)	(258)	(204)	(123)	

[1] Reversed from actual scoring to make a "liberal" response closer to "1" and a "conservative" response closer to "7."
[2] Numbers in parentheses are the totals upon which percentages are based.

Table 6-4   Apparent Issue Voting, 1984, and Comparisons with 1980, 1976, and 1972 (in percentages)[1]

Issue Scale	Placed Self on Issue Scale	Met All Four Issue Voting Criteria	Placed Self but Failed to Meet All Three Other Criteria
Government spending/			
services	74	84	42
Aid to minorities	68	76	54
Central America	54	64	37
Defense spending	60	64	42
Aid to women	68	76	53
Relations with Russia	60	69	43
Jobs and standard of living	72	80	54
Average			
1984	65	73	46
1980	63	71	48
1976	57	70	50
1972	66	76	55

The column group header reads: *Extent to Which Voter Met Issue Voting Criteria*

[1] An "apparent issue vote" is a vote for the candidate closer to one's own position on an issue scale. The closer candidate is determined by comparing self-placement to the median placement of the two candidates on the scale as a whole. Respondents who did not place themselves or who were equidistant from the two candidates were excluded from the calculations.

other two elections. There is substantial variation across issues. Again, the Central America issue scale is least strongly related to the vote. Slightly more than half, or what we would expect by chance, voted for the closer candidate on this issue.[16] Issues that measure the long-standing divisions between the two parties—government involvement in social services, jobs, and assistance to disadvantaged groups—were more strongly related to the vote, as between 68 percent and 74 percent voted for the closer candidate. The other two foreign and defense issues fall midway between these extremes. In sum, in 1976 apparent issue voting was relatively low, and in 1984, as in the other recent elections, about two of three voted for the closer candidate on the issues.

These figures do not tell the whole story, however, for those who placed themselves on an issue but failed to meet some other criterion were unlikely to have cast a vote based on that issue. In the second column, we report the percentage of those who voted for the closer candidate on each issue, among voters who met all four conditions on that issue. The third column reports the percentage voting for the closer candidate among voters who failed to meet all three of the remaining conditions. Obviously, those who met all four conditions were much more likely to vote for the closer candidate on any issue. On average, three of four did so, while for those who failed to meet all three of the latter three conditions, voting was essentially random with respect to the issues.

Clearly, voting consistently with issue preferences was stronger on all four domestic issues than any of the foreign and defense issues, a finding consistent with the oft-noted tendency of Americans to vote more heavily along domestic policy lines. This tendency may be traced to the relatively lower salience of such issues (particularly appropriate for the Central American problem) and to lesser certainty among voters about what to do about these often highly complex issues. Still, all issues were clearly related to voter choice for those voters with the information needed to cast an issue-based vote.

The similarity of all four election averages in the second and third columns suggests that the major reason that issue voting seems more prevalent in some elections than others depends primarily on the number of people who clearly perceive differences between the candidates. In all elections, nearly three of four who satisfied all four conditions voted consistently with their issue preferences, while in all elections, those who did not satisfy the conditions concerning candidate perceptions voted randomly with respect to the individual issues. Therefore, the relatively lower percentage of apparent issue voting in 1976, for instance, results from the perception of smaller differences between the two candidates. Those who saw differences in 1976 and favored one candidate over the other were no less likely to vote consistently with their issue-based preferences. There were simply fewer such people in 1976. Conversely, the high levels of apparent issue voting in 1984 result from the remarkable clarity with which most people saw the positions of Reagan and Mondale.

Overall Apparent Issue Voting

Most people held a more "liberal" position on the Central America issue than they saw either candidate espousing. If this were the only factor relevant to voter choice, Mondale would have won the election rather easily, because more people saw him rather than Reagan as closer to their own position. Thus, many of those who voted for Reagan did so even though they saw Mondale as the closer candidate on this issue. This reminds us that there are many factors involved in voting, and it is the rare voter that finds every factor consistently pushing him or her in one candidate's direction. In later chapters, we will compare the impact of these prospective issues with other factors in the election. Here, we will look at the entire set of these issues.

We constructed an overall assessment of these seven issue scales, what we call the "balance of issues measure," by giving individuals a score of +1 if their positions on an issue scale were closer to the average perception of Reagan, a −1 if their positions were closer to the average perception of Mondale, and a score of 0 if they were equally close to both candidates or if they had no preference on an issue. These scores were then added up for all seven issue scales, creating a measure that ranged from −7 to +7. For instance, respondents who had issue preferences on all seven scales and who were closer to the average perception of Mondale on every issue would receive a score of −7. A net negative score indicated that the respondent was, on balance, closer to the public's perception of Mondale, while a net positive score indicated the respondent was, overall, closer to the public's perception of Reagan.[17]

In Figure 6-3, we collapse this summary measure of prospective issues into seven categories, ranging from strongly Democratic to strongly Republican, and display the distribution of respondents on this measure for all four recent elections.[18] There is a consistent trend in the four elections. In 1972 the electorate stood closer, overall, to Richard Nixon than to George S. McGovern. While this was true in 1976 as well, Ford held less of an advantage than Nixon. Rather, there were more people in the neutral category than in any other and rather fewer, overall, closer to Ford than Carter, compared to four years earlier. By 1980 the relative conservatism of Reagan meant that even more people were in the neutral category than earlier and, consequently, fewer found that issues pushed them strongly in the Republican direction. Still, the Republican candidate had the advantage in 1980, as a greater proportion of the electorate was closer to the perception of his position than to Carter's.

For the first time, the Democratic candidate held a slight advantage on issues in 1984. In general, more were in the neutral category than in any other, as in the preceding two elections, and, as in 1980, the next most common categories were those near the neutral point. Still, 38 percent of the respondents were, on balance, closer to the Democratic candidate, while only 22 percent were closer to the Republican nominee. Mondale had suggested throughout the campaign that he was closer to more people than Reagan on the issues, and Figure 6-3 suggests he might have been right. Mondale's advantage, however, was relatively slight. Moreover, if we were to remove the Central America issue from the analysis, there would be virtually no advantage either way. Even so, an even split on the issues in 1984 must be considered an "advantage" that Mondale had in comparison to McGovern and Carter, who had to contend with electorates that, on the issues, favored the Republican candidates.

Figure 6-3 Distribution of Electorate on Net Balance of Issues, 1972-1984

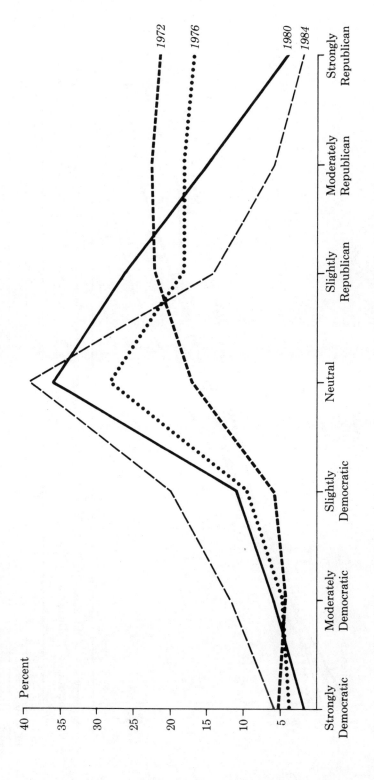

Figure 6-4 Major Party Voters Who Voted Democratic for President, by Net Balance of Issues Measure, 1972-1984

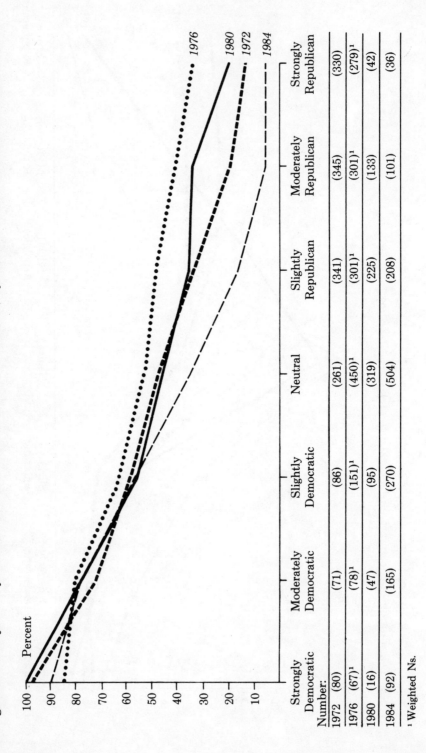

Number:	Strongly Democratic	Moderately Democratic	Slightly Democratic	Neutral	Slightly Republican	Moderately Republican	Strongly Republican
1972	(80)	(71)	(86)	(261)	(341)	(345)	(330)
1976[1]	(67)[1]	(78)[1]	(151)[1]	(450)[1]	(301)[1]	(301)[1]	(279)[1]
1980	(16)	(47)	(95)	(319)	(225)	(133)	(42)
1984	(92)	(165)	(270)	(504)	(208)	(101)	(36)

[1] Weighted Ns.

As can be seen in Figure 6-4, the relationship between the net balance of issues measure and the vote was strong in all four elections. In all elections, when these issues pushed the respondent strongly in one candidate's direction or the other, that voter was very likely to vote consistently with these issues. In 1984, for instance, about 9 of 10 in the strongly partisan categories voted consistently with their issue preferences, and 9 out of 10 voters who were moderately Republican voted consistently with their preferences. Among voters who were moderate Democrats, more than 3 out of 4 voted for Mondale, nearly twice the share Mondale received among voters as a whole. Perhaps the most remarkable finding is the consistency of the relationship for all four years. Still, voters who were neutral or in any of the Republican categories were less likely to vote Democratic in 1984 than in previous elections. This suggests that, unless the prospective issues consistently favored Mondale, the voters were more likely to look to factors other than these issues.

These findings suggest that Reagan's electoral landslide victory was not due to the role of prospective issues. Most people were located in between where they saw the two candidates standing. Indeed, on most issues, more people were relatively moderate, and the candidates were seen as more liberal and more conservative, respectively. In 1980 Carter lost because, compared with his 1976 victory, he fared worse among voters who were slightly Democratic, neutral, or who were slightly, moderately, or strongly pro-Republican. Except for voters who were slightly pro-Democratic, Mondale did even worse among these groups than Carter had done in 1980. This line of reasoning suggests, perhaps, that people voted against an unpopular incumbent in 1980, unless issues pushed strongly in his direction; they voted for a popular incumbent in 1984, unless issues strongly impelled them otherwise. In the next chapter we will see that such an interpretation seems most reasonable.

Notes

1. For more on the strategies of the candidates in 1980, see Paul R. Abramson, John H. Aldrich, and David W. Rohde, *Change and Continuity in the 1980 Elections*, rev. ed. (Washington, D.C.: CQ Press, 1983), Chap. 2.
2. Each respondent in the survey is asked the question in the text and encouraged to give up to three responses. Then, if more than one problem is raised, the respondent is asked which one is the single most important. The responses in Table 6-1 are from this latter question. Looking at the full array of responses, we find a broader range of alternatives suggested, yet the same outlines are apparent.

3. It is likely that respondents who cited "government spending" as the most important problem and were coded into this category wanted to see spending reduced to reduce the deficit. Otherwise, the response would probably have been coded into another category.

4. These measures, on which this chapter relies heavily, were developed by the Survey Research Center of the University of Michigan. They were first used in the 1968 study, but were used extensively in presidential election surveys beginning in 1972. The issue measures analyzed in Chap. 7 also were used extensively beginning in the 1970s. Therefore, in this chapter and in chapters 7 and 8, we restrict our attention to the last four elections at most. We also include only those respondents from whom a postelection survey was obtained.

5. The median is based on the assumption that respondents can be ranked from most conservative to most liberal. The number of respondents who are more liberal than median respondent is equal to the number who are more conservative. Likewise, the median ranking of a candidate is the point where an equal number of respondents place the candidate as more conservative than that point as place the candidate as more liberal. Because there are only seven points on the issue scales, and because many respondents will choose any given point, the median is computed using a procedure that derives a median for "grouped data." That procedure is described in many statistics texts.

6. Abramson, Aldrich, and Rohde, *Change and Continuity in the 1980 Elections*, rev. ed., 124-26.

7. Angus Campbell, Philip E. Converse, Warren E. Miller, and Donald E. Stokes, *The American Voter* (New York: John Wiley & Sons, 1960), 168-87.

8. The SRC-CPS interviewers did not ask those who failed to place themselves on an issue scale where they thought the candidates stood. Therefore, by definition, those who "failed" to meet the first criterion were not able to meet any of the remaining ones.

9. These criteria are critiqued by Morris P. Fiorina, *Retrospective Voting in American National Elections* (New Haven, Conn.: Yale University Press, 1981). Although many scholars have interpreted failure to meet these criteria as akin to failing a "test," he argues that the criteria imply no such thing. We agree. Failure to satisfy these criteria in no way impugns the citizen. As we will see, the "failure" to satisfy these criteria is related to the strategies followed by the candidates in the campaign.

10. For details, see Abramson, Aldrich, and Rohde, *Change and Continuity in the 1980 Elections*, rev. ed., Table 6-3, 130.

11. While this evidence indicates that most people *claim* to have issue preferences, it does not demonstrate that they *do*. For example, evidence indicates that some use the midpoint of the scale (point number 4) as a means of answering the question even if they have ill-formed preferences. See John H. Aldrich, Richard G. Niemi, George Rabinowitz, and David W. Rohde, "The Measurement of Public Opinion about Public Policy: A Report on Some New Issue Question Formats," *American Journal of Political Science* 26 (May 1982): 391-414.

12. Fiorina, *Retrospective Voting*.

13. The term "apparent issue voting" is used to emphasize several points. First,

there are too many factors to infer that closeness to a candidate on one issue was the cause of the voter's choice. In fact, the issue similarity may have been purely coincidental. Second, we use the median perception of the candidates rather than the individual's own reported perceptions. Third, there is a possibility of "rationalization." Voters may have decided to support a candidate for entirely different reasons and may also have altered their own issue preference to align more closely with the chosen candidate's positions or have misperceived the candidate's positions to be closer to their own preferences. See Richard A. Brody and Benjamin I. Page, "Comment: The Assessment of Policy Voting," *American Political Science Review* 66 (June 1972): 450-58.

14. Ibid.
15. We have eliminated, of course, those equidistant from the two candidate perceptions because they had no effective choice on that issue.
16. While this issue was not strongly related to the vote, Table 6-3 reveals that those with the least clear choice, such as those at points 3 and 4, make up the bulk of those who voted for the "wrong" candidate on this issue. Others who held preferences giving them a more clear-cut choice voted heavily for the closer of the two candidates.
17. This procedure counts every issue as equal in importance. It also assumes that all that matters is that the voter is closer to the candidate on an issue; it does not consider how much closer the citizen is to one candidate or the other.
18. Scores of $+6$ and $+7$ were called strongly Republican, while similarly negative scores were called strongly Democratic. Scores of $+4$ and $+5$ were considered moderately Republican (and -4 and -5 moderately Democratic). Scores of $+2$ and $+3$ were called slightly Republican, and scores of -2 and -3 were called slightly Democratic. Scores of -1, 0, and $+1$ were called neutral. Note that the number of issue scales differed from election to election, making comparisons across elections at least somewhat problematic. For details on our scaling procedures for 1972, 1976, and 1980, see Abramson, Aldrich, and Rohde, *Change and Continuity in the 1980 Elections*, rev. ed., 140.

Chapter 7

Presidential Performance and Candidate Choice

In 1980 Ronald Reagan claimed that his victory was a mandate for his campaign platform. In the preceding chapter, however, we saw that most people were not much closer to his positions than to Jimmy Carter's. Moreover, while the issues that concerned the electorate were related to the vote, the relationship was not particularly strong. Thus, Reagan's claim for a mandate was not supported by the evidence.

In 1984 people saw differences on issues between the two candidates even more clearly than four years earlier, and the issues were more strongly related to the vote. Once again, however, people were not much closer to one candidate than the other. The data indicate that the election was not a mandate for Reagan's policy promises. In fact, these issues cannot help us understand why he won handily in either election, especially in 1984. For, if these issues were the only factors in the election, the 1984 election should have been very close.

What can explain Reagan's easy victories? We attributed the Reagan victory of 1980 to the public's perception that Carter had not done a good enough job as president.[1] The 1984 election can be seen as just the reverse: people voted heavily for Reagan because they thought he had done a good job as president in his first term. This sort of voting decision is termed "retrospective" voting, and we will examine retrospective evaluations in this chapter.

What Is 'Retrospective' Voting?

An individual who voted for the incumbent because the incumbent was, in the voter's opinion, a particularly strong and successful president is said to have cast a retrospective vote. The voter decided that "one good term deserved another." If, instead, a voter cast a ballot for the opposition because, in the voter's opinion, the incumbent had been *un*successful in office, the voter also cast a retrospective vote, in this case to "throw the rascal out." In other words, retrospective voting decisions are based on evaluations of the course of politics over the last term in office and on evaluations of how much the incumbent should be held responsible for what good or ill occurred. V. O. Key, Jr., popularized this argument by suggesting that the voter might be a "rational god of vengeance and of reward." [2]

Obviously, retrospective voting is a stronger basis of choice the closer the candidate of one party can be tied to the actions of the incumbent. Thus, the incumbent president cannot escape such evaluations, and the incumbent vice president is often identified with (and often identifies himself with) the administration's performance. In 18 of the 22 presidential elections during this century (all but 1908, 1920, 1928, and 1952), an incumbent president or vice president stood for election.

As a result of the Twenty-second Amendment, Reagan will not be eligible to run for president in 1988. Assuming he is still president, the 1988 election will be the first one in two decades in which an incumbent president will not run. Of course, the incumbent vice president, George Bush, is very likely to run and is among the strong contenders for the Republican nomination. Should Bush gain the nomination, voters will once again be able to cast retrospective votes. Retrospective voters are outcome oriented and evaluate only the performance of the incumbent, all but ignoring the opposition. A "pure" retrospective voter evaluates what has been done, not what might be done in the future.

Anthony Downs presents a different view of retrospective voting. [3] He argues that voters look to the past to understand what an incumbent will do in the future. According to Downs, parties are basically consistent in their goals, methods, and ideologies over time. Therefore, past performance by both parties' candidates, especially that of the incumbent, may prove relevant for projections about future conduct. Because it takes time and effort to evaluate candidates' campaign promises and because promises are just words, the voters find it faster, easier, and safer to use past performance to infer the administration's actions for the next four years. Downs emphasizes that retrospective evaluations are used to make comparisons between the alternatives standing for election. Key's view is that of a retrospective referendum on the incumbent alone. Downs's view adds an emphasis on evaluations of the past as a guide to the future.

Another view of retrospective voting is advanced by Morris P. Fiorina. In many respects, his effort is an elaboration and extension of

Downs's point of view. Fiorina argues that "citizens monitor party promises and performances over time, encapsulate their observations in a summary judgment termed 'party identification,' and rely on this core of previous experience when they assign responsibility for current societal conditions and evaluate ambiguous platforms designed to deal with uncertain futures." [4]

Retrospective voting and voting according to issue positions, as analyzed in Chapter 6, differ significantly. The difference lies in how concerned people are with societal outcomes and how concerned they are about the means to achieve desired outcomes. For example, everyone prefers economic prosperity. The disagreement among political decision makers lies in how best to achieve it. At the voters' level, however, the central question is whether voters care only about achieving prosperity or whether they care, or even are able to judge, how to achieve this desired goal. Perhaps they looked at high inflation and interest rates in 1980 and said, "We tried Carter's approach, and it failed. Let's try something else—anything else." Or they noted the economic recovery of 1983-1984 and said, "Whatever Reagan's doing, it is working. Let's keep him in office." Or they agreed with Walter F. Mondale and said, "Sure, the recovery is terrific, but Reagan's programs have hurt—and will continue to hurt—some people in society. I believe that Mondale's program will be fairer to more people; let's try that approach."

Economic policies and many of the most discussed foreign affairs issues are often evaluated this way because they share several characteristics. First, the outcomes are clear, and most voters can judge whether they approve of the results. Inflation and unemployment are high or low; the economy is growing or it is not. The country is at war or peace; the world is stable or unstable. Second, there is often near consensus on what the desired outcomes are; no one disagrees with peace or prosperity, with world stability or low unemployment. Third, the means to achieve these ends are often very complex, and information is hard to understand; experts as well as candidates and parties disagree over specific ways to achieve the desired ends.

As issues, therefore, peace and prosperity differ sharply from policy areas, such as abortion and gun control, in which there is vigorous disagreement over ends. On still other issues, people value means as well as ends. The classic cases often ask whether it is appropriate for government to take action at all. President Reagan is fond of saying, "Government isn't the solution to our problems, government *is* the problem." For instance, should government provide national health insurance? Few disagree with the end, health protection, but they do disagree over the means to achieve it. Does affirmative action risk "reverse discrimination," and is that acceptable? The choice of means involves some of the basic philosophical and ideological differences that have divided the Republicans from the Democrats for decades.[5] For example, in 1984 Mondale did not argue that we were not in a period of economic prosperity or that prosperity is a bad thing. He argued that Reagan's policies were unfair to the disadvantaged. He also claimed that these policies, by creating a large deficit, were sowing the seeds for future woes. Disagreement was not over the ends, but over the means and the consequences that would result from following different means.

Two basic conditions are necessary for retrospective evaluations to affect voting choices. First, the individual must connect his or her concern (for example, the problem felt to be the most important one facing the nation) with the incumbent and the actions he took in office. One might blame the earlier administrations with sowing the seeds that grew into the huge deficits of the 1980s, or blame a profligate Congress, or even believe that deficits are totally beyond anyone's control. If not, the voter may blame the incumbent wholly or only in part. Second, the individual (in the Downs-Fiorina view) must compare that evaluation with what he or she believes the opposition would do. Even if the voter holds Reagan responsible for budget deficits, that voter might conclude that Mondale's programs would not be any better at reducing the deficit.

We will now examine some illustrative retrospective evaluations and study their impact on voter choice. As we look at the data, we must keep in mind that retrospective and prospective voting can be kept distinct in theory, but it is more difficult to maintain that distinction in practice.[6] In Chapter 6 we looked at issue scales designed to measure what the public saw the candidates promising to do in office in the next term. Of course, the public can evaluate not only the promises of the incumbent but also the actions of the first term. We will compare promises with performance in this chapter, but one must remember that the distinctions are not as sharp in practice as they are in principle. Of course, the Downs-Fiorina view is that past outcomes and projections about the future are necessarily intertwined.

Evaluations of Governmental Performance

What do you consider the "most important problem" facing the country, and how do you feel the "government in Washington" has been handling this problem? These questions are designed to measure retrospective judgments. The data in Table 7-1 compare evaluations of governmental performance on the single most important problem as mentioned by respondents from 1972 to 1984.[7] The most striking finding is that in 1984, and only somewhat less so in 1972, the public was more approving of governmental performance than in 1976 and 1980. Six respondents out of 10, for example, thought the government was doing a poor job in 1980, but only 4 in 10 thought so in 1984.[8]

Table 7-1 Evaluation of Governmental Performance on Most Important Problem and Major Party Vote, 1972-1984

A. Evaluation of Governmental Performance on Most Important Problem

Government Is Doing	1972[1]	1976	1980	1984
Good job	12%	8%	4%	16%
Only fair job	58	46	35	46
Poor job	30	46	61	39
Total percent	100%	100%	100%	101%
(N)	(993)	(2156)[2]	(1319)	(1797)

B. Percentage of Major Party Vote for Incumbent

Government Is Doing	1972[1] Nixon	1976[2] Ford	1980 Carter	1984 Reagan
Good job	85	72	81	89
(N)	(91)	(128)	(43)	(214)
Only fair job	69	53	55	65
(N)	(390)	(695)	(289)	(579)
Poor job	46	39	33	37
(N)	(209)	(684)	(505)	(494)

[1] These questions were asked of a randomly selected half of the sample in 1972. In 1972, the question wording and responses were different. Respondents were asked whether the government was being a) very helpful, b) somewhat helpful, or c) not helpful at all in solving this most important problem.
[2] Weighted Ns.
Note: Numbers in parentheses are the totals upon which percentages are based.

If the voter is a rational god of vengeance and reward, we would expect a strong relationship between the evaluation of government performance and the vote. Such is indeed the case for all four elections, as seen in Table 7-1B. From 7 to 9 people in 10 who thought the government was doing a good job on the most important problem voted for the incumbent in each election. In 1984 about two-thirds of those who thought the government's performance only fair supported Reagan, while only a bit more than 1 in 3 who thought the government was doing a poor job voted for Reagan.

According to Downs and Fiorina, it is important to know not just how things have been going, but also to know how that evaluation compares to the alternative. Table 7-2 shows that, in support of the Downs-Fiorina view, retrospective evaluations are useful for projective comparisons. Table 7-2A shows the percentages of the electorate who felt

Table 7-2   Evaluation of Party Seen as Better on Most Important
Problem and Major Party Vote, 1972-1984

A. Distribution of Responses on Party Better on Most Important Problems

Party Better	1972[1]	1976	1980	1984
Republican	28%	14%	43%	32%
No difference	46	50	46	44
Democratic	26	37	11	25
Total percent	100%	101%	100%	101%
(N)	(931)	(2054)[2]	(1251)	(1785)

B. Percentage of Major Party Voters Who Voted Democratic for President

Republican	6	3	12	5
(N)	(207)[1]	(231)[2]	(391)	(464)
No difference	32	35	63	41
(N)	(275)	(673)	(320)	(493)
Democratic	75	89	95	91
(N)	(180)	(565)	(93)	(331)

[1] These questions were asked of a randomly selected half of the sample in 1972. In 1972 respondents were asked which party would be more likely to get the government to be helpful in solving the most important problem.
[2] Weighted Ns.
Note: Numbers in parentheses are the totals upon which percentages are based.

that one party or the other would better handle the most important problem.[9] The question is clearly future oriented. These questions do not ask the respondent to evaluate policy alternatives, and thus responses are likely based on a retrospective comparison of how the incumbent party had handled things with a projection about how the opposition would fare. We therefore view this question as a measure of comparative retrospective evaluations.

By comparing Table 7-1A and 7-2A, we can see that twice as many people in 1984 thought the Republican party would be better at handling the most important problem as thought the government was doing a good job with it. Moreover, while 4 respondents in 10 thought the government was doing a poor job, only 1 in 4 thought the Democratic party would handle it better. These kinds of comparisons hold in each election year. In 1980, while only 1 American in 25 thought the government, headed by Democrat Carter, was doing a good job of handling the most important problem facing the country, nearly 1 in 8 thought the Democratic party would do a better job in handling it. In all years, nearly half the public thought it would make no difference which party was in power. Clearly, more is going on here than merely looking at the performance of the incumbent. The comparative assessment of the two parties' expected performance, while strongly related to the evaluation of the performance of the government, goes beyond merely repeating that judgment.

In all four elections the most frequent response was that neither party would do better, but 1984 differed from the three previous elections in one important respect. It was the best year for the incumbent party, for it was the only year in which the party holding the White House had a clear lead over the party out of office.

As Table 7-2B reveals, the relationship between the party seen as better on the most important problem and the vote is very strong—stronger than just the retrospective evaluations of government performance alone *(Table 7-1B)*. In 1984, for instance, more than 9 voters out of 10 chose the party they thought would better handle this concern. Moreover, in 1984, those who thought there would be no difference between the two parties gave Mondale the same percentage of the vote he received nationwide, suggesting that, for these voters, their comparative assessment made little difference in their voting behavior.[10]

The data presented in Table 7-1 and Table 7-2 have two limitations. First, as we saw in Chapter 6, there was considerable diversity, especially in 1984, over what problem most concerned respondents, and some of the problems were more clearly retrospective than others. It is therefore harder to make comparisons and interpret the findings. Second, in the first question the referent is to "the government" and not to the incumbent president, and it is to the "political party" and not the candidate in the second question. So, we will look a bit more carefully at the incumbent and at people's evaluations of comparable problems where there are data to permit such comparisons.

Economic Evaluations and the Vote for the Incumbent

More than any other, economic issues have received attention as retrospective-type issues. The impact of economic conditions on congressional and presidential elections has been studied extensively.[11] Popular evaluations of presidential effectiveness, John E. Mueller has pointed out, are strongly influenced by the economy.[12] Edward R. Tufte suggests that because the incumbent realizes his fate may hinge on the performance of the economy, he may attempt to manipulate it, leading to what is known as a "political business cycle."[13] Incumbent president Carter's fate in the 1980 election was due largely to the perception that economic

Table 7-3   Distribution of Responses Concerning Assessment of Personal Financial Situation, 1972-1984

Percentage of responses to the question, "Would you say that you (and your family here) are better off or worse off financially than you were a year ago?"

Response	1972[1]	1976	1980	1984
Better now	36%	34%	33%	44%
Same	42	35	25	28
Worse now	23	31	42	27
Total percent	101%	100%	100%	99%
(N)	(955)	(2828)[2]	(1393)	(1956)

[1] These questions were asked of a randomly selected half of the sample in 1972.
[2] Weighted N.

performance was weak during his administration. Reagan's rhetorical question in the 1980 debate with Carter, "Are you better off than you were four years ago?" indicates that politicians realize the power such arguments have with the electorate.

If people are concerned about economic outcomes, especially those that affect them directly, they should start by looking for an answer to the sort of question Reagan asked. Table 7-3 presents respondents' perceptions of whether they were financially better off then or one year earlier. From 1972 to 1980, about a third of the sample felt they were better off. However, over that period, more and more of the remainder felt they were worse off. By 1980 "worse now" was the most common response. By 1984 the economic recovery was felt by many, and more than two out of five felt they were better off than in the previous year; only little more than one in four felt worse off financially. These views were good news for Reagan, bad news for Mondale. In his two debates with Reagan, Mondale could not pose the telling question that Reagan had asked four years earlier, for he knew the answer. Most survey evidence available in the fall of 1984 showed that a majority of Americans felt economic conditions had improved.

People may "vote their pocketbooks," but people may also vote retrospectively, based on their judgment of how the economy as a whole has been faring. In 1980 far more (84 percent) thought the national economy was worse off than thought their own finances were. About 4 percent thought the nation's economy was better off, compared to the third of the sample who thought themselves better off. The 1984 election year, on the other hand, found much greater similarity between individual and national fortunes. Overall, in fact, the distributions of perceptions on the two measures were very similar. *(Compare the center column of Table 7-4 with the 1984 results in Table 7-3.)*

If, as in 1984, there was a general perception that national and personal finances were improving, then the next question is whether the public viewed that improvement as due to the government's policies. As you can see from the first column in Table 7-4, only one respondent in five thought the government's policies had made them better off, presumably attributing their financial success to their own hard work, luck, business conditions, or a source other than the government. Likewise only one in five felt that national policies had hurt them. The most common response by far was that government policies had made little difference in their personal financial situations. Not surprisingly, more thought the overall economy was affected by government policies, as nearly two in five said that economic policies had made the nation better off, while one in five said they had made it worse off. *(See the last column of Table 7-4.)*

To this point, we have looked at whether people felt they and the nation were better off economically and at whether the policies of the government in Washington had contributed to these economic circumstances. We have not yet looked at the extent to which such evaluations are attributed to the incumbent. In Table 7-5, we report responses to the question of whether people approved of Reagan's handling of the economy, along with similar questions measuring approval of other aspects of the Reagan incumbency to provide some basis of comparison.

Table 7-4 Public's Views of the State of the Economy and Government Economic Policy, 1984

Distribution of Responses to:

	Would you say that the economic policies of the federal government have made you:	*Would you say that over the past year the nation's economy has gotten:*	*Would you say that the economic policies of the federal government have made the nation's economy:*
Better [off]	19%	44%	38%
Stayed same/have not made much difference	59	33	40
Worse [off]	22	23	22
Total percent	100%	100%	100%
(N)	(1891)	(1904)	(1841)

Table 7-5 Public's Approval of Reagan's Handling of
Various Issues, 1984

	The Economy	Balancing the National Budget	Our Relations with Foreign Countries
Approve	58%	38%	53%
Disapprove	42	62	47
Total percent	100%	100%	100%
(N)	(1858)	(1735)	(1842)

As you can see, nearly three out of five respondents approved of Reagan's handling of the economy—more than approved of his handling of foreign relations and far more than approved of his handling of the budget deficit.

In Table 7-6 we report some comparisons of 1984 with other recent elections. These comparisons are very difficult to make because different questions were asked in each election survey. Still, even with different questions, it seems quite reasonable to conclude that the public held far more positive views of the performance of the Reagan administration than any of the three administrations preceding it. While a majority approved of Reagan's handling of the economy in 1984, less than one in four held positive views of economic performance in the Nixon, Ford, and Carter years. Clearly, Carter was perceived most negatively, but no other recent administration was seen nearly as positively as Reagan's.

The "bottom-line" question is whether these views are related to voter choice. As the data in Table 7-6 show, those who held positive views of governmental performance in economic affairs were very likely to vote for the incumbent, by percentages ranging from almost 80 and up. Large majorities of those with negative views voted to "throw the rascal out," and those with neutral or balanced views (in those years when such responses were possible) split their vote much more evenly. Note that those with balanced views were more likely to vote to retain the administration, possibly reflecting a desire to maintain a satisfactory performance in favor of taking a risk with an unknown quantity.

The 1972, 1976, and 1980 surveys contained questions that enabled us to measure comparative retrospective evaluations of the parties on key economic problems. Analysis of these questions suggested that people were able to make comparative assessments about which party would be better at handling the economy; that those assessments were related to, but still different from, the sorts of retrospective views examined here; and, most important, those comparative assessments were even more

Table 7-6 Evaluations of the Government/Incumbent's Handling of the Economy and Major Party Vote, 1972-1984

A. Distribution of Responses

| | Government Performance on Inflation/ Unemployment | | Approval of Incumbent's Handling of the Economy | |
	1972[1]	*1976*[2]	*1980*[3]	*1984*[4]
Positive view	22%	15%	18%	58%
Neutral/balanced	59	45	17	—
Negative view	19	39	65	42
Total percent	100%	99%	100%	100%
(N)	(941)	(2664)	(1097)	(1858)

B. Percentage of Major Party Voters Who Voted for the Incumbent for President

Positive view	91	79	88	86
(N)	(149)	(247)	(130)	(801)
Neutral/balanced	68	57	60	—
(N)	(401)	(688)	(114)	
Negative view	30	26	23	16
(N)	(122)	(597)	(451)	(515)

[1] Questions asked of randomly selected half sample, asking whether the government had done a good (positive), fair (neutral), or poor (negative) job on handling inflation and unemployment, combined.
[2] Weighted Ns. Two questions asked in fashion similar to 1972. A "positive [negative] view" was good [poor] on both, or on one, "fair" on the other. Neutral/balanced was any other combination of nonmissing responses.
[3] In 1980 the questions asked whether the respondent approved or disapproved of Carter's handling of inflation [unemployment]. A positive [negative] view was approve [disapprove] on both; balanced responses were approve on one, disapprove on the other.
[4] In 1984 responses were whether the respondent approved of Reagan's handling of the economy.

closely related to voter choice. The evidence, we conclude, supports the Downs-Fiorina view that retrospective voting is based on comparative evaluations.[14] While comparable questions were not included in the 1984 SRC-CPS survey, it still seems reasonable to conclude that available evidence favors the Downs-Fiorina view.

Other Retrospective Evaluations

Although economic concerns have been central to all recent elections and have dominated studies of retrospective voting, there are other retrospective judgments that also have influenced voters. Respondents in several surveys were asked whether there was then a greater chance of war than in the last few years, or a chance of a bigger war during the Korean and Vietnam war years. In 1984 they were asked whether they were worried that the United States would become involved in a conventional war and whether they were worried that the country would get into a nuclear war. About a third said they were very worried about "our country getting into a nuclear war at this time," another third said they were somewhat worried, and the final third said they were not worried. Fewer (about one in five) were very worried about getting into a conventional war, and the rest were about evenly divided between "somewhat worried" and "not worried." About half said they thought the two parties were about equally likely to keep the United States out of war, and just a few more picked the Republican party over the Democrats as better at keeping the country out of war. In all years, the retrospective evaluation is clearly related to the vote, but the comparative assessment of parties is related to the vote even more strongly. Thus, these questions show the same basic patterns as those about the economy.[15]

Specific events, policies, or problems also serve as a basis of retrospective evaluations. Examples are Gerald R. Ford's pardon of Richard Nixon and Carter's handling of the Iranian hostage crisis. In other words, the dominant attention on the economy as the source of retrospective evaluations is due to the nature of the times, to the overriding importance of economic concerns in the 1970s and early 1980s, and not due to economic issues being the sole basis on which the public can form retrospective judgments.

Evaluations of the Incumbent

Thus far we have considered two kinds of retrospective evaluations. Personal effects of social outcomes (such as one's financial status) and perceptions of the nation's economic well-being can be understood as "simple retrospective evaluations," according to Fiorina. Specific evaluations and comparisons of the performance of the president, government, and the political parties are "mediated retrospective evaluations"— evaluations mediated through the perceptions of political actors and institutions.[16]

As we have seen, the more politically mediated the question, the more closely responses align with voting behavior. Perhaps the ultimate in mediated evaluations is the so-called (and misnamed) "presidential popularity" question: "Do you approve or disapprove of the way [the incumbent] is handling his job as president?" From a retrospective voting standpoint, this evaluation is a summary of all aspects of his service in office. Table 7-7 reports the distribution of these evaluations and their

Table 7-7 Distribution of Responses on President's Handling of Job and Major Party Vote, 1972-1984

A. Distribution of Responses

Do you approve or disapprove of the way [the incumbent] is handling his job as president?	Election Year			
	1972	1976	1980	1984
Approve	71%	63%	41%	64%
Disapprove	29	37	59	36
Total percent	100%	100%	100%	100%
(N)	(1215)	(2439)[1]	(1279)	(1989)

B. Percentage of Major Party Voters Who Voted for the Incumbent

Approve	83	74	81	87
(N)[2]	(553)	(935)[1]	(315)	(863)
Disapprove	14	9	18	7
(N)	(203)	(523)[1]	(491)	(449)

[1] Weighted Ns.
[2] Numbers in parentheses are the totals upon which percentages are based.

Note: Question was asked of a randomly selected half sample in 1972. In 1984, only respondents interviewed in the full post-election survey are included.

relationship to major party voting in the last four elections.

As can be seen in Table 7-7A, the three Republican incumbents have enjoyed widespread approval whereas only 4 respondents in 10 approved of Carter's handling of his job. Carter's dilemma in 1980—and at least part of Reagan's advantage in 1984—is even clearer if we look at Table 7-7B, in which the very strong relationship to the vote is evident. Like previous incumbents, Reagan held the support of those who approved of his performance—and lost the votes of the vast majority of those who disapproved. Ford in 1976 presents the only anomaly. A clear majority approved of his performance, yet he was unable to hold that support as well as other incumbents.

The Impact of Retrospective Evaluations

Our evidence strongly suggests that retrospective voting was widespread in all recent elections. Moreover, as far as data permit us to judge, the evidence is clearly on the side of the Downs-Fiorina view. Retrospective evaluations appear to be used to make comparative judgments. Presumably, voters find it easier, less time consuming, and less risky to

Figure 7-1A Distribution of Electorate on Summary Measure of Retrospective Evaluations, 1976, 1980, 1984

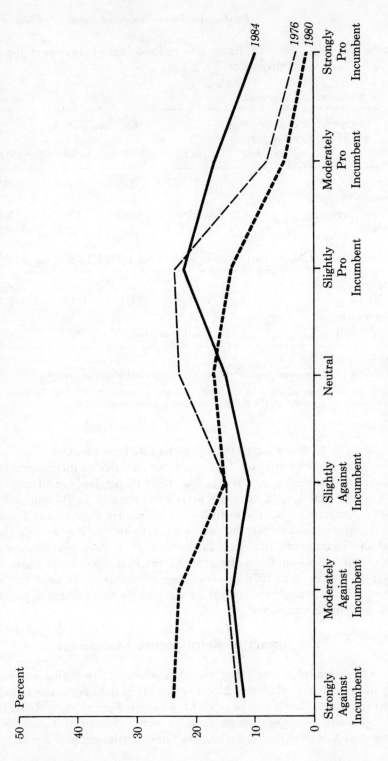

Total Number of Cases: 1976, 2,166 (weighted); 1980, 1,325; 1984, 1,814.

Figure 7-1B Percentage of Major Party Voters Who Voted for the Incumbent, by Summary Measure of Retrospective Evaluations, 1976, 1980, 1984

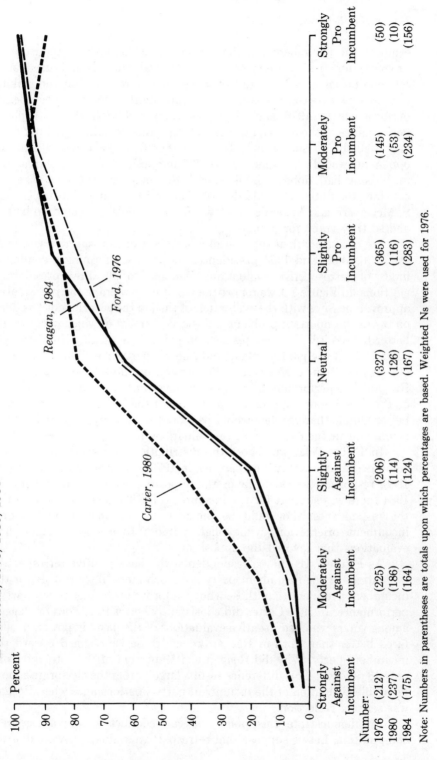

	Strongly Against Incumbent	Moderately Against Incumbent	Slightly Against Incumbent	Neutral	Slightly Pro Incumbent	Moderately Pro Incumbent	Strongly Pro Incumbent
Number:							
1976	(212)	(225)	(206)	(327)	(365)	(145)	(50)
1980	(237)	(186)	(114)	(126)	(116)	(53)	(10)
1984	(175)	(164)	(124)	(167)	(283)	(234)	(156)

Note: Numbers in parentheses are totals upon which percentages are based. Weighted Ns were used for 1976.

evaluate the incumbent on what he has done in the past than on his promises for the future. And yet, that evaluation is not used as a referendum, as a rational god of vengeance or reward, but for making comparisons between the two major contenders. When the incumbent's performance in 1976 and 1980 was compared with the anticipated performance of the opponent, most felt that the incumbent had not done very well, but a surprisingly large number of those believed that his opponent would do worse. In 1972 and 1984, many felt that the incumbent had done well, leaving little room for the challenger to convince the public he could do even better. Still, some—but for George S. McGovern and Mondale, too few—felt the challenger could do better, and so they voted for him.

We can strengthen the overall assessment of retrospective voting in the 1976, 1980, and 1984 presidential elections by forming a combined index of retrospective evaluations common to all three presidential elections. In Figure 7-1 we report the result of combining the presidential approval measure with the evaluation of the job the government has done on the most important problem and the assessment of which party would better handle it.[17] This creates a seven-point scale ranging from strongly supportive of the job the incumbent and his party have done to strongly opposed to that performance. For instance, those who approved of Reagan's job performance, thought the government was doing a good job on the most important problem, and thought the Republican party would better handle that problem would be scored as strongly supportive of the incumbent in their retrospective evaluations for 1984.

In Figure 7-1A we report the distribution of respondents on this combined measure.[18] As you can see, in 1976, and even more strongly in 1980, responses tended to favor the opposition over the incumbent. In 1984 there was support for the incumbent; for instance, virtually half of the respondents who could be included in the analysis had a pro-incumbent orientation, while slightly more than one in three had evaluations that favored the opposition.

As Figure 7-1B shows, respondents who have positive retrospective evaluations of the incumbent party are much more likely to vote for the incumbent president than those who disapprove of the incumbent party's performance. In 1980 Carter did consistently better than Ford or Reagan among voters who had negative evaluations of the party in power; he also fared better than Ford or Reagan among those who leaned toward the incumbent party. Why did Reagan win 59 percent of the vote and Ford only 48 percent? This difference results largely from the electorate's more favorable evaluation of the incumbent party's performance when Reagan was seeking reelection.

To demonstrate this point, we can conduct a simple algebraic computation. Let us suppose that retrospective evaluations were distributed the same way in 1984 as they were in 1976. Suppose, in other words, that retrospective evaluations were as unfavorable to the incumbent party as they were eight years earlier. Let us further suppose that among each of the seven subsets of voters, Reagan won precisely the same percentage of the vote that he actually won in the 1984 election. In other words, the same proportion of those who, for instance, strongly supported his and the Republican party's performance voted for him as they actually did, the difference being that there would be fewer people holding that view. If we make these assumptions, Reagan would have received only 50 percent of the vote, just a bit more than Ford received in 1976. Rather than a Reagan landslide, the 1984 election would have been a tossup that could have been won by either Reagan or Mondale.

In sum, it would seem reasonable to conclude that the 1976 election, with its razor-thin edge going to Carter, was a very narrow rejection of Ford's incumbency, and 1980 was a clear and strong rejection of Carter's. In 1984 Reagan won in large part because he was seen as having performed well and because Mondale was unable to convince the public he would do better.

There is obviously more to the differences between these elections than differences in retrospective evaluations alone. For one thing, Carter did better among those who disapproved of the Democratic incumbency than Ford or Reagan did among those who disapproved of their Republican incumbencies. And Reagan did somewhat better than Ford, even if we take into account that Reagan benefited from more favorable retrospective judgments.

Another difference may be found in the "balance of [prospective] issues" measure analyzed in Chapter 6. As you may recall, this measure was strongly related to the vote in 1984, apparently more so than in any election since 1972. *(See Figures 6-4 and 7-1B to compare the relationship of the balance of issues measure to voting choice with the relationship of the summary measure of retrospective evaluations to voting choice.)* Table 7-8 presents the joint relationship of both types of policy evaluation measures with the vote for Reagan, collapsing both summary measures into pro-Republican, neutral, and pro-Democratic categories. Clearly, if people had a partisan orientation to their retrospective judgments, that orientation was closely related to the vote— more closely related to the vote than was the balance of issues measure. Still, the balance of issues measure remains related to the vote. For the 1976 and 1980 elections, there was little relationship between issue preferences and the vote, once people's retrospective judgments were taken into account.[19] Thus, the 1984 election appears to be more like that of 1972, in that retrospective evaluations were more important than the issue preferences, but the latter remained an important factor in the vote.

Table 7-8 Percentage of Major Party Voters Who Voted for Reagan by Balance of Issues and Summary Retrospective Measures, 1984

Balance of Issues[1]	Repub- lican	(N)[3]	Neutral	(N)	Demo- cratic	(N)	Total	(N)
			Summary Retrospective:[2]					
Republican	97	(264)	69	(36)	26	(31)	87	(331)
Neutral	94	(269)	67	(72)	12	(132)	67	(473)
Democratic	82	(140)	54	(59)	4	(300)	32	(499)
Total	93	(673)	63	(167)	8	(463)	59	(1303)

[1] The neutral category is a score of −1, 0, or 1 on the full measure, while Republican [Democratic] is any score greater than 1 [less than −1] on the full measure.
[2] The neutral category is the same as on the full scale, while the Republican [Democratic] category is the combination of all three Republican [Democratic] categories on the full scale.
[3] Number is the total on which the percentages are based.

Notice that, in Table 7-8, those who had no partisan orientation on either measure still voted primarily for Reagan. This suggests that there is still more to the vote than either prospective or retrospective voting, and there are other signs of this in that table as well. More important, we have not accounted for why people had the views they did on these two measures. While we cannot provide a complete account of the origins of people's views, there is one important source we can examine. Party identification, a variable we already utilized in Chapters 1, 2, and 4, provides a powerful means for the typical citizen to reach preliminary judgments. As we will see, partisanship is strongly related to these judgments, especially to retrospective evaluations. Moreover, party iden-tification plays a central role in debates about partisan realignment because many political scientists believe that no realignment can be complete unless there are changes in party loyalties as well as changes in voting behavior. Therefore, to understand voter choice better and to assess future Republican prospects, we must examine the role of party loyalties, and it is to this task we turn in the next chapter.

Notes

1. Paul R. Abramson, John H. Aldrich, and David W. Rohde, *Change and Continuity in the 1980 Elections*, rev. ed. (Washington, D.C.: CQ Press, 1983), Chap. 7.

2. V. O. Key, Jr., *Politics, Parties, and Pressure Groups*, 5th ed. (New York: Thomas Y. Crowell Co., 1964), 568.
3. Anthony Downs, *An Economic Theory of Democracy* (New York: Harper & Row, 1957).
4. Morris P. Fiorina, *Retrospective Voting in American National Elections* (New Haven, Conn.: Yale University Press, 1981), 83. We will examine this view of partisanship more closely in Chapter 8.
5. See Benjamin I. Page, *Choices and Echoes in Presidential Elections: Rational Man and Electoral Democracy* (Chicago: University of Chicago Press, 1978). He argues that "party cleavages" distinguish the party at the candidate and mass levels.
6. Arthur H. Miller and Martin P. Wattenberg, "Throwing the Rascals Out: Policy and Performance Evaluations of Presidential Candidates, 1952-1980," *American Political Science Review* 79 (June 1985): 359-72.
7. Each respondent assesses governmental performance on the problem he or she considers most important. In 1976, 1980, and 1984, respondents were asked, "How good a job is the government doing in dealing with this problem—a good job, only fair, or a poor job?"
8. A negative evaluation is not surprising. After all, if you thought the government had done a good job with the problem, then it probably would not be your major concern.
9. In 1976, 1980, and 1984, respondents were asked, "Which political party do you think would be the most likely to get the government to do a better job in dealing with this problem—the Republicans, the Democrats, or wouldn't there be much difference between them?"
10. These responses might be subject to "rationalization." For example, a Republican in 1984 might have thought that Reagan had not done very well but that Mondale would do worse—because the voter was a Republican. Of course, the evaluation of the incumbent's performance may have been rationalized as well. As we will see in Chapter 8, these assessments are, indeed, closely related to partisanship, although that does not demonstrate by itself that the voters are "rationalizing" their responses. On rationalization, see Richard A. Brody and Benjamin I. Page, "Comment: The Assessment of Policy Voting," *American Political Science Review* 66 (June 1972): 450-58.
11. See Gerald H. Kramer, "Short-Term Fluctuations in U.S. Voting Behavior, 1896-1964," *American Political Science Review* 65 (March 1971): 131-43; Fiorina, *Retrospective Voting;* M. Stephen Weatherford, "Economic Conditions and Electoral Outcomes: Class Differences in the Political Response to the Recession," *American Journal of Political Science* 22 (November 1978): 917-38; and D. Roderick Kiewiet, *Macroeconomics and Micropolitics: The Electoral Effects of Economic Issues* (Chicago: University of Chicago Press, 1983).
12. John E. Mueller, *War, Presidents and Public Opinion* (New York: John Wiley & Sons, 1973).
13. Edward R. Tufte, *Political Control of the Economy* (Princeton, N.J.: Princeton University Press, 1978). For a perceptive critique of the business cycle formulation, see James E. Alt and K. Alec Chrystal, *Political Economics* (Berkeley: University of California Press, 1983).

14. Abramson, Aldrich, and Rohde, *Change and Continuity in the 1980 Elections*, rev. ed., 147-51.
15. Fiorina, *Retrospective Voting*. Fiorina also shows that these variables have an effect on the vote independent of the economic measures.
16. Fiorina, *Retrospective Voting*.
17. To construct this measure, we awarded respondents two points if respondents approved of the president's performance, one if they had no opinion, and no points if they disapproved. Second, respondents received two points if they thought the government was doing a good job in handling the most important problem facing the country, one point if they thought the government was doing only a fair job, and no points if they thought the government was doing a poor job. Finally, for 1976 and 1984 respondents received two points for saying the Republican party would do a better job solving the most important problem, one point if they said that there was no difference between the two parties, and no points if they said the Democrats would do a better job. For 1980, when Democrats were in office, scoring on this last question was reversed. For all three questions, "don't know" and "not ascertained" responses were scored as 1, but respondents with more than one such response were excluded from the analysis. Scores on our measure were the sums of the individual values for each of the three questions, and thus ranged from a low of 0 (strongly against the incumbent party) to a high of 6 (strongly for the incumbent party). Thus, this measure has seven possible values, corresponding to the seven categories in Figure 7-1.
18. This measure cannot be constructed for 1972. In the first place, the questions about governmental performance and the party that would do better were worded differently. More important, the 1972 SRC-CPS survey asked different questions to half of the respondents than to the other half. In particular, respondents who were asked to evaluate Nixon's performance as president were not asked the questions about governmental performance and which party would do better. There is, therefore, no way to combine responses to these three questions.
19. Abramson, Aldrich, and Rohde, *Change and Continuity in the 1980 Elections*, rev. ed., 155-57, Table 7-8. Note that different measures of retrospective evaluations were used in that book. Similar results obtain, however, when our new measure is compared with the balance of issues measure in 1976 and 1980.

Chapter 8

Party Loyalties, Policy Preferences, Performance Evaluations, and the Vote

Political parties are central institutions in our political and electoral system. Most citizens identify with a political party, and this identification influences their political attitudes and, ultimately, their behavior. In the fifties and sixties the authors of *The American Voter* along with other scholars began to emphasize the importance of party loyalties.[1] Although today few would deny that partisanship is central to political attitudes and behavior, many scholars have begun to question the interpretation of the evidence gathered during the last three decades. Indeed, what is party identification and how does it actually structure other attitudes and behavior? We will try to answer these questions before examining the role that party identification played in the 1984 presidential election.

Party Identification:
The Standard View

According to the authors of *The American Voter,* party identification is "the individual's affective orientation to an important group-object in his environment," in this case the political party.[2] In other words, an individual sees that there are two major political parties that play significant roles in elections and develops an affinity for one of them. Most Americans develop a liking for either the Republican or Democratic party. The remainder are mostly independents, who are not only unattached to a party but also relatively unattached to politics in general.[3] They are less interested, informed, and active than their attached peers. Partisanship is, therefore, an evaluation of the two parties, but its implications extend to a wider variety of political phenomena. Angus Campbell and his colleagues measured partisanship simply by asking with which party an individual identifies and how strongly that identification is held.[4] If the individual does not identify with either party, he or she may "lean" toward a party or, if not, be "purely" independent. The small percentage who cannot relate to the party identification questions is "apolitical."[5]

Partisan identification in this view becomes an attachment or loyalty not unlike that observed between the individual and other groups or organizations in society, such as a religious body, social class, or even a favorite sports team. As with loyalties to many of these groups, partisan affiliation often begins early. One of the first political attitudes children develop is party identification, and it develops well before they acquire policy preferences and many other political orientations. Furthermore, as with other group loyalties, once an attachment to a party develops, it tends to endure. Some people do switch parties, of course, but they usually do so only if their social situation changes, if there is an issue of overriding concern that sways their loyalties, or if the political parties themselves change substantially.

Party identification, then, stands as a base or core orientation to electoral politics. It is often formed at an early age and endures for most people throughout their entire lives.[6] Once formed, this core, predicated on a general evaluation of the two parties, affects many other specific orientations. Democratic loyalists tend to evaluate Democratic candidates and officeholders more highly than Republican candidates and officeholders, and vice versa. In effect, one is predisposed to evaluate the promises and performance of one's party leaders relatively higher. It follows, therefore, that Democrats are more likely to vote for Democratic candidates than are Republicans, and vice versa.

Party Identification: An Alternative View

In *The Responsible Electorate,* published in 1966, V. O. Key, Jr., argued that party loyalties contributed to electoral inertia, with many partisans voting as "standpatters" from election to election.[7] That is, in the absence of any information to the contrary, or if the attractions and disadvantages of the candidates are fairly evenly balanced, partisans are expected to vote in a manner consistent with their loyalty to a political party. In recent years, scholars have reexamined the reasons for such behavior. In this new view, citizens who consider themselves Democrats have a standing decision to vote for the Democratic nominee because of the past positions of Democrats compared to Republicans and because of their comparative past performances while in office. In short, this view of party identification presumes that it is a "running tally" of past experience (mostly in terms of policy and performance), a sort of summary expression of political memory.[8]

Furthermore, when in doubt about what, say, a Democratic candidate is likely to do on civil rights in comparison to the Republican opponent, it is reasonable to assume the Democrat would be more liberal than the Republican—at least unless the candidates indicate otherwise. Because the political parties tend to be consistent on the basic historical policy cleavages for lengthy periods of time, summary judgments of parties and their typical candidates will not change radically or often.[9] As a result, one's running tally serves as a good first approximation, changes rarely, and can be an excellent device for saving time that would be spent gathering information in the absence of this "memory."

Many of the major findings used in support of the conventional interpretation of party identification are completely consistent with this more policy-oriented view. We do not have the evidence to assert one view as superior to the other. Indeed, the two interpretations are not mutually exclusive and to choose between them calls for a very different sort of empirical research than is available at the present time. What is important is that, while party identification can be understood in different ways, both views emphasize the central role of party identification in shaping voters' decisions.

Party Identification in the Electorate

If partisan identification is a fundamental orientation for most citizens, then the distribution of party loyalties among the electorate is of crucial importance. As Table 8-1 shows, most people have a sense of party identification. In 1984 nearly two-thirds of the sample claimed to think of themselves as a Democrat or a Republican, and another 1 in 4, who initially said that they were independent or had no preference, nonetheless said they felt closer to one of the major parties than the other.[10] Only 1 in 10 were purely independent of party, and 1 in 50 were classified as "apolitical." There appears to be a general, if small, decline in the number of people identifying themselves as independents. Beginning in the mid-1960s, more and more people claimed to be independents.[11] However, by the late 1970s and through the early 1980s, this growth stopped and, if anything, began to decline to the levels found in the late 1960s and early 1970s. Still, as we saw in Chapter 4, the percentage of strong partisans is substantially lower than it was two decades ago.

Table 8-1 also shows that more people continue to think of themselves as Democrats rather than as Republicans. Over the past 32 years, the balance between the two parties has favored the Democrats by a range of about 55 to 45 to about 60 to 40. While the 1984 results still fall

Table 8-1 Party Identification, 1984

Party Identification	Preelection Survey	Postelection Survey
Strong Democrat	17%	18%
Weak Democrat	20	22
Independent, leans Democratic	11	10
Independent, no partisan leanings	11	7
Independent, leans Republican	13	14
Weak Republican	15	15
Strong Republican	13	15
Total Percent	100	101
(N)	(2198)	(1941)
Apolitical	2%	2%
(N)	(38)	(32)

within that historic range, they show a clear shift to the Republicans. In the 1980 Survey Research Center-Center for Political Studies preelection survey, 35 percent of the party identifiers were Republican, and in the postelection survey 37 percent were.[12] In the 1984 preelection survey 42 percent of the party identifiers were Republicans, and in the postelection survey 43 percent were. Moreover, if independents who "lean" to a party are counted as partisans, the percentage of Republicans would rise from 38 percent (1980 preelection) or 42 percent (1980 postelection) to 45 percent (1984 preelection) or 47 percent (1984 postelection).

This shift toward Republican identification was revealed in numerous other surveys, with studies suggesting that much of this pro-Republican shift occurred in the fall of 1984. For example, the General Social Survey, conducted by the National Opinion Research Center at the University of Chicago, found that the percentage calling themselves Republicans rose from 37 percent of the party identifiers in early 1980 to 40 percent in early 1984. If independents who leaned toward a major party were included, the percentage of Republicans would rise from 38 percent to 41 percent.[13] But Gallup polls, which have been monitoring party loyalties since 1937, found a sizable shift toward the Republicans in the fall of 1984.[14] For all of 1980, Gallup found that 46 percent called themselves Democrats, and only 24 percent said they were Republicans. By the fall of 1984, Gallup found that only 39 percent called themselves Democrats, and 35 percent said they were Republicans.[15] Because only about 300 respondents per month were sampled in the SRC-CPS continuous monitoring survey, these data must be used with caution, but

Table 8-2 Party Identification among Whites, 1952-1984

Party Identification[1]	Survey Year																
	1952	1954	1956	1958	1960	1962	1964	1966	1968	1970	1972	1974	1976	1978	1980	1982	1984
Strong Democrat	21%	22%	20%	26%	20%	22%	24%	17%	16%	17%	12%	15%	13%	12%	14%	16%	15%
Weak Democrat	25	25	23	22	25	23	25	27	25	22	25	20	23	24	23	24	18
Independent, leans Democratic	10	9	6	7	6	8	9	9	10	11	12	13	11	14	12	11	11
Independent, no partisan leanings	6	7	9	8	9	8	8	12	11	13	13	15	15	14	14	11	11
Independent, leans Republican	7	6	9	5	7	7	6	8	10	9	11	9	11	11	11	9	13
Weak Republican	14	15	14	17	14	17	14	16	16	16	14	15	16	14	16	16	17
Strong Republican	14	13	16	12	17	13	12	11	11	10	11	9	10	9	9	11	14
Apolitical	2	2	2	3	1	3	1	1	1	1	1	3	1	3	2	2	2
Total percent	99%	99%	99%	100%	100%	101%	99%	99%	100%	99%	99%	99%	100%	101%	101%	100%	101%
(N)	(1615)	(1015)	(1610)	(1638)[2]	(1739)[2]	(1168)	(1394)	(1131)	(1387)	(1395)	(2397)	(2246)[2]	(2490)[2]	(2006)[2]	(1405)	(1248)	(1931)

[1] The percentage supporting another party has not been presented; it usually totals less than 1 percent and never totals more than 1 percent.
[2] Weighted Ns

these telephone polls suggest that there was a substantial increase in the proportion of the electorate identifying as Republican in October 1984. The position of the Democrats as the majority party in the electorate had been seriously eroded.

The shift toward the Republican party is a phenomenon concentrated almost exclusively among white Americans. As we saw in Chapter 5, the sharpest social division in U.S. electoral politics is race, and this division has been reflected in partisan affiliations for decades. In Table 8-2 we report the party identification of whites between 1952 and 1984, and in Table 8-3 we report the affiliation of blacks. As you can see, black and white patterns in partisan affiliation have been very different throughout this period. There was a sharp shift in black loyalties in the mid-1960s. Before then, about 50 percent of blacks were strong or weak Democrats, but from that time, 60 percent, 70 percent, and even more blacks considered themselves Democrats.

The party affiliations of whites have changed more slowly. Still, the percentage of self-professed Democrats among whites declined in 1984, while the percentage of Republicans (especially strong Republicans) increased. In 1984, then, affiliation by race changed, this time due to shifts among whites. Looking at strong, weak, and independent partisan leaners, the balance between the two parties among whites is virtually even, while among blacks, there are still about nine Democrats for every one Republican. In 1977, before the vigorous Republican party efforts in the 1978 congressional elections, Gallup found that 46 percent of the whites surveyed said they were Democrats, and only 22 percent said they were Republicans. This two-to-one edge disappeared entirely. By the fall of 1984, Gallup found that only 34 percent of the whites said they were Democrats, and 38 percent said they were Republicans.[16]

Party identification among blacks, however, has changed substantially since 1952, as Table 8-3 makes clear. Between 1952 and 1962, the Democratic party received greater loyalty from blacks than did the Republican party, although about one black out of seven still supported the Republicans.

The 1964 election marked a point of rapid growth of Democratic loyalty among blacks: 52 percent of the black electorate considered themselves strong Democrats. Since then, around 70 percent have identified, either strongly or weakly, with the Democratic party. At the same time, Republican identification fell to just a trace. The jump in support for the Democratic party in 1964 can be attributed to the two presidential nominees. Lyndon B. Johnson's advocacy of civil rights legislation appealed directly to black voters, and his Great Society programs in general made an only slightly more indirect appeal. The Republican nominee, Barry M. Goldwater, voted against the 1964 Civil Rights Act in the Senate, a vote criticized even by his Republican peers.

Table 8-3 Party Identification among Blacks, 1952-1984

Party Identification[1]	Survey Year																
	1952	1954	1956	1958	1960	1962	1964	1966	1968	1970	1972	1974	1976	1978	1980	1982	1984
Strong Democrat	30%	24%	27%	32%	25%	35%	52%	30%	56%	41%	36%	40%	34%	37%	45%	53%	32%
Weak Democrat	22	29	23	19	19	25	22	31	29	34	31	26	36	29	27	26	31
Independent, leans Democratic	10	6	5	7	7	4	8	11	7	7	8	15	14	15	9	12	14
Independent, no partisan leanings	4	5	7	4	16	6	6	14	3	12	12	12	8	9	7	5	11
Independent, leans Republican	4	6	1	4	4	2	1	2	1	1	3	—[2]	1	2	3	1	6
Weak Republican	8	5	12	11	9	7	5	7	1	4	4	—[2]	2	3	2	2	1
Strong Republican	5	11	7	7	7	6	2	2	1	0	4	3	2	3	3	0	2
Apolitical	17	15	18	16	14	15	4	3	3	1	2	4	1	2	4	1	2
Total percent	100%	101%	100%	100%	101%	100%	100%	100%	101%	100%	100%	100%	99%	100%	100%	100%	99%
(N)	(171)	(101)	(146)	(161)[2]	(171)[3]	(110)	(156)	(132)	(149)	(157)	(267)	(224)[3]	(290)[3]	(230)	(187)	(148)	(247)

[1] The percentage supporting another party has not been presented; it usually totals less than 1 percent and never totals more than 1 percent.
[2] Less than 1 percent.
[3] Weighted Ns.

Party stances have not shifted since then, although the percentage of blacks who were strong Democrats declined somewhat after 1968.

The other notable change in black partisanship concerned the apolitical category. Between 1952 and 1962, 14 percent or more could not relate to the questions used to measure party identification. In 1964 this percentage plummeted to 4 percent and has hovered at the 1 to 4 percent range since then, quite comparable to the percentages of apoliticals among whites. This shift also can be attributed directly to the civil rights movement, the contest between Johnson and Goldwater, and passage of the Civil Rights Act. Civil rights activism stimulated many blacks, especially in the South, to become politically active. And the Voting Rights Act of 1965 enabled many blacks to vote for the first time.

The number of independents among blacks grew slightly in the post-1964 period, but this seems to represent more of a shift away from the apolitical and Republican categories. The percentage of pure independents increased in 1966, but fell massively in 1968, probably in response to George Wallace's American Independent party candidacy. It declined between 1976 and 1980. Today there are about one-half to two-thirds as many independents among blacks as among whites. Recent Gallup polls confirm both the low number of independents among blacks and their overwhelming support for the Democrats. In surveys of about 700 blacks conducted in the fall of 1984, only 13 percent of the blacks said they were independents, while 28 percent of the 5,000 whites surveyed did. Eighty percent of the blacks said they were Democrats, and only 7 percent said they were Republicans.[17]

In short, the Democratic character of black partisanship is unmistakable. There are virtually two electorates in America, a white majority that is somewhat more Democratic than Republican (or, by late 1984, about evenly divided) and a black minority that is overwhelmingly Democratic. Even among blacks, however, there was a sharp decline in the percentage identifying as strong Democrats in the 1984 SRC-CPS survey.

Party Identification and the Vote

As we saw in Chapter 4, partisanship is related to turnout. Strong supporters of either party are more likely to vote than weak supporters, and independents who lean toward a party are more likely to vote than independents without partisan leanings. Republicans are somewhat more likely to vote than Democrats. While partisanship influences whether people go to the polls, it is more strongly related to *how* people vote.

Table 8-4 reports the percentage of white, major party voters who voted for the Democratic candidate across all categories of partisanship since 1952. Clearly, a strong relationship exists between partisan affiliation and candidate choice. With the single exception of the 1972

Table 8-4 White Major Party Voters Who Voted Democratic for President, by Party Identification, 1952-1984 (in percentages)

Party Identification	Survey Year								
	1952	1956	1960	1964	1968	1972	1976	1980	1984
Strong Democrat	82	85	91	94	89	66	88	87	88
Weak Democrat	61	63	70	81	66	44	72	59	63
Independent, leans Democratic	60	65	89	89	62	58	73	57	77
Independent, no partisan leanings	18	15	50	75	28	26	41	23	21
Independent, leans Republican	7	6	13	25	5	11	15	13	5
Weak Republican	4	7	11	40	10	9	22	5	6
Strong Republican	2	—[1]	2	9	3	2	3	4	2

[1] Less than 1 percent.

Note: To approximate the numbers upon which these percentages are based, see Table 8-2. Actual Ns will be smaller than those that can be derived from Table 8-2 because respondents who did not vote (or who voted for a minor party) have been excluded from these calculations. Numbers also will be lower since the voting report is provided in the postelection interviews that usually contain about 10 percent fewer respondents than the preelection interviews in which party identification is measured.

election, the Democratic nominee has received more than 80 percent of the vote of strong Democrats and majority support from both weak Democratic partisans and Democratic leaders. The picture is even clearer among Republicans. Since 1952, strong Republicans have given the Democratic candidate less than 1 vote in 10, even in the face of the massive Democratic landslide in 1964. The other two Republican categories are also more loyal than their Democratic counterparts. The pure independent vote, which fluctuates substantially, tends to be Republican, with the exception of 50 percent for John F. Kennedy in 1960 and 75 percent for Johnson in 1964. In strong Republican years, their vote is clearly Republican.

Among whites, then, partisanship leads to loyalty in voting. The 1984 election, in fact, saw a resurgence in the importance of party identification at the polls. In this election, the relationship between party identification and presidential voting choices was as high as it had been in the 1950s, although it fell below the relationship attained in 1960. However, the relationship between party identification and presidential vote in 1984 was higher than in any of the five elections between 1964 and 1980.[18] This increase in the impact of partisanship upon voting choices is reflected in voting for other offices, too. As we will see in Chapter 10, the relationship between party identification and voting for Congress increased somewhat in 1984. Moreover, the proportion of people who said they voted strictly along party lines for state and local offices, a proportion that had declined significantly over the last 20 years, increased somewhat in 1984; almost half claimed to have been "straight ticket" voters, the highest percentage since 1970. The much discussed "decline" of parties in the United States appears to have ceased, and, indeed, the two parties may be gathering new strength in the public.

As we saw in Chapter 5, blacks have voted overwhelmingly Democratic since 1964. Because of this near unanimity, there is no meaningful relationship between party identification and the vote. Prior to 1964, more blacks identified with the Republican party. Nevertheless, the relationship between partisanship and the vote was weak because even blacks who said they were Republicans often voted Democratic.

Partisanship is related to the way people vote, but why do partisans support their party's candidates? As we shall see, party identification affects behavior because it helps structure the way voters view both policies and performance.

Policy Preferences and Performance Evaluations

In their study of voting in the 1948 presidential election, Bernard R. Berelson, Paul F. Lazarsfeld, and William N. McPhee discovered that Democratic voters attributed to their nominee, incumbent Harry S

Truman, positions on key issues that were consistent with their own beliefs—whether they were liberal, moderate, or conservative.[19] Similarly, Republicans tended to see their nominee, Gov. Thomas E. Dewey, taking whatever positions they preferred. Since then, research has emphasized the roles of party identification in the "projection" on the preferred candidate of positions similar to the voter's own views and in influencing policy preferences in the public.[20] We will use four examples to illustrate the strong relationship between partisan affiliation and perceptions, preferences, and evaluations of candidates and other election-specific factors.

First, most partisans evaluate a president of their party as having done a better job than do independents and those who identify with the other party. This is revealed in Figure 8-1, which shows the percentage of each of the seven partisan groups that approves of the way the incumbent has handled his job as president (as a proportion of those approving or disapproving) in the last four presidential elections. Strong Republicans have given overwhelming approval to the last three Republican incumbents, and even three of four strong Democrats gave their approval to the generally unpopular Carter presidency in 1980. In all four cases, the differences between Democrats and Republicans is very clear. The "pure" independents have favored the Republicans on this measure, giving majority approval to all Republican presidents—and nearly overwhelming approval to Ronald Reagan in 1984—but not giving their approval to Carter in 1980. Overall, partisanship is clearly not directly translated into approval or disapproval, but it is closely related to it.

Second, partisans' policy preferences tend to put them closer to the policy positions of their party's nominee. In Table 8-5 we present the relationship between partisan affiliation and our "balance of issues" measure, which summarizes the overall Democratic or Republican leanings of each respondent on the issue scale questions asked in each election survey and analyzed in Chapter 6.[21] As we saw there, these issues favored the Republicans in 1972, 1976, and 1980, but worked slightly to Mondale's advantage in 1984.

As the table shows, there is a moderate relationship between partisanship and the "balance of issues" measure in 1976, 1980, and 1984, and there was a similar, moderate relationship in 1972. Until 1984 the relationship had been stronger among Republicans than among Democrats. The 1984 election, for instance, was the only one in which Democratic identifiers were, on balance, closer to the samplewide perception of their party nominee's positions on issues than to the Republican nominee's. In the earlier elections, a majority of Republican identifiers were closer to where the Republican nominee was seen to stand, while only a handful were closer to the perceptions of the Democratic nominee's positions. By 1984 one Republican in five was closer to his or her

Figure 8-1 Partisan Groups Approving of Incumbent's Handling of Job, 1972, 1976, 1980, 1984

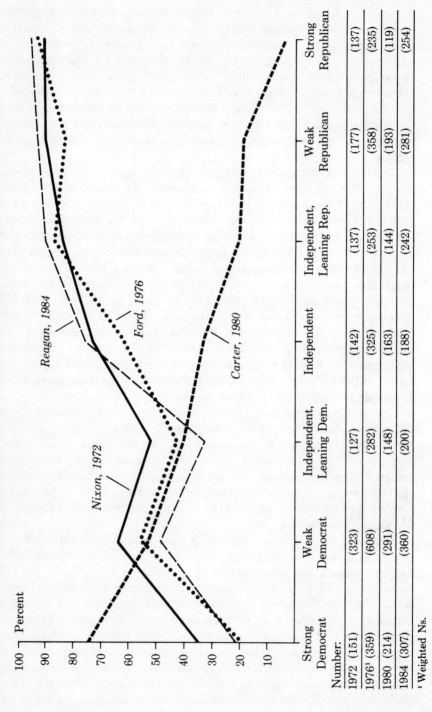

	Strong Democrat	Weak Democrat	Independent, Leaning Dem.	Independent	Independent, Leaning Rep.	Weak Republican	Strong Republican
Number:							
1972	(151)	(323)	(127)	(142)	(137)	(177)	(137)
1976[1]	(359)	(608)	(282)	(325)	(253)	(358)	(235)
1980	(214)	(291)	(148)	(163)	(144)	(193)	(119)
1984	(307)	(360)	(200)	(188)	(242)	(281)	(254)

[1] Weighted Ns.

Table 8-5 Balance of Issues Positions among Partisan Groups, 1976-1984

				Party Identification				
Issue Positions Closer to:	Strong Democrat	Weak Democrat	Independent, Leans Democrat	Independent	Independent, Leans Republican	Weak Republican	Strong Republican	Total
1976[1]								
Democratic candidate	28%	27%	22%	15%	12%	9%	3%	18%
Neutral[2]	32	26	37	29	27	23	27	29
Republican candidate	39	47	40	55	61	67	69	53
Total percent	99	100	99	99	100	99	99	100
(N)	(422)	(655)	(336)	(416)	(277)	(408)	(254)	(2778)
1980								
Democratic candidate	26%	23%	27%	20%	12%	10%	9%	19%
Neutral	34	37	33	43	40	43	31	37
Republican candidate	40	40	40	37	48	48	60	43
Total percent	100	100	100	100	100	101	100	99
(N)	(245)	(317)	(161)	(176)	(150)	(202)	(127)	(1378)
1984								
Democratic candidate	57%	49%	59%	35%	23%	29%	14%	39%
Neutral	32	37	28	48	46	40	39	38
Republican candidate	11	14	13	17	32	32	47	23
Total percent	100	100	100	100	101	101	100	100
(N)	(331)	(390)	(215)	(213)	(248)	(295)	(256)	(1948)

[1] Weighted Ns.

[2] The neutral category consists of those who were scored as 0 on the balance of issues measure or as 1 in a pro-Democratic or pro-Republican direction. A score of more than 1 in a pro-Democratic direction is considered as closer to the Democratic candidate, while more than 1 in a pro-Republican direction is considered as closer to the Republican candidate.

perception of Mondale's position, while the rest were evenly split between being closer to Reagan's position and being in the neutral category.

Why is the relationship between partisan affiliation and positions on issues usually clearer among Republicans? For the most part, the Republicans' ideology is more sharply defined than the Democrats', perhaps because they are a smaller and more cohesive political party.[22] This Republican advantage is balanced against the advantage enjoyed by the Democratic party—more identifiers. By 1984 the Reagan appeal reached out to a broad segment of the public, while Mondale's appeal was the more cohesive on party and on policy. A relationship does exist between partisan affiliation and positions on issues, but it is not overwhelming. That these relationships are moderate suggests that candidates themselves affect the way voters view the issues and that candidate behavior is more important than partisanship in influencing the effect of issues on the vote.

The relationship depicted in Table 8-6 between partisanship and the party or candidate seen to be better at handling economic issues is much closer than the tie between partisanship and the balance of issues measure. Again, we report the measure collapsed into three categories for 1976 to 1980 and two categories in 1984 (there being no neutral or middle category). Table 8-6 shows that distribution for all seven categories of partisan identification.[23]

The relationship between partisanship and the party judged as better on economic issues appears to be much stronger than that between party identification and positions on the issues. (A similar result occurred in the 1972 election data.) How we understand this relationship, however, depends upon which view of partisanship we follow. According to the standard view, partisans believe their party would do better because they are loyal to their party and because they are likely to be more receptive to their party's successes and less forgiving of the opposition's failures. According to the more recent interpretation of Morris P. Fiorina and others, partisans are partisans because they believe one party had been better at handling these and other problems. Either way, we find a strong tie between party loyalties and evaluations of the parties among the electorate.

Finally, we find a strong relationship between party identification and our summary measure of retrospective evaluations. We found that in 1976, 1980, and 1984 there was a strong relationship between party loyalties and evaluations of the incumbent party's performance (measured by the respondent's evaluation of the president's performance, the job the government is doing on the "most important problem," and which party he or she thinks would do the best job dealing with this problem).[24] Table 8-7 shows the basic relationships in these years, although we have simplified the presentation by dividing our summary measure into three

Table 8-6 Party Better on Economy among Partisan Groups, 1976-1984

Party/Candidate Better[1]	Strong Democrat	Weak Democrat	Independent, Leans Democrat	Party Identification — Independent	Independent, Leans Republican	Weak Republican	Strong Republican	Total
1976[2]								
Democratic	83%	55%	49%	15%	10%	10%	5%	38%
Neutral	16	38	48	78	56	61	36	46
Republican	2	6	3	6	34	28	58	16
Total percent	101	99	100	99	100	99	99	100
(N)	(386)	(638)	(296)	(329)	(256)	(349)	(225)	(2479)
1980								
Democratic	57%	27%	24%	6%	1%	3%	3%	21%
Neutral	37	57	63	72	35	35	21	47
Republican	6	16	13	22	65	62	75	33
Total percent	100	100	100	100	101	100	99	101
(N)	(228)	(286)	(147)	(149)	(139)	(191)	(118)	(1258)
1984								
Democratic	83%	59%	68%	32%	16%	14%	5%	42%
Neutral	—	—	—	—	—	—	—	—
Republican	17	41	32	68	84	86	95	58
Total percent	100	100	100	100	100	100	100	100
(N)	(309)	(367)	(207)	(179)	(245)	(277)	(249)	(1833)

[1] For the wording of each year's questions, see Table 7-6.
[2] Weighted Ns.

basic categories—pro-Democratic, neutral, and pro-Republican. In all three years, a majority of Republican identifiers tended to evaluate Republican performance favorably. Even in 1976, when only about one respondent in three was favorable to the Republicans, more than 60 percent of the Republicans were favorable. And in both 1976 and 1984, more than three Democratic identifiers out of five assessed the Democratic party favorably. In 1980 only 20 percent of the electorate gave favorable assessments of Democratic performance, but among all Democratic identifiers, 36 percent did. Among strong Democrats, 45 percent gave favorable evaluations, more than twice the level as the electorate as a whole.

Although party identification and retrospective evaluations are strongly related to each other, they still both contribute independently to the way people vote. We have examined the combined impact of party identification and retrospective evaluations upon voting choices in the last three presidential elections. To simplify the presentation we have regrouped party identification into three basic categories: strong and weak Republicans, all independents, and strong and weak Democrats. As with Table 8-7, we present results for the three basic categories on our summary measure of retrospective evaluations.

Table 8-8 shows the percentage of major party voters who voted Republican, controlling for both party identification and retrospective evaluations. Reading across each row reveals that in all three elections retrospective evaluations are strongly related to the vote, regardless of the respondents' party identification. Reading down each column shows that in all three elections party identification is related to the vote, regardless of retrospective evaluations. In all three elections, party identification exerts its strongest influence among respondents with neutral retrospective evaluations. Moreover, party identification and retrospective evaluations always have a strong combined impact upon how people voted. For example, in 1984 among Republican party identifiers with pro-Republican evaluations, 99 percent voted for Reagan: among Democratic identifiers with pro-Democratic evaluations, only 5 percent did.

In sum, partisanship appears to affect the way voters evaluate incumbents and their performance. Moreover, the projective inference about likely future performance on economic and, presumably, other issues is intimately bound up in party loyalties, at least where those measures could be examined. Positions on issues are rather different. While partisans are likely to be closer to their party's nominee and his policy platform, the connection between party identification and comparisons between partisans' preferences and candidates' positions on issues is less clear cut. Policy-related evaluations in general are partly

Table 8-7 Retrospective Evaluations among Partisan Groups, 1976-1984

Summary Measure of Retrospective Evaluation[1]	Party Identification							
	Strong Democrat	Weak Democrat	Independent, Leans Democrat	Independent	Independent, Leans Republican	Weak Republican	Strong Republican	Total
1976[2]								
Democratic	80%	53%	62%	39%	16%	19%	6%	42%
Neutral	11	23	24	28	28	25	23	23
Republican	10	24	15	33	56	57	71	35
Total percent	101	100	101	100	100	101	100	100
(N)	(314)	(535)	(249)	(293)	(238)	(314)	(206)	(2149)
1980								
Democratic	45%	29%	18%	11%	8%	7%	4%	20%
Neutral	26	21	25	22	8	9	2	17
Republican	29	50	57	68	85	84	93	62
Total percent	100	100	100	101	101	100	99	99
(N)	(229)	(294)	(157)	(160)	(144)	(197)	(123)	(1304)
1984								
Democratic	77%	54%	65%	27%	9%	9%	5%	37%
Neutral	12	17	13	22	15	18	5	14
Republican	12	29	21	52	76	73	90	49
Total percent	101	100	99	101	100	100	100	100
(N)	(303)	(356)	(197)	(181)	(241)	(270)	(239)	(1787)

[1] The neutral category is the same as that on the full scale, while the Democratic [Republican] category is the combination of all three Democratic [Republican] categories on the full scale.
[2] Weighted Ns.

Table 8-8 Percentage of Major Party Voters Who Voted for the Republican Candidate, by Party Identification and Summary Retrospective Measures, 1976, 1980, 1984

Party Identification[1]	Republican	(N)	Neutral	(N)	Democratic	(N)	Total	(N)
			Summary Retrospective[2]					

A. Percentage Who Voted for Ford, 1976[3]

Party Identification[1]	Republican	(N)	Neutral	(N)	Democratic	(N)	Total	(N)
Republican	96	(269)[4]	90	(98)	35	(54)	87	(421)
Independent	85	(183)	73	(133)	16	(187)	56	(503)
Democratic	53	(111)	30	(96)	5	(404)	18	(611)
Total	84	(563)	65	(327)	11	(645)	49	(1535)[4]

B. Percentage Who Voted for Reagan, 1980

Republican	100	(217)	75	(12)	33	(12)	95	(241)
Independent	82	(183)	36	(36)	24	(25)	69	(244)
Democratic	51	(135)	6	(78)	7	(140)	24	(353)
Total	81	(535)	21	(126)	11	(177)	58	(838)

C. Percentage Who Voted for Reagan, 1984

Republican	99	(344)	86	(42)	39	(18)	95	(404)
Independent	91	(230)	77	(62)	10	(110)	67	(402)
Democratic	72	(97)	32	(62)	5	(333)	22	(492)
Total	93	(671)	63	(166)	8	(461)	59	(1298)

[1] Democratic [Republican] identifiers were those classified as strong and weak Democrats [Republicans]. Independents include those who lean toward either party as well as "pure" independents.
[2] The neutral category is the same as that on the full scale, while the Democratic [Republican] category is the combination of all three Democratic [Republican] categories on the full scale.
[3] Weighted Ns.
[4] The numbers in parentheses are the totals upon which percentages are based.

influenced by history and political memory and partly by the candidate's campaign rhetoric. Partisan attachments, then, limit the ability of candidates to fully control their fate in the electorate, but they are not entirely rigid limits. Candidates may be fairly tightly constrained by prior performance, especially that of the incumbent, as seen in partisan terms, but they are less limited by partisanship in their ability to receive support based on issues.

Conclusion

Party loyalties affect how people vote, how they evaluate issues, and how they judge the performance of the incumbent and his party. In recent years, research has suggested that party loyalties not only affect behavior, but that behavior may affect party loyalties. Moreover, the relationship between party loyalties and issue preferences is more complex than any model assuming a one-way relationship would suggest. And doubtless, evaluations of incumbent performance may also affect party loyalties.[25]

As we saw in this chapter, there was a substantial shift toward Republican loyalties among the electorate between 1980 and 1984, and among whites the advantage the Democrats have enjoyed for the past four decades had been almost eliminated. To some extent, this shift in party loyalties must reflect Reagan's appeal, as well as his successful performance in office, at least as judged by the electorate. But it is still reasonable to ask the extent to which Reagan, when the 1984 election was finally held, benefited from that pro-Republican shift in party loyalties.

As we saw in Chapter 6, there was no shift toward the Republican party in the issue preferences of the electorate. But, as we saw in Chapter 7, there was a sizable shift among the electorate toward a favorable view of the incumbent party's performance. These retrospective evaluations were strongly related to voting choices, and, as we saw above, to party loyalties as well. Let us assume for the moment that party loyalties among the electorate did more to shape these retrospective evaluations than these evaluations did to shape partisanship. If so, how would those retrospective evaluations have been distributed in 1984 if the electorate had been as pro-Democratic in its partisan loyalties as it had been four years earlier?

In 1984, 49 percent of the electorate was pro-Republican on our summary measure of retrospective evaluations. We will assume that the distribution of party loyalties was the same in 1984 as it had been four years earlier, but that the percentage of each partisan group scoring as pro-Republican on our summary measure was the same as that we observed in 1984. Under these conditions, the overall percentage of the electorate favorable to the Republican party would have been 46 percent. To a small extent, then, the electorate was more favorable to the incumbent party in 1984 than it had been four years earlier because the electorate itself had become more Republican.

A more direct way to assess how much Reagan gained from the pro-Republican shift in party loyalties is to ask what share of the vote he would have received in 1984 if the partisan loyalties of the electorate were as Democratic as they had been four years earlier. This estimate is complicated because the relative turnout among partisan groups differed somewhat in the two elections. We will assume, however, that each party identification category had the same turnout in 1984 as that observed in the 1984 vote validation study, and that the percentage of each group voting for Reagan was the same as we observed in our 1984 survey. For example, in our hypothetical estimates Reagan would win the same support among strong Republicans in 1984 as he actually did win, but there would be fewer strong Republicans. According to our estimates, if there had been no shift in the party loyalties of the electorate, Reagan would have received only 53 percent of the vote in 1984, whereas he actually won 58 percent. Viewed from this perspective about 70 percent of Reagan's gains between 1980 and 1984 resulted from a shift in party loyalties among the electorate.

Clearly, party loyalties are still an important force in the electoral process. If anything, they were more strongly related to the vote in 1984 than in any election from 1964 through 1980. As we saw, party loyalties are related to issue preferences and are strongly related to retrospective evaluations. Given these relationships, the shift toward the Republican party identification among the electorate could have long-term consequences. One of the major advantages the Democrats enjoyed during the postwar years was a substantial lead in partisan loyalties. Because Republicans are somewhat more likely to vote than Democrats and because they are usually more loyal to their candidate than the Democrats are to theirs, this shift in party loyalties toward the Republicans could become an additional burden for the Democrats, at least in their quest to regain the presidency. Obviously, the Republicans hope to continue their gains in party loyalties. But even if they merely keep the gains they made between 1980 and 1984 they will have substantially improved their competitive position.

Notes

1. Angus Campbell, Philip E. Converse, Warren E. Miller, and Donald E. Stokes, *The American Voter* (New York: John Wiley & Sons, 1960).
2. Ibid., 121. See also Morris P. Fiorina, *Retrospective Voting in American National Elections* (New Haven, Conn.: Yale University Press, 1981), 85-86.
3. Only a very few identify with another party.
4. For the full wording of the party identification questions, see Chap. 4, note 40.
5. For the most detailed discussion of how the SRC-CPS creates its summary measure of party identification, see Arthur H. Miller and Martin P. Wattenberg, "Measuring Party Identification: Independent or No Partisan Preference?" *American Journal of Political Science* 27 (February 1983): 106-21.

6. For evidence on the relatively high level of partisan stability among individuals over time, see M. Kent Jennings and Gregory B. Markus, "Partisan Orientations over the Long Haul: Results from the Three-Wave Political Socialization Panel Study," *American Political Science Review* 78 (December 1984): 1000-18.
7. V. O. Key, Jr., *The Responsible Electorate: Rationality in Presidential Voting 1936-1960* (Cambridge, Mass.: Harvard University Press, 1966).
8. Morris P. Fiorina, "An Outline for a Model of Party Choice," *American Journal of Political Science* 21 (August 1977): 601-25; and Fiorina, *Retrospective Voting.*
9. Benjamin I. Page, *Choices and Echoes in Presidential Elections: Rational Man and Electoral Democracy* (Chicago: University of Chicago Press, 1978).
10. There is some controversy about how to classify these independent leaners. Some argue that they are mainly "hidden partisans" who should be considered to be identifiers. For the strongest statement of this position, see Bruce E. Keith et al., "The Partisan Affinities of Independent 'Leaners,'" *British Journal of Political Science,* forthcoming. In our view, however, the evidence on the proper classification of independent leaners is mixed. On balance, the evidence suggests that they are more partisan than independents with no partisan leanings, but less partisan than weak partisans. See Paul R. Abramson, *Political Attitudes in America: Formation and Change* (San Francisco: W. H. Freeman, 1983), 80-81; 95-96. For an excellent discussion of this question, see Herbert B. Asher, "Voting Behavior Research in the 1980s: An Examination of Some Old and New Problem Areas" in *Political Science: The State of the Discipline,* ed. Ada W. Finifter (Washington, D.C.: American Political Science Association, 1983), 357-60.

   For all the analyses in this book, we initially analyzed the results using the full seven-point party identification scale. In all those places where we combined partisan categories, we analyzed the results using all reasonable alternative combinations. In no case would an alternative regrouping of partisans have led to different substantive conclusions.
11. See, for example, Martin P. Wattenberg, *The Decline of American Political Parties, 1952-1980* (Cambridge, Mass.: Harvard University Press, 1984).
12. For the full distribution of party identification for the entire electorate in the 1980 pre- and postelection SRC-CPS surveys, see Paul R. Abramson, John H. Aldrich, and David W. Rohde, *Change and Continuity in the 1980 Elections,* rev. ed. (Washington, D.C.: CQ Press, 1983), Table 8-1, 161.
13. These are our calculations based upon codebooks for the General Social Surveys. These surveys of some 1,500 respondents have been conducted by the National Opinion Research Center of the University of Chicago since 1972 and have been carried out in every subsequent year except 1979. The basic party identification question used in these surveys is: "Generally speaking, do you usually think of yourself as a Republican, Democrat, Independent, or what?" Follow-up questions are used to distinguish between strong and weak partisans and among independents who lean toward one of the two major parties and those who do not.
14. The basic Gallup question is as follows: "In politics, as of today, do you consider yourself a Republican, a Democrat, or an Independent?" No follow-

up questions are used to distinguish between strong and weak partisans or among various categories of independents.

15. *Gallup Poll,* Nov. 25, 1984, 3.
16. Ibid.
17. Ibid.
18. Bear in mind that Table 8-4 presents results only for major party voters. The table thus tends to exaggerate the impact of party identification in 1968 and 1980, because in both of those elections there was a sizable third party vote. For the distribution of votes among whites for the three major candidates in 1968 and 1980, see Abramson, Aldrich, and Rohde, *Change and Continuity in the 1980 Elections,* rev. ed., 177.
19. Bernard R. Berelson, Paul F. Lazarsfeld, and William N. McPhee, *Voting: A Study of Opinion Formation in a Presidential Campaign* (Chicago: University of Chicago Press, 1954).
20. See Richard A. Brody and Benjamin I. Page, "Comment: The Assessment of Policy Voting," *American Political Science Review* 66 (June 1972): 450-58; Page and Brody, "Policy Voting and the Electoral Process: The Vietnam War Issue," *American Political Science Review* 66 (September 1972): 979-95; and Fiorina, "An Outline for a Model of Party Choice."
21. For a description of this measure, see Chap. 6. To conserve space, we have not presented the relationship between party identification and issue preferences in 1972. For those relationships, see *Change and Continuity in the 1980 Elections,* rev. ed., Table 8-5, 171.
22. Sidney Verba and Norman H. Nie, *Participation in America: Political Democracy and Social Equality* (New York: Harper & Row, 1972).
23. To conserve space we have not presented the relationship between party identification and views about which party would do better in handling economic problems in 1972. For these relationships, see Abramson, Aldrich, and Rohde, *Change and Continuity in the 1980 Elections,* rev. ed., Table 8-6, 173.
24. As we explained in Chap. 7, this measure cannot be employed for the 1972 SRC-CPS survey.
25. For two important articles assessing some of these relationships, see Gregory B. Markus and Philip E. Converse, "A Dynamic Simultaneous Equation Model of Electoral Choice," *American Political Science Review* 73 (December 1979): 1055-70; and Benjamin I. Page and Calvin C. Jones, "Reciprocal Effects of Policy Preferences, Party Loyalties and the Vote," *American Political Science Review* 73 (December 1979): 1071-89. For a brief discussion of these articles, see Richard G. Niemi and Herbert F. Weisberg, *Controversies in Voting Behavior,* 2d ed., (Washington, D.C.: CQ Press, 1984), 89-94. For an excellent discussion of complex models of voting behavior and the role of party identification in these models, see Asher, "Voting Behavior Research in the 1980s," 341-54.

The 1984 Congressional Election

So far the focus of this book has been the presidential contest, the major event of interest in the 1984 elections. The president, however, does not govern alone, but shares responsibility and power with Congress, which must approve major appointments and enact the legislative program. Having concluded our analysis of Ronald Reagan's reelection, we now turn to the selection of the Congress that serves with him. In Part III we will consider the similarities and differences in the selection of these offices and the policy implications of the electorate's choices.

There were many elections in 1984. In addition to 13 governors and thousands of other state and local officials, the electorate chose 33 U.S. senators and the 435 members of the House of Representatives. Unlike 1980, when the Republicans unexpectedly won control of the Senate, the 1984 congressional election held no major surprises. Neither did it deliver a clear message. The Republicans retained control of the Senate for a second straight election—a success the party has not enjoyed since it lost control of that chamber in 1932. At the same time, however, the Republicans lost two Senate seats and began the 99th Congress with a slim 53-47 margin over the Democrats. Because the Republicans must defend 22 Senate seats in 1986 and the Democrats only 12, even this modest loss jeopardized their future hold on the Senate. The Republicans gained 14 seats in the House, but this did not make up for the 26 seats they had lost in the 1982 midterm elections. The Republicans thus began the 99th Congress with only 182 seats to the Democrats' 253.

The overall pattern in 1984 was remarkably similar to the results in 1972. Richard Nixon, like Reagan, won 49 of 50 states. In 1972 the Republicans also lost two Senate seats, while gaining 12 seats in the House. But in 1972 Nixon had run a highly personal campaign, ignoring the Republican National Committee and refusing to work for Republican congressional candidates. Reagan, on the other hand, had worked more closely with his party and had tried to help fellow Republicans in congressional races. The president won in a landslide, but the Republican party had only modest success.

Why did Republican congressional candidates have such limited success in 1984? What are the likely policy consequences of this mixed pattern of results? What are Republican prospects in future Senate and House races? In Part III we will address these questions.

Chapter 9 examines candidates' resources and their effect on electoral outcomes. The most crucial factor in determining congressional success—especially in House races—is incumbency. We begin by looking at patterns of success for incumbents, studying change over the past three decades. Although the Republicans have not become the majority party in the House, there have been dramatic changes in the regional bases of support for the two major parties; regional shifts have been even more dramatic for the Senate. We will examine change in regional patterns over the past three decades and show how the erosion of regional differences affected congressional as well as presidential voting. We will then study factors that affect the likelihood of success in congressional races—the background of the candidates, incumbency, and campaign spending. Next, we will study the likely impact of the 1984 congressional election upon public policy. Last, we will speculate on the outcome of the 1986 midterm election and on the longer-term prospects for the GOP.

Many political scientists argue that a pro-Republican realignment will not be complete unless the GOP gains a majority in the House. Failing this, they argue, the Republicans cannot be considered a majority party. We will show that the Republicans have some advantages, especially in campaign funding, that might ultimately gain them control of the House. The GOP can also look forward to the reapportionment and redistricting that will follow the 1990 census. We will show that, despite these advantages, prospects for Republican control of the House are not great, even for the 103d Congress that will be elected in 1992.

Chapter 10 explores the way voters make congressional voting choices—one of the most exciting and rapidly growing areas of research since the University of Michigan's Survey Research Center-Center for Political Studies introduced new questions in 1978 to study congressional voting behavior. Because the composition of the Senate's electorate changes more radically from election to election, our analysis will focus on voting for the House. Chapter 10 examines how social factors influence voters' choices and compares the relationship of these forces in congressional and presidential voting. The effect of issue preferences, partisan loyalties, and incumbency on voters' decisions are also assessed. As we will see, issue preferences do affect congressional voting choices, although they have less impact than party identification. We will then consider the thesis that a congressional voting choice is a referendum on the performance of the individual member of Congress as well as on the president and will examine the effect of Reagan's "coattails" in helping Republican congressional candidates. Last, we will present additional evidence about the importance of campaign spending and additional insights about the advantages of incumbency.

Chapter 9

Candidates and Outcomes

The 1984 election afforded Ronald Reagan an enormous victory in both popular and electoral votes, but that victory did not extend to Republican congressional candidates. The American electorate, as it had so many times since the 1950s, again endorsed divided government. The Republicans retained control of the Senate, which they had won so surprisingly in the 1980 election, but they suffered a net loss of two seats. This gave them a 53 to 47 seat majority, a slender margin that might be vulnerable to Democratic reversal in 1986. In the House of Representatives, the Republicans gained 14 seats, a good deal less than they had hoped for in light of Reagan's widely anticipated landslide. The Democrats retained the majority, 253-182, giving the Republicans 10 fewer seats than Reagan had carried with him when he won his first term. Indeed, the Republican share of House seats, 41.8 percent, was the lowest proportion won by the party of a victorious presidential candidate in our country's history.[1]

Thus, while the presidential election of 1984 offered much good news for the Republicans, the congressional elections carried a more divided message. In this chapter we will consider the pattern of congressional outcomes for 1984 and how they related to outcomes of previous decades. We seek to explain why the 1984 results took the shape they did—what factors led to the overwhelming success of incumbents and what permitted those challengers who defeated incumbents to be successful. We also try to predict the impact these results are likely to have on the politics of the 99th Congress. Finally, we attempt to anticipate the implications of these results for the 1986 midterm elections and for subsequent elections through the 1990s.

Election Outcomes in 1984

Patterns of Incumbency Success

The overwhelming majority of congressional elections involve incumbents, and the overwhelming majority of incumbents are reelected. Table 9-1 presents the election outcomes for House and Senate races involving incumbents between 1954 and 1984.[2] During this period, an average of 92 percent of House incumbents and 80 percent of Senate incumbents who sought reelection were successful. Most of the incumbent defeats that have occurred were in general elections rather than in primaries.

Between 1964 and 1980 House incumbents were more likely to be successful than Senate incumbents, and rates of success for the two groups were moving in opposite directions.[3] In the three elections between 1976 and 1980, House incumbent success averaged more than 90 percent, and Senate incumbent success was around 60 percent. The data for 1982 and 1984, however, show a change. In those elections, incumbent success was similar for the House and Senate.

It appears that these results are the consequence of at least two factors, the first primarily statistical and the second substantive. The statistical factor simply involves the number of cases: House elections routinely involve about 400 incumbents, and Senate races routinely involve fewer than 30. A comparatively small number of cases is more likely to produce volatile results over time. Thus, the proportion of successful incumbents in Senate races tends to "jump around" more than for the House. The substantive factor is that a Senate race is more likely to be vigorously contested than a House race. In 1984, for example, 59 House incumbents (or about 15 percent) had no opponent from the other major party, and a large share of the remainder had opponents who were inexperienced or underfunded or both. In Senate races, on the other hand, only one incumbent, J. Bennett Johnston of Louisiana, was unopposed. The opponents of most Senate incumbents had previously won elective office and were reasonably well funded. Thus, a large number of House races involve incumbents who are virtually guaranteed reelection. Had all House races been as heavily contested as Senate races in the late 1970s, the rate of defeat for House incumbents might have been as high as that for senators. We will consider the substantive point again later in this chapter.

Turning from incumbency to party, we find in Figure 9-1 the proportion of seats in the House and Senate won by Democrats in each election since 1952, the last time that Republicans won a majority of the seats in both houses of Congress. The data show that in 1982 and 1984 the Democrats stopped the precipitous decline they had been suffering in earlier elections. However, they have not been able to retake the Senate, leaving control of the Congress split between the parties. The Democratic

Table 9-1 House and Senate Incumbents and Election Outcomes, 1954-1984

Year	Incumbents Running (N)	Primary Defeats (N)	Percent	General Election Defeats (N)	Percent	Reelected (N)	Percent
House							
1954	(407)	(6)	1.5	(22)	5.4	(379)	93.1
1956	(410)	(6)	1.5	(15)	3.7	(389)	94.9
1958	(394)	(3)	0.8	(37)	9.4	(354)	89.8
1960	(405)	(5)	1.2	(25)	6.2	(375)	92.6
1962	(402)	(12)	3.0	(22)	5.5	(368)	91.5
1964	(397)	(8)	2.0	(45)	11.3	(344)	86.6
1966	(411)	(8)	1.9	(41)	10.0	(362)	88.1
1968	(409)	(4)	1.0	(9)	2.2	(396)	96.8
1970	(401)	(10)	2.5	(12)	3.0	(379)	94.5
1972	(392)	(13)	3.3	(13)	3.3	(366)	93.4
1974	(391)	(8)	2.0	(40)	10.2	(343)	87.7
1976	(383)	(3)	0.8	(12)	3.1	(368)	96.1
1978	(382)	(5)	1.3	(19)	5.0	(358)	93.7
1980	(398)	(6)	1.5	(31)	7.8	(361)	90.7
1982	(393)	(10)	2.5	(29)	7.4	(354)	90.1
1984	(411)	(3)	0.7	(16)	3.9	(392)	95.4
Senate							
1954	(27)	(0)	—	(4)	15	(23)	85
1956	(30)	(0)	—	(4)	13	(26)	87
1958	(26)	(0)	—	(9)	35	(17)	65
1960	(28)	(0)	—	(1)	4	(27)	96
1962	(30)	(0)	—	(3)	10	(27)	90
1964	(30)	(0)	—	(2)	7	(28)	93
1966	(29)	(2)	7	(1)	3	(26)	90
1968	(28)	(4)	14	(4)	14	(20)	71
1970	(28)	(1)	4	(3)	11	(24)	86
1972	(26)	(1)	4	(5)	19	(20)	77
1974	(26)	(1)	4	(2)	8	(23)	88
1976	(25)	(0)	—	(9)	36	(16)	64
1978	(22)	(1)	5	(6)	27	(15)	68
1980	(29)	(4)	14	(9)	31	(16)	55
1982	(30)	(0)	—	(2)	7	(28)	93
1984	(29)	(0)	—	(3)	10	(26)	90

Figure 9-1   Democratic Share of Seats in the House and Senate, 1953-1985

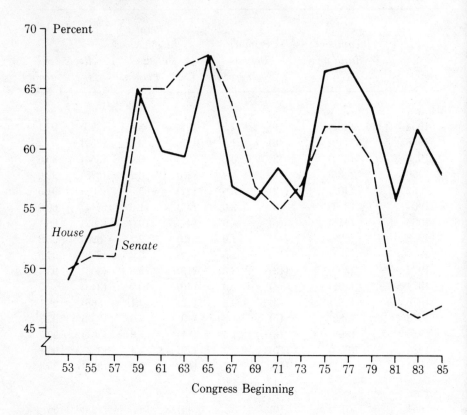

gain of two Senate seats in 1984 puts them within striking distance of regaining control of the Senate, but we will demonstrate that there are good reasons not to expect significant changes from the recent pattern of outcomes in the near future.

The combined effect of party and incumbency is shown in Table 9-2. The Democrats won 58 percent of the seats in the House, and the Republicans 52 percent of the seats in the Senate. As in 1980, Republicans were quite successful in retaining seats previously held by their party. Only four formerly Republican seats were lost in the House, and three in the Senate. Unlike in 1980, however, the Republicans were not able to make substantial inroads into Democratic seats. In Senate races four years earlier, the Republicans had won almost half of the seats held by Democratic incumbents and more than half of the open seats that were previously Democratic. In 1984 the Republicans were able to move only a single Democratic Senate seat into the Republican column, with

Table 9-2   House and Senate Election Outcomes, by Party and
Incumbency, 1984

1984 Winners	Democratic Incumbent	No Incumbent (Seat Was Democratic)	No Incumbent (Seat Was Republican)	Republican Incumbent	Total
		1984 Candidates			
House					
Democrats	95%	62%	7%	2%	58%
Republicans	5	38	93	98	42
Total Percent	100	100	100	100	100
(N)	(254)	(13)	(14)	(154)	(435)
Senate					
Democrats	92%	100%	50%	12%	48%
Republicans	8	0	50	88	52
Total Percent	100	100	100	100	100
(N)	(12)	(2)	(2)	(17)	(33)

the defeat of Democratic incumbent Walter D. Huddleston of Kentucky
by Mitch McConnell. In House races, the proportion of Democratic
incumbents defeated for reelection was cut by more than half, compared
to 1980. Only in open House seats that were formerly Democratic were
the Republicans able to repeat their 1980 success, and their performance
was virtually identical to that in 1980 in terms of proportion of seats won.
Because, however, there were fewer than half as many such seats at stake
in 1984 (13 open Democratic seats versus 27), even this success yielded
them a much smaller gain.

Regional Bases of Power

The geographic pattern of 1984 election outcomes in the House and
Senate can be seen in the partisan breakdowns by region presented in
Table 9-3.[4] For comparison we also present breakdowns for 1979 (before
the Republicans won Senate control) and for 1953 (the last completely
Republican Congress). In the House the Reagan years have brought
noticeable Republican gains in the East, West, and South. Paradoxically,
Republicans actually lost ground in the Midwest, which historically has
been the heartland of Republican strength and where in 1953 the
Republicans controlled 76 percent of the seats. Despite the banner
Republican year at the presidential level in 1984, the Democrats won a
majority of the seats in all five regions.

Table 9-3   Party Shares of Regional Delegations in the House and Senate, 1953, 1979, 1985

	1953			1979			1985		
Region	*% Dem.*	*% Rep.*	*(N)*	*% Dem.*	*% Rep.*	*(N)*	*% Dem.*	*% Rep.*	*(N)*
House									
East	35	65	(116)	66	34	(105)	57	43	(96)
Midwest	23	76	(118)[1]	51	49	(111)	54	46	(104)
West	33	67	(57)	62	38	(76)	52	48	(85)
South	94	6	(106)	71	29	(108)	63	37	(116)
Border	68	32	(38)	77	23	(35)	74	26	(34)
Total	49	51	(435)	64	36	(435)	58	42	(435)
Senate									
East	25	75	(20)	55	45	(20)	50	50	(20)
Midwest	14	86	(22)	59	41	(22)	50	50	(22)
West	45	55	(22)	46	54	(26)	31	69	(26)
South	100	0	(22)	73	27	(22)	55	45	(22)
Border	70	30	(10)	70	30	(10)	60	40	(10)
Total	49	51	(96)	59	41	(100)	47	53	(100)

[1] Includes one independent

Note: The figures are for the opening of the Congress each year.

The pattern is somewhat different in the Senate, reflecting the Republican majority there. Between 1979 and 1985 the Republicans have made significant gains in both the West and the South, the core of Reagan's strength. Only in the South and Border States do the Democrats retain a majority of the seats. The West is heavily Republican, and the East and Midwest are evenly split.

The 1985 results are even more interesting when viewed from the longer historical perspective. In 1953 there were sharp regional differences in party success in both houses. In the intervening years these differences have largely disappeared. The most obvious changes occurred in the South. The percentage of southern seats in the House held by Democrats declined from 94 percent in 1953 to 63 percent in 1985. In 1953 the Democrats held all 22 Senate seats from the South, but in 1985 they controlled only 55 percent of them. While the regional shift is not as drastic as in presidential elections, the South is no longer a Democratic stronghold for congressional candidates.

This change in the partisan share of the South's seats in Congress has had an important impact on that region's influence within the two parties. The South used to be the backbone of Democratic congressional representation. This, and the tendency of southern members of Congress to build seniority, gave southerners disproportionate power within the Democratic party in Congress. Because of the decline in Democratic electoral success, the numerical strength of southern Democrats in Congress has waned. In 1947, with the Republicans in control of both houses of Congress, southerners accounted for about half of the Democratic seats in the House and Senate. During the late 1940s and the 1950s, southern strength was fairly stable at something over 40 percent. It then began to decline, and by the 1970s it stabilized again at about one-fourth of the Democratic seats in the Congress.

A consideration of the South's share of Republican congressional representation presents the reverse picture. Minuscule or nonexistent at the end of World War II, it steadily began to grow, reaching about 20 percent in 1981 and later. As a consequence of these changes, southern influence has declined in the Democratic party and grown in the GOP. Because southerners of both parties tend to be more conservative than their colleagues from other regions, these shifts in strength have tended to make the Democratic party in Congress somewhat more liberal and the Republican party somewhat more conservative.

Other regional changes since 1953, while not as striking as those in the South, are also significant. In the 1953 House, the Republicans controlled the East and West by two-to-one margins, and the Midwest by a margin of three to one; in 1985, they controlled none of these regions, and the party proportions were very similar among the three. In the 1953 Senate, the Republicans had a massive lead in the East and Midwest and a slight lead in the West; by 1985, party control was evenly split in both the East and West, although Republican strength in the West had increased somewhat. On balance, what we have witnessed in the last three decades is the "de-regionalization" of congressional elections. Although some regional variations are still apparent, the similarities are much more striking than the differences. The Congress of 1985 is regionally homogeneous compared to that of 1953.

Candidates' Resources and Election Outcomes

Congressional elections are vigorous contests in which candidates use whatever resources they have available. To understand elections we must consider the comparative advantages and disadvantages of both sides. In this section we will consider the most significant resources available to candidates and their impact on the outcomes of congressional elections.

Candidate Quality

One of the major resources a candidate can bring to bear is political ability in an electoral environment.[5] Because few constituencies are any longer completely safe for one party or another, election outcomes usually depend heavily on candidate quality. A strong, capable candidate is a significant asset; a weak, inept one is a disability that is difficult to overcome. In his study of the activities of House members in their districts, Richard F. Fenno, Jr., describes how members try to build support within their constituencies, establishing bonds of trust between constituent and representative.[6] Members attempt to convey to their constituents a sense that they are qualified for their job, a sense that they identify with their constituents, and a sense of empathy with them. Challengers of incumbents and candidates for open seats engage in similar activities to win support. The winner of a contested congressional election will usually be the candidate who is better able to establish these bonds of support among constituents and convince them that he or she is the person for the job.

One indicator of candidate quality is previous success at winning elective office. The more important the office a candidate has held, the more likely it is that he or she had to overcome significant opposition to obtain that office. Moreover, the visibility and reputation for performance that usually accompany public office can itself be a significant electoral asset. For example, a state legislator running for a House seat can appeal to the electorate on the basis that his or her prior experience was a good preparation for congressional service because of the similarities between the two offices. A state legislator also would have previously constructed a successful electoral organization that could be useful in the campaign. Finally, success in an electoral arena suggests that these candidates are more likely to be able to run strong campaigns. Less adept candidates have already been "screened out" at lower levels of competition. For these and other reasons, an experienced candidate would have an electoral advantage over a candidate who had held no previous elective office. Moreover, the higher the office previously held, the stronger the candidate will likely be in the congressional contest.

Table 9-4 presents data on which candidates were successful in 1984 House and Senate elections, controlling for previous experience, party, and incumbency. In House races, the Republicans were more successful than the Democrats in the case of almost every kind of background in office. Moreover, candidates with experience in higher offices usually were more successful than those who had held less important offices, particularly in open races. In those no-incumbent races, for both Democrats and Republicans, state legislators were notably more successful than candidates with other backgrounds. In Senate races the small number of cases relative to the number of categories offers less clear results. Overall, however, two of the three victorious challengers against incumbents and all four of the winners of open seats had either statewide elective office or the office of U.S. representative as their last experience before running.

Table 9-4   Success in House and Senate Elections, Controlling for Office Background, Party, and Incumbency, 1984

Candidate's Last Office	Opponent of Democratic Incumbent %	(N)	Opponent of Republican Incumbent %	(N)	(No Incumbent in District) Democratic Candidate %	(N)	Republican Candidate %	(N)
					Candidate Is			
House								
State legislature or U.S. House	24	(25)	7	(15)	50	(6)	91	(11)
Other elective office	0	(10)	10	(10)	43	(7)	50	(4)
No elective office	4	(166)	1	(115)	21	(14)	54	(11)
Senate								
U.S. House	0	(2)	67	(3)	100	(1)	100	(1)
Statewide elective office	—	(0)	0	(5)	100	(2)	—	(0)
Other elective office	25	(4)	0	(4)	0	(1)	0	(1)
No elective office	0	(5)	0	(5)	—	(0)	0	(2)

Note: Percentages show the proportion of candidates in each category who won; numbers in parentheses are the totals on which percentages are based.

Whether experienced politicians actually run for the House or Senate is, of course, not an accident. These are significant strategic decisions made by politicians with much to lose if they make the wrong choice. The choices will be governed by a host of factors that relate to the perceived chances of success, the potential value of the new office relative to what will be lost if the candidate fails, and the costs of running.[7] The chances of success of the two major parties vary from election to election both locally and nationally. Therefore, each election offers a different mix of experienced and inexperienced candidates from the two parties for the House and Senate.

In House elections, for example, substantially more experienced nonincumbent candidates ran in 1980 than in 1984. In 1980 the Democrats ran 61 experienced candidates, and the Republicans 57 for a total of 118; in 1984 the numbers were 38 and 50 respectively for a total of 88.[8] There is evidence that potential candidates of both parties decided to bypass 1984 and wait for another year, and in a number of cases the political parties did not try to persuade them to change their minds. In 1982 many southern Republican party organizations recruited congressional candidates even in districts where their chances were not perceived to be particularly good. Many Republican strategists now believe this was a mistake because their party not only failed to win in the vast majority of such races, but in the process they also stimulated a heavy Democratic turnout that might have cost the Republicans other races.[9] In 1984 these Republican organizations sought to recruit candidates for Congress only where their chances of winning were good.

Some of the negative decisions on running by potential candidates were due to the redistricting process before the 1982 elections. In California, for example, a strongly pro-Democratic districting was imposed. As a result neither party sees much chance of taking any significant portion of the other party's districts for the near future. As one conservative activist put it, in California "they may as well not even have elections. . . . Democrats have taken about 43 districts out of the political process."[10] Thus, few experienced California politicians were willing to challenge incumbents, and the consequences were about as observers had anticipated. Twenty-eight Democratic incumbents sought reelection; only one was defeated, and only four others received less than 60 percent of the vote. Of the 17 Republican incumbents who sought reelection, each received at least 60 percent of the vote, and 11 won more than 70 percent.

Many Democrats decided to bypass 1984 because they thought that 1986 would be a better year for their party. In 1984 President Reagan looked strong and there did not appear to be any pro-Democratic tide. As we will see, the second midterm election of a presidency is usually a good year for the opposition party in congressional elections. Whatever the reasons, fewer experienced challengers of incumbents should lead to less party turnover and, comparing 1984 to 1980, that is what happened.

Incumbency

Another significant resource is incumbency. Actually, incumbency is not a single resource, but rather a status that usually gives a candidate a variety of benefits. In some respects, incumbency works to a candidate's advantage automatically. For example, incumbents tend to be more visible to voters and to be viewed more favorably than their challengers.[11] Moreover, the plurality of the electorate in many districts will identify with the incumbent's political party, as in the case of the California districting just discussed. In other respects, incumbents can *use* their status to gain advantages. Incumbents usually raise and spend more campaign funds than challengers, and they usually have a more developed and experienced campaign organization. They also have assets, provided at public expense, that are supposed to assist in performing their jobs, but which provide electoral advantages.

Since the mid-1960s the *margins* by which incumbents have been reelected have increased (although the pattern is less clear and more erratic in the case of Senate elections).[12] These changing patterns have interested analysts both for their own sake and because it was believed that the disappearance of "marginal" incumbents would mean less congressional turnover and a "locking-in" of current office occupants.

One explanation of the increased incumbent margins was offered by Edward R. Tufte, who argued that it was largely due to redistricting, which protected incumbents of both parties.[13] This argument seemed plausible because the increase in margins occurred around the same time as the massive redistricting produced by Supreme Court reapportionment decisions, but other analysts showed that incumbents had won by larger margins both in states that had redistricted and those that had not, as well as in Senate races.[14] Thus, redistricting cannot be the dominant reason for the change.

Another explanation of the increased incumbency advantage was that it was a consequence of the growth in the perquisites of members—and of the greater complexity of government. Morris P. Fiorina has noted that in the post-New Deal period the level of federal services and the bureaucracy that administers them have grown tremendously.[15] More complex government has meant more problems encountered by the people for whom the services are targeted, and people who have problems with the delivery of services frequently contact their representative to complain. Fiorina contends that in the mid-1960s new members of Congress placed greater emphasis on such constituency problem solving than did their predecessors. This expanded constituency service was translated into a reservoir of electoral support. Although analyses of the electoral impact of constituency services have produced mixed conclusions, it is likely that the growth of these services offers a partial explanation for changing incumbent vote margins and for the incumbency advantage generally.[16]

A change in voting habits offers a third explanation for the growth in incumbent vote margins. Until the mid-1960s there was a very strong linkage between party identification and congressional voting behavior: most people tended to identify with a political party, these identifications tended to be strong, and most voters supported the candidate of their chosen party. Since then, however, the impact of party identification has decreased. John A. Ferejohn, drawing on data from national election surveys, has shown that the strength of party ties has generally weakened and that within any given party identification category the propensity to support the candidate of one's party is less.[17] An analysis by Albert D. Cover shows that between 1958 and 1974 voters who did not identify with the party of a congressional incumbent were increasingly more likely to defect from their party and support the incumbent, while there had been no increase in defections from party identification by voters who are of the same party as incumbents.[18] Thus, in effect, weakened party ties produce a substantial net electoral benefit for incumbents. While the evidence regarding the change in voter behavior is strong, these analyses do not explain *why* voters have moved to support incumbents who are not of their party. We will shortly present an argument that we believe accounts for the change, but first we must consider a new analysis that offers a different perspective on the pattern of change and its significance.

Gary C. Jacobson has argued that although incumbents' margins have indeed increased, observers have been off the mark in characterizing this as an increase in incumbency safeness.[19] To the contrary, Jacobson's data show that an incumbent in the 1970s who had won the preceding election by 65 percent of the vote was no more likely to win reelection than was a 1950s incumbent who had won with 60 percent of the vote. What we have had, then, is an inflation in victory margins without any corresponding increase in security. These findings have important implications for the analysis of congressional elections. As Jacobson said, "The dependent variable is recast. The phenomenon to be explained is not a decline in competition for incumbent-held House seats; it is, rather, the greater idiosyncrasy and volatility of district-level voting that can expand re-election margins without making incumbents any safer." [20]

Campaign Spending

In our view the "artificial" inflation of incumbent margins has been caused largely by the patterns of campaign spending. The impact of campaign spending on congressional elections has received a great deal of attention in recent years as a consequence of the availability of more dependable data,[21] but little of this analysis has been related to the study of increased election margins. Because research shows that there is linkage between election outcomes and campaign spending, and because incumbents generally outspend their opponents by a significant margin, this would seem to be a reasonable factor to study. For example, 1982 data show that in House races Democratic incumbents outspent their challengers by an average of 91 percent, and Republican incumbents did so by 125 percent. Senate challengers tend to be better funded, so the incumbent spending advantage in 1982 Senate races was only 64 percent for Democrats and 40 percent for Republicans.[22] Patterns are similar for elections stretching back at least to 1972.

These disparities in campaign spending are linked to the increase in incumbent election margins. Beginning in the 1960s, congressional campaigns began to rely more heavily on campaign strategies that cost money—for example, media time, campaign consulting, and direct mailing—and over time these items became more and more expensive. At the same time, candidates were progressively less likely to have available pools of campaign workers from established party organizations or from interest groups, making expensive media and direct mail strategies relatively more important. Many challengers, however, are unable to raise significant campaign funds. Neither the individuals nor groups who are interested in the outcomes of congressional elections like to throw money away; before making contributions they usually need to be convinced that the candidate has a chance. Yet we have seen that over time few incumbents are beaten. Thus, potential contributors are difficult to convince and contributions are often not forthcoming. The consequence is that many challengers are unable to raise sufficient funds to wage a competitive campaign.

The ability to compete, rather than the simple question of relative amounts of spending, is the core of the issue. We have noted that incumbents have many inherent advantages that the challenger must overcome if he or she hopes to win. But often the money is not there to overcome them. In 1982, for example, more than a third of challengers spent $25,000 or less.[23] Similarly, in 1976, a third of the challengers of House incumbents spent less than $10,000.[24] With such small amounts of money available, challengers would be unable to make themselves visible to the electorate or to convey a convincing message. Under such circumstances, most voters—being unaware of the positions, or perhaps even the existence, of the challenger—would probably vote for the incumbent.

Available data on campaign spending and election outcomes seem consistent with this argument. Table 9-5 shows the relationship between the incumbent's share of the two-party vote in the 1982 House elections and the amount of money spent by challengers. It is clear that there is a strong negative relationship between how much challengers spend and how well incumbents do. In races where challengers spent less than $26,000, every incumbent received at least 60 percent of the vote. At the other end of the spectrum, in races where challengers spent $200,000 or more, almost three-fourths of the incumbents received less than 60 percent of the vote, and more than 4 incumbents in 10 won under 55 percent. These results are consistent with earlier House races for which comparable data are available.[25]

It is, of course, true that challengers who appear to have good prospects will find it easier to raise money than those whose chances seem dim. Thus, one might wonder whether these data are simply a reflection of the fulfillment of expectations, in which money flows to challengers who would have done well regardless of spending. Other research, however, indicates that this is probably not the case. In an analysis of the 1972 and 1974 congressional elections, Jacobson concludes, "Our evidence is that campaign spending helps candidates, particularly non-incumbents, by bringing them to the attention of voters; it is *not* the case that well-known candidates simply attract more money; rather, money buys attention." [26] Those two elections offer an example, in the Fourth District of Georgia, that demonstrates the extremes the hypothe-

Table 9-5   Incumbents' Share of the Vote in the 1982 House Elections, by Challenger Campaign Spending

Challenger Spending (in thousands of dollars)	Incumbents' Share of the Two-Party Vote					
	70 percent or more	60-69 percent	55-59 percent	Less than 55 percent	Total percent	(N)
0-25	67.9%	32.1	0.0	0.0	100.0%	(109)
26-75	33.9%	48.2	16.1	1.8	100.0%	(56)
76-125	0.0%	53.3	30.0	16.7	100.0%	(30)
126-199	13.0%	26.1	23.9	37.0	100.0%	(46)
200 or more	2.7%	23.3	30.1	43.8	99.9%	(73)
All	32.2%	34.1	16.2	17.5	100.0%	(314)

sized relationship can manifest. In 1972 Republican incumbent Ben B. Blackburn was reelected to a fourth term with 75.9 percent of the vote. His opponent was a retired government employee who spent less than $4,000 on his campaign. (Blackburn spent $34,000.) In 1974 Blackburn was opposed by Elliott H. Levitas, a Democratic state representative. Blackburn outspent his opponent $160,000 to $121,000, but lost anyway with 44.9 percent of the vote. Moving from a situation with an under-financed political newcomer as an opponent to a contest with a well-funded experienced opponent, Blackburn's share of the vote dropped 31 percent. Moreover, Levitas was rated a comparatively strong opponent, but his chances of defeating Blackburn were still considered slim. Therefore, it would seem more reasonable to conclude that adequate funding made Blackburn's defeat possible, rather than to conclude that the funding flowed to a candidate who was destined to win.

From this perspective, adequate funding is a necessary but not a sufficient condition for a closely fought election contest. This does not mean that heavily outspending one's opponent guarantees victory; we do not believe elections can be bought. If an incumbent outspends the challenger, the incumbent can still lose if the challenger is adequately funded. The 1982 elections offer clear evidence of this. In 21 of the 23 House races where incumbents lost, the loser outspent the winner. In these races, incumbents outspent challengers by an average of more than 50 percent. Nor is a spending advantage any kind of guarantee to a challenger. In an extreme example from 1982, in the Seventh District of New Jersey Democrat Adam Levin spent $2.3 million in his race against Republican incumbent Matthew J. Rinaldo, who spent about $700,000. Levin received only 43 percent of the vote. Instead, our view can be summarized as follows: if a challenger is to attain visibility and get his or her message across to the voters—overcoming the incumbent's advantages in name recognition and perquisites of office—the challenger needs to be adequately funded. If both sides in a race are adequately funded, the outcome of the race will tend to turn on factors other than money, and it will matter little whether one candidate heavily outspends another.

This argument carries us full circle back to our discussion at the beginning of this section and leads us to bring together the three elements that we have been considering—candidate experience, incumbency, and campaign spending. Table 9-6 presents data on the combination of the three elements. We have categorized challenger experience as weak or strong depending on whether the challenger previously had held a significant elective office;[27] challenger spending was classed as low or high depending on whether it was less than or more than $125,000. The data show that each of the elements exerts its own independent effect. When challengers have weak experience and low spending, all incumbents win, and the vast majority win with more than 60 percent of the vote. In the opposite situation, where the challenger has both strong experience and substantial spending, a majority of the races are quite close, and more than a fourth of the incumbents were defeated. The intermediate circumstances each yield similar results, with the incumbents being less likely either to win overwhelmingly or to be contested very closely. The data suggest, however, that challenger spending may be a more important variable, because with high spending and weak experience about one incumbent in nine is defeated, and in the opposite case no incumbents lost.

This combination of factors also helps to explain the greater volatility of outcomes in Senate races. Previous analysis has shown that data on campaign spending in Senate races is consistent with what we have found true for House races: if challenger spending is above a certain threshold level, the race is likely to be quite close; if it is below that level, the incumbent is likely to win by a large margin.[28] In Senate races, however, the mix of well-funded and inadequately funded challengers is different. Senate challengers are more likely than House challengers to be able to raise significant amounts of money. Senate challengers, moreover, are also more likely to possess significant experience in office. Thus, in Senate races incumbents will face well-funded and experienced challengers more often than their House counterparts, and the stage is then set for their defeat in greater numbers if other circumstances work against them.

In 1980 a larger number of incumbent Democratic senators faced challengers with significant experience and substantial campaign funds. As a result many of the races were closely contested, and—whether because of Reagan's personal popularity, a Republican surge, or simple coincidence—most of the close races tipped in the Republicans' favor and

Table 9-6   Incumbents' Share of the Vote in the 1982 House Elections, by Challenger Campaign Spending and Office Background

Challenger Experience	Challenger Spending	Incumbents' Share of the Two-Party Vote						% of Incumbents Defeated
		70% or More	60-69 %	55-59 %	Less than 55%	Total	(N)	
Weak	Low	52.6%	40.5	5.2	1.7	100.0%	(73)	0%
Strong	Low	9.1%	36.4	40.9	13.6	100.0%	(22)	0%
Weak	High	10.4%	28.4	28.4	32.8	100.0%	(67)	11.9%
Strong	High	1.9%	19.2	26.9	51.9	99.9%	(52)	28.9%
All		32.2%	34.1	16.2	17.5	100.0%	(314)	7.3%

almost half of the incumbent Democrats lost. While it is extremely rare for results to be this one-sided, the conditions for this possibility are much more likely to occur in Senate races than in House elections, where so many incumbents are insulated from significant challenge.

The 1984 Election: The Impact on Congress

When Reagan was first elected president, the impact of the congressional elections on Congress was substantial. The Republican party had unexpectedly taken control of the Senate from the Democrats and had gained 33 seats in the House of Representatives. Most of the incoming Republican senators and representatives were extremely conservative, shifting the ideological balance of Congress noticeably to the right. The massive Reagan victory and Republican gain also had an impact on the behavior of many Democrats from the South. Reagan's popularity in their region and their own conservative inclinations led many southern Democrats to support Reagan's early policy initiatives on taxes and the budget. Southern Democratic support provided the margin of victory on those measures.[29]

The results of the 1984 elections were very different. With a gain of only 14 House seats for the Republicans and 2 seats for the Democrats in the Senate, the degree of partisan change is very small. The ideological change is also small. In 1980 not only were many of the new members far more conservative than those whom they replaced, but also in both houses the incumbents who were reelected tended to be more conservative than their fellow partisans who departed. Thus the liberals in the Democratic party in the Senate were damaged in three ways: their party lost control, their party became noticeably more conservative, and the Republican conservatives were substantially strengthened. In the House, only the last of these changes occurred. For 1984 an examination of the degree of support for the conservative coalition among members who left Congress and those who stayed on indicates virtually no differences for northern Democrats, southern Democrats, or Republicans in either house.[30]

Because there is little ideological difference between departing and holdover members, and because there was no change in the party control of either house, the ideological impact of the 1984 election is largely limited to the degree of replacement of members of one party by members of the other, and that was very small. In the House, moreover, the ideological impact is muted even further because half of the Republican gain of 14 seats was in the South. Thus, in many instances, we have fairly conservative Democrats replaced by only somewhat more conservative Republicans.

Because of the small impact of membership change, the greatest effects of the 1984 elections on Congress will be to accentuate the tendency toward stalemate in the federal government, and perhaps to exacerbate the differences within the political parties—particularly the Republican party—as President Reagan's status as a "lame-duck" becomes more developed and the 1986 elections approach. When Reagan began his first term, he made a series of bold policy initiatives in fiscal matters. He got his way because he received overwhelming support from members of his own party in Congress and the support of enough Democrats to carry the day. As he began his second term, his party's position in the House was numerically weaker and the amount of dependable support on fiscal and other matters had declined.

Within the Republican party, significant differences are surfacing among traditional fiscal conservatives, "supply-siders," social conservatives, and more moderate members. The fiscal conservative/supply-sider disagreement manifested itself in the struggle over the fiscal 1986 budget. During the summer of 1985, the projected deficit for the budget was in the $170-180 billion range, and the president refused to consider any tax increase that would close the gap. The Democrats, on the other hand, resisted further cuts in social programs desired by the president, and they particularly opposed limitations proposed by the Republicans on Social Security increases. As a consequence, any significant reduction in the deficit was unlikely, and many Republicans worried about the political impact of this course. One freshman Republican in the House said, "Our class may be the most vulnerable class in history because of the deficit." Another added, "If we don't take a substantial look at the debt, as far as I am concerned, there will be a lot of loose cannons on the ship." [31]

The problem in the Senate was worsened in July 1985 when Reagan abandoned the proposal for a one-year freeze on Social Security benefits. Republican senators had supported the proposal—an act they regarded as a significant political risk—and they were angry because they felt they had been left out on a limb. Thus, many party members, particularly freshmen in the House and the Senate Republicans who hold seats that are up for reelection in 1986, may go their own way on the budget. In December of 1985, about four-fifths of Senate Republicans united to support the Senate-initiated Gramm-Rudman-Hollings balanced budget bill, which Reagan also backed. This was not a clear partisan issue, however, because half the Senate Democrats also voted for it. (In the House, Republican support was a bit higher and Democratic support a bit lower.) In early 1986, moreover, there were indications that Senate Republicans were threatening to hold Reagan's tax reform plan hostage until there was some compromise resolution of the deficit problem.

In addition to budgeting problems, Republicans face problems dealing with the "social issues." Social conservatives want the Congress to take action on a variety of matters such as abortion, school prayer, and busing, but the Reagan administration and the Senate Republican leadership prefer (as they did in the first term) to delay consideration of these matters until Congress finishes action on the budget and on tax reform. Because that delay might mean putting off those matters until the 100th Congress, social conservatives are less likely to be as accommodating as they were during Reagan's first term. Many supporters of the conservative social agenda want to force votes on these issues, even though they recognize that they are even less likely to win than they were in the two previous Congresses. They view these symbolic votes as a weapon against Democrats in the upcoming elections. One conservative activist said, "If you don't raise these issues again vigorously through battles in the Congress, we are going to lose our cutting edge and the 1986 election is going to be a disaster." [32]

Democrats, on the other hand—because they anticipate the possibility of significant gains in the midterm elections and because Reagan's popularity did not translate into substantial losses for the Democrats in 1984—are likely to be more unified and less prone to support the president than in the past. The Conservative Democratic Forum (the organization of southern Democratic conservatives in the House) has fewer members than in 1981 and is more inclined to work with the Democratic leadership. After the 1984 election House Republican leader Robert H. Michel said people "should not expect too many victories" in the House for the president. And in the Senate, one Republican observer indicated that those Republicans up for reelection will be increasingly independent: "The shots will be called by 22 people who will be saying to the President, 'Hey, I'd like to be loyal, but if it doesn't sell in my neck of the woods, forget it.' " [33] In summary, in the 99th Congress neither party may have the capacity to get its way, and policy conflicts are likely to result in compromise or deadlock or both at least until 1987, and probably 1989.

The 1986 Congressional Election and Beyond

The Election of 1986

One reason the Republicans were able to make such substantial Senate gains in 1980 was that the Democrats had 24 seats at stake and the Republicans had 10. In 1986 that same set of seats will be up again, but, because of the previous Republican victories, the numerical balance now favors the Democrats: the Republicans have 22 seats at stake and the Democrats only 12. In assessing which seats will be most vulnerable in November 1986, there are certain systematic forces and individual circumstances we can take into account.

Two important considerations in assessing vulnerability are previous election margin and length of service of incumbents. As of early 1986, 27 incumbents were seeking reelection, 18 Republicans and 9 Democrats. While, as we have seen, large margins of victory may not guarantee the next win, narrow wins frequently mean future vulnerability because they tend to attract strong, well-funded challengers. First-term incumbents also tend to be more vulnerable than long-serving members who have had greater time to solidify their positions. Thirteen of the Republican incumbents seeking reelection are freshmen who were elected with less than 55 percent of the vote; none of the Democratic incumbents are in the same category. Among the nonfreshmen, one Democrat and one Republican seeking reelection were last elected by similarly small margins. Another important consideration in assessing whether a seat is likely to switch parties involves whether it has an incumbent in the first place; for 1986 three of the open seats belong to the Democrats and four to the Republicans.

Does the combination of these factors mean that Democrats are likely to gain the four seats they need to retake control of the Senate? Not necessarily. The disparity in numbers alone is unlikely to be enough to guarantee a Democratic Senate. First-term and marginal incumbents may be *more* vulnerable than other incumbents, but that does not necessarily make them *very* vulnerable. Many of the first-term Republicans are capable politicians who beat strong Democrats to get into the Senate. They have used the intervening years to build strong ties with their constituents and to develop reputations for independence and the ability to bring home federal dollars.[34] Moreover, the Democrats need 51 seats to control the Senate; the Republicans can retain control with only 50 seats because Vice President George Bush can vote with them in case of a tie. Unless there is a strong national tide in favor of the Democrats— a possibility we discuss below—Democratic gains may fall short of a majority. However, the contest for control of the Senate is likely to be close, and, if the Democrats are lucky in a few key races, they could win control.

In the House, outcomes are more likely to be sensitive to national forces and there may be a comparatively large number of open seats. These factors raise the possibility of greater numerical change than in the Senate. The number of House members considering retirement appears to be about the same for both parties, but the large number of Republican Senate seats up in 1986 and the correspondingly large number of Democratic representatives interested in them may result in a somewhat larger number of open Democratic House seats.[35] Democratic incumbents heavily outnumber Republican incumbents, but organizing and fund-raising efforts by the national Republican party make it likely that many Republican challengers will have adequate funds to wage serious campaigns. On the other hand, because 1986 may not be a good year for Republicans, many potentially strong Republican House candidates may decide to wait for a better year, as many Democrats did in 1984. Because House races are fought on a district-by-district basis, it appears that here too significant change is likely to occur only if there is a substantial impact from national forces.

What then of national trends? The party opposing the president tends to do better in midterm elections if the president is relatively unpopular and if economic conditions are poor. However, even if the president is popular and the economy is strong, the president's party tends to lose seats. By examining the 10 midterm elections in the postwar years, we may gain some insight about both parties' chances in 1986. Table 9-7 shows that since World War II the average seat loss was 29.2 seats in midterm elections for the party that controlled the presidency. But the table also shows that there was a tremendous range in outcomes, from a 4-seat loss in 1962 to a 55-seat loss in 1946.

Adding another consideration related to the president permits us to narrow the range of expected outcomes. If a president is facing his first midterm, he can make a plausible appeal that he has had little time to bring about substantial change or to secure many achievements. Many presidents will approach their first midterm election, as Reagan did in 1982, with appeals like "stay the course," or "give us a chance." Four years later, if the president is fortunate enough to face a second midterm, such appeals are far less plausible or persuasive. A president will then have had six years in office, and if the economy or foreign policy are not going well, the voters may seek a change in policy by reducing the number of the president's partisans in Congress.

The second part of Table 9-7 shows that this is the case. (Earlier research indicates that for these purposes voters may tend to regard a president who has succeeded another who has died or resigned from office as a continuation of the first president's administration. Therefore, these data are organized by term of administration, rather than term of president.)[36] Looked at from this perspective, House seat losses in

Table 9-7 House Seat Losses by Party of the President in Midterm
Elections, 1946-1982

All Elections

1946:	55 Democrats	1966:	47 Democrats
1950:	29 Democrats	1970:	12 Republicans
1954:	18 Republicans	1974:	43 Republicans
1958:	47 Republicans	1978:	11 Democrats
1962:	4 Democrats	1982:	26 Republicans
		Average:	29.2

By Term of Administration

First Term		Later Term	
1954:	18 Republicans	1946:	55 Democrats
1962:	4 Democrats	1950:	29 Democrats
1970:	12 Republicans	1958:	47 Republicans
1978:	11 Democrats	1966:	47 Democrats
1982:	26 Republicans	1974:	43 Republicans
Average:	14.2	Average:	44.2

midterm elections reveal two fairly homogeneous sets of outcomes that
are sharply different from one another. In the five midterm elections that
took place during a first term, the president's party lost between 4 and 26
seats, with an average loss of 14.2. In the five elections after the first
term, the range of losses was between 29 and 55 seats with an average of
44.2. These results are rather clear cut. There is no overlap between the
two sets, the difference between the averages is large (30 seats), and the
variation within each set is comparatively small (a 22-seat range in the
first midterm set and 26 seats in the second set).

This analysis suggests that both history and a conception of the
different appeals of national parties in the first and second midterms of
the presidency should lead us to anticipate fairly substantial seat losses in
the House for the Republicans. (As befits the greater visibility of
individual campaigns, the impact of these forces on Senate races does not
seem to be as great.) Furthermore, even if Reagan remains very popular
in 1986, the Republicans may still lose many House seats. In the past, the
party of the incumbent president has suffered significant losses even
when that president was popular. In 1958, when the Republicans lost 47
seats in the House, President Dwight D. Eisenhower had an approval
rating in the Gallup poll of 52 percent positive and 30 percent negative.[37]
Even in 1974, at the time of the "Watergate Landslide," President Gerald

R. Ford's approval outweighed disapproval, 47 to 33, but the Republicans lost 43 seats.

With a relatively good economy to back them, the national Republican party and the Republican campaign committees in Congress began campaigning early to wage a national campaign to mitigate the midterm effect. In the House, for example, the Republican campaign committee planned to spend between four and five million dollars to attack the legislative records of 25 to 30 incumbent Democrats.[38] On the other hand, Democrats were also trying to improve their party image nationally. On July 1, 1985, Gov. Charles S. Robb of Virginia, saying that he was "tired of hearing this party and those who represent this party described as wimps," traveled to five Texas cities, along with other members of a new group called the Democratic Leadership Council, to defend their party's ideas on matters such as defense and the economy.[39]

Another consideration is the small number of seats the GOP now holds. In both 1958 and 1974 the Republicans lost 24 percent of their seats; starting with a smaller number in the 99th Congress, a similar percentage loss would cost them 41 seats. Taking all of these factors into account, it would appear that—barring some significant deterioration in the economy—Republican losses in the House are likely to be held to a smaller number than the historical standard for second midterm elections would lead us to expect. In the Senate there is likely to be a Democratic gain, and the chances for each party to control that body seem about equal.

Republican Prospects in Congressional Elections

To close this chapter we examine the likelihood of a national partisan realignment, the prospects for continued Republican control of the Senate, and the Republican outlook in the House. As we have said, the connection between partisan identification and congressional voting is weaker today than it used to be. Thus, even if the shift toward the Republicans in party identification we discussed in Chapter 8 proves to be long lasting, it is unlikely to produce a stable voting bloc that will guarantee continuing Republican majorities in Congress. For Senate elections, we argue that this means that outcomes will continue to be volatile and erratic, influenced to some degree by national trends, but even more so by the one-on-one competition of strong, well-funded Republican candidates facing strong, well-funded Democratic candidates in most elections. For the House, there are a number of other factors, including party organizations, gerrymandering, and presidential coattails, that we must consider before rendering a judgment.

The Republican party's supposed comparative advantage in terms of national organization in House elections has received a good deal of attention.[40] In the 1982 House races, for example, the Republican party outspent the Democratic party almost six to one in direct contributions and coordinated spending for House elections.[41] The $5 million in early Republican spending for the 1986 campaign, already mentioned, and party plans to widely utilize computerized lists of voters categorized by demographic groups, developed in the Reagan reelection campaign, are other examples of Republican efforts in this area.

Yet things are not so one-sided or simple as this summary would suggest. Even though the Republicans were first to organize and develop their national congressional campaign organization, the Democrats are catching up. The party improved its fund raising and organization in 1984 and appears likely to improve them even more for the future. Moreover, the Democrats have followed other strategies that do not show up in the kind of spending figures we have cited. For example, the Democratic congressional campaign committee has concentrated on helping candidates get money from political action committees (PACs) rather than simply raising it themselves and donating it to candidates. Democrats argue that their party controls the House and will continue to do so for the rest of the century, so the PACs would be well advised to support their candidates. The strategy appears to be working. The *Wall Street Journal* analyzed the 77 House races that were deemed to be very close before the 1984 election. Even though candidate spending for the two parties was virtually equal in those races, PACs provided 43 percent of funds for Democratic candidates but only 30 percent for Republicans.[42]

Another factor that many think is related to the potential for future Republican success is the pattern of House districting in the United States. Republicans believe that Democrats have drawn district lines to their advantage and against the Republicans, depriving the GOP of their rightful share of House seats according to their national vote. Citing 1984 as an example, Republicans point out that they got 47 percent of the national House vote but only 42 percent of the House seats. Republicans have, therefore, made it a high priority to win state legislative seats so they can increase their control of House redistricting after the 1990 census.

To be sure, some states are gerrymandered against Republican candidates; we have already cited California as an example. However, other states (Indiana, for example) are gerrymandered in the opposite direction, and in still other states, mostly where political control of the state government was divided between the parties, districts were drawn to the advantage of incumbents of both parties.[43] The net effect of redrawn congressional districts would seem to be less one-sided than Republicans suggest.

Even if current districting were one-sided, moreover, Republican chances of significantly altering the situation in their favor seem limited. The chances of partisan benefit from reapportionment and redistricting are usually best for a party if it controls the governorship and *both* houses of the state legislature.[44] After the 1984 election the Republicans held this kind of control in only 4 states with a total of 16 House seats, while the Democrats controlled 18 states with a total of 151 representatives.[45] Of course, the important question is the balance of partisan control after the 1990 election, for that is when the next reapportionment will take place. But the Republicans have a long way to go before they will be well positioned to take advantage of the redistricting that will result from the 1990 census.

Norman J. Ornstein has pointed out that the gap between the share of seats and share of the vote for the Republicans seems to be more a consequence of the single-member district system employed in this country and the higher turnout among Republicans.[46] The single-member district system means that a party can win a seat with 51 percent of the vote as well as with 80 percent. If one party wins districts across the country by larger margins than the other party, the former party will "waste" a lot of votes even if there is no bias in districting. Districts are, moreover, apportioned on the basis of population, not voter turnout. As Table 9-8 shows, Democrats tend to do very well in districts in which relatively few people vote, and Republicans win a lot of districts with higher turnout. When these votes are aggregated nationally the total vote of the two parties is closer than it would be if turnout were equal in all districts. Thus the Republican "disadvantage" appears to be more a consequence of our electoral system than of deliberate Democratic design, and Republican hopes for substantial gains when districts are redrawn after 1990 may turn out to be little more than wishful thinking.

Table 9-8   Election Outcomes by Party in 1984 House Races, by Total Vote Cast in District

Winner	Less than 125,000	125,000- 150,000	150,000- 175,000	175,000- 200,000	200,000- 225,000	More than 225,000
Dem.	93%	93%	73%	57%	42%	50%
Rep.	7	7	27	43	58	50
Total	100	100	100	100	100	100
(N)	(27)	(30)	(51)	(91)	(121)	(98)

Source: Adapted from Norman J. Ornstein, "Genesis of a Gerrymander," *Wall Street Journal*, May 7, 1985, 34.

Note: Because there is relatively little difference in the size of the voting-age population among congressional districts, the total number of votes cast provides a rough measure of the relative turnout among the districts. Uncontested seats have been excluded from these calculations.

A third consideration relevant to evaluation of the Republican party's future in House elections is the link between House outcomes and the presidential vote in 1984. Or perhaps the better way to express it is the lack of a link because, despite his tremendous victory, Reagan was remarkably unsuccessful in pulling Republican House candidates in with him. As we said at the beginning of the chapter, the outcome in 1984 represents the smallest share of House seats won by the party of a victorious presidential candidate in the history of our country. Ronald Reagan ran ahead of Walter F. Mondale in 372 congressional districts in 1984, but Democratic House candidates won a majority (191) of them. Moreover, Reagan worked hard to link his campaign to the national Republican congressional effort, and personally campaigned for many congressional candidates. Because the Republicans were unable to win a substantial share of Democratic seats in a strong Republican year, running with a popular president when the economy was in very good shape, it is difficult to see how they can hope to win many Democratic seats in the near future when conditions may not be as favorable. As Walter Dean Burnham has argued, "If Ronald Reagan could not provide the incentive for straight party voting, who will be able to do so in the future?" [47]

Just as the Republicans have been unable to capitalize on the popularity of their president, in the future they may also be unable to capitalize further on the unpopularity of Congress and its presumed reflection on the Democratic party. Approval ratings of Congress have been strongly negative for a number of years, but that may be changing. A comparison of Harris polls shows that Congress received a 32 percent positive rating in 1984, but a 53 percent positive rating in 1985. [48] Nor is this simply the reflection of a confusion among respondents about which party controls Congress, because there has been only a small positive shift among Republicans. The shift in evaluation instead has taken place among Democrats (from 33 percent positive in 1984 to 65 percent in 1985) and independents (23 percent in 1984 to 48 percent in 1985). It is much too early to conclude that Democrats in Congress are receiving a positive endorsement from the electorate because of resistance to Reagan administration programs, but if this were to turn out to be the case it would not bode well for the Republicans in 1986 and later.

After consideration of all these factors, one must conclude that the likelihood of the Republicans winning control of the House of Representatives in the near future, say through 1992, is relatively small. The Republicans would have to make a net gain of 36 House seats over the number they held at the beginning of the 99th Congress to take control. But after the 1986 midterm contest, the Republicans might need 50 or more seats for control. It is not easy to see where such substantial Republicans gains are likely to come from over the three elections after 1986. We must therefore conclude that, barring any strong pro-Republican national tide, which seems unlikely, the Democratic hold on control of the House is likely to be fairly secure.

Notes

1. Walter Dean Burnham, "A Continuing Political Gridlock," *Wall Street Journal,* June 24, 1985, 14.
2. The definition of incumbent here is limited to elected incumbents. This includes all members of the House because the only way to become a representative is by election. In the case of the Senate, however, vacancies may be filled by appointment. These senators are not counted as incumbents. There is no obvious ground on which to choose a beginning date for the study of congressional change. Here we will use 1954 because, beginning with that year, more reliable data are readily available, and it is the first opportunity for reelection for members elected after the first postwar reapportionment of congressional seats.
3. Paul R. Abramson, John H. Aldrich, and David W. Rohde, *Change and Continuity in the 1980 Elections,* rev. ed. (Washington, D.C.: CQ Press, 1983), 192-93.
4. The regional breakdowns used in this chapter are as follows: East: Connecticut, Delaware, Maine, Massachusetts, New Hampshire, New Jersey, New York, Pennsylvania, Rhode Island, and Vermont; Midwest: Illinois, Indiana, Iowa, Kansas, Michigan, Minnesota, Nebraska, North Dakota, Ohio, South Dakota, and Wisconsin; West: Alaska, Arizona, California, Colorado, Hawaii, Idaho, Montana, Nevada, New Mexico, Oregon, Utah, Washington, and Wyoming; South: Alabama, Arkansas, Florida, Georgia, Louisiana, Mississippi, North Carolina, South Carolina, Tennessee, Texas, and Virginia; Border: Kentucky, Maryland, Missouri, Oklahoma, and West Virginia. This classification differs somewhat from the one we used in other chapters, but it is commonly used for congressional analysis.
5. See Gary C. Jacobson and Samuel Kernell, *Strategy and Choice in Congressional Elections,* 2d ed. (New Haven, Conn.: Yale University Press, 1983), especially Chaps. 2-4 for a corroborating analysis.
6. Richard F. Fenno, Jr., *Home Style: House Members in Their Districts* (Boston: Little, Brown, 1978).
7. See Jacobson and Kernell, *Strategy and Choice;* Gary C. Jacobson, "Strategic Politicians and Congressional Elections, 1946-1980" (Paper delivered at the Annual Meeting of the American Political Science Association, New York, Sept. 3-6, 1981); Jon R. Bond, Gary Covington, and Richard Fleisher, "Explaining Challenger Quality in Congressional Elections," *Journal of Politics* 47 (May 1985): 510-29; and David W. Rohde, "Risk-Bearing and Progressive Ambition: The Case of Members of the United States House of Representatives," *American Journal of Political Science* 23 (February 1979): 1-26.
8. These figures compare the data in Table 9-4 to data from the corresponding table in Abramson, Aldrich, and Rohde, *Change and Continuity in the 1980 Elections,* rev. ed., 198.
9. "House Campaigns Quiet as Few Seek to Run," *Congressional Quarterly Weekly Report,* March 24, 1984, 657-58.

10. Ibid., 658; see also Abramson, Aldrich, and Rohde, *Change and Continuity in the 1980 Elections,* rev. ed., 258-63.
11. See Thomas E. Mann and Raymond E. Wolfinger, "Candidates and Parties in Congressional Elections," *American Political Science Review* 74 (September 1980): 617-32.
12. See David R. Mayhew, "Congressional Elections: The Case of the Vanishing Marginals," *Polity* 6 (Spring 1974): 295-317; Robert S. Erikson, "The Advantage of Incumbency in Congressional Elections," *Polity* 3 (Spring 1971): 395-405; Robert S. Erikson, "Malapportionment, Gerrymandering, and Party Fortunes in Congressional Elections," *American Political Science Review* 66 (December 1972): 1234-45; and Warren Lee Kostroski, "Party and Incumbency in Postwar Senate Elections: Trends, Patterns, and Models," *American Political Science Review* 67 (December 1973): 1213-34.
13. Edward R. Tufte, "Communication," *American Political Science Review* 68 (March 1974): 211-13. The communication involved a discussion of Tufte's earlier article, "The Relationship Between Seats and Votes in Two-Party Systems," *American Political Science Review* 67 (June 1973): 540-54.
14. See John A. Ferejohn, "On the Decline of Competition in Congressional Elections," *American Political Science Review* 71 (March 1977): 166-76; Albert D. Cover, "One Good Term Deserves Another: The Advantage of Incumbency in Congressional Elections," *American Journal of Political Science* 21 (August 1977): 523-41; and Albert D. Cover and David R. Mayhew, "Congressional Dynamics and the Decline of Competitive Congressional Elections," in *Congress Reconsidered,* 2d ed., edited by Lawrence C. Dodd and Bruce I. Oppenheimer (Washington, D.C.: CQ Press, 1981), 62-82.
15. Morris P. Fiorina, *Congress: Keystone of the Washington Establishment* (New Haven, Conn.: Yale University Press, 1977), especially Chaps. 4-6.
16. See several conflicting arguments and conclusions in the *American Journal of Political Science* 25 (August 1981): John R. Johannes and John C. McAdams, "The Congressional Incumbency Effect: Is It Casework, Policy Compatibility, or Something Else? An Examination of the 1978 Election," 512-42; Morris P. Fiorina, "Some Problems in Studying the Effects of Resource Allocation in Congressional Elections," 543-67; Diana Evans Yiannakis, "The Grateful Electorate: Casework and Congressional Elections," 568-80; and John C. McAdams and John R. Johannes, "Does Casework Matter? A Reply to Professor Fiorina," 581-604. See also John R. Johannes, *To Serve the People: Congress and Constituency Service* (Lincoln: University of Nebraska Press, 1984), especially Chap. 8; and Albert D. Cover and Bruce S. Brumberg, "Baby Books and Ballots: The Impact of Congressional Mail on Constituent Opinion," *American Political Science Review* 76 (June 1982): 347-59. The evidence in Cover and Brumberg for a positive electoral effect is quite strong, although the result may be applicable only to limited circumstances.
17. Ferejohn, "On the Decline in Competition," 174.
18. Cover, "One Good Term," 535.
19. Gary C. Jacobson, "The Marginals Never Vanished: Incumbency and Competition in Elections to the U.S. House of Representatives, 1952-1982" (Paper delivered at the Annual Meeting of the Midwest Political Science Association, Chicago, Ill., April 17-20, 1985).
20. Ibid., 7.
21. The body of literature has now grown to be quite large. Some salient examples are: Gary C. Jacobson, "The Effects of Campaign Spending in Congressional Elections," *American Political Science Review* 72 (June 1978):

469-91; Jacobson, *Money in Congressional Elections* (New Haven, Conn.: Yale University Press, 1980); Jacobson, "Parties and PACs in Congressional Elections," in *Congress Reconsidered,* 3d ed., edited by Lawrence C. Dodd and Bruce I. Oppenheimer (Washington, D.C.: CQ Press, 1985), 131-60: Jacobson, "Money in the 1980 and 1982 Congressional Elections," in Michael J. Malbin, ed., *Money and Politics in the United States* (Chatham, N.J.: Chatham House, 1984), 38-69; Jacobson and Kernell, *Strategy and Choice;* John A. Ferejohn and Morris P. Fiorina, "Incumbency and Realignment in Congressional Elections," in John E. Chubb and Paul E. Peterson, *The New Direction in American Politics* (Washington, D.C.: The Brookings Institution, 1985), 91-115.

22. Jacobson, "Money in the 1980 and 1982 Congressional Elections," 56-57. The analysis includes only incumbents with major party opposition.

23. The 1982 election was the last for which complete spending data were available at the time this analysis was conducted, so we will rely primarily on that year. Data were taken from Michael Barone and Grant Ujifusa, *The Almanac of American Politics, 1984* (Washington, D.C.: National Journal, 1983). The analysis excludes races with no major party opposition and those in which both candidates were incumbents.

24. Abramson, Aldrich, and Rohde, *Change and Continuity in the 1980 Elections,* rev. ed., 201.

25. Ibid., 200-203.

26. Gary C. Jacobson, "Campaign Spending and Voter Awareness of Congressional Candidates" (Paper presented at the Annual Meeting of the Public Choice Society, New Orleans, La., May 11-13, 1977, 16).

27. Significant elective offices included U.S. representative, statewide office, state legislature, countywide (supervisor or prosecutor) or citywide (mayor or prosecutor) offices.

28. Abramson, Aldrich, and Rohde, *Change and Continuity in the 1980 Elections,* rev. ed., 202-203.

29. Ibid., 204-207.

30. This is the standard measure of ideological views in congressional research. The conservative coalition is the voting coalition of a majority of Republicans and a majority of southern Democrats. The ratio is a measure of how frequently a member supports this coalition. It is computed by dividing the frequency of support by the sum of the frequency of support and the frequency of opposition. Higher support ratios indicate greater conservatism. These figures are published annually in the *Congressional Quarterly Almanac.*

31. Quoted in Jeffrey L. Pasley, "New House GOP Freshman Class Wary of Following Reagan's Budget Lead," *National Journal,* March 16, 1985, 584.

32. Quoted in Ronald Brownstein, "Conservatives Split on Social Agenda Tactics," *National Journal,* June 29, 1985, 1503.

33. These quotations are from Helen Dewar, "Congress Less Compliant Than One Elected in '80," *Washington Post,* Nov. 8, 1984, A1, A53.

34. Examples are the Republican senators from the farm states. See Jack W. Germond and Jules Witcover, "Incumbency May Save Farmbelt GOP Senators," *National Journal,* March 16, 1985, 600.

35. Richard E. Cohen, "Many House Seats Could Switch Party in 1986," *National Journal,* March 30, 1985, 679, 702.

36. See Abramson, Aldrich, and Rohde, *Change and Continuity in the 1980 Elections,* rev. ed., 252-53.

37. All approval data used in this chapter, unless otherwise indicated, are taken from George H. Gallup, *The Gallup Poll: Public Opinion, 1935-1971,* 3 vols.

(New York: Random House, 1972) for years through 1970, and various issues of *The Gallup Opinion Index* (Princeton, N.J.: American Institute of Public Opinion) for later years. Respondents were asked whether they approve or disapprove of the way the president is handling his job.

38. Hedrick Smith, "G.O.P. Plans Early Drive to Unseat 30 House Democrats," *New York Times*, Feb. 28, 1985, 16.
39. Tom Sherwood, "Robb Leads Democrats on Texas Blitz," *Washington Post*, July 2, 1985, A8.
40. See, for example, Gary C. Jacobson and Samuel Kernell, "Party Organization and the Efficient Distribution of Campaign Resources: Republicans and Democrats in 1982" (Paper presented at the Weingart-Caltech Conference on Institutional Context of Elections, California Institute of Technology, Pasadena, Calif., Feb. 16-18, 1984); and Gary C. Jacobson, "The Republican Advantage in Campaign Finance," in Chubb and Peterson, *The New Direction in American Politics*, 175-200.
41. Jacobson, "The Republican Advantage," 156.
42. Brooks Jackson, "Democrats Credit Wins to Funding," *Wall Street Journal*, Nov. 12, 1984, 50. These activities demonstrate how party organizations can become stronger despite the fact (or perhaps because of the fact) that the ties of party identification are becoming weaker. See Joseph A. Schlesinger, "The New American Political Party," *American Political Science Review* 79 (December 1985): 1152-69.
43. See Abramson, Aldrich, and Rohde, *Change and Continuity in the 1980 Elections*, rev. ed., 256-63.
44. Ibid., 261-63. See also Alan I. Abramowitz, "Partisan Redistricting and the 1982 Congressional Elections," *Journal of Politics* 45 (August 1983): 767-70.
45. *Congressional Quarterly Weekly Report*, Nov. 17, 1984, 2944-45. These numbers remained the same after the New Jersey and Virginia elections in November 1985.
46. Norman J. Ornstein, "Genesis of a 'Gerrymander,'" *Wall Street Journal*, May 7, 1985, 34.
47. Burnham, "A Continuing Political Gridlock."
48. Louis Harris, "Positive Congress Rating, First Time in Twenty Years," *The Harris Survey*, June 19, 1985, 3. These results are based upon responses to the following question: "How would you rate the job being done by Congress—excellent, pretty good, only fair or poor?" "Excellent" and "pretty good" replies were scored as positive.

Chapter 10

The Congressional Electorate

In the previous chapter we viewed congressional elections at the district and state level and saw how those outcomes aggregate to form a national result. In this chapter we consider congressional elections from the point of view of the individual voter, using the same national survey by the University of Michigan's Survey Research Center-Center for Political Studies that we employed to consider presidential voting. We discuss how social forces, issues, partisan loyalties, incumbency, and evaluations of congressional and presidential performance influence the decisions of voters in congressional elections. We also try to determine the existence and extent of presidential "coattails" and to shed additional light on the effects of adequate or inadequate campaign resources on the part of challengers.

Social Forces and the Congressional Vote

In general, social forces relate to the congressional vote in much the same way they do to the presidential vote. But in 1984 Democratic congressional candidates did better than the presidential candidate, Walter F. Mondale, in every single category used in the presidential vote analysis *(Table 5-1.)* [1] Consider the relationship between voting and race, for example. Democratic candidates for the House of Representatives ran 16 points better than Mondale among white voters and 2 points better even among black voters, from whom Mondale had received 89 percent of the vote. While Mondale received only a little over a third of the vote among whites, Democratic House candidates won a majority of these voters with 52 percent.

Keeping in mind the gap in relative support that we have discussed, we find that presidential and congressional voting patterns are similar not only with respect to race, but also for other social categories, including occupation, family income, education, union membership, age, and religion. (Except for voting by race, the discussion here, as in Chapter 5, is limited to white voters.) Members of union families were 10 percentage points more likely to vote Democratic than voters from non-union families; working-class voters were 4 points more Democratic than middle-class voters. Catholics were 14 points more likely to vote Democratic than Republican. The gap between voters with annual family incomes of less than $10,000 and families that earned $60,000 or more is very large: 27 points. Like presidential voting, however, most of the difference in voting on this variable is captured by these two extreme categories. If we exclude them, there is comparatively little variation in congressional vote by party along the income spectrum. For these and the other social forces, the comparison to the Democratic presidential vote is similar: in virtually every instance the direction of the relationship is the same, but the strength of the relationship is weaker.

Even with respect to voting by gender, this generalization holds, although we found the relationship reversed four years ago. In 1980 women were more likely than men to vote Democratic for president, but for the House of Representatives, men were more likely to vote Democratic. In 1984, on the other hand, women were more likely to vote Democratic for both president and Congress, although the gender gap in House voting was only 3 points.

The one exception to this general relationship is the impact of region on voting, and here the presidential pattern is reversed. Among whites, Ronald Reagan fared best in the South, and Mondale did best in the Mountain and Pacific region. In House voting, the highest rate of support for Democrats was in the South and in the New England and Middle Atlantic states at 56 percent. In the Mountain and Pacific region, Democratic House candidates received 49 percent of the vote. Despite the shattering of southern Democratic party ties at the presidential level, southern voters still tend to support Democratic congressional candidates. It should be noted, however, that here too the relationship is weaker at the congressional level than at the presidential level. The gap between the highest region of Democratic support and the lowest is 15 points in presidential voting; in the House vote it is only 7 points.

Issues and the Congressional Vote

In Chapter 6 we analyzed the impact of issues on the presidential vote in 1984. Any attempt to conduct a parallel analysis for congressional elections is hampered by limited data. Because we do have data on voters' positions on many issues, one approach we can take is to see whether those positions are systematically related to the portion of the congressional vote going to one party or another.

Table 10-1 depicts the relationship between issue position and voting for the House on seven issues.[2] Because we would expect a relationship between issue position and party identification and between party identification and congressional vote, we control for party identification in Table 10-1. Reading across each row, we see that although there is some variation in the strength of the relationship, the issues present a consistent picture: the more liberal the position of the voter, the more likely the voter is to vote Democratic. Furthermore, this relationship is not merely the consequence of party identification; it holds for almost all identification groups. Reading down each column, however, shows that party identification is consistently and strongly related to the way people vote regardless of a respondent's position on these issues. Party identification categories consistently produce greater voting differences than do varying issue positions.

A more interesting perspective on issues in the congressional vote is to ask whether voters are affected by their perceptions of where candidates stand on the issues. Previous analysis has shown that there was a relationship between voter perception of House candidates' position on that scale and the voter's choice.[3] Unfortunately, the SRC-CPS 1984 survey does not contain similar questions on the perceived position of House candidates on issues. We can, however, draw on other research to shed further light on this question. In two articles Alan I. Abramowitz demonstrated a relationship between candidate ideology and voter choice in both House and Senate elections.[4] For the 1978 Senate election, Abramowitz classified the contests according to the clarity of the ideological choice the two major party candidates offered to voters. He found that the higher the ideological clarity of the race, the more likely voters were to perceive some difference between the candidates on a liberalism-conservatism scale, and the stronger the relationship was between voter position on that scale and the vote. Indeed, in races with a very clear choice, ideology had approximately the same impact on the vote as party identification. In an analysis of House races in 1980 and 1982, Abramowitz found that ideology had a positive impact on voting in both cases (in other words, the more liberal the voter the more likely the voter was to vote Democratic), but that the relationship was statistically significant only in 1982.

Another point of view is offered in an analysis by Robert S. Erikson and Gerald C. Wright.[5] They examined the positions of 1982 House candidates on a variety of issues (expressed in response to a *New York Times*/CBS News poll) and found that, on most issues, most of the districts were presented with a liberal Democrat and a conservative

Table 10-1 Percentage Voting Democratic for the House, 1984,
Controlling for Party Identification and Positions on
Seven Issues

Party Identification[1]	Issue		

Government Spending/Services

	Liberal	Middle	Conservative
Democrat	88 (57)[2]	76 (267)	60 (30)
Independent	62 (39)	54 (206)	43 (53)
Republican	38 (13)	20 (196)	22 (114)

Aid to Minorities

	Liberal	Middle	Conservative
Democrat	90 (81)	74 (233)	73 (48)
Independent	81 (31)	54 (213)	43 (61)
Republican	30 (23)	23 (211)	17 (88)

Central America

	Liberal	Middle	Conservative
Democrat	83 (150)	70 (141)	68 (28)
Independent	55 (92)	54 (151)	44 (39)
Republican	33 (54)	20 (189)	14 (44)

Defense Spending

	Liberal	Middle	Conservative
Democrat	85 (103)	76 (218)	59 (32)
Independent	69 (61)	51 (209)	41 (41)
Republican	35 (17)	21 (239)	23 (79)

Aid to Women

	Liberal	Middle	Conservative
Democrat	92 (107)	72 (206)	66 (41)
Independent	58 (52)	55 (187)	51 (51)
Republican	41 (32)	22 (210)	14 (76)

Relations with Russia

	Liberal	Middle	Conservative
Democrat	87 (108)	74 (178)	70 (67)
Independent	65 (65)	55 (181)	34 (61)
Republican	22 (32)	23 (195)	18 (92)

Jobs and Standard of Living

	Liberal	Middle	Conservative
Democrat	94 (79)	75 (225)	57 (49)
Independent	76 (33)	52 (190)	49 (79)
Republican	38 (24)	23 (155)	18 (142)

[1] In this table and in Tables 10-3 through 10-8, independents who lean to one of the parties are classified as independents, strong and weak Democrats as Democrats, and strong and weak Republicans as Republicans.

[2] Numbers in parentheses are totals on which percentages are based. For each of the scales we group positions 1 and 2, positions 3 through 5, and positions 6 and 7. The "liberal" positions on these issues are: favor government spending and services; favor aid to minorities; oppose greater involvement in Central America; for reducing defense spending; for aid to women; for cooperation with Russia; and for government action on jobs and standard of living. See Figure 6-2 for more information on the scales.

Republican. They also found that moderate candidates did better in attracting votes than more extreme candidates.

So far, we have seen that both issue positions and party identification appear to have an independent impact on voter choice in congressional elections, with the impact of partisanship consistently being stronger. It is also clear, however, that neither of these factors, nor both together, account for all the variation in voting, so we must also consider other influences on the vote. Before moving on, we will provide a little more detail on the effect of party identification on House voting.

Party Identification and the Congressional Vote

As our discussion in the preceding chapters demonstrates and data presented here indicate, party identification has a significant effect on voters' decisions, although the relationship is weaker today than in the past. Table 10-2, which corresponds to Table 8-4 on the presidential vote, reports the percentage of whites voting Democratic for the House across all categories of partisanship from 1952 through 1984. Even a casual inspection of the data reveals that the proportion of voters who cast ballots in accordance with their party identification has declined substantially over time.

Consider first the strong identifier categories. In every election between 1952 and 1964, at least 9 strong party identifiers out of 10 supported the candidate of their party. After that, the percentage dropped, falling to 4 out of 5 in 1980. There was, however, some resurgence of support in these categories in 1982 and 1984. The relationship between party and voting among weak party identifiers shows a similar decline over time, and the rates of defection are higher. By 1984 fully a third of the weak identifiers in both parties were voting for House candidates of the opposition. Independents who lean to one party or the other show a more erratic pattern, although here too defection rates tend to be higher since the 1970s than earlier.

Despite this increase in defections from party identification since the mid-1960s, strong party identifiers continue to be more likely to vote in accord with their party than weak identifiers. Weak Republicans are usually more likely to vote Republican than independents who lean toward the Republicans. Weak Democrats were more likely to vote Democratic than independents who leaned Democratic in most of the elections between 1952 and 1978, although in the last three elections this pattern was reversed.

As we saw in Chapter 8, however, the proportion of the electorate that falls in the strong party identification categories has declined. Thus strong Democrats, for example, not only are less likely to vote Democratic

Table 10-2 Percentage of White Major Party Voters Who Voted Democratic for the House, by Party Identification, 1952-1984

Party Identification	1952	1954	1956	1958	1960	1962	1964	1966	1968	1970	1972	1974	1976	1978	1980	1982	1984
Strong Democrat	90	97	94	96	92	96	92	92	88	91	91	89	86	83	82	90	87
Weak Democrat	76	77	86	88	85	83	84	81	72	76	79	81	76	79	66	73	66
Independent, leans Democratic	63	70	82	75	86	74	78	54	60	74	78	87	76	60	69	84	76
Independent, no partisan leanings	25	41	35	46	52	61	70	49	48	48	54	54	55	56	57	31	59
Independent, leans Republican	18	6	17	26	26	28	28	31	18	35	27	38	32	36	32	36	39
Weak Republican	10	6	11	22	14	14	34	22	21	17	24	31	28	34	26	20	33
Strong Republican	5	5	5	6	8	6	8	12	8	4	15	14	15	19	22	12	15

Note: To approximate the numbers upon which these percentages are based, see Table 8-2. Actual Ns will be smaller than those that can be derived from Table 8-2 because respondents who did not vote (or who voted for a minor party) have been excluded from these calculations. Numbers also will be lower for the presidential election years because the voting report is provided in the postelection interviews that usually contain about 10 percent fewer respondents than the preelection interviews in which party identification was measured. The 1954 survey measured voting intention shortly before the election. Except for 1954, the off-year election surveys are based upon a postelection interview.

than before, but also fewer voters identify themselves as strong Democrats. The impact of party on voting, therefore, has suffered a double weakening.

If party identifiers have been defecting more frequently in House elections, to whom have they been defecting? As one might expect from the preceding chapter, the answer is: to incumbents.

Incumbency and the Congressional Vote

In Chapter 9 we mentioned Albert D. Cover's analysis of congressional voting behavior between 1958 and 1974.[6] Cover compared the rates of defection from party identification between voters who were of the same party as the incumbent and those who were of the same party as the challenger. The analysis showed no systematic increase over time in defection among voters who shared identification with incumbents, and the proportions defecting varied between 5 percent and 14 percent. Among voters who identified with the same party as challengers, however, the rate of defection—that is, the proportion voting for the incumbent instead of the candidate of their own party—increased steadily from 16 percent in 1958 to 56 percent in 1972, then dropped to 49 percent in 1974. Thus the decline in the strength of the relationship between party identification and House voting appears to be attributed in a large measure to increased support for incumbents.

Data on the percentage of respondents who voted Democratic for the House and Senate in 1984, controlling for party identification and incumbency, are presented in Table 10-3. In House voting we find the same relationship that Cover did. The proportion of voters defecting from their party identification is comparatively lower when that identification is shared by the incumbent: 9 percent among Democrats and 5 percent among Republicans.[7] When, however, the incumbent belongs to the other party, the rates are much higher: 60 percent among Democrats and 38 percent among Republicans. Note also that the support of the independents is skewed sharply in favor of the incumbent. When there was an incumbent Democrat running, two-thirds of the independents voted Democratic; when there was an incumbent Republican, three independents out of four voted Republican. For open seats, independents went two to one for Republicans.

A similar pattern is apparent from the data on Senate voting, although the pull of incumbency appears to be substantially weaker upon Democratic party identifiers. When given the opportunity to support a Republican House incumbent, 60 percent of the Democratic identifiers defected. Faced with the opportunity to support an incumbent Republican senator, only 30 percent defected. Because the proportion of the electorate that has the chance to vote for Democratic and Republican

Table 10-3　Percentage Voting Democratic for the House and Senate, 1984, by Party Identification and Incumbency

Incumbency	Democrat	(N)	Party Identification Independent	(N)	Republican	(N)
House						
Democrat	91	(284)	68	(208)	38	(177)
None	59	(27)	33	(42)	7	(43)
Republican	40	(87)	24	(75)	5	(136)
Senate						
Democrat	92	(71)	57	(90)	34	(70)
None	89	(84)	45	(53)	22	(37)
Republican	70	(122)	43	(96)	10	(110)

Note: Numbers in parentheses are the totals upon which percentages are based.

senatorial candidates will vary greatly from election to election, it is difficult to make generalizations about the overall effects of incumbency in Senate contests. But the results in Table 10-3 show that in the House elections the Democrats are the clear beneficiaries of the pro-incumbent bias. Nearly half of all Republican identifiers lived in a district in which a Democratic incumbent was seeking reelection. On the other hand, just over a fifth of the Democratic identifiers lived in a district with a Republican incumbent running. Among independents, 64 percent lived in a district with a Democratic incumbent seeking reelection and 23 percent in a district with a Republican incumbent. In the remainder of this chapter we will further explore this relationship among party identification, incumbency, and congressional voting.

The Congressional Vote as a Referendum

In Chapter 7 we analyzed the effect of perceptions of presidential performance on the vote for president in 1984, more or less viewing that election as a referendum on Reagan's job performance. A similar conception can be applied here, employing different perspectives. On one hand, a congressional election can be considered a referendum on the performance of a particular member of Congress in office; on the other, it can be viewed as a referendum on the performance of the president. We will consider both possibilities here.

For some time, public opinion surveys have shown that the approval ratings of the performance of congressional incumbents are very high, even when judgments on the performance of Congress as an institution are not. While traveling with House incumbents in their districts, Richard F. Fenno, Jr., noted that the people he met overwhelmingly approved of the performance of their own representative, although at the time the public generally disapproved of the job the institution was doing.[8] Data in the 1984 SRC-CPS survey again indicate widespread approval of House incumbents: among respondents who had an opinion, an average of 88 percent endorsed their members' job performance. Approval was widespread, regardless of the party identification of the voter or the party of the incumbent. Indeed, an examination of all combinations of these two variables shows that the *lowest* approval rate for incumbents is the 79 percent level achieved by Democratic members among Republican party identifiers.[9]

Further evidence indicates, moreover, that the level of approval is electorally consequential. Table 10-4 shows the level of pro-incumbent voting among voters who share the incumbent's party and among those who are of the opposite party, controlling for whether they approve or disapprove of the incumbent's job performance. If voters approve of the member's performance and share his or her party identification, support is almost complete. At the opposite pole, among voters from the opposite party who disapprove, support is virtually nil. In both of the mixed categories, just a little more than three voters out of five support the incumbent. Approval rates are very high even among members of the opposite party, and it is easy to see why most incumbents are reelected by large margins.

In Chapter 9 we pointed out that midterm congressional elections were influenced by public evaluations of the president's job performance. Voters who think the president is doing a good job are more likely to support the congressional candidate of the president's party. Little scholarly

Table 10-4 Percentage of Voters Supporting Incumbents in House Voting, 1984, by Party and Attitude toward Incumbent's Performance

Incumbent Is	Voter's Attitude toward Incumbent's Job Performance			
	Approve	*(N)*	*Disapprove*	*(N)*
Same party as voter	95	(350)	62	(21)
Opposite party	64	(165)	5	(44)

Note: Numbers in parentheses are the totals upon which percentages are based. The total number of cases is markedly lower than for previous tables because we have excluded respondents who did not evaluate the performance of the incumbent and those who live in a district with no incumbent running.

attention has been given to this phenomenon in presidential election years, but the 1984 election survey provides us with the data needed to explore the question.

On the surface at least, there would appear to be a strong relationship. Among voters who approved of Reagan's job performance, only 37 percent voted Democratic for the House; among those who disapproved of the president's performance, 87 percent supported Democrats. In 1980 there was a similar relationship between the two variables, but when controls were introduced for party identification and incumbency, the relationship all but disappeared.[10] Approval of Carter increased the Democratic House vote by a small amount among Democrats, but had virtually no effect among independents and Republicans. In 1984, however, the results are very different. Table 10-5 presents the relevant data on House voting, controlling for party identification, incumbency, and evaluation of Reagan's job performance. We find that even with these controls, there is still a noticeable impact on House voting from evaluations of the president's job. To be sure, Democrats are still more likely both to disapprove of Reagan and to vote Democratic than are Republicans. Yet even after controlling for the pull of incumbency, within each party identification category, those who disapprove of Reagan's job performance are noticeably more likely to vote Democratic for the House than are those who approve, and the difference in every category is larger than the corresponding difference in 1980. Further research is necessary to reconcile these sharply conflicting findings in two consecutive presidential elections. At this point, all we know is that in the two elections a popular incumbent appeared to be of some substantial benefit to House candidates of his party, while an unpopular incumbent seemed to have little negative effect on his party's candidates.

Table 10-5   Percentage Voting Democratic for the House, 1984, Controlling for Attitude toward Reagan's Performance, Party Identification, and Incumbency

| Party Identification | Incumbent Is Republican | | | | Incumbent Is Democrat | | | |
| | Attitude toward Reagan's Job | | | | | | | |
	Approve	(N)	Disapprove	(N)	Approve	(N)	Disapprove	(N)
Democrat	21	(38)	53	(47)	78	(92)	97	(182)
Independent	11	(54)	55	(20)	60	(146)	88	(59)
Republican	4	(129)	[2]	(3)	35	(163)	83	(12)

Note: Numbers in parentheses are the totals upon which percentages are based. The number in brackets is the number voting Democratic where the total N is less than 10.

Presidential Coattails
and the Congressional Vote

Another perspective on the congressional vote, somewhat related to the presidential referendum concept we have just considered, is the impact of the voter's presidential vote decision, or the "length" of a presidential candidate's coattails. That is, does a voter's decision to support a presidential candidate make him or her more likely to support a congressional candidate of the same party, permitting the congressional candidate, as the saying goes, to ride into office on the president's coattails?

Expectations regarding presidential coattails have been shaped in substantial measure by the period of the New Deal realignment. Franklin D. Roosevelt won by landslide margins in 1932 and 1936 and swept enormous congressional majorities into office with him. Research has indicated, however, that such strong pulling power by presidential candidates may have been a historical aberration, and, in any event, that candidates' pulling power has declined in recent years.[11] In an analysis of the coattail effect since 1868, John A. Ferejohn and Randall L. Calvert point out that the effect is a combination of two factors: how many voters a presidential candidate can pull to congressional candidates of his party and how many congressional seats can be shifted between the parties by the addition of those voters.[12] (The second aspect is called the seats-votes relationship, or the swing ratio.)

Ferejohn and Calvert discovered that the relationship between presidential voting and congressional voting between 1932 and 1948 was virtually the same as it was between 1896 and 1928 and that the impact of coattails was strengthened by an increase in the swing ratio. In other words, the same proportion of votes pulled in by a presidential candidate produced more congressional seats than in the past. After 1948, they argue, the coattail effect declined because the relationship between presidential and congressional voting decreased. Analyzing data from presidential elections from 1956 through 1980, Ferejohn and Calvert reached similar conclusions about the length of presidential coattails.[13] They found that although every election during the period exhibited significant coattail voting, over time the extent of such voting probably declined.

Data on the percentage of respondents who voted Democratic for the House and Senate in 1984, controlling for their presidential vote and their party identification, are presented in Table 10-6. For both congressional offices, a strong relationship is apparent. Within each party identification category, the proportion of Reagan voters who supported Democratic congressional candidates is substantially lower than the proportion of Mondale voters who cast their congressional ballots that way.

Table 10-6   Percentage of Respondents Voting Democratic for House and Senate, 1984, Controlling for Party Identification and Presidential Vote

| *Presidential* | *Party Identification* | | | | | |
Vote	*Democrat*	*(N)*	*Independent*	*(N)*	*Republican*	*(N)*
House						
Reagan	52	(95)	43	(231)	22	(344)
Mondale	88	(343)	82	(114)	77	(13)
Senate						
Reagan	49	(51)	35	(158)	19	(205)
Mondale	90	(217)	77	(74)	[4]	(9)

Note: Numbers in parentheses are the totals upon which percentages are based. The number in brackets is the number voting Democratic for the Senate when the total N is less than 10.

Because we know that this apparent relationship could be just an accidental consequence of the distribution of different types of voters among Democratic and Republican districts, in Table 10-7 we present the same data on House voting in 1984, but this time controlling for the party of the House incumbent. Despite this additional control, the relationship holds up very well. Within every category, Reagan voters support Democratic candidates at substantially lower rates than do Mondale voters. The conclusion from these data is that Reagan was a significant electoral asset to Republican congressional candidates in 1984. Unfortunately for the Republicans, the net impact of this asset yielded relatively few additional Republican seats in the House. It is also important to note that the results in both Table 10-6 and 10-7 are very similar to the corresponding data from 1980. Within the various categories of party identification and congressional incumbency, the relationship between presidential voting and congressional voting seems to be substantially the same in both elections.[14]

Incumbency and Candidate Resources Revisited

In Chapter 9 and this one, we have consistently seen the impact of incumbency both on congressional election outcomes and on the decisions of individual voters. In Chapter 9 we discussed the relationship between incumbency and candidate resources and argued that the larger victory margins of House incumbents, observed since the mid-1960s, may be primarily the consequence of the challengers' inability to raise enough money to compete effectively. The 1984 SRC-CPS election study con-

Table 10-7 Percentage of Respondents Voting Democratic for the House, 1984, Controlling for Presidential Vote, Party Identification, and Incumbency

Party Identification	Incumbent Is Democrat				Incumbent Is Republican			
	Presidential Vote							
	Mondale	*(N)*	*Reagan*	*(N)*	*Mondale*	*(N)*	*Reagan*	*(N)*
Democrat	97	(227)	63	(48)	56	(57)	11	(27)
Independent	94	(68)	57	(131)	50	(26)	10	(48)
Republican	[6]	(8)	37	(164)	[2]	(3)	4	(129)

Note: Numbers in parentheses are the totals upon which percentages are based. Numbers in brackets are the number voting Democratic for the House where the total N is less than 10.

tains a number of questions that provide, we believe, further support for this position.

In addition to the various questions about attitudes and voting behavior we have employed so far, respondents in the 1984 survey were asked a number of questions about contacts they had with incumbents and challengers in House races.[15] Recalling our earlier discussion of incumbency and resources, we would expect that most voters were contacted in some way by their House incumbent, but that a large share of the electorate was not contacted by challengers, because many of the challengers lacked the resources to do so. There are as many as 400,000 persons of voting age in each district, and contacting them is an expensive task. The survey data bear out this expectation. Among congressional voters who live in contested districts with incumbents running, 44 percent report some contact with both candidates, but an additional 43 percent remember only contact with the incumbent. Eleven percent of the voters report no contact with either candidate, and fewer than 2 percent report being contacted only by the challenger. These results are also consistent with the earlier survey research studies on name recognition advantages of incumbents that we discussed in Chapter 9.

The next step is to assess whether these patterns of contact have electoral consequences. Table 10-8 presents data on voter support for incumbents controlling for party identification and contacts between voters and congressional candidates. (Because there were so few cases where voters were contacted only by the challenger, this category is excluded.) The results appear to be fairly strong and consistent with our expectations. When voters share partisanship with the incumbent, support rates tend to be very high across all categories, although there is

Table 10-8 Percentage Supporting House Incumbents, 1984, Controlling for Party of Voter and Incumbent and for Contact by Incumbent and Challenger

	Voter Is Contacted by		
Voter Is	*Only the Incumbent (N)*	*Both Candidates (N)*	*Neither Candidate (N)*
Same party as incumbent	96 (105)	91 (78)	83 (23)
Independent	93 (56)	64 (74)	46 (13)
Opposite party	60 (57)	26 (68)	33 (18)

Note: Numbers in parentheses are the totals upon which percentages are based. This question was asked only of respondents in the in-person postelection interview.

some slippage when the incumbent and the challenger both fail to contact the voter. Among independents and voters who identify with the same party as the challenger, however, the variations across categories are substantial. When only the incumbent contacts independent voters, the support level is more than 90 percent. Support for the incumbent falls below two-thirds when both candidates contact the voter, and it splits virtually evenly among the few respondents contacted by neither candidate. Similarly, among voters of the challenger's party, the defection rate is 60 percent when only the incumbent has contacted the voter, but only about one in four when both candidates have contacted the voter. These results seem to provide support for our hypothesis that a significant part of the electoral advantage of House incumbents is due to the inability of challengers to get their message across to voters.

Conclusion

In this chapter we have considered a variety of possible influences on voters' decisions in congressional elections. We found that social forces, with the exception of race, have a modest impact on that choice. Party identification and issues both apparently have an effect, with the former generally stronger than the latter.

Consistent with our discussion in the preceding chapter, incumbency has a major and consistent impact on voters' choices. It solidifies the support of the incumbent's partisans, attracts independents, and leads to defections by members of the opposite party. Incumbent support is linked to positive evaluation of the representative's job by the voters and apparently also to greater contact with voters. The tendency to favor incumbents appears to be of particular benefit to the Democratic party in

House races. Within the context of this incumbency effect, voters' choices also seem to be affected by their evaluations of the job the president is doing and by their vote choice for president.

Notes

1. We will confine our attention in this section to voting for the House because this group of voters is more directly comparable to the presidential electorate. Except for our comparison of whites and blacks, our social comparisons refer to white voters only. We here employ the same definitions for social and demographic categories used in Chapter 5.
2. To simplify the presentation, we have eliminated from consideration votes for minor party candidates in all the tables in this chapter. Furthermore, to ensure that our study of choice is meaningful, in all tables except Table 10-2 we include only voters who lived in districts or states in which both major parties ran candidates.
3. Paul R. Abramson, John H. Aldrich, and David W. Rohde, *Change and Continuity in the 1980 Elections*, rev. ed. (Washington, D.C.: CQ Press, 1983), 215-16.
4. Alan I. Abramowitz, "Choices and Echoes in the 1978 U.S. Senate Elections: A Research Note," *American Journal of Political Science* 25 (February 1981): 112-18; and "National Issues, Strategic Politicians, and Voting Behavior in the 1980 and 1982 Congressional Elections," *American Journal of Political Science* 28 (November 1984): 710-21.
5. Robert S. Erikson and Gerald C. Wright, "Voters, Candidates, and Issues in Congressional Elections," in Lawrence C. Dodd and Bruce I. Oppenheimer, eds., *Congress Reconsidered*, 3d ed. (Washington, D.C.: CQ Press, 1985), 87-108.
6. Albert D. Cover, "One Good Term Deserves Another: The Advantage of Incumbency in Congressional Elections," *American Journal of Political Science* 21 (August 1977): 523-41. Cover includes in his analysis not only strong and weak partisans, but also independents with partisan leanings.
7. The defection rate among Democrats is the percentage who do not vote Democratic. Because the table shows the percentage voting Democratic, the defection rate is 100 percent minus 91 percent or 9 percent.
8. Richard F. Fenno, Jr., "If, as Ralph Nader Says, Congress Is 'the Broken Branch,' How Come We Love Our Congressmen So Much?" in Norman J. Ornstein, ed., *Congress in Change: Evolution and Reform* (New York: Praeger Publishers, 1975), 277-87. This theme is expanded and analyzed in Richard F. Fenno, Jr., *Home Style: House Members in Their Districts* (Boston: Little, Brown & Co., 1978).
9. The 1984 survey shows one notable shift in this regard from previous years. Bearing out the shift in Harris survey data reported in Chapter 9, there has been a significant positive shift in the approval level of the job Congress has

been doing. In the 1980 survey there was only a 41 percent approval level, while in 1984, 60 percent of the respondents approved.

10. Abramson, Aldrich and Rohde, *Change and Continuity in the 1980 Elections*, rev. ed., 220-21.

11. Opinion on this last point is not unanimous, however. See Richard Born, "Reassessing the Decline of Presidential Coattails: U.S. House Elections from 1952-80," *Journal of Politics* 46 (February 1984): 60-79.

12. John A. Ferejohn and Randall L. Calvert, "Presidential Coattails in Historical Perspective," *American Journal of Political Science* 28 (February 1984): 127-46.

13. Randall L. Calvert and John A. Ferejohn, "Coattail Voting in Recent Presidential Elections," *American Political Science Review* 77 (June 1983): 407-19.

14. See Abramson, Aldrich and Rohde, *Change and Continuity in the 1980 Elections*, rev. ed., 222-23, for the corresponding data on 1980.

15. Researchers have argued that the SRC-CPS surveys from 1978 through 1982 have a built-in bias among the respondents in favor of incumbents because the question on congressional voting is preceded by a set of questions about the respondent's perceptions of and contacts with the incumbent, and in many of these questions the incumbent is mentioned by name. See Robert B. Eubank and David John Gow, "The Pro-Incumbent Bias in the 1978 and 1980 National Election Studies," *American Journal of Political Science* 27 (February 1983): 122-39; and David John Gow and Robert B. Eubank, "The Pro-Incumbent Bias in the 1982 National Election Study," *American Journal of Political Science* 28 (February 1984): 224-30. This problem has been alleviated in the 1984 survey because the incumbent-perception and contact questions were asked after the voting behavior questions.

PART IV

The 1984 Elections in Perspective

Chapter 11

The 1984 Elections and the Future of American Politics

The 1984 presidential election assured the continuation of the Reagan administration begun on January 20, 1981. But Ronald Reagan's second term differs fundamentally from his first. Immediately upon reelection, Reagan became constitutionally ineligible to run again because the Twenty-second Amendment states that "No person shall be elected to the office of the President more than twice." Like Dwight D. Eisenhower in 1957 and Richard Nixon in 1973, Reagan began his second term as a "lame duck," a politician who cannot or will not seek reelection. However great a margin of victory a lame-duck president may have attained, members of Congress know that this president will not be leading the party in the next presidential election.

Reagan's lame-duck status may prove a major barrier to future policy changes. This did not dampen his enthusiasm in calling for a "new American Emancipation" to further reduce government involvement in the economy.[1] But a realistic assessment of Reagan's second term suggests that the prospects for continuity are greater than the prospects for change. Thus, an examination of the likely policy consequences of the 1984 elections must begin by assessing the changes wrought by the 1980 elections.

The 1980 elections led to major policy changes. Although Reagan's own margin of victory was smaller than in 1984, the 1980 elections produced a more sweeping Republican victory. The Republicans won 33 seats in the U.S. House of Representatives and 12 seats in the Senate, gaining control of the Senate for the first time since they lost it in the 1954 midterm election. Along with the support of conservative Democrats in the House, Reagan reduced taxes, cut spending on domestic programs, greatly increased defense spending, and reduced federal revenue sharing to the states. Reagan also introduced policy changes through his administrative appointments. His appointees made decisions to reduce government protection of the environment, to promote business interests, and to reduce the government's involvement in the economy. The Department of Justice reversed Democratic policies that promoted "affirmative action" to aid minority groups and even went to court against hiring plans that promoted "reverse discrimination." [2]

Reagan's policy triumphs came mainly within the first year and a half of his administration, and his greatest triumph, approval of the Economic Recovery Act of 1981, came within the first seven months. Congress not only approved large cuts in domestic spending, but also passed a 25 percent cut in federal income taxes and a revised tax formula that benefited wealthy Americans. This change largely implemented the 30 percent cut in taxes Reagan had called for in his 1980 election campaign. In addition, Congress added indexing, a provision that was not part of the original Reagan tax plan. Starting in 1985 the federal income tax schedule would be linked to the Consumer Price Index and automatically adjusted to take inflation into account. Given the relatively low inflation during 1985, the effects of indexing were modest, but indexing removed a source of increased government revenues in times of inflation. If the president and Congress want to increase revenues, they must make an explicit decision to raise taxes.

The logic behind the Economic Recovery Act was that lowering taxes would lead to greater individual productivity, that economic growth would accelerate, and that, as a result, government revenues would increase. Most economists thought it would be impossible for productivity to rise fast enough to compensate for the lower tax rates and higher defense spending. For once, the economists were right. In fiscal year 1980 the federal budget deficit was $59.6 billion, and in 1981 it was $57.9. But in fiscal year 1982, the first year of a Reagan budget, the deficit rose to $110.7 billion, rising to $195.4 billion in 1983, falling in 1984 to $175.3 billion, and rising to $202.8 billion for fiscal year 1985. [3] According to Paul E. Peterson, the real value of the national debt (taking inflation into account) did not increase between 1947 and 1981. Between 1981 and 1985, however, the real value of the national debt increased 54 percent. [4]

Walter F. Mondale tried to make the growing federal deficit the key focus of his presidential campaign. He failed, partly because he was not a credible candidate to raise this issue. But the deficit has become the chief focus of Reagan's second term, and, for the president, both a blessing and a curse. In some respects, a large budget deficit is a long-term asset because it discourages introduction of new social programs. The Democrats proposed no new major spending programs in 1984, proving the extent to which Reagan has shaped the policy agenda. Continuing deficits may force future administrations also to avoid new social programs, even if the Democrats regain the White House in the 1988 presidential election. On the other hand, the deficit makes it more difficult for Reagan to gain acceptance for new policies of his own, such as tax simplification and the Strategic Defense Initiative.

Policy Consequences of the 1984 Elections

The 1984 elections gave voters the opportunity to reject the new direction in American public policy. By reelecting Reagan, they turned down this opportunity. But, as we saw in Chapter 2, Reagan had proposed no new policy directions for a second term, choosing instead to run a "feel good" campaign that emphasized his past accomplishments. Considering Mondale's explicit promise to raise taxes and his own insistence that taxes would be raised only as a last resort, Reagan could claim to have a mandate to avoid new taxes. But because he had avoided spelling out new policies, including specific proposals to reduce the budget deficit, it would be difficult to convince Congress that it should follow new leads.

Reagan's reelection has policy consequences because of the office's great administrative powers. Through his appointments Reagan can continue policies that favor business and reduce government involvement in the economy. The Department of Justice, under Attorney General Edwin Meese, can be expected to follow a pro-business course and to pursue social goals supported by conservatives. If Reagan has the opportunity to make several Supreme Court appointments, he may affect the course of U.S. policy for decades to come. His influence will be greatest if he has the chance to replace liberal justices such as Thurgood Marshall, who was 76 when Reagan's second term began, or William J. Brennan, Jr., who was 78, or Harry A. Blackmun, who was 76 and who sometimes votes with the liberals.[5] By the fall of 1985, Reagan had already appointed more than 200 district and appeals court judges, and it seemed likely that by the end of a second term Reagan may have named half of the nation's federal judges.[6] His reelection may have important foreign policy consequences because he is likely to continue to favor U.S. involvement in Central America, to be wary of arms control agreements, and to resist pressures to impose restrictions on foreign trade.

Reagan began his second term with a budget proposal in February 1985 calling for major new cuts in domestic spending and further increases in defense spending, and in May he advanced proposals for major changes in the tax code to provide for "tax simplification." Reagan's proposed budget was essentially "dead on arrival" when it reached the Congress, and the House and Senate developed their own budget proposals. The compromise budget resolution passed by Congress on August 1, 1985, largely ignored Reagan's budget. The congressional budget resolution limited increases in defense spending to the rate of inflation, providing a far smaller increase than Reagan had requested. Most of the specific domestic spending cuts proposed by Reagan were viewed as politically unrealistic when they were made. The congressional budget resolution called for relatively small cuts in federal benefits.

Not only did Congress reject most of Reagan's budget recommendations, but in the course of the budget process the president severely strained relations with the Republican leadership in the Senate. By the time the congressional budget resolution had passed, most congressional leaders were convinced that Reagan had abandoned any serious attempt to reduce the deficit. Even with the proposed budget compromise, the projected deficit for the 1986 fiscal year would be $172 billion. And although the budget plan called for a deficit reduced to $113 billion by fiscal year 1988, many believed that this estimate was based upon unrealistically optimistic projections about the economy.

In a more direct attempt to produce a balanced budget, Republican senators Phil Gramm of Texas and Warren B. Rudman of New Hampshire and Democratic senator Ernest F. Hollings of South Carolina proposed a new plan. By December 1985 Gramm-Rudman-Hollings, with some modifications, was enacted into law. According to the law, the budget would be automatically balanced in stages, with the deficit being cut to zero by 1991. If Congress and the president could not agree on spending cuts or if they could not agree to raise taxes, automatic across-the-board spending cuts were to be implemented. Because about 70 percent of the total budget, including Social Security, some poverty programs, and interest on the national debt, are exempt from these cuts, reductions must be made from the remaining 30 percent of the budget and divided about equally between military and domestic programs.

If Gramm-Rudman-Hollings remains in force through 1990, it will have major policy consequences, leading to the elimination of many domestic programs and to a dramatic change in the current budgetary process. But there are several reasons why the law is unlikely to have such far-reaching effects. First, the constitutionality of the reform has been challenged, with opponents arguing that it transfers spending powers to bureaucratic agencies. Second, even if Gramm-Rudman-Hollings survives such challenges, Congress can suspend the budget balancing process if it concludes that an economic or foreign policy emergency exists. Third, the cuts necessitated by the plan may be so objectionable that Congress will vote to raise taxes. Indeed, some Democrats supported Gramm-Rudman-Hollings because they believed that Reagan would ultimately agree to raise taxes before allowing major cuts in military spending. Last, Congress may find so many problems with Gramm-Rudman-Hollings that the plan itself may be scrapped.

Passage of Gramm-Rudman-Hollings may ultimately complicate the major policy initiative of Reagan's second term—his proposal for tax reform. Indeed, as 1985 ended, Reagan's proposals for tax simplification also appeared to be in serious trouble. While tax simplification is an idea hailed by Democrats and Republicans alike, there were many objections to Reagan's specific proposals. By repealing deductions on state and local taxes, his plan would be costly to residents of states with high taxes. Proposals to reduce capital gains taxes had greater appeal in states with growing service industries, but proposals to reduce investment tax credits or curtail accelerated depreciation write-offs would harm states with large capital intensive manufacturing plants.[7] In addition, there were many proposals that faced strong opposition from specific interest groups. For example, the real estate lobby objected to the proposal to disallow interest deductions on second homes.

Despite the appeal of tax simplification, many members of Congress were willing to consider a tax overhaul only as a means to raise revenues and to reduce the deficit. The president had insisted that any tax reform must be "revenue neutral." When Congress adjourned in December 1985, tax reform was still alive, but the House had passed a tax bill that was shaped largely by the House Ways and Means Committee, chaired by Democrat Dan Rostenkowski of Illinois. Reagan had won a last-minute reprieve for tax reform by persuading some House Republicans to support the Democratic reform package. The Republican-controlled Senate may find it difficult to agree to tax reform that is acceptable to the House, and Reagan had promised to veto any bill that he found unacceptable. Thus, as 1986 began, the outlook for tax reform was questionable, and the prospect for a plan similar to Reagan's original reform package seemed bleak.

Nor did the chances seem bright for Reagan's one new defense proposal, the Strategic Defense Initiative, popularly called "Star Wars." The technology necessary to destroy incoming enemy missiles is complex, untested, and staggeringly expensive. Many believe that actually deploying such a technology, which is not even contemplated during Reagan's second term, would destabilize the present arms race. One way to overcome an anti-missile system is to launch a very large number of missiles, to overload that system, and to assure that enough missiles penetrated the defense to devastate the enemy. One logical Soviet response to SDI would be to build a very large number of missiles. In any event, given Congress's unwillingness to go along with major increases in defense spending, the best Reagan can hope for is modest funding for research into anti-missile technologies.

In short, Reagan's second term seems unlikely to yield any important new policy initiatives. The more likely result is a stalemate between the president and Congress, along with continued battles over the budget. If the Democrats make substantial gains in the House of Representatives in the 1986 midterm election, the chances for stalemate will grow, even if the Republicans retain control of the Senate. Major policy changes would then wait until 1989 when a newly elected president takes office.

Toward Realignment?

Even if the policy outcomes of the 1984 election prove to be limited, the election does have implications for the future of American party politics. The Republicans are now the dominant party in controlling the presidency, but that dominance is part of an overall pattern of electoral volatility. Will this pattern continue, or will the Republicans extend their dominance to the end of this century? Can a Republican presidential majority be translated into a Republican majority at other levels of government? In particular, is the GOP likely to gain control of Congress? The Democrats are no longer the majority party, but can they at least become more competitive at the presidential level? Can they once again become the majority party? Will partisan conflict continue to be confined to the Republican and Democratic parties?

These questions raise the issue of partisan realignment. Has there been a realignment, and, if not, is a realignment imminent? The answer to both questions is yes, no, or maybe—depending upon the definition of realignment one chooses. Debates about definitions are usually uninformative. If one relies upon traditional definitions of partisan realignment and expects a single party to dominate across all branches of government and at both the federal and state level, clearly there has been no realignment. Nor is there likely to be one. Past realignments probably were based upon electorates with strong partisan attachments. Most voters could be expected to vote a straight party ticket and seldom waver in their party commitments. But an electorate of loyal partisans no longer exists. Considering the relatively highly educated population, the inexpensive nonpartisan information available through the mass media, and new technologies of campaigning, it seems unlikely that there will ever be such an electorate again.

We saw in Chapter 9 that, despite a presidential landslide of historic proportions, the Republicans gained only 14 seats in the House and lost 2 seats in the Senate. This is almost identical to the 1972 result, when Nixon won 49 of 50 states. The Republicans won only 12 seats in the House and lost 2 seats in the Senate. But there are two major differences between these elections. In 1984 Reagan tried to help Republican congressional candidates, but Nixon bypassed the Republican National Committee and virtually ignored other Republican candidates. Moreover, the 1984 election was *preceded* by a marked shift in party loyalties to the Republicans, whereas no such shift took place 12 years earlier. That the

Republicans gained so little despite Reagan's efforts on their behalf and despite the pro-Republican shift in partisan loyalties suggests that they may face formidable obstacles in winning control of the House. It seems highly unlikely that the Republicans will have a majority in the House by 1990. They may be aided somewhat by the reapportionment that will take place before the 1992 elections, but, unless they make substantial gains in the number of states in which they control the governorship and both houses of the state legislature, they are unlikely to benefit greatly from the reapportionment and redistricting that will follow the 1990 census.

The Republican domination of the presidency and the Democratic control of the House for the past 30 years have led Kevin Phillips to call the present configuration of political forces a "split-level" realignment.[8] If this description is accurate, the present differs markedly from the past, for past realignments were characterized by single party control of both houses of Congress as well as the presidency.

Our remaining analysis will focus on the future prospects for the presidency. Here we see four possibilities. First, the Republicans may continue to dominate in presidential elections, clearly ending the pattern of postwar volatility. Second, despite their present doldrums, the Democrats could reemerge as a majority party. Third, a new political party could be successful, especially if the Democrats move to the center of the American political spectrum. Last, there is the possibility of continued electoral volatility.

Continued Republican Dominance

The Republicans now have won four of the last five presidential elections. But what of the future? Can they continue their dominance for the remaining three elections of this century and into the year 2000? Perhaps not, but who can blame Republican leaders for optimism? "We are on the threshold of a golden era in Republican politics," Republican senator Paul Laxalt of Nevada asserted in early 1985. "We've got Ronald Reagan and the economy, plus a solid Sun Belt base while the traditional coalitions in the Northeast are crumbling."[9] According to Frank Fahrenkopf, chairman of the Republican party, "The prospects and outlook are perhaps the best we've had in 50 years."[10] Reagan has made even stronger claims; according to him, "Realignment is real."[11]

There are reasons for Republican optimism. At the presidential level they are the dominant party. Although they have not won three elections in a row—a clear sign of electoral dominance—they came close to doing so. Even after the Watergate scandal, Gerald R. Ford, the unelected Republican incumbent who had pardoned Nixon, came close to holding the White House.[12] But even with a four-year Democratic presidency, by

January 20, 1989, when Reagan's second term ends, the GOP will have held the presidency for 16 of the last 20 years. As we saw in Chapter 3, there are many states, especially in the West, that the Republicans consistently win, giving them a substantial electoral vote "base." There is not a single large state that the Democrats have won in even four of the last six elections, and, as 1984 demonstrates, they have a solid electoral vote base of only three votes. And, as we saw in Chapter 5, the New Deal coalition appears to be crumbling, with a major component, southern whites, voting solidly Republican.

Many political scientists think that the most positive development for future Republican prospects is the shift in party identification toward the Republicans. Indeed, some believe that this shift, if it persists, could extend the party's dominance beyond the White House. As we saw in Chapter 8, the Republicans have pulled nearly even with the Democrats in party identification, a shift that occurred before the 1984 election and which was registered in the Michigan Survey Research Center-Center for Political Studies preelection survey. The Michigan party identification scale is highly regarded because it is specifically designed to measure long-term commitment to a political party.[13] In 1980 the Michigan surveys found no evidence of a shift in party loyalties to the GOP, even in the survey conducted shortly after the election. In 1984 these surveys registered a sizable pro-Republican shift. Admittedly, the Democrats still held a slight edge in party identification. But because Republicans are consistently more likely to vote than Democrats, Republican parity in party loyalties might be enough to make the GOP the majority party.

The shift toward Republican party loyalties appears to be greatest among the young and first-time voters. The evidence here is not very firm, for the number of young people sampled in most surveys is usually small, and samples of people below the age of 25 may be somewhat unrepresentative. Still, as Thomas E. Cavanagh and James L. Sundquist stated, "[T]he data show exactly the pattern that would appear if a substantial partisan realignment were in progress."[14] Of course, the durability of this shift has not been established. But, Cavanagh and Sundquist concluded, "If the current trends persist into 1988, one would probably be justified in declaring that a realignment—not one as decisive as that of the 1930s but one of a second order of magnitude—had occurred."[15]

Seeking to extend these gains, the Republicans have been waging a concerted effort to persuade prominent Democrats to switch to the Republican party. The best-known convert is Jeane J. Kirkpatrick, the former U.N. ambassador, who had maintained her nominal Democratic affiliation through Reagan's first term. Another notable convert is Gramm, who was a leading Democratic conservative and a supporter of Reagan's policies in the 97th Congress. Gramm was stripped of his seniority by the Democratic House Caucus after he was reelected in 1982. He not only changed parties, but also resigned from the House— something he had no obligation to do. He then ran as a Republican in a special election for the seat he had resigned and was elected again. In 1984 he won the Senate seat being vacated by retiring Republican John Tower. Other new Republicans are not as well known, but the conversion of William Lucas, the county executive of Wayne County, Mich., which includes Detroit, attracted considerable attention for one simple reason: Lucas is black. Moreover, Lucas was considered likely to run for governor in 1986, and many Republican leaders were expected to support him.

Republicans are also attempting to get rank-and-file Democrats to switch their party registration. Special efforts are being made to recruit the young. Teen Age Republicans, an organization for 13- to 19-year-olds, claims 100,000 members, many of whom move on to become College Republicans and Young Republicans.[16] According to William Belk, president of the Young Democrats, "The Republican Party is reeling them in like fish. . . . The Democrats have sat back and let them do it." [17]

But while the Republicans may well remain dominant, their future is by no means assured. George Orwell pointed out that it is an intellectual weakness to believe that the future will merely be "a continuation of the thing that is happening." [18] Still, Orwell warned, for some, "Whoever is winning at the moment will always seem to be invincible." [19] But the Republicans are not invincible, even at the presidential level.

It is true that the Republicans appear to have a substantial electoral vote base. But that base is not so impressive if one considers California a potentially competitive state. It is true that the Republicans have won two elections of the last five by massive landslides, carrying 49 of 50 states in both 1972 and 1984. But this, too, is somewhat deceptive. Because of the decline in regional differences in voting since World War II, electoral vote landslides are easier to attain. Before the war, a Republican landslide of these proportions was impossible because the Democrats could count on the "Solid South." In 1920, for example, Warren G. Harding, the Republican winner, gained 60.3 percent of the popular vote, while his Democratic opponent, James M. Cox, received only 34.2 percent. But Cox still carried every former Confederate state except Tennessee, as well as Kentucky, winning nearly a fourth of the electoral votes. Today, either party is probably capable of a near sweep. The West, for example, is considered "Reagan country." But in 1964, Lyndon B. Johnson carried every western state except Arizona, Barry M. Goldwater's home state.

The shift toward the Republicans in party identification is important and probably contributed to Reagan's margin of victory, as we saw in Chapter 8. But this shift has not made the Republicans a majority party; it has only pulled them close to even with the Democrats. Moreover, it remains to be seen whether this shift is durable. Gallup polls through the first three months of 1985 showed that 37 percent of the electorate call themselves Democrats, 35 percent Republicans, and 28 percent independents, sustaining, but not extending, the Republican gains registered in late 1984. After that, the Republicans suffered a slight slippage. During the third quarter of 1985 (July through September), support for the Democrats remained at 37 percent, but the Republicans fell to 32 percent, and the percentage calling themselves independents rose to 31.[20] A *New York Times*/CBS News poll conducted in September 1985 found that 34 percent were Democrats, 31 percent Republicans, and 36 percent independents.[21] A *Washington Post*/ABC News poll conducted in October 1985 found that 34 percent were Democrats, 31 percent Republicans, and 35 percent were independents.[22]

Not all the polls show the Republicans to be this strong, however. Louis Harris reports that his polls suggest that the case for realignment has been overstated. Harris, like Gallup, found a substantial erosion of Democratic loyalties in late 1984. A 24-point Democratic advantage in Democratic identification in 1976 had been cut to a 7-point advantage by late 1984. But Harris found a Democratic rebound after the 1984 election. Based upon polls through the first eight months of 1985, Harris reported that 39 percent of the adult population claimed to be Democratic, 29 percent identified as Republican, 26 percent were independent, and the remaining 6 percent were classified as "other" or "not sure." [23] And the General Social Survey conducted by the National Opinion Research Center in early 1985 found a Democratic lead very close to that reported by Harris: 39 percent of the sample identified as Democrats, 30 percent as Republicans, and 31 percent were independents—a 9-point Democratic margin. If independent leaners were classified as partisans, the Democratic lead was 50 percent to 40 percent—rounding to a 9-point Democratic margin.[24] Admittedly, this is a slight gain for the Republicans over their standing in the 1984 General Social Survey.[25] Among all identifiers, 43 percent were Republicans; if independent leaners were classified as partisans, 45 percent were. But the Democrats still enjoyed a clear lead in this highly regarded academic survey.

Just as we must await further evidence on party identification, we must also wait to see whether the shift of prominent Democrats to the Republicans continues and whether Republican support among the young is just a sign of trendy behavior by an age group susceptible to fads. Moreover, the Republicans have suffered setbacks as well as successes. A registration drive that targeted Florida, Louisiana, North Carolina, and Pennsylvania in the summer of 1985 fell short of its goal of persuading 100,000 Democrats to switch to the Republican party.[26] And in a special election in August 1985, the Republicans spent more than $1 million, but failed to win a seat in the Texas First Congressional District, a traditionally Democratic district in eastern Texas that Reagan had won with 61 percent of the vote the previous November.[27]

Despite their strengths, the Republicans have liabilities as well. We see three potential sources of weakness. First, the Republicans have moved so far to the right that they are far more conservative than the electorate. To many Republicans, Reagan is too moderate. At the Republican nominating convention in Dallas, conservatives drafted a party platform that was not in line with Reagan's publicly stated positions. For example, Reagan was willing to consider a tax increase as a "last resort," but the platform promised, "We will continue our efforts to further reduce tax rates and now foresee no economic circumstances which would call for increased taxation." [28] On abortion, a key social issue, the platform not only called for a constitutional amendment extending Fourteenth Amendment protections to the unborn, but also for "the appointment of judges at all levels of the judiciary who respect traditional family values and the sanctity of innocent human life." [29]

As we observed in Chapter 6, Reagan is seen by the electorate as more conservative than the average voter views himself or herself. On balance, however, neither Reagan nor Mondale benefited very much from the issues because Mondale was seen as more liberal than the average voter. However, if the Republicans nominate a hard-line conservative in 1988 and if the Democrats move to the political center, the Democrats could easily field a candidate who would be closer to the average policy preferences of the electorate.

Second, the Republicans may not be as united as the 1984 contest made them appear. Although most Republican leaders are economically conservative, they are divided about the importance of and the solution to the budget deficits. Some, like Senate majority leader Robert Dole of Kansas, believe that tax increases are necessary to reduce the deficit, while others, like New York representative Jack F. Kemp, claim that economic growth will solve the problem. Some Republicans also question Reagan's commitment to free trade, arguing that U.S. trade deficits result largely from unfair practices by America's trading partners. Moreover, not all Republicans are concerned about the controversial social issues.

Reagan has been an extremely skilled politician, paying lip service to the demands of social conservatives, such as fundamentalist Protestants and "right-to-life" Catholics, while expending his actual political energies for his economic policies. For most voters economic issues are clearly more important. Many young voters may see the Republicans as the party of economic opportunity, and future Republican success may depend on holding their loyalties. But many young voters have fairly liberal social views. If Republican leaders begin to push seriously for social legislation, they would jeopardize their support among the young and the upper-middle-class voters who have benefited from Reagan's economic policies. But the Republicans also rely on southern support, and their support in the South depends partly upon the votes of fundamentalist Protestants. Few politicians would have Reagan's ability to reconcile these potentially conflicting forces in the Republican elector- ate. Of course, coalitions made up of potentially antagonistic groups can endure for a long time. The New Deal coalition brought together southern whites, northern blacks, farmers, and trade unionists. Skilled leaders often can hold conflicting interests together, but it remains to be seen whether future Republican leaders can.

Last, we find it difficult to designate any party as a clear majority party when only 55 percent of the potential electorate votes. For the Republicans the large body of nonvoters poses a potential danger because nonvoters are found disproportionately among those social groups that might be expected to vote Democratic. But the 1984 election demon- strated that these nonvoters may be very difficult to mobilize. Moreover, there is no reasonable scenario in which increased turnout by the disadvantaged would have altered the presidential election result. Even in 1980, when Reagan won by a smaller margin, increased turnout by pro- Democratic groups would probably have had little effect on the out- come.[30] But in a closer contest the Democrats might benefit from increased turnout by blacks, Hispanics, and poor whites. The Democrats, however, might face a problem getting these groups to the polls without losing support among working-class and middle-class whites. While it is unrealistic for the Democrats to pin their hopes upon higher turnout, the potential for increased participation among disadvantaged Americans still poses a danger for the Republicans.

A Resurgent Democratic Party

The Democratic party has survived since 1828 when Andrew Jackson defeated the incumbent president, National Republican John Quincy Adams, and it would be foolish to ignore its chances to return to dominance. Admittedly, those chances currently look poor. The Demo- crats lack a regional base to regain the presidency and would need to rely upon an across-the-board win that would somehow earn them 270 electoral votes. The New Deal coalition that provided electoral domi- nance from the 1930s through 1964 seems defunct, with one of its major components, southern whites, voting heavily Republican for president. One of the major Democratic assets, a solid lead in party identification, appears to have substantially narrowed. Moreover, the party is currently leaderless. Competing leaders recognize the need to change the Demo- cratic party's appeals, but cannot agree on an appropriate strategy.

Indeed, no clear strategy is available, and, even if it were, there would be no easy way to implement it. The basic problem is that the

Democratic party is internally divided. These divisions were illustrated by the 1984 Democratic nomination struggle. The three final candidates symbolized the competing forces within the party. Mondale represented the traditional wing of the party, drawing major support from organized labor and support from the white working class. Gary Hart represented the younger, more affluent Democrats who reject traditional Democratic leadership, especially the influence of organized labor. And Jesse Jackson represented an increasingly active black constituency, which made up about one voter out of five in the Democratic primaries and about one Democratic party identifier out of five. These groups have different policy goals, with many union leaders demanding protectionism in the form of import quotas or domestic content legislation and with upper-middle-class Democrats stressing support for technological innovation to assure economic growth. Jackson stood far to the left of Hart and Mondale, demanding increased federal spending to benefit disadvantaged Americans, cuts in defense spending, and major changes in U.S. foreign policy, including a less pro-Israel Middle East policy. Three moderate Democrats who sought the Democratic nomination, John Glenn, Ernest F. Hollings, and Reubin Askew, all had been winnowed out of the delegate selection process very early, and moderate and conservative Democrats played virtually no visible role at the Democratic convention in San Francisco, except for a brief appearance by Jimmy Carter. And yet most Democratic leaders now believe that the party needs to become more moderate and to shed its image as a mere representative of competing interest group claims.

Even the widely recognized liberal, Edward M. Kennedy, has advanced a plea for moderation. In a speech delivered five months after the Reagan landslide, he said, "As Democrats, we must understand that there is a difference between being a party that cares about labor and being a labor party. . . . There is a difference between being a party that cares about women and being the women's party. And we can and we must be a party that cares about minorities, without becoming a minority party. We are citizens first and constituencies second." [31]

Some symbolic steps have been taken to begin the transformation of the party's image. For example, the new Democratic National Committee chairman, Paul G. Kirk, Jr., abolished some of the official caucuses within the party. In addition, Kirk allowed a black who was not officially endorsed by the DNC black caucus to run for a leadership position within the committee. This led to the defeat for a DNC post of Mayor Richard G. Hatcher of Gary, Indiana, a Jackson supporter. But these steps are not very important. What is important is finding a presidential candidate who can unite the competing factions within the party. And if that leader tries to move the party to the center, it may be difficult to hold the support of black Democrats, who have the option of abstaining, if they also find the Republican party unacceptable.

The Democratic problems seem so fundamental that it is difficult to imagine what a newly dominant Democratic party would look like. Of course, the Democrats could be aided by adverse economic conditions, as in the 1982 midterm elections. Indeed, as of late 1982, with the nation in its worst postwar recession, Democratic prospects for 1984 appeared to improve.[32] And truly disastrous developments could once again transform the Democrats into the majority party. Nor are such disasters difficult to envision. The most serious potential problems are found in the current pattern of international debt, with several Third World countries, most notably Argentina, Brazil, and Mexico, heavily in debt to major international banks based in New York. It is widely recognized that these countries may never be able to repay the principal. The interest rate on these international loans fluctuates, with rates tied to the prime interest rate in the United States. If interest rates rise, these countries could not afford to repay the interest on that principal without new loans that also have very little prospect of being repaid. Despite Reagan's denial of any linkage, high government deficits do put upward pressure on U.S. interest rates, because a growing share of the gross national product is needed just to pay the interest on the national debt.

No one knows the potential impact of a major international default or the effects of a major debtor nation simply repudiating its debt. But it is obvious that the U.S. banking system is potentially unstable. Even without such a default, the nation's eighth largest holding bank, the Continental Bank of Illinois, was forced to restructure in 1984. The U.S. Federal Deposit Insurance Corporation was able to rescue the bank, at the price of taking over 80 percent of its assets, but the FDIC does not have the resources to cope with a nationwide banking collapse.

If major economic problems emerge, it would be difficult for the Republicans to blame them on Democratic policies. It would be hard to persuade voters that these problems did not result largely from Reagan's economic policies and the unprecedented budget deficits they produced. While budget deficits and the national debt may be only vague abstractions to most voters in times of economic prosperity, the electorate might well blame the Republicans if the deficit and the national debt led to higher inflation, unemployment, or both.

Barring major economic difficulties, the Democrats' best hope is for a protracted and divisive nomination struggle within the Republican party, a sharp move to the right by the GOP, and a weak candidate becoming the Republican standard-bearer. Republican weaknesses might not make the Democrats the majority party, but they could greatly increase the Democratic prospects for recapturing the presidency. Even as of early 1985, just half a year after Reagan's landslide, those prospects did not look particularly bleak. In April 1985 a Harris poll showed both Hart and Kennedy running even in a potential presidential race with Republican front-runner George Bush.[33] Kennedy actually led Bush 50 percent to 48 percent. And a Gallup poll conducted in July 1985 showed Kennedy and Bush running even, with each receiving 46 percent of the vote, although Gallup showed Bush leading Hart 50 percent to 39 percent.[34] Of course, this does not mean that Kennedy would actually run a close race against Bush. Indeed, Kennedy's decision not to run for president, announced in December 1985, was probably based partly on his assessment that he would not win the 1988 general election. But if there has been or is-about to be a clearly pro-Republican realignment, it seems difficult to account for the relative strength in the polls of a well-known liberal Democrat against the current Republican front-runner.

A New Political Party

The political struggle need not be confined to the Republican and Democratic parties. Admittedly, no new political party has emerged to capture the presidency since the Republicans replaced the Whigs in the 1850s. But third parties have three sources of hope. First, approximately one-third of all Americans of voting age claim to have no party ties. Second, and perhaps more important, only 3 adults in 10 claim to be strongly committed to either of the two major parties. Third, there are about 80 million nonvoters who, if brought to the polls, could transform any political movement into a majority party. In principle, then, a massive number of Americans are available to support a third party candidate. Even though all minor party candidates together won only 620,000 votes in 1984 (roughly .7 percent of the votes cast), four years earlier John B. Anderson, an independent candidate, won 5,700,000 votes or 6.6 percent of the total. Clearly a new political party could emerge, but how likely is such a development, and what would such a party's ideological stripe be?

The only third parties since World War II that have gained a single electoral vote have been parties of the political right—the States' Rights Democrats in 1948 and the American Independent party in 1968—with all these votes coming from states of the old Confederacy. But it is hard to see how a conservative political party can compete with the Republicans. Admittedly, some Americans believe that even the Republicans favor too much government involvement. The Libertarian party represents such a position and favors very little government interference in either the economy or in the lives of individuals. In 1980 Ed Clark, the Libertarian presidential candidate, was on the ballot in all 50 states and gained 920,000 votes—only 1 percent of the votes cast. He finished behind Reagan, Carter, and Anderson in every state but Alaska, where he finished third behind Reagan and Carter. Even in Alaska, he gained only 12 percent of the vote. In 1984 the Libertarians won only 230,000 votes *(Table 3-1)*. Once again, they fared best in Alaska, but won only 3 percent of the vote. As we saw in Chapter 6, Reagan is viewed as far more conservative than the average voter views himself or herself. A party that favors even less government involvement in the economy and even less support for social programs is unlikely to have a large potential pool of supporters.

There is probably a far greater number of social conservatives who are dissatisfied with the failure of Reagan and other Republican leaders to push for constitutional amendments banning abortion and legalizing school prayer. Reagan has espoused these goals, but he has expended little political capital to achieve them. In principle, a third party could emphasize these social issues. But because most voters are concerned with economic issues, parties that push for social or moral issues are probably doomed to failure.[35] Most social conservatives are likely to continue supporting the Republicans, although they could become disaffected if the Republicans choose a candidate who does not show adequate concern for their cause. But there seems to be little basis for a successful political party based on social issues.

Anderson's candidacy of 1980 illustrates the problems facing a third party of the center. According to Anthony Downs, the center is the logical place for each party to strive, yet one of the two major parties is likely to hold that space already.[36] A third party of the center finds it difficult to present a distinctive policy agenda. On most issues a majority of the electorate did not know where Anderson stood, despite his attempts to articulate clear policy positions.[37] A centrist party has a chance only if the two major parties veer too far to the right and left simultaneously or if both major parties nominate unpopular candidates. Moreover, even when the major parties have moved to the right or left, it is usually easy for at least one of them to recapture some of the center ground.

A left-wing party has plenty of room on the American political landscape and would find even more space if the Democrats move toward the center, which is likely. A leftist party could draw support from disadvantaged social groups that have had very low turnout in recent elections. However, a party of the left faces severe organizational difficulties. To be successful it must extend its reach beyond the upper-middle-class liberals who may have supported a candidate like Eugene McCarthy (independent) in 1976 or Barry Commoner (Citizens party) in 1980. Rather, it must win support from blacks, the poor, and from working-class whites.

Where could the organizational impetus for such a party come from? In his bid for the Democratic presidential nomination, Jackson relied heavily upon black churches. But even though about one-fifth of all the

Democratic party identifiers are black, Jackson had no chance of winning the Democratic presidential nomination. Jackson could have hoped to win enough delegates to influence the Democratic platform and, under ideal conditions for his cause, could have held the balance of votes between Mondale and Hart. But there is no logical basis for a black third party presidential candidacy. Blacks make up only 11 percent of the electorate, and, even in the most heavily black state, Mississippi, they make up only 31 percent. A black political party running a national campaign would probably win only the three electoral votes of the District of Columbia. Even if the Democrats stop supporting policies favored by blacks, this segment of the electorate may have no attractive alternatives. Of course, blacks could vote Republican, but this is unlikely, at least in 1988. Blacks could support a black third party candidate, but, except for the message this might convey, such a vote would have the same effect as abstaining.

For a party of the left to succeed it would have to be a multiracial coalition. Ira Katznelson reminded us in an essay written shortly after the 1980 election, "Over three decades ago C. Wright Mills observed that the only mass, multiracial, progressive organizations in the United States were trade unions; and the future of social policy depended heavily on the zeal of their members and the choices of their leaders." [38] Mills was pessimistic about the prospects for unions taking a lead in social reforms, and, according to Katznelson, there was less reason for optimism in the early 1980s than there was in the 1950s. As Katznelson concludes, "[O]rganized labor has become increasingly disinclined to engage in larger political battles." [39]

In fact, organized labor did become more politically involved after 1980, but only as a traditional force within the Democratic party. In October 1983 the AFL-CIO formally endorsed Mondale, and labor unions provided major organizational and financial support that helped him win the nomination. A majority of union members voted for Mondale in the general election, but approximately two union members out of five voted against him *(Table 5-1 and Figure 5-3)*. Many politicians view organized labor as discredited; it pushed strongly for a losing candidate and then did not deliver a solid union vote. But labor remains a strong force within the Democratic party. To many union leaders, controlling the nomination process may seem more important than winning the general election. Organized labor may have no clear choice in 1988—indeed, Paul Kirk has asked the AFL-CIO not to endorse a Democratic presidential candidate before the nominating convention.[40] But even if labor leaders are disappointed with the 1988 Democratic nominee, it seems unlikely that they would support a left-of-center movement. In many respects unions and blacks have differing interests. Union leaders are often interested in protecting the privileges of their members, and black leaders are more likely to make broader claims for the redistribution of resources. This is seen most concretely in the insistence of union leaders that seniority be the major criterion for job security, while black leaders often demand preferential treatment for minority group members to compensate for past injustices.

The absence of any social structure that could provide the organizational basis for a third party of the left greatly reduces the chance that there will be a successful third party movement—even if the Democrats become more moderate in 1988. But there are also structural features to the American electoral system that tend to protect the Republican and Democratic parties from new political parties.

Most obviously, there is the electoral college system that requires a party to receive a plurality of the vote within a state or D.C. to attain any electoral votes. This rule places any new party at a great disadvantage unless it has a regional base. But there are other features as well. Third parties have difficulty getting on the ballot, despite court decisions that have made it somewhat easier.[41] In 1984 the Libertarians, the most successful third party, were on the ballot in only 38 states and D.C. Even more difficult is raising money, and here the federal election laws place an additional burden on third party candidates. Democratic and Republican nominees are guaranteed full federal funding merely by gaining their party's nomination, but third party candidates can receive funding only if they attain 5 percent of the total vote in the November election. Thus, in 1980 Anderson was forced to ask supporters to lend him money with no guarantee that it would be repaid.[42] Given the importance of money for polling, travel, media, and organizational expenses, the built-in federal funding for major party nominees provides a tremendous advantage.

Even more important, nomination by a major political party provides a huge bonus of votes because, at the very least, a major party nominee can count on the votes of strong party identifiers. This bonus, already large in 1980, has grown substantially for the Republicans because of the increasing percentage of strong Republican identifiers. How many votes can a major party nominee count on? Assuming there are 167.7 million citizens of voting age,[43] there are about 28 million strong Democratic identifiers. If we assume that three-fifths of these Democrats actually vote and that 7 out of 10 vote Democratic (a smaller percentage than has ever supported a Democratic presidential candidate in any Michigan SRC survey), these voters would provide the Democratic candidate with nearly 12 million votes. There are fewer strong Republican identifiers, but they are more likely to vote and are more consistently loyal to their party. Assuming that two-thirds of these Republicans vote and that about 9 out of 10 vote Republican (the SRC surveys have always registered at least 90 percent support), these Republicans would provide their nominee with 13 million votes.[44] Of course, neither the Democratic nor Republican candidate can win the presidency with only 12 or 13 million votes—but this is a substantial base with which to start.

A third party candidate has no base of support. Even Americans who call themselves independents felt no loyalty to third party candidates, such as George C. Wallace in 1968 or Anderson in 1980, who use the label of "independent." Although such candidates do fare better among independents than among partisan identifiers, Wallace received only a fifth of the vote among independents with no partisan leanings (his best category), and Anderson received just over a fifth of the vote among independents who leaned Democratic (the category in which he fared best).[45]

Last, the very weakness of the current party system dictates that most candidates who wish to become president will seek their goal by first earning the Democratic or Republican party nomination. The party reforms introduced by the Democrats between 1968 and 1972 made it far more difficult for elected political leaders to influence the choice of nominee. Perhaps this is why Wallace, who earned nearly 10 million votes as the American Independent party candidate in 1968, decided four years later to seek the Democratic party nomination. The nomination of George S. McGovern in 1972 and of Carter in 1976 attest to the openness of the system. The creation of "superdelegates" in 1984 slightly increased the influence of elected officials, and, even though this reform was relatively minor, it may have provided Mondale's margin of victory. Even so, Hart's strong showing demonstrates that the system is still relatively open. Although the Republican party did not engage in a similar series of reforms, it was affected by many of the changes wrought by the Democrats, and in 1984 three Republican delegates out of five were chosen by primaries.

Wresting a party's nomination away from an incumbent president is still a formidable task. Even an unelected president, Ford, was able to hold off Reagan in 1976, and four years later Carter was able to outrun Kennedy. But at least one party's nomination is always open, and sometimes both will be. The relatively weak structure of the two major parties makes aiming at a major party nomination the most reasonable strategy for any presidential candidate and contributes to the absence of attractive candidates to lead third party movements.[46]

Future Electoral Volatility

As we have seen, Reagan's reelection may lead to a pro-Republican realignment, although perhaps not to a classic realignment in which a single party dominates all elected branches of government. A less likely possibility is a resurgent Democratic party that regains majority party status. The least likely is the emergence of a new political party as a major political force. But even though the Democrats may not regain their majority party status, they can win presidential elections under circumstances that favor their cause. If the Democrats win in 1988, a clear pattern of electoral volatility would be reestablished.

From 1952 through 1984 neither party has been able to win more than two elections in a row. The greatest volatility occurred in 1976 and 1980 when the party controlling the White House lost two elections in a row—the only two successive losses for the incumbent party in this century *(Table 3-2)*. Moreover, there have been wide swings in the presidential vote from election to election, the most dramatic being the 24 percentage point drop in the Democratic vote between 1964 and 1972.

Despite the Reagan landslide of 1984 there are several factors that suggest the electorate may continue to be volatile. First, even though party loyalties became somewhat stronger between 1980 and 1984, they are considerably weaker than they were between 1952 and 1964—the years Philip E. Converse labeled the "steady-state" period in American party loyalties.[47] During that period, 22 percent of the electorate was classified as independent; in the 1984 SRC-CPS preelection survey, 34 percent were.[48] While being an independent does not necessarily signify commitment to "independence" as a principle, it does reveal a lack of commitment to a party.[49] Moreover, even though the percentage of strong partisans grew between 1980 and 1984 (due to an increase in strong Republicans), the percentage of strong partisans was substantially lower than during the steady-state period. In the period from 1952 through 1964, 36 percent of the electorate claimed to have strong partisan ties; in the 1984 preelection survey, only 29 percent did. Weak partisans and self-classified independents are much more volatile in their voting choices than individuals who claim strong party ties.

Second, the evidence strongly suggests that most of the gains in Republican partisanship occurred very suddenly in the fall of 1984. Even though there is some evidence that this shift has persisted through late 1985, the evidence is mixed, with Gallup polls showing a slight weakening in support for the Republicans. In any event, there must be a very large number of Republican identifiers with very recent Republican loyalties. These new Republicans cannot have developed a pattern of habitual partisan voting that, according to *The American Voter* thesis, would contribute to strong party ties.[50] Of course, the shift toward the Republicans may turn out to be durable. But we should remember that the substantial Republican gains in partisan loyalties that were registered in early 1981 had vanished by the end of 1982.[51] These recent fluctuations suggest that the electorate has relatively volatile partisan loyalties.

Third, social forces (other than race) have less and less influence on voting behavior—a trend that is likely to contribute to electoral volatility. Today, few voters are bound to a party by social class, ethnic, or religious ties. This increases the proportion of the electorate that is likely to switch parties from election to election.

Fourth, as our analysis in Chapter 7 demonstrates, Reagan's landslide was grounded very largely in positive retrospective evaluations. The electorate was much more favorable about the performance of the incumbent president and of the government than it had been in 1976 and 1980, and to a very large extent Reagan's 1984 victory resulted from these evaluations. Despite Reagan's claims, his victory did not result from a commitment to Republican or conservative principles. As we saw above, it is not difficult to imagine fairly disastrous economic conditions during the next several years. But even if there is only a moderate deterioration in the economy and if this decline is blamed on massive government deficits and the doubling of the national debt during Reagan's presidency, the Democrats will have a strong chance of regaining the White House. High levels of unemployment hurt the Republicans in the 1982 midterm elections, but then the Republicans could still point to Jimmy Carter and urge voters to "stay the course." Carter was an ineffective president, but he was not Herbert Hoover. The Democrats could run against memories of Hoover for two decades, but by 1988 it will be impossible to run against Carter or the "Carter-Mondale" administration. If future economic difficulties occur, it will be difficult for the Republicans to escape the blame, for they will have held power since 1981.

Last, in a world of uncertainty, there is one certainty: Ronald Reagan will not be the Republican presidential candidate in 1988. Of course, Reagan may not be president in 1988, a prospect that would be raised by his age (he was born in 1911) even without the discovery of colon cancer in July 1985. If Bush is president in 1988, the Republicans will probably face a contested nomination, especially if Bush becomes president after the midpoint of Reagan's current term.[52] If Reagan completes his term, we expect a large number of Republicans to seek the presidential nomination, and divisions within the GOP that were concealed by Reagan's uncontested nomination may be laid bare.

If Reagan is president at election time or if Bush is president and does not get the party nomination, the Republicans will have to try to hold the White House without running an incumbent president. There have been three elections of this type since World War II. Adlai E. Stevenson was the Democratic nominee in 1952, Richard Nixon was the Republican nominee in 1960, and Hubert H. Humphrey was the Democratic nominee in 1968. All were defeated. The last time the incumbent party won without running their incumbent president was when the Republicans ran Hoover in 1928—60 years before the 1988 election. If the Republicans field a nonincumbent and win, a period of electoral volatility will be over. A clear pattern of Republican party dominance will have been established.

Notes

1. "President Reagan's 2nd Inaugural Address," *Congressional Quarterly Weekly Report,* Jan. 26, 1985, 160.
2. There have been extensive discussions of the policy consequences of the 1980 presidential election. For two excellent studies, see John L. Palmer and Isabel V. Sawhill, eds., *The Reagan Record: An Assessment of America's Changing Domestic Priorities* (Cambridge, Mass.: Ballinger, 1984); and John E. Chubb and Paul E. Peterson, eds., *The New Direction in American Politics* (Washington, D.C.: The Brookings Institution, 1985).
3. U.S. Department of the Treasury, *Treasury Bulletin,* Fall 1985, 3.
4. Paul E. Peterson, "The New Politics of Deficits," in *The New Direction in American Politics,* 367-68.
5. Robert H. Birkby, "The Courts: 40 More Years?" in *The Elections of 1984,* edited by Michael Nelson (Washington, D.C.: CQ Press, 1985), 242-43. See also Jeffrey A. Segal and Harold J. Spaeth, "If a Supreme Court Vacancy Occurs, Will the Senate Confirm a Reagan Nominee?" *Judicature* 69 (December/January 1986): 186-90.
6. Robert Friedman and Stephen Wermiel, "Reagan Appointments to the Federal Bench Worry U.S. Liberals," *Wall Street Journal,* Sept. 6, 1985, 1, 8; Steven V. Roberts, "Democrats Judicially Frustrated, *New York Times,* Nov. 6, 1985, A20.
7. Robert W. Merry, "Great Divide: North Carolina Finds President's Tax Plan Fairer Than Ohio Does," *Wall Street Journal,* Aug. 1, 1985, 1, 10.
8. This concept is discussed in Kevin Phillips's biweekly newsletter, *The American Political Report* 14 (Jan. 11, 1985).
9. Hedrick Smith, "Republicans See Opportunity," *New York Times,* Feb. 4, 1985, A1.
10. Ibid., A1, 17.
11. Phil Gailey, "Republicans Start to Worry About Signs of Slippage," *New York Times,* Aug. 25, 1985, E5.
12. Our analysis of the 1976 SRC-CPS election survey strongly suggests that Ford's pardon of Nixon cost Ford votes. See Paul R. Abramson, John H. Aldrich, and David W. Rohde, *Change and Continuity in the 1980 Elections,* rev. ed., (Washington, D.C.: CQ Press, 1983), 151-52.
13. Philip E. Converse and Roy Pierce, "Measuring Partisanship" (Paper delivered at the World Congress of the International Political Science Association, Paris, July 15-20, 1985.) For the exact wording of the questions the Michigan SRC uses to measure party identification, see Chap. 4, note 40.
14. Thomas E. Cavanagh and James L. Sundquist, "The New Two-Party System," in *The New Direction in American Politics,* 42.
15. Ibid., 42-43.
16. "Republican Party Is Attracting Teen-Agers," *New York Times,* June 23, 1985, 21.
17. Ibid.
18. George Orwell, "Second Thoughts on James Burnham," in *Collected Essays: George Orwell* (London: Mercury Books, 1961), 382.

19. Ibid., 384.
20. George Gallup, Jr., "Republican Party Allegiance Slips from Earlier Peaks," *Gallup Poll,* Dec. 19, 1985, 1. Gallup relies upon a single question: "In politics, as of today do you consider yourself a Republican, a Democrat, or an Independent?"
21. "Opinion Roundup, Is It Realignment? Surveying the Evidence," *Public Opinion* 8 (October/November 1985): 57. These results are based upon party identifiers. Independent leaners have been classified as independents.
22. Ibid. As with the *New York Times*/CBS News polls, these results are based upon party identifiers.
23. Louis Harris, "Democrats Still Maintain Wide Lead in Party Preference," *Harris Survey,* Sept. 9, 1985, 1-2. The Harris question is, "Regardless of how you may vote, what do you usually consider yourself—a Republican, a Democrat, an independent, or what?"
24. We are grateful to Everett Carll Ladd, executive director of the Roper Center for Public Opinion Research, for providing us with the party identification results for the 1985 General Social Survey.
25. For a discussion of the General Social Survey results for 1980 and 1984, see Chap. 8.
26. Larry Eichel, "GOP Claims Success Converting Democrats," *Detroit Free Press,* Aug. 23, 1985, 7D.
27. "Texas 1st Clings to Tradition, Elects Democrat," *Congressional Quarterly Weekly Report,* Aug. 10, 1985, 1605-1606.
28. "Text of 1984 Republican Party Platform," *Congressional Quarterly Weekly Report,* Aug. 25, 1984, 2097.
29. Ibid., 2110-11.
30. See Abramson, Aldrich, and Rohde, *Change and Continuity in the 1980 Elections,* rev. ed., 88-89.
31. Patricia O'Brien, "Kennedy Urges a New Party Trail," *Detroit Free Press,* March 30, 1985, A1.
32. See Abramson, Aldrich, and Rohde, *Change and Continuity in the 1980 Elections,* rev. ed., 282-92.
33. Louis Harris, "For 1988 Presidential Race, Bush Even With Hart, Kennedy," *Harris Survey,* April 25, 1985. Both Harris and Gallup polls in mid-1985 showed Bush to be the leading candidate among Republicans and former U.S. senator Howard H. Baker, Jr., of Tennessee to be second. Both polls showed Kennedy to be the leading candidate among Democrats and Hart to be second.
34. George Gallup, Jr., "Bush, Kennedy Tied For Lead in Test for Presidency in '88," *Gallup Poll,* Aug. 11, 1985, 2.
35. The Republicans emerged as a major party in the 1850s by opposing extension of slavery into the territories, but for both northern farmers and southern slave owners this was an economic issue that would determine the availability of western land.
36. Anthony Downs, *An Economic Theory of Democracy* (New York: Harper & Row, 1957). As Steven J. Brams points out, there are disadvantages to the middle position in multicandidate races. See *The Presidential Election Game* (New Haven, Conn.: Yale University Press, 1978), 13-18.

37. Abramson, Aldrich, and Rohde, *Change and Continuity in the 1980 Elections*, rev. ed., 178-80.
38. Ira Katznelson, "A Radical Departure: Social Welfare and the Election," in *The Hidden Election: Politics and Economics in the 1980 Presidential Campaign*, ed. Thomas Ferguson and Joel Rogers (New York: Pantheon Books), 331.
39. Ibid., 332.
40. Kenneth B. Noble, "Kirk Urges Labor to Delay Endorsements in 1988," *New York Times*, March 26, 1985, A23.
41. For a discussion of restrictions to ballot access, see Steven J. Rosenstone, Roy L. Behr, and Edward H. Lazarus, *Third Parties in America: Citizen Response to Major Party Failure* (Princeton, N.J.: Princeton University Press, 1984), 19-25.
42. Anderson received $4.2 million dollars in federal funding after the campaign. The Federal Election Commission ruled that Anderson's National Unity party would be entitled to limited federal funding in 1984, but Anderson did not run for president and endorsed Mondale. No third party will be eligible for advance federal funding in 1988. For an additional discussion of the adverse impact of federal funding on third parties, see ibid., 25-27.
43. In estimating turnout, we used the U.S. Bureau of the Census projection of the voting-age population, 173,936,000. But because the SRC surveys are of the politically eligible population and because noncitizens could not vote without changes in state law, we here use the voting-age citizen population in these calculations. We are using Walter Dean Burnham's estimate of the size of the politically eligible population in 1984, which he provided in a personal communication, Sept. 9, 1985.
44. In similar estimates based upon the voting-age population in 1980 and the distribution of party identification in the 1980 SRC-CPS preelection survey, we projected a Democratic base of nearly 12 million votes and a Republican base of more than 8 million votes. See Abramson, Aldrich, and Rohde, *Change and Continuity in the 1980 Elections*, rev. ed., 176.
45. See ibid., 177. Table 8-8 is based upon whites, but including blacks would have little effect on the overall percentage of Wallace or Anderson voters among these partisan categories.
46. We are grateful to Joseph A. Schlesinger for this insight.
47. Philip E. Converse, *The Dynamics of Party Support: Cohort-Analyzing Party Identification* (Beverly Hills, Calif.: Sage Publications, 1976).
48. Our result for 1952 through 1964 is based upon the mean proportion of strong partisans among the entire electorate in the seven surveys conducted during this period. All seven surveys were weighted equally.
49. For the strongest evidence supporting this conclusion, see Martin P. Wattenberg, *The Decline of American Political Parties: 1952-1980* (Cambridge, Mass.: Harvard University Press, 1984), 50-72.
50. See Angus Campbell, Philip E. Converse, Warren E. Miller, and Donald E. Stokes, *The American Voter* (New York: John Wiley & Sons, 1960), 161-65. Morris P. Fiorina, on the other hand, views the relationship between length of attachment to a party and strength of partisan identification as more problematic. See *Retrospective Voting in American National Elections* (New

Haven, Conn.: Yale University Press, 1981), 91.
51. For a review of this evidence, see Abramson, Aldrich, and Rohde, *Change and Continuity in the 1980 Elections*, rev. ed., 286-87.
52. If Bush became president after January 20, 1987, he would be eligible to serve two full additional terms. If Bush were elected in 1988, a Republican hopeful might then have to wait until 1996 to run for president without facing an incumbent of his own party. That might encourage some Republicans to challenge Bush. If Bush became president before the midpoint in Reagan's term, and were elected in 1988, a Republican hopeful would not have to face an incumbent of his or her own party in 1992. Republican hopefuls might therefore be more inclined to sit out the 1988 contest.

Suggested Readings

(Starred readings include discussions of the 1984 elections.)

Chapter 1: The Nomination Struggle

Aldrich, John H. *Before the Convention: Strategies and Choices in Presidential Nomination Campaigns.* Chicago: University of Chicago Press, 1980.

Brams, Steven J. *The Presidential Election Game.* New Haven, Conn.: Yale University Press, 1978, 1-79.

*Crotty, William, and John S. Jackson III. *Presidential Primaries and Nominations.* Washington, D.C.: CQ Press, 1985.

*Germond, Jack W., and Jules Witcover. *Wake Us When It's Over: Presidential Politics of 1984.* New York: Macmillan, 1985.

*Goldman, Peter, and Tony Fuller, with others. *The Quest for the Presidency— 1984.* New York: Bantam Books, 1985.

*Jones, Charles O. "Renominating Ronald Reagan: The Compleat Politician at Work." In *The American Elections of 1984,* edited by Austin Ranney. Durham, N.C.: Duke University Press, 1985, 66-99.

*Mann, Thomas E. "Elected Officials and the Politics of Presidential Selection." In *The American Elections of 1984,* edited by Austin Ranney. Durham, N.C.: Duke University Press, 1985, 100-28.

*Orren, Gary R. "The Nomination Process: Vicissitudes of Candidate Selection." In *The Elections of 1984,* edited by Michael Nelson. Washington, D.C.: CQ Press, 1985, 27-82.

Polsby, Nelson W. *Consequences of Party Reform.* New York: Oxford University Press, 1983.

*_____. "The Democratic Nomination and the Evolution of the Party System." In *The American Elections of 1984,* edited by Austin Ranney. Durham, N.C.: Duke University Press, 1985, 36-65.

Polsby, Nelson W., and Aaron Wildavsky. *Presidential Elections: Strategies of American Electoral Politics.* 6th ed. New York: Charles Scribner's Sons, 1984, 93-146.

*Pomper, Gerald M. "The Nominations." In *The Election of 1984: Reports and Interpretations,* Gerald M. Pomper, with colleagues. Chatham, N.J.: Chatham House, 1985, 1-34.

Stone, Walter J., and Alan I. Abramowitz. "Winning May Not Be Everything, But It's More than We Thought: Presidential Party Activists in 1980." *American Political Science Review* 77 (December 1983): 945-56.

Wayne, Stephen J. *The Road to the White House: The Politics of Presidential Elections.* 2d ed. New York: St. Martin's Press, 1984, 81-163.

Chapter 2: The General Election Campaign

Asher, Herbert B. *Presidential Elections and American Politics: Voters, Candidates, and Campaigns since 1952.* 3d ed. Homewood, Ill.: Dorsey Press, 1984, 215-80.

Brams, Steven J. *The Presidential Election Game.* New Haven, Conn.: Yale University Press, 1978, 80-133.

*Frankovic, Kathleen A. "The 1984 Election: The Irrelevance of the Campaign." *PS* 18 (Winter 1985): 39-47.

*Germond, Jack W., and Jules Witcover. *Wake Us When It's Over: Presidential Politics of 1984.* New York: Macmillan, 1985.

*Goldman, Peter, and Tony Fuller, with others. *The Quest for the Presidency— 1984.* New York: Bantam Books, 1985, 245-374.

*Hunt, Albert R. "The Campaign and the Issues." In *The American Elections of 1984,* edited by Austin Ranney. Durham, N.C.: Duke University Press, 1985, 129-65.

*Light, Paul C., and Celinda Lake. "The Election: Candidates, Strategies, and Decisions." In *The Elections of 1984,* edited by Michael Nelson. Washington, D.C.: CQ Press, 1985, 83-110.

Polsby, Nelson W., and Aaron Wildavsky. *Presidential Elections: Strategies of American Electoral Politics.* 6th ed. New York: Charles Scribner's Sons, 1984, 147-207.

Wayne, Stephen J. *The Road to the White House: The Politics of Presidential Elections.* 2d ed. New York: St. Martin's Press, 1984, 167-278.

West, Darrell M. *Making Campaigns Count: Leadership and Coalition Building in 1980.* Westport, Conn.: Greenwood, 1984.

Chapter 3: The Election Results

America Votes 16: A Handbook of Contemporary American Election Statistics, compiled and edited by Richard M. Scammon and Alice V. McGillivray. Washington, D.C.: Congressional Quarterly, 1985.

Burnham, Walter Dean. *Critical Elections and the Mainsprings of American Politics.* New York: W. W. Norton & Co., 1970.

Clubb, Jerome M., William H. Flanigan, and Nancy H. Zingale. *Partisan Realignment: Voters, Parties, and Government in American History.* Beverly Hills, Calif.: Sage Publications, 1980.

Kelley, Stanley, Jr. *Interpreting Elections.* Princeton, N.J.: Princeton University Press, 1983.

Key, V. O., Jr. *Southern Politics in State and Nation.* New York: Alfred A. Knopf, 1949.

Lamis, Alexander P. *The Two-Party South.* New York: Oxford University Press, 1984.

*Pomper, Gerald M. "The Presidential Election." In *The Election of 1984: Reports and Interpretations,* Gerald M. Pomper, with colleagues. Chatham, N.J.: Chatham House, 1985, 60-90.

Presidential Elections Since 1789. 3d ed. Washington, D.C.: Congressional Quarterly, 1983.
Rosenstone, Steven J., Roy L. Behr, and Edward H. Lazarus. *Third Parties in America: Citizen Response to Major Party Failure.* Princeton, N.J.: Princeton University Press, 1984.
Sundquist, James L. *Dynamics of the Party System: Alignment and Realignment of Political Parties in the United States.* rev. ed. Washington, D.C.: The Brookings Institution, 1983.

Chapter 4: Who Voted

Abramson, Paul R., and John H. Aldrich. "The Decline of Electoral Participation in America." *American Political Science Review* 76 (September 1982): 502-21.
*Abramson, Paul R., and William Claggett. "Race-Related Differences in Self-Reported and Validated Turnout in 1984." *Journal of Politics* 48 (May 1986), forthcoming.
Aldrich, John H. "Some Problems in Testing Two Rational Models of Participation." *American Journal of Political Science* 20 (November 1976): 713-33.
Burnham, Walter Dean. *The Current Crisis in American Politics.* New York: Oxford University Press, 1982.
*Conway, M. Margaret. *Political Participation in the United States.* Washington, D.C.: CQ Press, 1985.
Ferejohn, John A., and Morris P. Fiorina, "The Paradox of Not Voting: A Decision Theoretic Analysis." *American Political Science Review* 68 (June 1974): 525-36.
Kleppner, Paul. *Who Voted? The Dynamics of Electoral Turnout, 1870-1980.* New York: Praeger, 1982.
Riker, William H., and Peter C. Ordeshook. "A Theory of the Calculus of Voting." *American Political Science Review* 62 (March 1968): 25-42.
Rosenstone, Steven J. "Economic Adversity and Voter Turnout." *American Journal of Political Science* 26 (February 1982): 25-46.
*U.S. Department of Commerce, Bureau of the Census, *Voting and Registration in the Election of November 1984 (Advance Report).* Washington, D.C.: U.S. Government Printing Office, Series P-20, No. 397, January 1985.
Wolfinger, Raymond E., and Steven J. Rosenstone. *Who Votes?* New Haven, Conn.: Yale University Press, 1980.

Chapter 5: Social Forces and the Vote

Abramson, Paul R. *Generational Change in American Politics.* Lexington, Mass.: D. C. Heath & Co., 1975.
Alford, Robert R. *Party and Society: The Anglo-American Democracies.* Chicago: Rand McNally & Co., 1963.
Axelrod, Robert. "Where the Votes Come From: An Analysis of Electoral Coalitions, 1952-1968." *American Political Science Review* 66 (March 1972): 11-20.
*_____. "Presidential Election Coalitions in 1984." *American Political Science Review* 80 (March 1986): 281-84.

Hamilton, Richard F. *Class and Politics in the United States.* New York: John Wiley & Sons, 1972.

Jackman, Mary R., and Robert W. Jackman. *Class Awareness in the United States.* Berkeley: University of California Press, 1983.

Lipset, Seymour Martin. *Political Man: The Social Bases of Politics.* Expanded edition. Baltimore: Johns Hopkins University Press, 1981.

*"Opinion Roundup, The 1984 Election Results: Patterns in Group Voting." *Public Opinion* 7 (December/January 1985): 30-35.

Petrocik, John R. *Party Coalitions: Realignment and the Decline of the New Deal Party System.* Chicago: University of Chicago Press, 1981.

*Schneider, William. "The Jewish Vote in 1984: Elements in a Controversy." *Public Opinion* 7 (December/January 1985): 18-19, 58.

*Vote By Groups in Presidential Elections Since 1952." *The Gallup Report,* Report No. 230, November 1984, 8-9.

Chapter 6: Issues, Candidates, and Voter Choice

Asher, Herbert B. *Presidential Elections and American Politics: Voters, Candidates, and Campaigns since 1952.* 3d ed. Homewood, Ill.: Dorsey Press, 1984, 79-179.

Brody, Richard A., and Benjamin I. Page. "Comment: The Assessment of Policy Voting." *American Political Science Review* 66 (June 1972): 450-58.

Campbell, Angus, Philip E. Converse, Warren E. Miller, and Donald E. Stokes. *The American Voter.* New York: John Wiley & Sons, 1960, 168-265.

Enelow, James M., and Melvin J. Hinich. *The Spatial Theory of Voting: An Introduction.* New York: Cambridge University Press, 1984.

Kessel, John H. *Presidential Parties.* Homewood, Ill.: Dorsey Press, 1984.

*Lipset, Seymour Martin. "The Elections, the Economy, and Public Opinion." *PS* 18 (Winter 1985): 28-38.

*Opinion Roundup, The 1984 Election Results: Issues in Campaign '84." *Public Opinion* 7 (December/January 1985): 36-37.

Page, Benjamin I. *Choices and Echoes in Presidential Elections: Rational Man and Electoral Democracy.* Chicago: University of Chicago Press, 1978.

*Plotkin, Henry A. "Issues in the Campaign." In *The Election of 1984: Reports and Interpretations,* Gerald M. Pomper, with colleagues. Chatham, N.J.: Chatham House, 1985, 35-59.

Pomper, Gerald M. *Voters' Choice: Varieties of American Electoral Behavior.* New York: Dodd, Mead & Co., 1975.

Chapter 7: Presidential Performance and Candidate Choice

*Adams, William C. "Recent Fables about Ronald Reagan." *Public Opinion* 7 (October/November 1984): 6-9.

*Cronin, Thomas E. "The Presidential Election of 1984." In *Election 84: Landslide Without a Mandate?* edited by Ellis Sandoz and Cecil V. Crabb, Jr. New York: New American Library, 1985, 28-65.

Downs, Anthony. *An Economic Theory of Democracy.* New York: Harper & Row, 1957.

Fiorina, Morris P. *Retrospective Voting in American National Elections.* New Haven, Conn.: Yale University Press, 1981.

Key, V. O., Jr. *The Responsible Electorate: Rationality in Presidential Voting, 1936-1960.* Cambridge, Mass.: Harvard University Press, 1966.

Kiewiet, D. Roderick. *Macroeconomics and Micropolitics: The Electoral Effects of Economic Issues.* Chicago: University of Chicago Press, 1983.

*Kiewiet, D. Roderick, and Douglas Rivers. "The Economic Basis of Reagan's Appeal." In *The New Direction in American Politics,* edited by John E. Chubb and Paul E. Peterson. Washington, D.C.: The Brookings Institution, 1985, 69-90.

*Keeter, Scott. "Public Opinion in 1984." In *The Election of 1984: Reports and Interpretations,* Gerald M. Pomper, with colleagues. Chatham, N.J.: Chatham House, 1985, 91-111.

Miller, Arthur H., and Martin P. Wattenberg. "Throwing the Rascals Out: Policy and Performance Evaluations of Presidential Candidates, 1952-1980." *American Political Science Review* 79 (June 1985): 359-72.

*Quirk, Paul J. "The Economy: Economists, Electoral Politics, and Reagan Economics." In *The Elections of 1984,* edited by Michael Nelson. Washington, D.C.: CQ Press, 1985, 155-87.

Riker, William H. *Liberalism Against Populism: A Confrontation Between the Theory of Democracy and the Theory of Social Choice.* San Francisco: W. H. Freeman & Co., 1982.

Tufte, Edward R. *Political Control of the Economy.* Princeton, N.J.: Princeton University Press, 1978.

Chapter 8: Party Loyalties, Policy Preferences, Performance Evaluations, and the Vote.

Abramson, Paul R. *Political Attitudes in America: Formation and Change.* San Francisco: W. H. Freeman & Co., 1983.

Asher, Herbert B. "Voting Behavior Research in the 1980s: An Examination of Some Old and New Problem Areas." In *Political Science: The State of the Discipline,* edited by Ada W. Finifter. Washington, D.C.: American Political Science Association, 1983, 339-88.

Beck, Paul Allen. "The Dealignment Era in America." In *Electoral Change in Advanced Industrial Democracies: Realignment or Dealignment?* edited by Russell J. Dalton, Scott C. Flanagan, and Paul Allen Beck. Princeton, N.J.: Princeton University Press, 1984. 240-66.

Campbell, Angus, Philip E. Converse, Warren E. Miller, and Donald E. Stokes. *The American Voter.* New York: John Wiley & Sons, 1960, 120-67.

Jennings, M. Kent, and Gregory B. Markus. "Partisan Orientations over the Long Haul: Results from the Three-Wave Political Socialization Panel Study." *American Political Science Review* 78 (December 1984): 1000-18.

Kinder, Donald R., and David O. Sears. "Public Opinion and Political Action." In *Special Fields and Applications,* vol. 2 of *Handbook of Social Psychology.* 3d ed., edited by Gardner Lindzey and Elliot Aronson. New York: Random House, 1985, 659-741.

Norpoth, Helmut, and Jerrold G. Rusk. "Partisan Dealignment in the American Electorate: Itemizing the Deductions since 1964." *American Political Science Review* 76 (September 1982): 522-37.

*Opinion Roundup, "Is it Realignment? Surveying the Evidence." *Public Opinion* 8 (October/November 1985): 21-31.

Wattenberg, Martin P. *The Decline of American Political Parties, 1952-1980.* Cambridge, Mass.: Harvard University Press, 1984.

Chapter 9: Candidates and Outcomes

Bond, Jon R., Cary Covington, and Richard Fleisher. "Explaining Candidate Quality in Congressional Elections." *Journal of Politics* 47 (May 1985): 510-29.

Fenno, Richard F., Jr. *Home Style: House Members in Their Districts.* Boston: Little, Brown, 1978.

*Ferejohn, John A., and Morris P. Fiorina. "Incumbency and Realignment in Congressional Elections." In *The New Direction in American Politics,* edited by John E. Chubb and Paul E. Peterson. Washington, D.C.: The Brookings Institution, 1985, 91-115.

Fiorina, Morris P. *Congress: Keystone of the Washington Establishment.* New Haven, Conn.: Yale University Press, 1977.

Hershey, Marjorie Randon. *Running for Office: The Political Education of Campaigners.* Chatham, N.J.: Chatham House, 1984.

*Jacob, Charles E. "The Congressional Elections." In *The Election of 1984: Reports and Interpretations,* Gerald M. Pomper, with colleagues. Chatham, N.J.: Chatham House, 1985, 112-32.

*Jacobson, Gary C. "Congress: Politics After a Landslide Without Coattails." In *The Elections of 1984,* edited by Michael Nelson. Washington, D.C.: CQ Press, 1985, 215-37.

*Jones, Charles O. "The Voters Say Yes: The 1984 Congressional Elections." In *Election 84: Landslide Without a Mandate?* edited by Ellis Sandoz and Cecil V. Crabb, Jr. New York: New American Library, 1985, 86-124.

*Ornstein, Norman J. "Changing Congress's Course: Republicans Still in the Wings." *Public Opinion* 7 (December/January 1985): 12-14.

_____. "The Elections for Congress." In *The American Elections of 1984,* edited by Austin Ranney. Durham, N.C.: Duke University Press, 1985, 245-76.

Rohde, David W. "Risk-Bearing and Progressive Ambition: The Case of Members of the United States House of Representatives." *American Journal of Political Science* 23 (February 1979): 1-26.

Schlesinger, Joseph A. *Ambition and Politics: Political Careers in the United States.* Chicago: Rand McNally & Co., 1966.

*_____. "The New American Political Party." *American Political Science Review* 79 (December 1985): 1152-69.

Chapter 10: The Congressional Electorate

Abramowitz, Alan I. "National Issues, Strategic Politicians, and Voting Behavior in the 1980 and 1982 Congressional Elections." *American Journal of Political Science* 28 (November 1984): 710-21.

Born, Richard. "Reassessing the Decline of Presidential Coattails: U.S. House Elections from 1952-80." *Journal of Politics* 46 (February 1984): 60-79.

Calvert, Randall L., and John A. Ferejohn. "Coattail Voting in Recent Presidential Elections." *American Political Science Review* 77 (June 1983): 407-19.

Cover, Albert D. "One Good Term Deserves Another: The Advantage of Incumbency in Congressional Elections." *American Journal of Political Science* 21 (August 1977): 523-41.

Erikson, Robert S., and Gerald C. Wright. "Voters, Candidates, and Issues in Congressional Elections." In *Congress Reconsidered.* 3d ed., edited by Lawrence C. Dodd and Bruce I. Oppenheimer. Washington, D.C.: CQ Press, 1985, 87-108.

Fenno, Richard F., Jr. "If, as Ralph Nader Says, Congress Is 'the Broken Branch,' How Come We Love Our Congressmen So Much?" In *Congress in Change: Evolution and Reform,* edited by Norman J. Ornstein. New York: Praeger Publishers, 1975, 277-87.

Ferejohn, John A., and Randall L. Calvert. "Presidential Coattails in Historical Perspective." *American Journal of Political Science* 28 (February 1984): 127-46.

Hinckley, Barbara. *Congressional Elections.* Washington, D.C.: CQ Press, 1981.

Jacobson, Gary C. *The Politics of Congressional Elections.* Boston: Little, Brown, 1983.

McAdams, John C., and John R. Johannes. "The 1980 House Elections: Reexamining Some Theories in a Republican Year." *Journal of Politics* 45 (February 1983): 143-62.

Chapter 11: The 1984 Elections and the Future of American Politics

*Brady, David W., and Patricia A. Hurley. "The Prospects for Contemporary Partisan Realignment." *PS* 18 (Winter 1985): 63-68.

*Burnham, Walter Dean. "The 1984 Election and the Future of American Politics." In *Election 84: Landslide Without a Mandate?* edited by Ellis Sandoz and Cecil V. Crabb, Jr. New York: New American Library, 1985, 204-60.

*Cavanagh, Thomas E., and James L. Sundquist. "The New Two-Party System." In *The New Direction in American Politics,* edited by John E. Chubb and Paul E. Peterson. Washington, D.C.: The Brookings Institution, 1985, 33-67.

*Chubb, John E., and Paul E. Peterson. "Realignment and Institutionalization." In *The New Direction in American Politics,* edited by John E. Chubb and Paul E. Peterson. Washington, D.C.: The Brookings Institution, 1985, 1-30.

*Ginsberg, Benjamin, and Martin Shefter. "A Critical Realignment? The New Politics, the Reconstituted Right, and the 1984 Election." In *The Elections of 1984,* edited by Michael Nelson. Washington, D.C.: CQ Press, 1985, 1-25.

*Huntington, Samuel P. "The Visions of the Democratic Party." *The Public Interest* 79 (Spring 1985): 63-78.

*Ladd, Everett Carll. "On Mandates, Realignments, and the 1984 Presidential Election." *Political Science Quarterly* 100 (Spring 1985): 1-25.

*Lowi, Theodore J. "An Aligning Election, A Presidential Plebiscite." In *The Elections of 1984,* edited by Michael Nelson. Washington, D.C.: CQ Press, 1985, 277-301.

*McWilliams, Wilson Carey. "The Meaning of the Election." In *The Election of 1984: Reports and Interpretations,* Gerald M. Pomper, with colleagues. Chatham, N.J.: Chatham House, 1985, 157-83.

*Schneider, William. "The November 6 Vote for President: What Did It Mean?" In *The American Elections of 1984,* edited by Austin Ranney. Durham, N.C.: Duke University Press, 1985, 203-44.

*Wolfinger, Raymond E. "Dealignment, Realignment, and Mandates in the 1984 Election." In *The American Elections of 1984,* edited by Austin Ranney. Durham, N.C.: Duke University Press, 1985, 277-96.

Index